THE BIG BOOK OF ALCOHOLICS ANONYMOUS

BY DR. BOB SMITH AND BILL WILSON

The Story of

How Many Thousands of Men and Women

Have Recovered from Alcoholism

SPECIAL 2013 EDITION

LARK PUBLISHING LLC

Dr. Bob Smith (1879 – 1950)
Bill Wilson (1895 – 1971)
The Big Book of Alcoholics Anonymous
Special 2013 Edition
First Published in 1939

Published by Lark Publishing LLC

ISBN-13: 978-1483907253
ISBN-10: 1483907252

CONTENTS

PREFACE

This is the special edition of the book, *Alcoholics Anonymous*, which made its first appearance in April, 1939.

Because this book has become the basic text for our Society and has helped such large numbers of alcoholic men and women to recovery, there exists a sentiment against any radical changes being made in it. Therefore the first portion of this volume, describing the A.A. recovery program, has been left largely untouched.

But the personal history section has been considerably revised and enlarged in order to present a more accurate representation of our membership as it is today. When the book was first printed, we had scarcely 100 members all told, and every one of them was an almost hopeless case of alcoholism. This has changed. A.A. now helps alcoholics in all stages of the disease. It reaches into every level of life and into nearly all occupations. Our membership now includes many young people. Women, who were at first very reluctant to approach A.A., have come forward in large numbers. Therefore the range of the story section has been broadened so that every alcoholic reader may find a reflection of him or herself in it.

As a souvenir of our past, the original Foreword has been preserved and is followed by a second one describing Alcoholics Anonymous of 1955.

Following the Forewords, there appears a section called "The Doctor's Opinion." This also has been kept intact, just as it was originally written in 1939 by the late Dr. William D. Silkworth, our Society's great medical benefactor. Besides Dr. Silkworth's original statement, there have been added, in the Appendices, a number of the medical and religious endorsements which have come to us in recent years.

On the last pages of this edition will be found the Twelve Traditions of Alcoholics Anonymous, the principles upon which our A.A. groups function, together with directions for getting in touch with A.A.

FOREWORD TO FIRST EDITION

This is the Foreword as it appeared in the first printing of the first edition in 1939.

WE, OF Alcoholics Anonymous, are many thousands of men and women who have recovered from a seemingly hopeless state of mind and body. To show other alcoholics *precisely how we have recovered* is the main purpose of this book. For them, we hope these pages will prove so convincing that no further authentication will be necessary. We think this account of our experiences will help everyone to better understand the alcoholic. Many do not comprehend that the alcoholic is a very sick person. And besides, we are sure that our way of living has its advantages for all.

It is important that we remain anonymous because we are too few, at present to handle the overwhelming number of personal appeals which may result from this publication. Being mostly business or professional folk, we could not well carry on our occupations in such an event. We would like it understood that our alcoholic work is an avocation.

When writing or speaking publicly about alcoholism, we urge each of our Fellowship to omit his personal name, designating himself instead as "a member of Alcoholics Anonymous."

Very earnestly we ask the press also, to observe this request, for otherwise we shall be greatly handicapped.

We are not an organization in the conventional sense of the word. There are no fees or dues whatsoever. The only requirement for membership is an honest desire to stop drinking. We are not allied with any particular faith, sect or denomination, nor do we oppose anyone. We simply wish to be helpful to those who are afflicted.

We shall be interested to hear from those who are getting results from this book, particularly from those who have commenced work with other alcoholics. We should like to be helpful to such cases.

Inquiry by scientific, medical, and religious societies will be welcomed.

ALCOHOLICS ANONYMOUS

FOREWORD TO SECOND EDITION

Figures given in this foreword describe the Fellowship as it was in 1955.

SINCE the original Foreword to this book was written in 1939, a wholesale miracle has taken place. Our earliest printing voiced the hope "that every alcoholic who journeys will find the Fellowship of Alcoholics Anonymous at his destination. Already," continues the early text, "twos and threes and fives of us have sprung up in other communities."

Sixteen years have elapsed between our first printing of this book and the presentation in 1955 of our second edition. In that brief space, Alcoholics Anonymous has mushroomed into nearly 6,000 groups whose membership is far above 150,000 recovered alcoholics. Groups are to be found in each of the United States and all of the provinces of Canada. A.A. has flourishing communities in the British Isles, the Scandinavian countries, South Africa, South America, Mexico, Alaska, Australia and Hawaii. All told, promising beginnings have been made in some 50 foreign countries and U.S. possessions. Some are just now taking shape in Asia. Many of our friends encourage us by saying that this is but a beginning, only the augury of a much larger future ahead.

The spark that was to flare into the first A.A. group was struck at Akron, Ohio, in June 1935, during a talk between a New York stockbroker and an Akron physician. Six months earlier, the broker had been relieved of his drink obsession by a sudden spiritual experience, following a meeting with an alcoholic friend who had been in contact with the Oxford Groups of that day. He had also been greatly helped by the late Dr. William D. Silkworth, a New York specialist in alcoholism who is now accounted no less than a medical saint by A.A. members, and whose story of the early days of our Society appears in the next pages. From this doctor, the broker had learned the grave nature of alcoholism. Though he could not accept all the tenets of the Oxford Groups, he was convinced of the need for moral inventory, confession of personality defects, restitution to those harmed, helpfulness to others, and the necessity of belief in and dependence upon God.

Prior to his journey to Akron, the broker had worked hard with many alcoholics on the theory that only an alcoholic could help an alcoholic, but he had succeeded only in keeping sober himself. The broker had gone to Akron on a business venture which had collapsed, leaving him greatly in fear that he might start drinking again. He suddenly realized that in order to save himself he must carry his message to another alcoholic. That alcoholic turned out to be the Akron physician.

This physician had repeatedly tried spiritual means to resolve his alcoholic dilemma but had failed. But when the broker gave him Dr. Silkworth's description of alcoholism and its hopelessness, the physician began to pursue the spiritual remedy for his malady with a willingness he had never before been able to muster. He sobered, never to drink again up to the moment of his death in 1950. This seemed to prove that one alcoholic could affect another as no nonalcoholic could. It also indicated that strenuous work, one alcoholic with another, was vital to permanent recovery.

Hence the two men set to work almost frantically upon alcoholics arriving in the ward of the Akron City Hospital. Their very first case, a desperate one, recovered immediately and became A.A. number three. He never had another drink. This work at Akron continued through the summer of 1935. There were many failures, but there was an occasional heartening success. When the broker returned to New York in the fall of 1935, the first A.A. group had actually been formed, though no one realized it at the time.

A second small group promptly took shape at New York, to be followed in 1937 with the start of a third at Cleveland. Besides these, there were scattered alcoholics who had picked up the basic ideas in Akron or New York who were trying to form groups in other cities. By late 1937, the number of members having substantial sobriety time behind them was sufficient to convince the membership that a new light had entered the dark world of the alcoholic.

It was now time, the struggling groups thought, to place their message and unique experience before the world. This determination bore fruit in the spring of 1939 by the publication of this volume. The membership had then reached about 100 men and women. The fledgling society, which had been nameless, now began to be called Alcoholics Anonymous, from the title of its own book. The flying-blind period ended and A.A. entered a new phase of its pioneering time.

With the appearance of the new book a great deal began to happen. Dr. Harry Emerson Fosdick, the noted clergyman, reviewed it with approval. In the fall of 1939 Fulton Oursler, then editor of *Liberty*, printed a piece in his magazine, called "Alcoholics and God." This brought a rush of 800 frantic inquiries into the little New York office which meanwhile had been established. Each inquiry was painstakingly answered; pamphlets and books were sent out. Businessmen, traveling out of existing groups, were referred to these prospective newcomers. New groups started up and it was found, to the astonishment of everyone, that A.A.'s message could be transmitted in the mail as well as by word of mouth. By the end of 1939 it was estimated that 800 alcoholics were on their way to recovery.

In the spring of 1940, John D. Rockefeller, Jr. gave a dinner for many of his friends to which he invited A.A. members to tell their stories. News of this got on the world wires; inquiries poured in again and many people went to the bookstores to get the book *Alcoholics Anonymous*. By March 1941 the membership had shot up to 2,000. Then Jack Alexander wrote a feature article in the *Saturday Evening Post* and placed such a compelling picture of A.A. before the general public that alcoholics in need of help really deluged us. By the close of 1941, A.A. numbered 8,000 members. The mushrooming process was in full swing. A.A. had become a national institution.

Our Society then entered a fearsome and exciting adolescent period. The test that it faced was this: Could these large numbers of erstwhile erratic alcoholics successfully meet and work together? Would there be quarrels over membership, leadership and money? Would there be strivings for power and prestige? Would there be schisms which would split A.A. apart? Soon A.A. was beset by these very problems on every side and in every group. But out of this frightening and at first disrupting experience the conviction grew that A.A.'s had to hang together or die separately. We had to unify our Fellowship or pass off the scene.

As we discovered the principles by which the individual alcoholic could live, so we had to evolve principles by which the A.A. groups and A.A. as a whole could survive and function effectively. It was thought that no alcoholic man or woman could be excluded from our Society; that our leaders might serve but never govern; that each group was to be autonomous and there was to be no professional class of therapy. There were to be no fees or dues; our expenses were to be met by our own voluntary contributions. There was to be the least possible organization, even in our service centers. Our public relations were to be based upon attraction rather than promotion. It was decided that all members ought to be anonymous at the level of press, radio, TV and films. And in no circumstances should we give endorsements, make alliances or enter public controversies.

This was the substance of A.A.'s Twelve Traditions, which are stated in full at the end of this book. Though none of these principles had the force of rules or laws, they had become so widely accepted by 1950 that they were confirmed by our first International Conference held at Cleveland. Today the remarkable unity of A.A. is one of the greatest assets that our Society has.

While the internal difficulties of our adolescent period were being ironed out, public acceptance of A.A. grew by leaps and bounds. For this there were two principal reasons: the large numbers of recoveries and reunited homes. These made their impressions everywhere. Of alcoholics who came to A.A. and really tried, 50 percent got sober at once and remained that way; 25 percent sobered up after some relapses, and among the remainder, those who stayed on with A.A. showed improvement. Other thousands came to a few A.A. meetings and at first decided they didn't want the program. But great numbers of these–about two out of three–began to return as time passed.

Another reason for the wide acceptance of A.A. was the ministration of friends–friends in medicine, religion, and the press, together with innumerable others who became our able and persistent advocates. Without such support, A.A. could have made only the slowest progress. Some of the recommendations of A.A.'s early medical and religious friends will be found further on in this book.

Alcoholics Anonymous is not a religious organization. Neither does A.A. take any particular medical point of view, though we cooperate widely with the men of medicine as well as with the men of religion.

Alcohol being no respecter of persons, we are an accurate cross section of America, and in distant lands, the same democratic evening-up process is now going on. By personal religious affiliation, we include Catholics, Protestants, Jews, Hindus, and a sprinkling of Moslems and Buddhists. More than 15 percent of us are women.

At present, our membership is pyramiding at the rate of about 20 percent a year. So far, upon the total problem of several million actual and potential alcoholics in the world, we have made only a scratch. In all probability, we shall never be able to touch more than a fair fraction of the alcohol problem in all its ramifications. Upon therapy for the alcoholic himself, we surely have no monopoly. Yet it is our great hope that all those who have as yet found no answer may begin to find one in the pages of this book and will presently join us on the high road to a new freedom.

THE DOCTOR'S OPINION

WE OF Alcoholics Anonymous believe that the reader will be interested in the medical estimate of the plan of recovery described in this book. Convincing testimony must surely come from medical men who have had experience with the sufferings of our members and have witnessed our return to health. A well-known doctor, chief physician at a nationally prominent hospital specializing in alcoholic and drug addiction, gave Alcoholics Anonymous this letter:

To Whom It May Concern:

I have specialized in the treatment of alcoholism for many years.

In late 1934 I attended a patient who, though he had been a competent businessman of good earning capacity, was an alcoholic of a type I had come to regard as hopeless.

In the course of his third treatment he acquired certain ideas concerning a possible means of recovery. As part of his rehabilitation he commenced to present his conceptions to other alcoholics, impressing upon them that they must do likewise with still others. This has become the basis of a rapidly growing fellowship of these men and their families. This man and over one hundred others appear to have recovered.

I personally know scores of cases who were of the type with whom other methods had failed completely.

These facts appear to be of extreme medical importance; because of the extraordinary possibilities of rapid growth inherent in this group they may mark a new epoch in the annals of alcoholism. These men may well have a remedy for thousands of such situations.

You may rely absolutely on anything they say about themselves.

Very truly yours,
William D. Silkworth, M.D.

The physician who, at our request, gave us this letter, has been kind enough to enlarge upon his views in another statement which follows. In this statement he confirms what we who have suffered alcoholic torture must believe–that the body of the alcoholic is quite as abnormal as his mind. It did not satisfy us to be told that we could not control our drinking just because we were maladjusted to life, that we were in full flight from reality, or were outright mental defectives. These things were true to some extent, in fact, to a considerable extent with some of us. But we are sure that our bodies were sickened as well. In our belief, any picture of the alcoholic which leaves out this physical factor is incomplete.

The doctor's theory that we have an allergy to alcohol interests us. As laymen, our opinion as to its soundness may, of course, mean little. But as ex-problem drinkers, we can say that his explanation makes good sense. It explains many things for which we cannot otherwise account.

Though we work out our solution on the spiritual as well as an altruistic plane, we favor hospitalization for the alcoholic who is very jittery or befogged. More often than not, it is imperative that a man's brain be cleared before he is approached, as he has then a better chance of understanding and accepting what we have to offer.

The doctor writes:

The subject presented in this book seems to me to be of paramount importance to those afflicted with alcoholic addiction.

I say this after many years' experience as Medical Director of one of the oldest hospitals in the country treating alcoholic and drug addiction.

There was, therefore, a sense of real satisfaction when I was asked to contribute a few words on a subject which is covered in such masterly detail in these pages.

We doctors have realized for a long time that some form of moral psychology was of urgent importance to alcoholics, but its application presented difficulties beyond our conception. What with our ultra-modern standards, our scientific approach to everything, we are perhaps not well equipped to apply the powers of good that lie outside our synthetic knowledge.

Many years ago one of the leading contributors to this book came under our care in this hospital and while here he acquired some ideas which he put into practical application at once.

Later, he requested the privilege of being allowed to tell his story to other patients here and with some misgiving, we consented. The cases we have followed through have been most interesting; in fact, many of them are amazing. The unselfishness of these men as we have come to know them, the entire absence of profit motive, and their community spirit, is indeed inspiring to one who has labored long and wearily in this alcoholic field. They believe in themselves, and still more in the Power which pulls chronic alcoholics back from the gates of death.

Of course an alcoholic ought to be freed from his physical craving for liquor, and this often requires a definite hospital procedure, before psychological measures can be of maximum benefit.

We believe, and so suggested a few years ago, that the action of alcohol on these chronic alcoholics is a manifestation of an allergy; that the phenomenon of craving is limited to this class and never occurs in the average temperate drinker. These allergic types can never safely use alcohol in any form at all; and once having formed the habit and found they cannot break it, once having lost their self- confidence, their reliance upon things human, their problems pile up on them and become astonishingly difficult to solve.

Frothy emotional appeal seldom suffices. The message which can interest and hold these alcoholic people must have depth and weight. In nearly all cases, their ideals must be grounded in a power greater than themselves, if they are to re-create their lives.

If any feel that as psychiatrists directing a hospital for alcoholics we appear somewhat sentimental, let them stand with us a while on the firing line, see the tragedies, the despairing wives, the little children; let the solving of these problems become a part of their daily work, and even of their sleeping moments, and the most cynical will not wonder that we have accepted and encouraged this movement. We feel, after many years of experience, that we have found nothing which has contributed more to the rehabilitation of these men than the altruistic movement now growing up among them.

Men and women drink essentially because they like the effect produced by alcohol. The sensation is so elusive that, while they admit it is injurious, they cannot after a time differentiate the true from the false. To them, their alcoholic life seems the only normal one. They are restless, irritable and discontented, unless they can again experience the sense of ease and comfort which comes at once by taking a few drinks–drinks which they see others taking with impunity. After they have succumbed to the desire again, as so many do, and the phenomenon of craving develops, they pass through the well-known stages of a spree, emerging remorseful, with a firm resolution not to drink again. This is repeated over and over, and unless this person can experience an entire psychic change there is very little hope of his recovery.

On the other hand–and strange as this may seem to those who do not understand–once a psychic change has occurred, the very same person who seemed doomed, who had so many problems he despaired of ever solving them, suddenly finds himself easily able to control his desire for alcohol, the only effort necessary being that required to follow a few simple rules.

Men have cried out to me in sincere and despairing appeal: "Doctor, I cannot go on like this! I have everything to live for! I must stop, but I cannot! You must help me!"

Faced with this problem, if a doctor is honest with himself, he must sometimes feel his own inadequacy. Although he gives all that is in him, it often is not enough. One feels that something more than human power is needed to produce the essential psychic change. Though the aggregate of recoveries resulting from psychiatric effort is considerable, we physicians must admit we have made little impression upon the problem as a whole. Many types do not respond to the ordinary psychological approach.

I do not hold with those who believe that alcoholism is entirely a problem of mental control. I have had many men who had, for example, worked a period of months on some problem or business deal which was to be settled on a certain date, favorably to them. They took a drink a day or so prior to the date, and then the phenomenon of craving at once became paramount to all other interests so that the important appointment was not met. These men were not drinking to escape; they were drinking to overcome a craving beyond their mental control.

There are many situations which arise out of the phenomenon of craving which cause men to make the supreme sacrifice rather than continue to fight.

The classification of alcoholics seems most difficult, and in much detail is outside the scope of this book. There are, of course, the psychopaths who are emotionally unstable. We are all familiar with this type. They are always "going on the wagon for keeps." They are over-remorseful and make many resolutions, but never a decision.

There is the type of man who is unwilling to admit that he cannot take a drink. He plans various ways of drinking. He changes his brand or his environment. There is the type who always believes that after being entirely free from alcohol for a period of time he can take a drink without danger. There is the manic-depressive type, who is, perhaps, the least understood by his friends, and about whom a whole chapter could be written.

Then there are types entirely normal in every respect except in the effect alcohol has upon them. They are often able, intelligent, friendly people.

All these, and many others, have one symptom in common: they cannot start drinking without developing the phenomenon of craving. This phenomenon, as we have suggested, may be the manifestation of an allergy which differentiates these people, and sets them apart as a distinct entity. It has never been, by any treatment with which we are familiar, permanently eradicated. The only relief we have to suggest is entire abstinence.

This immediately precipitates us into a seething caldron of debate. Much has been written pro and con, but among physicians, the general opinion seems to be that most chronic alcoholics are doomed.

What is the solution? Perhaps I can best answer this by relating one of my experiences.

About one year prior to this experience a man was brought in to be treated for chronic alcoholism. He had but partially recovered from a gastric hemorrhage and seemed to be a case of pathological mental deterioration. He had lost everything worthwhile in life and was only living, one might say, to drink. He frankly admitted and believed that for him there was no hope. Following the elimination of alcohol, there was found to be no permanent brain injury. He accepted the plan outlined in this book. One year later he called to see me, and I experienced a very strange sensation. I knew the man by name, and partly recognized his features, but there all resemblance ended. From a trembling, despairing, nervous wreck, had emerged a man brimming over with self-reliance and contentment. I talked with him for some time, but was not able to bring myself to feel that I had known him before. To me he was a stranger, and so he left me. A long time has passed with no return to alcohol.

When I need a mental uplift, I often think of another case brought in by a physician prominent in New York. The patient had made his own diagnosis, and deciding his situation hopeless, had hidden in a deserted barn determined to die. He was rescued by a searching party, and, in desperate condition, brought to me. Following his physical rehabilitation, he had a talk with me in which he frankly stated he thought the treatment a waste of effort, unless I could assure him, which no one ever had, that in the future he would have the "will power" to resist the impulse to drink.

His alcoholic problem was so complex, and his depression so great, that we felt his only hope would be through what we then called "moral psychology," and we doubted if even that would have any effect.

However, he did become "sold" on the ideas contained in this book. He has not had a drink for a great many years. I see him now and then and he is as fine a specimen of manhood as one could wish to meet.

I earnestly advise every alcoholic to read this book through, and though perhaps he came to scoff, he may remain to pray.

William D. Silkworth, M.D.

Chapter I

BILL'S STORY

WAR FEVER ran high in the New England town to which we new, young officers from Plattsburg were assigned, and we were flattered when the first citizens took us to their homes, making us feel heroic. Here was love, applause, war; moments sublime with intervals hilarious. I was part of life at last, and in the midst of the excitement I discovered liquor. I forgot the strong warnings and the prejudices of my people concerning drink. In time we sailed "Over There." I was very lonely and again turned to alcohol.

We landed in England. I visited Winchester Cathedral. Much moved, I wandered outside. My attention was caught by a doggerel on an old tombstone:

"Here lies a Hampshire Grenadier
Who caught his death
Drinking cold small beer.
A good soldier is ne'er forgot
Whether he dieth by musket
Or by pot."

Ominous warning–which I failed to heed.

Twenty-two, and a veteran of foreign wars, I went home at last. I fancied myself a leader, for had not the men of my battery given me a special token of appreciation? My talent for leadership, I imagined, would place me at the head of vast enterprises which I would manage with the utmost assurance.

I took a night law course, and obtained employment as an investigator for a surety company. The drive for success was on. I'd prove to the world I was important. My work took me about Wall Street and little by little I became interested in the market. Many people lost money–but some became very rich. Why not I? I studied economics and business as well as law. Potential alcoholic that I was, I nearly failed my law course. At one of the finals I was too drunk to think or write. Though my drinking was not yet continuous, it disturbed my wife. We had long talks when I would still her forebodings by telling her that men of genius conceived their best projects when drunk; that the most majestic construction of philosophic thought were so derived.

By the time I had completed the course, I knew the law was not for me. The inviting maelstrom of Wall Street had me in its grip. Business and financial leaders were my heroes. Out of this alloy of drink and speculation, I commenced to forge the weapon that one day would turn in its flight like a boomerang and all but cut me to ribbons. Living modestly, my wife and I saved $1,000. It went into certain securities, then cheap and rather unpopular. I rightly imagined that they would some day have a great rise. I failed to persuade my broker friends to send me out looking over factories and managements, but my wife and I decided to go anyway. I had developed a theory that most people lost money in stocks through ignorance of markets. I discovered many more reasons later on.

We gave up our positions and off we roared on a motorcycle, the sidecar stuffed with tent, blankets, a change of clothes, and three huge volumes of a financial reference service. Our friends thought a lunacy commission should be appointed. Perhaps they were right. I had had some success at speculation, so we had little money, but we once worked on a farm for a month to avoid drawing on our small capital. That was the last honest manual labor on my part for many a day. We covered the whole eastern United States in a year. At the end of it, my reports to Wall Street procured me a position there and the use of a large expense account. The exercise of an option brought in more money, leaving us with a profit of several thousand dollars for that year.

For the next few years fortune threw money and applause my way. I had arrived. My judgment and ideas were followed by many to the tune of paper millions. The great boom of the late twenties was seething and swelling. Drink was taking an important and exhilarating part in my life. There was loud talk in the jazz places uptown. Everyone spent in thousands and chattered in millions. Scoffers could scoff and be damned. I made a host of fair-weather friends.

My drinking assumed more serious proportions, continuing all day and almost every night. The remonstrances of my friends terminated in a row and I became a lone wolf. There were many unhappy scenes in our sumptuous apartment. There had been no real infidelity, for loyalty to my wife, helped at times by extreme drunkenness, kept me out of those scrapes.

In 1929 I contracted golf fever. We went at once to the country, my wife to applaud while I started out to overtake Walter Hagen. Liquor caught up with me much faster than I came up behind Walter. I began to be jittery in the morning. Golf permitted drinking every day and every night. It was fun to carom around the exclusive course which had inspired such awe in me as a lad. I acquired the impeccable coat of tan one sees upon the well-to-do. The local banker watched me whirl fat checks in and out of his till with amused skepticism.

Abruptly in October 1929 hell broke loose on the New York stock exchange. After one of those days of inferno, I wobbled from a hotel bar to a brokerage office. It was eight o'clock–five hours after the market closed. The ticker still clattered. I was staring at an inch of the tape which bore the inscription XYZ-32. It had been 52 that morning. I was finished and so were many friends. The papers reported men jumping to death from the towers of High Finance. That disgusted me. I would not jump. I went back to the bar. My friends had dropped several million since ten o'clock–so what? Tomorrow was another day. As I drank, the old fierce determination to win came back.

Next morning I telephoned a friend in Montreal. He had plenty of money left and thought I had better go to Canada. By the following spring we were living in our accustomed style. I felt like Napoleon returning from Elba. No St. Helena for me! But drinking caught up with me again and my generous friend had to let me go. This time we stayed broke.

We went to live with my wife's parents. I found a job; then lost it as a result of a brawl with a taxi driver. Mercifully, no one could guess that I was to have no real employment for five years, or hardly draw a sober breath. My wife began to work in a department store, coming home exhausted to find me drunk. I became an unwelcome hanger-on at brokerage places.

Liquor ceased to be a luxury; it became a necessity. "Bathtub" gin, two bottles a day, and often three, got to be routine. Sometimes a small deal would net a few hundred dollars, and I would pay my bills at the bars and delicatessens. This went on endlessly, and I began to waken very early in the morning shaking violently. A tumbler full of gin followed by half a dozen bottles of beer would be required if I were to eat any breakfast. Nevertheless, I still thought I could control the situation, and there were periods of sobriety which renewed my wife's hope.

Gradually things got worse. The house was taken over by the mortgage holder, my mother-in-law died, my wife and father-in-law became ill.

Then I got a promising business opportunity. Stocks were at the low point of 1932, and I had somehow formed a group to buy. I was to share generously in the profits. Then I went on a prodigious bender, and that chance vanished.

I woke up. This had to be stopped. I saw I could not take so much as one drink. I was through forever. Before then, I had written lots of sweet promises, but my wife happily observed that this time I meant business. And so I did.

Shortly afterward I came home drunk. There had been no fight. Where had been my high resolve? I simply didn't know. It hadn't even come to mind. Someone had pushed a drink my way, and I had taken it. Was I crazy? I began to wonder, for such an appalling lack of perspective seemed near being just that.

Renewing my resolve, I tried again. Some time passed, and confidence began to be replaced by cocksureness. I could laugh at the gin mills. Now I had what it takes! One day I walked into a cafe to telephone. In no time I was beating on the bar asking myself how it happened. As the whisky rose to my head I told myself I would manage better next time, but I might as well get good and drunk then. And I did.

The remorse, horror and hopelessness of the next morning are unforgettable. The courage to do battle was not there. My brain raced uncontrollably and there was a terrible sense of impending calamity. I hardly dared cross the street, lest I collapse and be run down by an early morning truck, for it was scarcely daylight. An all night place supplied me with a dozen glasses of ale. My writhing nerves were stilled at last. A morning paper had told me the market had gone to hell again. Well, so had I. The market would recover, but I wouldn't. That was a hard thought. Should I kill myself? No–not now. Then a mental fog settled down. Gin would fix that. So two bottles, and–oblivion.

The mind and body are marvelous mechanisms, for mine endured this agony two more years. Sometimes I stole from my wife's slender purse when the morning terror and madness were on me. Again I swayed dizzily before an open window, or the medicine cabinet where there was poison, cursing myself for a weakling. There were flights from city to country and back, as my wife and I sought escape. Then came the night when the physical and mental torture was so hellish I feared I would burst through my window, sash and all. Somehow I managed to drag my mattress to a lower floor, lest I suddenly leap. A doctor came with a heavy sedative. Next day found me drinking both gin and sedative. This combination soon landed me on the rocks. People feared for my sanity. So did I. I could eat little or nothing when drinking, and I was forty pounds under weight.

My brother-in-law is a physician, and through his kindness and that of my mother I was placed in a nationally-known hospital for the mental and physical rehabilitation of alcoholics. Under the so-called belladonna treatment my brain cleared. Hydrotherapy and mild exercise helped much. Best of all, I met a kind doctor who explained that though certainly selfish and foolish, I had been seriously ill, bodily and mentally.

It relieved me somewhat to learn that in alcoholics the will is amazingly weakened when it comes to combating liquor, though it often remains strong in other respects. My incredible behavior in the face of a desperate desire to stop was explained. Understanding myself now, I fared forth in high hope. For three or four months the goose hung high. I went to town regularly and even made a little money. Surely this was the answer–self-knowledge.

But it was not, for the frightful day came when I drank once more. The curve of my declining moral and bodily health fell off like a ski-jump. After a time I returned to the hospital. This was the finish, the curtain, it seemed to me. My weary and despairing wife was informed that it would all end with heart failure during delirium tremens, or I would develop a wet brain, perhaps within a year. She would soon have to give me over to the undertaker or the asylum.

They did not need to tell me. I knew, and almost welcomed the idea. It was a devastating blow to my pride. I, who had thought so well of myself and my abilities, of my capacity to surmount obstacles, was cornered at last. Now I was to plunge into the dark, joining that endless procession of sots who had gone on before. I thought of my poor wife. There had been much happiness after all. What would I not give to make amends. But that was over now.

No words can tell of the loneliness and despair I found in that bitter morass of self-pity. Quicksand stretched around me in all directions. I had met my match. I had been overwhelmed. Alcohol was my master.

Trembling, I stepped from the hospital a broken man. Fear sobered me for a bit. Then came the insidious insanity of that first drink, and on Armistice Day 1934, I was off again. Everyone became resigned to the certainty that I would have to be shut up somewhere, or would stumble along to a miserable end. How dark it is before the dawn! In reality that was the beginning of my last debauch. I was soon to be catapulted into what I like to call the fourth dimension of existence. I was to know happiness, peace, and usefulness, in a way of life that is incredibly more wonderful as time passes.

Near the end of that bleak November, I sat drinking in my kitchen. With a certain satisfaction I reflected there was enough gin concealed about the house to carry me through that night and the next day. My wife was at work. I wondered whether I dared hide a full bottle of gin near the head of our bed. I would need it before daylight.

My musing was interrupted by the telephone. The cheery voice of an old school friend asked if he might come over. *He was sober.* It was years since I could remember his coming to New York in that condition. I was amazed. Rumor had it that he had been committed for alcoholic insanity. I wondered how he had escaped. Of course he would have dinner, and then I could drink openly with him. Unmindful of his welfare, I thought only of recapturing the spirit of other days. There was that time we had chartered an airplane to complete a jag! His coming was an oasis in this dreary desert of futility. The very thing–an oasis! Drinkers are like that.

The door opened and he stood there, fresh-skinned and glowing. There was something about his eyes. He was inexplicably different. What had happened?

I pushed a drink across the table. He refused it. Disappointed but curious, I wondered what had got into the fellow. He wasn't himself.

"Come, what's all this about?" I queried.

He looked straight at me. Simply, but smilingly, he said, "I've got religion."

I was aghast. So that was it–last summer an alcoholic crackpot; now, I suspected, a little cracked about religion. He had that starry-eyed look. Yes, the old boy was on fire all right. But bless his heart, let him rant! Besides, my gin would last longer than his preaching.

But he did no ranting. In a matter of fact way he told how two men appeared in court, persuading the judge to suspend his commitment. They had told of a simple religious idea and a practical program of action. That was two months ago and the result was self-evident. It worked!

He had come to pass his experience along to me–if I cared to have it. I was shocked, but interested. Certainly I was interested. I had to be, for I was hopeless.

He talked for hours. Childhood memories rose before me. I could almost hear the sound of the preacher's voice as I sat, on still Sundays, way over there on the hillside; there was that proffered temperance pledge I never signed; my grandfather's good natured contempt of some church folk and their doings; his insistence that the spheres really had their music; but his denial of the preacher's right to tell him how he must listen; his fearlessness as he spoke of these things just before he died; these recollections welled up from the past. They made me swallow hard.

That war-time day in old Winchester Cathedral came back again.

I had always believed in a Power greater than myself. I had often pondered these things. I was not an atheist. Few people really are, for that means blind faith in the strange proposition that this universe originated in a cipher and aimlessly rushes nowhere. My intellectual heroes, the chemists, the astronomers, even the evolutionists, suggested vast laws and forces at work. Despite contrary indications, I had little doubt that a mighty purpose and rhythm underlay all. How could there be so much of precise and immutable law, and no intelligence? I simply had to believe in a Spirit of the Universe, who knew neither time nor limitation. But that was as far as I had gone.

With ministers, and the world's religions, I parted right there. When they talked of a God personal to me, who was love, superhuman strength and direction, I became irritated and my mind snapped shut against such a theory.

To Christ I conceded the certainty of a great man, not to closely followed by those who claimed Him. His moral teaching–most excellent. For myself, I had adopted those parts which seemed convenient and not too difficult; the rest I disregarded.

The wars which had been fought, the burnings and chicanery that religious dispute had facilitated, made me sick. I honestly doubted whether, on balance, the religions of mankind had done any good. Judging from what I had seen in Europe and since, the power of God in human affairs was negligible, the Brotherhood of Man a grim jest. If there was a Devil, he seemed the Boss Universal, and he certainly had me.

But my friend sat before me, and he made the point-blank declaration that God had done for him what he could not do for himself. His human will had failed. Doctors had pronounced him incurable. Society was about to lock him up. Like myself, he had admitted complete defeat. Then he had, in effect, been raised from the dead, suddenly taken from the scrap heap to a level of life better than the best he had ever known!

Had this power originated in him? Obviously it had not. There had been no more power in him than there was in me at that minute; and this was none at all.

That floored me. It began to look as though religious people were right after all. Here was something at work in a human heart which had done the impossible. My ideas about miracles were drastically revised right then. Never mind the musty past; here sat a miracle directly across the kitchen table. He shouted great tidings.

I saw that my friend was much more than inwardly reorganized. He was on a different footing. His roots grasped a new soil.

Despite the living example of my friend there remained in me the vestiges of my old prejudice. The word God still aroused a certain antipathy. When the thought expressed that there might be a God personal to me this feeling was intensified. I didn't like the idea. I could go for such conceptions as Creative Intelligence, Universal Mind or Spirit of Nature, but I resisted the thought of a Czar of the Heavens, however loving His sway might be. I have since talked with scores of men who felt the same way.

My friend suggested what then seemed a novel idea. He said, "*Why don't you choose your own conception of God?*"

That statement hit me hard. It melted the icy intellectual mountain in whose shadow I had lived and shivered many years. I stood in the sunlight at last.

It was only a matter of being willing to believe in a power greater than myself. Nothing more was required of me to make my beginning. I saw that growth could start from that point. Upon a foundation of complete willingness I might build what I saw in my friend. Would I have it? Of course I would!

Thus was I convinced that God is concerned with us humans when we want Him enough. At long last I saw, I felt, I believed. Scales of pride and prejudice fell from my eyes. A new world came into view.

The real significance of my experience in the Cathedral burst upon me. For a brief moment, I had needed and wanted God. There had been a humble willingness to have Him with me–and He came. But soon the sense of His presence had been blotted out by worldly clamors, mostly those within myself. And so it had been ever since. How blind I had been.

At the hospital I was separated from alcohol for the last time. Treatment seemed wise, for I showed signs of delirium tremens.

There I humbly offered myself to God, as I then understood Him, to do with me as He would. I placed myself unreservedly under His care and direction. I admitted for the first time that of myself I was nothing; that without Him I was lost. I ruthlessly faced my sins and became willing to have my new-found Friend take them away, root and branch. I have not had a drink since.

My schoolmate visited me, and I fully acquainted him with my problems and deficiencies. We made a list of people I had hurt or toward whom I felt resentment. I expressed my entire willingness to approach these individuals, admitting my wrong. Never was I to be critical of them. I was to right all such matters to the utmost of my ability.

I was to test my thinking by the new God-consciousness within. Common sense would thus become uncommon sense. I was to sit quietly when in doubt, asking only for direction and strength to meet my problems as He would have me. Never was I to pray for myself, except as my requests bore on my usefulness to others. Then only might I expect to receive. But that would be in great measure.

My friend promised when these things were done I would enter upon a new relationship with my Creator; that I would have the elements of a way of living which answered all my problems. Belief in the power of God, plus enough willingness, honesty and humility to establish and maintain the new order of things, were the essential requirements.

Simple, but not easy; a price had to be paid. It meant destruction of self-centeredness. I must turn in all things to the Father of Light who presides over us all.

These were revolutionary and drastic proposals, but the moment I fully accepted them, the effect was electric. There was a sense of victory, followed by such a peace and serenity as I had ever known. There was utter confidence. I felt lifted up, as though the great clean wind of a mountain top blew through and through. God comes to most men gradually, but His impact on me was sudden and profound.

For a moment I was alarmed, and called my friend, the doctor, to ask if I were still sane. He listened in wonder as I talked.

Finally he shook his head saying, "Something has happened to you I don't understand. But you had better hang on to it. Anything is better than the way you were." The good doctor now sees many men who have such experiences. He knows that they are real.

While I lay in the hospital the thought came that there were thousands of hopeless alcoholics who might be glad to have what had been so freely given me. Perhaps I could help some of them. They in turn might work with others.

My friend had emphasized the absolute necessity of demonstrating these principles in all my affairs. Particularly was it imperative to work with others as he had worked with me. Faith without works was dead, he said. And how appallingly true for the alcoholic! For if an alcoholic failed to perfect and enlarge his spiritual life through work and self-sacrifice for others, he could not survive the certain trials and low spots ahead. If he did not work, he would surely drink again, and if he drank, he would surely die. Then faith would be dead indeed. With us it is just like that.

My wife and I abandoned ourselves with enthusiasm to the idea of helping other alcoholics to a solution of their problems. It was fortunate, for my old business associates remained skeptical for a year and a half, during which I found little work. I was not too well at the time, and was plagued by waves of self-pity and resentment. This sometimes nearly drove me back to drink, but I soon found that when all other measures failed, work with another alcoholic would save the day. Many times I have gone to my old hospital in despair. On talking to a man there, I would be amazingly lifted up and set on my feet. It is a design for living that works in rough going.

We commenced to make many fast friends and a fellowship has grown up among us of which it is a wonderful thing to feel a part. The joy of living we really have, even under pressure and difficulty. I have seen hundreds of families set their feet in the path that really goes somewhere; have seen the most impossible domestic situations righted; feuds and bitterness of all sorts wiped out. I have seen men come out of asylums and resume a vital place in the lives of their families and communities. Business and professional men have regained their standing. There is scarcely any form of trouble and misery which has not been overcome among us. In one western city and its environs there are one thousand of us and our families. We meet frequently so that newcomers may find the fellowship they seek. At these informal gatherings one may often see from 50 to 200 persons. We are growing in numbers and power.

An alcoholic in his cups is an unlovely creature. Our struggles with them are variously strenuous, comic, and tragic. One poor chap committed suicide in my home. He could not, or would not, see our way of life.

There is, however, a vast amount of fun about it all. I suppose some would be shocked at our seeming worldliness and levity. But just underneath there is deadly earnestness. Faith has to work twenty-four hours a day in and through us, or we perish.

Most of us feel we need look no further for Utopia. We have it with us right here and now. Each day my friend's simple talk in our kitchen multiplies itself in a widening circle of peace on earth and good will to men.

Chapter II

THERE IS A SOLUTION

WE, OF ALCOHOLICS ANONYMOUS, know thousands of men and women who were once just as hopeless as Bill. Nearly all have recovered. They have solved the drink problem.

We are average Americans. All sections of this country and many of its occupations are represented, as well as many political, economic, social, and religious backgrounds. We are people who normally would not mix. But there exists among us a fellowship, a friendliness, and an understanding which is indescribably wonderful. We are like the passengers of a great liner the moment after rescue from shipwreck when camaraderie, joyousness and democracy pervade the vessel from steerage to Captain's table. Unlike the feelings of the ships passengers, however, our joy in escape from disaster does not subside as we go our individual ways. The feeling of having shared in a common peril is one element in the powerful cement which binds us. But that in itself would never have held us together as we are now joined.

The tremendous fact for every one of us is that we have discovered a common solution. We have a way out on which we can absolutely agree, and upon which we can join in brotherly and harmonious action. This is the great news this book carries to those who suffer from alcoholism.

An illness of this sort–and we have come to believe it an illness–involves those about us in a way no other human sickness can. If a person has cancer all are sorry for him and no one is angry or hurt. But not so with the alcoholic illness, for with it there goes annihilation of all the things worth while in life. It engulfs all whose lives touch the sufferer's. It brings misunderstanding, fierce resentment, financial insecurity, disgusted friends and employers, warped lives of blameless children, sad wives and parents–anyone can increase the list.

We hope this volume will inform and comfort those who are, or who may be affected. There are many.

Highly competent psychiatrists who have dealt with us have found it sometimes impossible to persuade an alcoholic to discuss his situation without reserve. Strangely enough, wives, parents and intimate friends usually find us even more unapproachable than do the psychiatrist and the doctor.

But the ex-problem drinker who has found this solution, who is properly armed with facts about himself, can generally win the entire confidence of another alcoholic in a few hours. Until such an understanding is reached, little or nothing can be accomplished.

That the man who is making the approach has had the same difficulty, that he obviously knows what he is talking about, that his whole deportment shouts at the new prospect that he is a man with a real answer, that he has no attitude of Holier Than Thou, nothing whatever except the sincere desire to be helpful; that there are no fees to pay, no axes to grind, no people to please, no lectures to be endured–these are the conditions we have found most effective. After such an approach many take up their beds and walk again.

None of us makes a sole vocation of this work, nor do we think its effectiveness would be increased if we did. We feel that elimination of our drinking is but a beginning. A much more important demonstration of our principles lies before us in our respective homes, occupations and affairs. All of us spend much of our spare time in the sort of effort which we are going to describe. A few are fortunate enough to be so situated that they can give nearly all their time to the work.

If we keep on the way we are going there is little doubt that much good will result, but the surface of the problem would hardly be scratched. Those of us who live in large cities are overcome by the reflection that close by hundreds are dropping into oblivion every day. Many could recover if they had the opportunity we have enjoyed. How then shall we present that which has been so freely given us?

We have concluded to publish an anonymous volume setting forth the problem as we see it. We shall bring to the task our combined experience and knowledge. This should suggest a useful program for anyone concerned with a drinking problem.

Of necessity there will have to be discussion of matters medical, psychiatric, social, and religious. We are aware that these matters are from their very nature, controversial. Nothing would please us so much as to write a book which would contain no basis for contention or argument. We shall do our utmost to achieve that ideal. Most of us sense that real tolerance of other people's shortcomings and viewpoints and a respect for their opinions are attitudes which make us more useful to others. Our very lives, as ex-problem drinkers, depend upon our constant thought of others and how we may help meet their needs.

You may already have asked yourself why it is that all of us became so very ill from drinking. Doubtless you are curious to discover how and why, in the face of expert opinion to the contrary, we have recovered from a hopeless condition of mind and body. If you are an alcoholic who wants to get over it, you may already be asking–"What do I have to do?"

It is the purpose of this book to answer such questions specifically. We shall tell you what we have done. Before going into a detailed discussion, it may be well to summarize some points as we see them.

How many time people have said to us: "I can take it or leave it alone. Why can't he?" "Why don't you drink like a gentleman or quit?" "That fellow can't handle his liquor." "Why don't you try beer and wine?" "Lay off the hard stuff." "His will power must be weak." "He could stop if he wanted to." "She's such a sweet girl, I should think he'd stop for her sake." "The doctor told him that if he ever drank again it would kill him, but there he is all lit up again."

Now these are commonplace observations on drinkers which we hear all the time. Back of them is a world of ignorance and misunderstanding. We see that these expressions refer to people whose reactions are very different from ours.

Moderate drinkers have little trouble in giving up liquor entirely if they have good reason for it. They can take it or leave it alone.

Then we have a certain type of hard drinker. He may have the habit badly enough to gradually impair him physically and mentally. It may cause him to die a few years before his time. If a sufficiently strong reason–ill health, falling in love, change of environment, or the warning of a doctor–becomes operative, this man can also stop or moderate, although he may find it difficult and troublesome and may even need medical attention.

But what about the real alcoholic? He may start off as a moderate drinker; he may or may not become a continuous hard drinker; but at some stage of his drinking career he begins to lose all control of his liquor consumption, once he starts to drink.

Here is a fellow who has been puzzling you, especially in his lack of control. He does absurd, incredible, tragic things while drinking. He is a real Dr. Jekyll and Mr. Hyde. He is seldom mildly intoxicated. He is always more or less insanely drunk. His disposition while drinking resembles his normal nature but little. He may be one of the finest fellows in the world. Yet let him drink for a day, and he frequently becomes disgustingly, and even dangerously anti-social. He has a positive genius for getting tight at exactly the wrong moment, particularly when some important decision must be made or engagement kept. He is often perfectly sensible and well balanced concerning everything except liquor, but in that respect he is incredibly dishonest and selfish. He often possesses special abilities, skills, and aptitudes, and has a promising career ahead of him. He uses his gifts to build up a bright outlook for his family and himself, and then pulls the structure down on his head by a senseless series of sprees. He is the fellow who goes to bed so intoxicated he ought to sleep the clock around. Yet early next morning he searches madly for the bottle he misplace the night before. If he can afford it, he may have liquor concealed all over his house to be certain no one gets his entire supply away from him to throw down the wastepipe. As matters grow worse, he begins to use a combination of high-powered sedative and liquor to quiet his nerves so he can go to work. Then comes the day when he simply cannot make it and gets drunk all over again. Perhaps he goes to a doctor who gives him morphine or some sedative with which to taper off. Then he begins to appear at hospitals and sanitariums.

This is by no means a comprehensive picture of the true alcoholic, as our behavior patterns vary. But this description should identify him roughly.

Why does he behave like this? If hundreds of experiences have shown him that one drink means another debacle with all its attendant suffering and humiliation, why is it he takes that one drink? Why can't he stay on the water wagon? What has become of the common sense and will power that he still sometimes displays with respect to other matters?

Perhaps there never will be a full answer to these questions. Opinions vary considerably as to why the alcoholic reacts differently from normal people. We are not sure why, once a certain point is reached, little can be done for him. We cannot answer the riddle.

We know that while the alcoholic keeps away from drink, as he may do for months or years, he reacts much like other men. We are equally positive that once he takes any alcohol whatever into his system, something happens, both in the bodily and mental sense, which makes it virtually impossible for him to stop. The experience of any alcoholic will abundantly confirm this.

These observations would be academic and pointless if our friend never took the first drink, thereby setting the terrible cycle in motion. Therefore, the main problem of the alcoholic centers in his mind, rather than in his body. If you ask him why he started on that last bender, the chances are he will offer you any one of a hundred alibis. Sometimes these excuses have a certain plausibility, but none of them really makes sense in the light of the havoc an alcoholic's drinking bout creates. They sound like the philosophy of the man who, having a headache, beats himself on the head with a hammer so that he can't feel the ache. If you draw this fallacious reasoning to the attention of an alcoholic, he will laugh it off, or become irritated and refuse to talk.

Once in a while he may tell the truth. And the truth, strange to say, is usually that he has no more idea why he took that first drink than you have. Some drinkers have excuses with which they are satisfied part of the time. But in their hearts they really do not know why they do it. Once this malady has a real hold, they are a baffled lot. There is the obsession that somehow, someday, they will beat the game. But they often suspect they are down for the count.

How true this is, few realize. In a vague way their families and friends sense that these drinkers are abnormal, but everybody hopefully awaits the day when the sufferer will rouse himself from his lethargy and assert his power of will.

The tragic truth is that if the man be a real alcoholic, the happy day may not arrive. He has lost control. At a certain point in the drinking of every alcoholic, he passes into a state where the most powerful desire to stop drinking is of absolutely no avail. This tragic situation has already arrived in practically every case long before it is suspected.

The fact is that most alcoholics, for reasons yet obscure, have lost the power of choice in drink. Our so-called will power becomes practically nonexistent. We are unable, at certain times, to bring into our consciousness with sufficient force the memory of the suffering and humiliation of even a week or a month ago. We are without defense against the first drink.

The almost certain consequences that follow taking even a glass of beer do not crowd into the mind to deter us. If these thoughts occur, they are hazy and readily supplanted with the old threadbare idea that this time we shall handle ourselves like other people. There is a complete failure of the kind of defense that keeps one from putting his hand on a hot stove.

The alcoholic may say to himself in the most casual way, "It won't burn me this time, so here's how!" Or perhaps he doesn't think at all. How often have some of us begun to drink in this nonchalant way, and after the third or fourth, pounded on the bar and said to ourselves, "For God's sake, how did I ever get started again?" Only to have that thought supplanted by "Well, I'll stop with the sixth drink." Or "What's the use anyhow?"

When this sort of thinking is fully established in an individual with alcoholic tendencies, he has probably placed himself beyond human aid, and unless locked up, may die or go permanently insane. These stark and ugly facts have been confirmed by legions of alcoholics throughout history. But for the grace of God, there would have been thousands more convincing demonstrations. So many want to stop but cannot.

There is a solution. Almost none of us liked the self-searching, the leveling of our pride, the confession of shortcomings which the process requires for its successful consummation. But we saw that it really worked in others, and we had come to believe in the hopelessness and futility of life as we had been living it. When, therefore, we were approached by those in whom the problem had been solved, there was nothing left for us but to pick up the simple kit of spiritual tools laid at our feet. We have found much of heaven and we have been rocketed into a fourth dimension of existence of which we had not even dreamed.

The great fact is just this, and nothing less: That we have had deep and effective spiritual experiences [*Fully explained–Appendix II.*] which have revolutionized our whole attitude toward life, toward our fellows and toward God's universe. The central fact of our lives today is the absolute certainty that our Creator has entered into our hearts and lives in a way which is indeed miraculous. He has commenced to accomplish those things for us which we could never do by ourselves.

If you are as seriously alcoholic as we were, we believe there is no middle-of-the-road solution. We were in a position where life was becoming impossible, and if we had passed into the region from which there is no return through human aid, we had but two alternatives: One was to go on to the bitter end, blotting out the consciousness of our intolerable situation as best we could; and the other, to accept spiritual help. This we did because we honestly wanted to, and were willing to make the effort.

A certain American business man had ability, good sense, and high character. For years he had floundered from one sanitarium to another. He had consulted the best known American psychiatrists. Then he had gone to Europe, placing himself in the care of a celebrated physician (the psychiatrist, Dr. Jung) who prescribed for him. Though experience had made him skeptical, he finished his treatment with unusual confidence. His physical and mental condition were unusually good. Above all, he believed he had acquired such a profound knowledge of the inner workings of his mind and its hidden springs that relapse was unthinkable. Nevertheless, he was drunk in a short time. More baffling still, he could give himself no satisfactory explanation for his fall.

So he returned to this doctor, whom he admired, and asked him point-blank why he could not recover. He wished above all things to regain self-control. He seemed quite rational and well-balanced with respect to other problems. Yet he had no control whatever over alcohol. Why was this?

He begged the doctor to tell him the whole truth, and he got it. In the doctor's judgment he was utterly hopeless; he could never regain his position in society and he would have to place himself under lock and key or hire a bodyguard if he expected to live long. That was a great physician's opinion.

But this man still lives, and is a free man. He does not need a bodyguard nor is he confined. He can go anywhere on this earth where other free men may go without disaster, provided he remains willing to maintain a certain simple attitude.

Some of our alcoholic readers may think they can do without spiritual help. Let us tell you the rest of the conversation our friend had with his doctor.

The doctor said: "You have the mind of a chronic alcoholic. I have never seen one single case recover, where that state of mind existed to the extent that it does in you." Our friend felt as though the gates of hell had closed on him with a clang.

He said to the doctor, "Is there no exception?"

"Yes," replied the doctor, "there is. Exceptions to cases such as yours have been occurring since early times. Here and there, once in a while, alcoholics have had what are called vital spiritual experiences. To me these occurrences are phenomena. They appear to be in the nature of huge emotional displacements and rearrangements. Ideas, emotions, and attitudes which were once the guiding forces of the lives of these men are suddenly cast to one side, and a completely new set of conceptions and motives begin to dominate them. In fact, I have been trying to produce some such emotional rearrangement within you. With many individuals the methods which I employed are successful, but I have never been successful with an alcoholic of your description." [*For amplification–see Appendix II (Spiritual Experiences)*.]

Upon hearing this, our friend was somewhat relieved, for he reflected that, after all, he was a good church member. This hope, however, was destroyed by the doctor's telling him that while his religious convictions were very good, in his case they did not spell the necessary vital spiritual experience.

Here was the terrible dilemma in which our friend found himself when he had the extraordinary experience, which as we have already told you, made him a free man.

We, in our turn, sought the same escape with all the desperation of drowning men. What seemed at first a flimsy reed, has proved to be the loving and powerful hand of God. A new life has been given us or, if you prefer, "a design for living" that really works.

The distinguished American psychologist, William James, in his book "Varieties of Religious Experience," indicates a multitude of ways in which men have discovered God. We have no desire to convince anyone that there is only one way by which faith can be acquired. If what we have learned and felt and seen means anything at all, it means that all of us, whatever our race, creed, or color are the children of a living Creator with whom we may form a relationship upon simple and understandable terms as soon as we are willing and honest enough to try. Those having religious affiliations will find here nothing disturbing to their beliefs or ceremonies. There is no friction among us over such matters.

We think it no concern of ours what religious bodies our members identify themselves with as individuals. This should be an entirely personal affair which each one decides for himself in the light of past associations, or his present choice. Not all of us join religious bodies, but most of us favor such memberships.

In the following chapter, there appears an explanation of alcoholism, as we understand it, then a chapter addressed to the agnostic. Many who once were in this class are now among our members. Surprisingly enough, we find such convictions no great obstacle to a spiritual experience.

Further on, clear-cut directions are given showing how we recovered. These are followed by three dozen personal experiences.

Each individual, in the personal stories, describes in his own language and from his own point of view the way he established his relationship with God. These give a fair cross section of our membership and a clear-cut idea of what has actually happened in their lives.

We hope no one will consider these self-revealing accounts in bad taste. Our hope is that many alcoholic men and women, desperately in need, will see these pages, and we believe that it is only by fully disclosing ourselves and our problems that they will be persuaded to say, "Yes, I am one of them too; I must have this thing."

Chapter III

MORE ABOUT ALCOHOLISM

MOST OF US have been unwilling to admit we were real alcoholics. No person likes to think he is bodily and mentally different from his fellows. Therefore, it is not surprising that our drinking careers have been characterized by countless vain attempts to prove we could drink like other people. The idea that somehow, someday he will control and enjoy his drinking is the great obsession of every abnormal drinker. The persistence of this illusion is astonishing. Many pursue it into the gates of insanity or death.

We learned that we had to fully concede to our innermost selves that we were alcoholics. This is the first step in recovery. The delusion that we are like other people, or presently may be, has to be smashed.

We alcoholics are men and women who have lost the ability to control our drinking. We know that no real alcoholic *ever* recovers control. All of us felt at times that we were regaining control, but such intervals–usually brief–were inevitably followed by still less control, which led in time to pitiful and incomprehensible demoralization. We are convinced to a man that alcoholics of our type are in the grip of a progressive illness. Over any considerable period we get worse, never better.

We are like men who have lost their legs; they never grow new ones. Neither does there appear to be any kind of treatment which will make alcoholics of our kind like other men. We have tried every imaginable remedy. In some instances there has been brief recovery, followed always by a still worse relapse. Physicians who are familiar with alcoholism agree there is no such thing as making a normal drinker out of an alcoholic. Science may one day accomplish this, but it hasn't done so yet.

Despite all we can say, many who are real alcoholics are not going to believe they are in that class. By every form of self-deception and experimentation, they will try to prove themselves exceptions to the rule, therefore nonalcoholic. If anyone who is showing inability to control his drinking can do the right-about-face and drink like a gentleman, our hats are off to him. Heaven knows, we have tried hard enough and long enough to drink like other people!

Here are some of the methods we have tried: Drinking beer only, limiting the number of drinks, never drinking alone, never drinking in the morning, drinking only at home, never having it in the house, never drinking during business hours, drinking only at parties, switching from scotch to brandy, drinking only natural wines, agreeing to resign if ever drunk on the job, taking a trip, not taking a trip, swearing off forever (with and without a solemn oath), taking more physical exercise, reading inspirational books, going to health farms and sanitariums, accepting voluntary commitment to asylums–we could increase the list ad infinitum.

We do not like to pronounce any individual as alcoholic, but you can quickly diagnose yourself. Step over to the nearest barroom and try some controlled drinking. Try to drink and stop abruptly. Try it more than once. It will not take long for you to decide, if you are honest with yourself about it. It may be worth a bad case of jitters if you get a full knowledge of your condition.

Though there is no way of proving it, we believe that early in our drinking careers most of us could have stopped drinking. But the difficulty is that few alcoholics have enough desire to stop while there is yet time. We have heard of a few instances where people, who showed definite signs of alcoholism, were able to stop for a long period because of an overpowering desire to do so. Here is one.

A man of thirty was doing a great deal of spree drinking. He was very nervous in the morning after these bouts and quieted himself with more liquor. He was ambitious to succeed in business, but saw that he would get nowhere if he drank at all. Once he started, he had no control whatever. He made up his mind that until he had been successful in business and had retired, he would not touch another drop. An exceptional man, he remained bone dry for twenty-five years and retired at the age of fifty-five, after a successful and happy business career. Then he fell victim to a belief which practically every alcoholic has–that his long period of sobriety and self-discipline had qualified him to drink as other men. Out came his carpet slippers and a bottle. In two months he was in a hospital, puzzled and humiliated. He tried to regulate his drinking for a little while, making several trips to the hospital meantime. Then, gathering all his forces, he attempted to stop altogether and found he could not. Every means of solving his problem which money could buy was at his disposal. Every attempt failed. Though a robust man at retirement, he went to pieces quickly and was dead within four years.

This case contains a powerful lesson. Most of us have believed that if we remained sober for a long stretch, we could thereafter drink normally. But here is a man who at fifty-five years found he was just where he had left off at thirty. We have seen the truth demonstrated again and again: "Once an alcoholic, always an alcoholic." Commencing to drink after a period of sobriety, we are in a short time as bad as ever. If we are planning to stop drinking, there must be no reservation of any kind, nor any lurking notion that someday we will be immune to alcohol.

Young people may be encouraged by this man's experience to think that they can stop, as he did, on their own will power. We doubt if many of them can do it, because none will really want to stop, and hardly one of them, because of the peculiar mental twist already acquired, will find he can win out. Several of our crowd, men of thirty or less, had been drinking only a few years, but they found themselves as helpless as those who had been drinking twenty years.

To be gravely affected, one does not necessarily have to drink a long time nor take the quantities some of us have. This is particularly true of women. Potential female alcoholics often turn into the real thing and are gone beyond recall in a few years. Certain drinkers, who would be greatly insulted if called alcoholics, are astonished at their inability to stop. We, who are familiar with the symptoms, see large numbers of potential alcoholics among young people everywhere. But try and get them to see it!

As we look back, we feel we had gone on drinking many years beyond the point where we could quit on our will power. If anyone questions whether he has entered this dangerous area, let him try leaving liquor alone for one year. If he is a real alcoholic and very far advanced, there is scant chance of success. In the early days of our drinking we occasionally remained sober for a year or more, becoming serious drinkers again later. Though you may be able to stop for a considerable period, you may yet be a potential alcoholic. We think few, to whom this book will appeal, can stay dry anything like a year. Some will be drunk the day after making their resolutions; most of them within a few weeks.

For those who are unable to drink moderately the question is how to stop altogether. We are assuming, of course, that the reader desires to stop. Whether such a person can quit upon a nonspiritual basis depends upon the extent to which he has already lost the power to choose whether he will drink or not. Many of us felt that we had plenty of character. There was a tremendous urge to cease forever. Yet we found it impossible. This is the baffling feature of alcoholism as we know it–this utter inability to leave it alone, no matter how great the necessity or the wish.

How then shall we help our readers determine, to their own satisfaction, whether they are one of us? The experiment of quitting for a period of time will be helpful, but we think we can render an even greater service to alcoholic sufferers and perhaps to the medical fraternity. So we shall describe some of the mental states that precede a relapse into drinking, for obviously this is the crux of the problem.

What sort of thinking dominates an alcoholic who repeats time after time the desperate experiment of the first drink? Friends who have reasoned with him after a spree which has brought him to the point of divorce or bankruptcy are mystified when he walks directly into a saloon. Why does he? Of what is he thinking?

Our first example is a friend we shall call Jim. This man has a charming wife and family. He inherited a lucrative automobile agency. He had a commendable World War record. He is a good salesman. Everybody likes him. He is an intelligent man, normal so far as we can see, except for a nervous disposition. He did no drinking until he was thirty-five. In a few years he became so violent when intoxicated that he had to be committed. On leaving the asylum he came into contact with us.

We told him what we knew of alcoholism and the answer we had found. He made a beginning. His family was re-assembled, and he began to work as a salesman for the business he had lost through drinking. All went well for a time, but he failed to enlarge his spiritual life. To his consternation, he found himself drunk half a dozen times in rapid succession. On each of these occasions we worked with him, reviewing carefully what had happened. He agreed he was a real alcoholic and in a serious condition. He knew he faced another trip to the asylum if he kept on. Moreover, he would lose his family for whom he had a deep affection.

Yet he got drunk again. We asked him to tell us exactly how it happened. This is his story: "I came to work on Tuesday morning. I remember I felt irritated that I had to be a salesman for a concern I once owned. I had a few words with the boss, but nothing serious. Then I decided to drive to the country and see one of my prospects for a car. On the way I felt hungry so I stopped at a roadside place where they have a bar. I had no intention of drinking. I just thought I would get a sandwich. I also had the notion that I might find a customer for a car at this place, which was familiar for I had been going to it for years. I had eaten there many times during the months I was sober. I sat down at a table and ordered a sandwich and a glass of milk. Still no thought of drinking. I ordered another sandwich and decided to have another glass of milk.

"*Suddenly the thought crossed my mind that if I were to put an ounce of whiskey in my milk it couldn't hurt me on a full stomach. I ordered a whiskey and poured it into the milk. I vaguely sensed I was not being any too smart, but felt reassured as I was taking the whiskey on a full stomach.* The experiment went so well that I ordered another whiskey and poured it into more milk. That didn't seem to bother me so I tried another."

Thus started one more journey to the asylum for Jim. Here was the threat of commitment, the loss of family and position, to say nothing of that intense mental and physical suffering which drinking always caused him. *He had much knowledge about himself as an alcoholic. Yet all reasons for not drinking were easily pushed aside in favor of the foolish idea that he could take whiskey if only he mixed it with milk!*

Whatever the precise definition of the word may be, we call this plain insanity. How can such a lack of proportion, of the ability to think straight, be called anything else?

You may think this an extreme case. To us it is not far-fetched, for this kind of thinking has been characteristic of every single one of us. We have sometimes reflected more than Jim did upon the consequences. But there was always the curious mental phenomenon that parallel with our sound reasoning there inevitably ran some insanely trivial excuse for taking the first drink. Our sound reasoning failed to hold us in check. The insane idea won out. Next day we would ask ourselves, in all earnestness and sincerity, how it could have happened.

In some circumstances we have gone out deliberately to get drunk, feeling ourselves justified by nervousness, anger, worry, depression, jealousy or the like. But even in this type of beginning we are obliged to admit that our justification for a spree was insanely insufficient in the light of what always happened. We now see that when we began to drink deliberately, instead or casually, there was little serious or effective thought during the period of premeditation of what the terrific consequences might be.

Our behavior is as absurd and incomprehensible with respect to the first drink as that of an individual with a passion, say, for jay-walking. He gets a thrill out of skipping in front of fast-moving vehicles. He enjoys himself for a few years in spite of friendly warnings. Up to this point you would label him as a foolish chap having queer ideas of fun. Luck then deserts him and he is slightly injured several times in succession. You would expect him, if he were normal, to cut it out. Presently he is hit again and this time has a fractured skull. Within a week after leaving the hospital a fast-moving trolley car breaks his arm. He tells you he has decided to stop jay-walking for good, but in a few weeks he breaks both legs.

On through the years this conduct continues, accompanied by his continual promises to be careful or to keep off the streets altogether. Finally, he can no longer work, his wife gets a divorce and he is held up to ridicule. He tries every known means to get the jay-walking idea out of his head. He shuts himself up in an asylum, hoping to mend his ways. But the day he comes out he races in front of a fire engine, which breaks his back. Such a man would be crazy, wouldn't he?

You may think our illustration is too ridiculous. But is it? We, who have been through the wringer, have to admit if we substituted alcoholism for jay-walking, the illustration would fit exactly. However intelligent we may have been in other respects, where alcohol has been involved, we have been strangely insane. It's strong language–but isn't it true?

Some of you are thinking: "Yes, what you tell us is true, but it doesn't fully apply. We admit we have some of these symptoms, but we have not gone to the extremes you fellows did, nor are we likely to, for we understand ourselves so well after what you have told us that such things cannot happen again. We have not lost everything in life through drinking and we certainly do not intend to. Thanks for the information."

That may be true of certain nonalcoholic people who, though drinking foolishly and heavily at the present time, are able to stop or moderate, because their brains and bodies have not been damaged as ours were. But the actual or potential alcoholic, with hardly any exception, will be *absolutely unable to stop drinking on the basis of self-knowledge.* This is a point we wish to emphasize and re-emphasize, to smash home upon our alcoholic readers as it has been revealed to us out of bitter experience. Let us take another illustration.

Fred is a partner in a well-known accounting firm. His income is good, he has a fine home, is happily married and the father of promising children of college age. He has so attractive a personality that he makes friends with everyone. If ever there was a successful business man, it is Fred. To all appearance he is a stable, well balanced individual. Yet, he is alcoholic. We first saw Fred about a year ago in a hospital where he had gone to recover from a bad case of jitters. It was his first experience of this kind, and he was much ashamed of it. Far from admitting he was an alcoholic, he told himself he came to the hospital to rest his nerves. The doctor intimated strongly that he might be worse than he realized. For a few days he was depressed about his condition. He made up his mind to quit drinking altogether. It never occurred to him that perhaps he could not do so, in spite of his character and standing. Fred would not believe himself an alcoholic, much less accept a spiritual remedy for his problem. We told him what we knew about alcoholism. He was interested and conceded that he had some of the symptoms, but he was a long way from admitting that he could do nothing about it himself. He was positive that this humiliating experience, plus the knowledge he had acquired, would keep him sober the rest of his life. Self-knowledge would fix it.

We heard no more of Fred for a while. One day we were told that he was back in the hospital. This time he was quite shaky. He soon indicated he was anxious to see us. The story he told is most instructive, for here was a chap absolutely convinced he had to stop drinking, who had no excuse for drinking, who exhibited splendid judgment and determination in all his other concerns, yet was flat on his back nevertheless.

Let him tell you about it: "I was much impressed with what you fellows said about alcoholism, and I frankly did not believe it would be possible for me to drink again. I rather appreciated your ideas about the subtle insanity which precedes the first drink, but I was confident it could not happen to me after what I had learned. I reasoned I was not so far advanced as most of you fellows, that I had been usually successful in licking my other personal problems, and that I would therefore be successful where you men failed. I felt I had every right to be self-confident, that it would be only a matter of exercising my will power and keeping on guard.

"In this frame of mind, I went about my business and for a time all was well. I had no trouble refusing drinks, and began to wonder if I had not been making too hard work of a simple matter. One day I went to Washington to present some accounting evidence to a government bureau. I had been out of town before during this particular dry spell, so there was nothing new about that. Physically, I felt fine. Neither did I have any pressing problems or worries. My business came off well, I was pleased and knew my partners would be too. It was the end of a perfect day, not a cloud on the horizon.

"I went to my hotel and leisurely dressed for dinner. *As I crossed the threshold of the dining room, the thought came to mind that it would be nice to have a couple of cocktails with dinner. That was all. Nothing more.* I ordered a cocktail and my meal. Then I ordered another cocktail. After dinner I decided to take a walk. When I returned to the hotel it struck me a highball would be fine before going to bed, so I stepped into the bar and had one. I remember having several more that night and plenty next morning. I have a shadowy recollection of being in an airplane bound for New York, and of finding a friendly taxicab driver at the landing field instead of my wife. The driver escorted me for several days. I know little of where I went or what I said and did. Then came the hospital with the unbearable mental and physical suffering.

"As soon as I regained my ability to think, I went carefully over that evening in Washington. *Not only had I been off guard, I had made no fight whatever against the first drink. This time I had not thought of the consequences at all.* I had commenced to drink as carelessly as though the cocktails were ginger ale. I now remembered what my alcoholic friends had told me, how they prophesied that if I had an alcoholic mind, the time and place would come–I would drink again. They had said that though I did raise a defense, it would one day give way before some trivial reason for having a drink. Well, just that did happen and more, for what I had learned of alcoholism did not occur to me at all. I knew from that moment that I had an alcoholic mind. I saw that will power and self-knowledge would not help in those strange mental blank spots. I had never been able to understand people who said that a problem had them hopelessly defeated. I knew then. It was the crushing blow.

"Two of the members of Alcoholics Anonymous came to see me. They grinned, which I didn't like so much, and then asked me if I thought myself alcoholic and if I were really licked this time. I had to concede both propositions. They piled on me heaps of evidence to the effect that an alcoholic mentality, such as I had exhibited in Washington, was hopeless condition. They cited cases out of their own experience by the dozen. This process snuffed out the last flicker of conviction that I could do the job myself.

"Then they outlined the spiritual answer and program of action which a hundred of them had followed successfully. Though I had been only a nominal churchman, their proposals were not, intellectually, hard to swallow. But the program of action, though entirely sensible, was pretty drastic. It meant I would have to throw several lifelong conceptions out of the window. That was not easy. But the moment I made up my mind to go through with the process, I had the curious feeling that my alcoholic condition was relieved, as in fact it proved to be.

"Quite as important was the discovery that spiritual principles would solve all my problems. I have since been brought into a way of living infinitely more satisfying and, I hope, more useful than the life I lived before. My old manner of life was by no means a bad one, but I would not exchange its best moments for the worst I have now. I would not go back to it even if I could."

Fred's story speaks for itself. We hope it strikes home to thousands like him. He had felt only the first nip of the wringer. Most alcoholics have to be pretty badly mangled before they really commence to solve their problems.

Many doctors and psychiatrists agree with our conclusions. One of these men, staff member of a world-renowned hospital, recently made this statement to some of us: "What you say about the general hopelessness of the average alcoholic's plight is, in my opinion, correct. As to two of you men, whose stories I have heard, there is no doubt in my mind that you were 100 percent hopeless, apart from divine help. Had you offered yourselves as patients at this hospital, I would not have taken you, if I had been able to avoid it. People like you are too heartbreaking. Though not a religious person, I have profound respect for the spiritual approach in such cases as yours. For most cases, there is virtually no other solution."

Once more: The alcoholic at certain times has no effective mental defense against the first drink. Except in a few cases, neither he nor any other human being can provide such a defense. His defense must come from a Higher Power.

Chapter IV

WE AGNOSTICS

IN THE PRECEDING chapters you have learned something of alcoholism. We hope we have made clear the distinction between the alcoholic and the non-alcoholic. If, when you honestly want to, you find you cannot quit entirely, or if when drinking, you have little control over the amount you take, you are probably alcoholic. If that be the case, you may be suffering from an illness which only a spiritual experience will conquer.

To one who feels he is an atheist or agnostic such an experience seems impossible, but to continue as he is means disaster, especially if he is an alcoholic of the hopeless variety. To be doomed to an alcoholic death or to live on a spiritual basis are not always easy alternatives to face.

But it isn't so difficult. About half our original fellowship were of exactly that type. At first some of us tried to avoid the issue, hoping against hope we were not true alcoholics. But after a while we had to face the fact that we must find a spiritual basis of life–or else. Perhaps it is going to be that way with you. But cheer up, something like half of us thought we were atheists or agnostics. Our experience shows that you need not be disconcerted.

If a mere code of morals or a better philosophy of life were sufficient to overcome alcoholism, many of us would have recovered long ago. But we found that such codes and philosophies did not save us, no matter how much we tried. We could wish to be moral, we could wish to be philosophically comforted, in fact, we could will these things with all our might, but the needed power wasn't there. Our human resources, as marshalled by the will, were not sufficient; they failed utterly.

Lack of power, that was our dilemma. We had to find a power by which we could live, and it had to be a *Power greater than ourselves.* Obviously. But where and how were we to find this Power?

Well, that's exactly what this book is about. Its main object is to enable you to find a Power greater than yourself which will solve your problem. That means we have written a book which we believe to be spiritual as well as moral. And it means, of course, that we are going to talk about God. Here difficulty arises with agnostics. Many times we talk to a new man and watch his hope rise as we discuss his alcoholic problems and explain our fellowship. But his face falls when we speak of spiritual matters, especially when we mention God, for we have re-opened a subject which our man thought he had neatly evaded or entirely ignored.

We know how he feels. We have shared his honest doubt and prejudice. Some of us have been violently anti-religious. To others, the word "God" brought up a particular idea of Him with which someone had tried to impress them during childhood. Perhaps we rejected this particular conception because it seemed inadequate. With that rejection we imagined we had abandoned the God idea entirely. We were bothered with the thought that faith and dependence upon a Power beyond ourselves was somewhat weak, even cowardly. We looked upon this world of warring individuals, warring theological systems, and inexplicable calamity, with deep skepticism. We looked askance at many individuals who claimed to be godly. How could a Supreme Being have anything to do with it all? And who could comprehend a Supreme Being anyhow? Yet, in other moments, we found ourselves thinking, when enchanted by a starlit night, "Who, then, made all this?" There was a feeling of awe and wonder, but it was fleeting and soon lost.

Yes, we of agnostic temperament have had these thoughts and experiences. Let us make haste to reassure you. We found that as soon as we were able to lay aside prejudice and express even a willingness to believe in a Power greater than ourselves, we commenced to get results, even though it was impossible for any of us to fully define or comprehend that Power, which is God.

Much to our relief, we discovered we did not need to consider another's conception of God. Our own conception, however inadequate, was sufficient to make the approach and to effect a contact with Him. As soon as we admitted the possible existence of a Creative Intelligence, a Spirit of the Universe underlying the totality of things, we began to be possessed of a new sense of power and direction, provided we took other simple steps. We found that God does not make too hard terms with those who seek Him. To us, the Realm of Spirit is broad, roomy, all inclusive; never exclusive or forbidding to those who earnestly seek. It is open, we believe, to all men.

When, therefore, we speak to you of God, we mean your own conception of God. This applies, too, to other spiritual expressions which you find in this book. Do not let any prejudice you may have against spiritual terms deter you from honestly asking yourself what they mean to you. At the start, this was all we needed to commence spiritual growth, to effect our first conscious relation with God as we understood Him. Afterward, we found ourselves accepting many things which then seemed entirely out of reach. That was growth, but if we wished to grow we had to begin somewhere. So we used our own conception, however limited it was.

We needed to ask ourselves but one short question. "Do I now believe, or am I even willing to believe, that there is a Power greater than myself?" As soon as a man can say that he does believe, or is willing to believe, we emphatically assure him that he is on his way. It has been repeatedly proven among us that upon this simple cornerstone a wonderfully effective spiritual structure can be built. [*Please be sure to read Appendix II on "Spiritual Experience."*]

That was great news to us, for we had assumed we could not make use of spiritual principles unless we accepted many things on faith which seemed difficult to believe. When people presented us with spiritual approaches, how frequently did we all say, "I wish I had what that man has. I'm sure it would work if I could only believe as he believes. But I cannot accept as surely true the many articles of faith which are so plain to him." So it was comforting to learn that we could commence at a simpler level.

Besides a seeming inability to accept much on faith, we often found ourselves handicapped by obstinacy, sensitiveness, and unreasoning prejudice. Many of us have been so touchy that even casual reference to spiritual things made us bristle with antagonism. This sort of thinking had to be abandoned. Though some of us resisted, we found no great difficulty in casting aside such feelings. Faced with alcoholic destruction, we soon became as open minded on spiritual matters as we had tried to be on other questions. In this respect alcohol was a great persuader. It finally beat us into a state of reasonableness. Sometimes this was a tedious process; we hope no one else will be prejudiced for as long as some of us were.

The reader may still ask why he should believe in a Power greater than himself. We think there are good reasons. Let us have a look at some of them.

The practical individual of today is a stickler for facts and results. Nevertheless, the twentieth century readily accepts theories of all kinds, provided they are firmly grounded in fact. We have numerous theories, for example, about electricity. Everybody believes them without a murmur of doubt. Why this ready acceptance? Simply because it is impossible to explain what we see, feel, direct, and use, without a reasonable assumption as a starting point.

Everybody nowadays, believes in scores of assumptions for which there is good evidence, but no perfect visual proof. And does not science demonstrate that visual proof is the weakest proof? It is being constantly revealed, as mankind studies the material world, that outward appearances are not inward reality at all. To illustrate:

The prosaic steel girder is a mass of electrons whirling around each other at incredible speed. These tiny bodies are governed by precise laws, and these laws hold true throughout the material world. Science tells us so. We have no reason to doubt it. When, however, the perfectly logical assumption is suggested that underneath the material world and life as we see it, there is an All Powerful, Guiding, Creative Intelligence, right there our perverse streak comes to the surface and we laboriously set out to convince ourselves it isn't so. We read wordy books and indulge in windy arguments, thinking we believe this universe needs no God to explain it. Were our contentions true, it would follow that life originated out of nothing, means nothing, and proceeds nowhere.

Instead of regarding ourselves as intelligent agents, spearheads of God's ever advancing Creation, we agnostics and atheists chose to believe that our human intelligence was the last word, the alpha and the omega, the beginning and end of all. Rather vain of us, wasn't it?

We, who have traveled this dubious path, beg you to lay aside prejudice, even against organized religion. We have learned that whatever the human frailties of various faiths may be, those faiths have given purpose and direction to millions. People of faith have a logical idea of what life is all about. Actually, we used to have no reasonable conception whatever. We used to amuse ourselves by cynically dissecting spiritual beliefs and practices when we might have observed that many spiritually-minded persons of all races, colors, and creeds were demonstrating a degree of stability, happiness and usefulness which we should have sought ourselves.

Instead, we looked at the human defects of these people, and sometimes used their shortcomings as a basis of wholesale condemnation. We talked of intolerance, while we were intolerant ourselves. We missed the reality and the beauty of the forest because we were diverted by the ugliness of some its trees. We never gave the spiritual side of life a fair hearing.

In our personal stories you will find a wide variation in the way each teller approaches and conceives of the Power which is greater than himself. Whether we agree with a particular approach or conception seems to make little difference. Experience has taught us that these are matters about which, for our purpose, we need not be worried. They are questions for each individual to settle for himself.

On one proposition, however, these men and women are strikingly agreed. Every one of them has gained access to, and believe in, a Power greater than himself. This Power has in each case accomplished the miraculous, the humanly impossible. As a celebrated American statesman put it, "Let's look at the record."

Here are thousands of men and women, worldly indeed. They flatly declare that since they have come to believe in a Power greater than themselves, to take a certain attitude toward that Power, and to do certain simple things, there has been a revolutionary change in their way of living and thinking. In the face of collapse and despair, in the face of the total failure of their human resources, they found that a new power, peace, happiness, and sense of direction flowed into them. This happened soon after they wholeheartedly met a few simple requirements. Once confused and baffled by the seeming futility of existence, they show the underlying reasons why they were making heavy going of life. Leaving aside the drink question, they tell why living was so unsatisfactory. They show how the change came over them. When many hundreds of people are able to say that the consciousness of the Presence of God is today the most important fact of their lives, they present a powerful reason why one should have faith.

This world of ours has made more material progress in the last century than in all the millenniums which went before. Almost everyone knows the reason. Students of ancient history tell us that the intellect of men in those days was equal to the best of today. Yet in ancient times material progress was painfully slow. The spirit of modern scientific inquiry, research and invention was almost unknown. In the realm of the material, men's minds were fettered by superstition, tradition, and all sort of fixed ideas. Some of the contemporaries of Columbus thought a round earth preposterous. Others came near putting Galileo to death for his astronomical heresies.

We asked ourselves this: Are not some of us just as biased and unreasonable about the realm of the spirit as were the ancients about the realm of the material? Even in the present century, American newspapers were afraid to print an account of the Wright brothers' first successful flight at Kitty Hawk. Had not all efforts at flight failed before? Did not Professor Langley's flying machine go to the bottom of the Potomac River? Was it not true that the best mathematical minds had proved man could never fly? Had not people said God had reserved this privilege to the birds? Only thirty years later the conquest of the air was almost an old story and airplane travel was in full swing.

But in most fields our generation has witnessed complete liberation in thinking. Show any longshoreman a Sunday supplement describing a proposal to explore the moon by means of a rocket and he will say, "I bet they do it–maybe not so long either." Is not our age characterized by the ease with which we discard old ideas for new, by the complete readiness with which we throw away the theory or gadget which does not work for something new which does?

We had to ask ourselves why we shouldn't apply to our human problems this same readiness to change our point of view. We were having trouble with personal relationships, we couldn't control our emotional natures, we were a prey to misery and depression, we couldn't make a living, we had a feeling of uselessness, we were full of fear, we were unhappy, we couldn't seem to be of real help to other people–was not a basic solution of these bedevilments more important than whether we should see newsreels of lunar flight? Of course it was.

When we saw others solve their problems by a simple reliance upon the Spirit of the Universe, we had to stop doubting the power of God. Our ideas did not work. But the God idea did.

The Wright brothers' almost childish faith that they could build a machine which would fly was the mainspring of their accomplishment. Without that, nothing could have happened. We agnostics and atheists were sticking to the idea that self-sufficiency would solve our problems. When others showed us that "God-sufficiency" worked with them, we began to feel like those who had insisted the Wrights would never fly.

Logic is great stuff. We like it. We still like it. It is not by chance we were given the power to reason, to examine the evidence of our sense, and to draw conclusions. That is one of man's magnificent attributes. We agnostically inclined would not feel satisfied with a proposal which does not lend itself to reasonable approach and interpretation. Hence we are at pains to tell why we think our present faith is reasonable, why we think it more sane and logical to believe than not to believe, why we say our former thinking was soft and mushy when we threw up our hands in doubt and said, "We don't know."

When we became alcoholics, crushed by a self-imposed crisis we could not postpone or evade, we had to fearlessly face the proposition that either

God is everything or else He is nothing. God either is, or He isn't. What was our choice to be?

Arrived at this point, we were squarely confronted with the question of faith. We couldn't duck the issue. Some of us had already walked far over the Bridge of Reason toward the desired shore of faith. The outlines and the promise of the New Land had brought lustre to tired eyes and fresh courage to flagging spirits. Friendly hands had stretched out in welcome. We were grateful that Reason had brought us so far. But somehow, we couldn't quite step ashore. Perhaps we had been leaning too heavily on Reason that last mile and we did not like to lose our support.

That was natural, but let us think a little more closely. Without knowing it, had we not been brought to where we stood by a certain kind of faith? For did we not believe in our own reasoning? Did we not have confidence in our ability to think? What was that but a sort of faith? Yes, we had been faithful, abjectly faithful to the God of Reason. So, in one way or another, we discovered that faith had been involved all the time!

We found, too, that we had been worshippers. What a state of mental goose-flesh that used to bring on! Had we not variously worshipped people, sentiment, things, money, and ourselves? And then, with a better motive, had we not worshipfully beheld the sunset, the sea, or a flower? Who of us had not loved something or somebody? How much did these feelings, these loves, these worships, have to do with pure reason? Little or nothing, we saw at last. Were not these things the tissue out of which our lives were constructed? Did not these feelings, after all, determine the course of our existence? It was impossible to say we had no capacity for faith, or love, or worship. In one form or another we had been living by faith and little else.

Imagine life without faith! Were nothing left but pure reason, it wouldn't be life. But we believed in life–of course we did. We could not prove life in the sense that you can prove a straight line is the shortest distance between two points, yet, there it was. Could we still say the whole thing was nothing but a mass of electrons, created out of nothing, meaning nothing, whirling on to a destiny of nothingness? Or course we couldn't. The electrons themselves seemed more intelligent than that. At least, so the chemist said.

Hence, we saw that reason isn't everything. Neither is reason, as most of us use it, entirely dependable, thought it emanate from our best minds. What about people who proved that man could never fly?

Yet we had been seeing another kind of flight, a spiritual liberation from this world, people who rose above their problems. They said God made these things possible, and we only smiled. We had seen spiritual release, but liked to tell ourselves it wasn't true.

Actually we were fooling ourselves, for deep down in every man, woman, and child, is the fundamental idea of God. It may be obscured by calamity, by pomp, by worship of other things, but in some form or other it is there. For faith in a Power greater than ourselves, and miraculous demonstrations of that power in human lives, are facts as old as man himself.

We finally saw that faith in some kind of God was a part of our make-up, just as much as the feeling we have for a friend. Sometimes we had to search fearlessly, but He was there. He was as much a fact as we were. We found the Great Reality deep down within us. In the last analysis it is only there that He may be found. It was so with us.

We can only clear the ground a bit. If our testimony helps sweep away prejudice, enables you to think honestly, encourages you to search diligently within yourself, then, if you wish, you can join us on the Broad Highway. With this attitude you cannot fail. The consciousness of your belief is sure to come to you.

In this book you will read the experience of a man who thought he was an atheist. His story is so interesting that some of it should be told now. His change of heart was dramatic, convincing, and moving.

Our friend was a minister's son. He attended church school, where he became rebellious at what he thought an overdose of religious education. For years thereafter he was dogged by trouble and frustration. Business failure, insanity, fatal illness, suicide–these calamities in his immediate family embittered and depressed him. Post-war disillusionment, ever more serious alcoholism, impending mental and physical collapse, brought him to the point of self-destruction.

One night, when confined in a hospital, he was approached by an alcoholic who had known a spiritual experience. Our friend's gorge rose as he bitterly cried out: "If there is a God, He certainly hasn't done anything for me!" But later, alone in his room, he asked himself this question: "Is it possible that all the religious people I have known are wrong?" While pondering the answer he felt as though he lived in hell. Then, like a thunderbolt, a great thought came. It crowded out all else:

"*Who are you to say there is no God?*"

This man recounts that he tumbled out of bed to his knees. In a few seconds he was overwhelmed by a conviction of the Presence of God. It poured over and through him with the certainty and majesty of a great tide at flood. The barriers he had built through the years were swept away. He stood in the Presence of Infinite Power and Love. He had stepped from bridge to shore. For the first time, he lived in conscious companionship with his Creator.

Thus was our friend's cornerstone fixed in place. No later vicissitude has shaken it. His alcoholic problem was taken away. That very night, years ago, it disappeared. Save for a few brief moments of temptation the thought of drink has never returned; and at such times a great revulsion has risen up in him. Seemingly he could not drink even if he would. God had restored his sanity.

What is this but a miracle of healing? Yet its elements are simple. Circumstances made him willing to believe. He humbly offered himself to his Maker–then he knew.

Even so has God restored us all to our right minds. To this man, the revelation was sudden. Some of us grow into it more slowly. But He has come to all who have honestly sought Him.

When we drew near to Him He disclosed Himself to us!

Chapter V

HOW IT WORKS

RARELY HAVE we seen a person fail who has thoroughly followed our path. Those who do not recover are people who cannot or will not completely give themselves to this simple program, usually men and women who are constitutionally incapable of being honest with themselves. There are such unfortunates. They are not at fault; they seem to have been born that way. They are naturally incapable of grasping and developing a manner of living which demands rigorous honesty. Their chances are less than average. There are those, too, who suffer from grave emotional and mental disorders, but many of them do recover if they have the capacity to be honest.

Our stories disclose in a general way what we used to be like, what happened, and what we are like now. If you have decided you want what we have and are willing to go to any length to get it–then you are ready to take certain steps.

At some of these we balked. We thought we could find an easier, softer way. But we could not. With all the earnestness at our command, we beg of you to be fearless and thorough from the very start. Some of us have tried to hold on to our old ideas and the result was nil until we let go absolutely.

Remember that we deal with alcohol–cunning, baffling, powerful! Without help it is too much for us. But there is One who has all power–that One is God. May you find Him now!

Half measures availed us nothing. We stood at the turning point. We asked His protection and care with complete abandon.

Here are the steps we took, which are suggested as a program of recovery:

1. We admitted we were powerless over alcohol–that our lives had become unmanageable.
2. Came to believe that a Power greater than ourselves could restore us to sanity.
3. Made a decision to turn our will and our lives over to the care of God *as we understood Him.*
4. Made a searching and fearless moral inventory of ourselves.
5. Admitted to God, to ourselves, and to another human being the

exact nature of our wrongs.

6. Were entirely ready to have God remove all these defects of character.
7. Humbly asked Him to remove our shortcomings.
8. Made a list of all persons we had harmed, and became willing to make amends to them all.
9. Made direct amends to such people wherever possible, except when to do so would injure them or others.
10. Continued to take personal inventory and when we were wrong promptly admitted it.
11. Sought through prayer and meditation to improve our conscious contact with God *as we understood Him*, praying only for knowledge of His will for us and the power to carry that out.
12. Having had a spiritual awakening as the result of these steps, we tried to carry this message to alcoholics, and to practice these principles in all our affairs.

Many of us exclaimed, "What an order! I can't go through with it." Do not be discouraged. No one among us has been able to maintain anything like perfect adherence to these principles. We are not saints. The point is, that we are willing to grow along spiritual lines. The principles we have set down are guides to progress. We claim spiritual progress rather than spiritual perfection.

Our description of the alcoholic, the chapter to the agnostic, and our personal adventures before and after make clear three pertinent ideas:

(a) That we were alcoholic and could not manage our own lives.
(b) That probably no human power could have relieved our alcoholism.
(c) That God could and would if He were sought.

Being convinced, *we were at Step Three*, which is that we decided to turn our will and our life over to God as we understood Him. Just what do we mean by that, and just what do we do?

The first requirement is that we be convinced that any life run on self-will can hardly be a success. On that basis we are almost always in collision with something or somebody, even though our motives are good. Most people try to live by self-propulsion. Each person is like an actor who wants to run the whole show; is forever trying to arrange the lights, the ballet, the scenery and the rest of the players in his own way. If his arrangements would only stay put, if only people would do as he wished, the show would be great. Everybody, including himself, would be pleased. Life would be wonderful. In trying to make these arrangements our actor may sometimes be quite virtuous. He may be kind, considerate, patient, generous; even modest and self-sacrificing. On the other hand, he may be mean, egotistical, selfish and dishonest. But, as with most humans, he is more likely to have varied traits.

What usually happens? The show doesn't come off very well. He begins to think life doesn't treat him right. He decides to exert himself more. He becomes, on the next occasion, still more demanding or gracious, as the case may be. Still the play does not suit him. Admitting he may be somewhat at fault, he is sure that other people are more to blame. He becomes angry, indignant, self-pitying. What is his basic trouble? Is he not really a self-seeker even when trying to be kind? Is he not a victim of the delusion that he can wrest satisfaction and happiness out of this world if he only manages well? Is it not evident to all the rest of the players that these are the things he wants? And do not his actions make each of them wish to retaliate, snatching all they can get out of the show? Is he not, even in his best moments, a producer of confusion rather than harmony?

Our actor is self-centered–ego-centric, as people like to call it nowadays. He is like the retired business man who lolls in the Florida sunshine in the winter complaining of the sad state of the nation; the minister who sighs over the sins of the twentieth century; politicians and reformers who are sure all would be Utopia if the rest of the world would only behave; the outlaw safe cracker who thinks society has wronged him; and the alcoholic who has lost all and is locked up. Whatever our protestations, are not most of us concerned with ourselves, our resentments, or our self-pity?

Selfishness–self-centeredness! That, we think, is the root of our troubles. Driven by a hundred forms of fear, self-delusion, self-seeking, and self-pity, we step on the toes of our fellows and they retaliate. Sometimes they hurt us, seemingly without provocation, but we invariably find that at some time in the past we have made decisions based on self which later placed us in a position to be hurt.

So our troubles, we think, are basically of our own making. They arise out of ourselves, and the alcoholic is an extreme example of self-will run riot, though he usually doesn't think so. Above everything, we alcoholics must be rid of this selfishness. We must, or it kills us! God makes that possible. And there often seems no way of entirely getting rid of self without His aid. Many of us had moral and philosophical convictions galore, but we could not live up to them even though we would have liked to. Neither could we reduce our self-centeredness much by wishing or trying on our own power. We had to have God's help.

This is the how and why of it. First of all, we had to quit playing God. It didn't work. Next, we decided that hereafter in this drama of life, God was going to be our Director. He is the Principal; we are His agents. He is the Father, and we are His children. Most Good ideas are simple, and this concept was the keystone of the new and triumphant arch through which we passed to freedom.

When we sincerely took such a position, all sorts of remarkable things followed. We had a new Employer. Being all powerful, He provided what we needed, if we kept close to Him and performed His work well. Established on such a footing we became less and less interested in ourselves, our little plans and designs. More and more we became interested in seeing what we could contribute to life. As we felt new power flow in, as we enjoyed peace of mind, as we discovered we could face life successfully, as we became conscious of His presence, we began to lose our fear of today, tomorrow or the hereafter. We were reborn.

We were now at Step Three. Many of us said to our Maker, *as we understood Him:* "God, I offer myself to Thee–to build with me and to do with me as Thou wilt. Relieve me of the bondage of self, that I may better do Thy will. Take away my difficulties, that victory over them may bear witness to those I would help of Thy Power, Thy Love, and Thy Way of life. May I do Thy will always!" We thought well before taking this step making sure we were ready; that we could at last abandon ourselves utterly to Him.

We found it very desirable to take this spiritual step with an understanding person, such as our wife, best friend, or spiritual adviser. But it is better to meet God alone than with one who might misunderstand. The wording was, of course, quite optional so long as we expressed the idea, voicing it without reservation. This was only a beginning, though if honestly and humbly made, an effect, sometimes a very great one, was felt at once.

Next we launched out on a course of vigorous action, the first step of which is a personal housecleaning, which many of us had never attempted. Though our decision was vital and crucial step, it could have little permanent effect unless at once followed by a strenuous effort to face, and to be rid of, the things in ourselves which had been blocking us. Our liquor was but a symptom. So we had to get down to causes and conditions.

Therefore, we started upon a personal inventory. *This was Step Four.* A business which takes no regular inventory usually goes broke. Taking commercial inventory is a fact-finding and a fact-facing process. It is an effort to discover the truth about the stock-in-trade. One object is to disclose damaged or unsalable goods, to get rid of them promptly and without regret. If the owner of the business is to be successful, he cannot fool himself about values.

We did exactly the same thing with our lives. We took stock honestly. First, we searched out the flaws in our make-up which caused our failure. Being convinced that self, manifested in various ways, was what had defeated us, we considered its common manifestations.

Resentment is the "number one" offender. It destroys more alcoholics than anything else. From it stem all forms of spiritual disease, for we have been not only mentally and physically ill, we have been spiritually sick. When the spiritual malady is overcome, we straighten out mentally and physically. In dealing with resentments, we set them on paper. We listed people, institutions or principles with whom we were angry. We asked ourselves why we were angry. In most cases it was found that our self-esteem, our pocketbooks, our ambitions, our personal relationships (including sex) were hurt or threatened. So we were sore. We were "burned up."

On our grudge list we set opposite each name our injuries. Was it our self-esteem, our security, our ambitions, our personal, or sex relations, which had been interfered with?

We were usually as definite as this example:

I'm resentful at: Mr. Brown
The Cause: His attention to my wife.
Affects my: Sex relations. Self-esteem (fear).
The Cause: Told my wife of my mistress.
Affects my: Sex relations. Self-esteem (fear).
The Cause: Brown may get my job at the office.
Affects my: Security. Self-esteem (fear).

I'm resentful at: Mrs. Jones
The Cause: She's a nut–she snubbed me. She committed her husband for drinking. He's my friend. She's a gossip.
Affects my: Personal relationship. Self-esteem (fear).

I'm resentful at: My employer
The Cause: Unreasonable–Unjust–Overbearing–Threatens to fire me for drinking and padding my expense account.
Affects my: Self-esteem (fear). Security.

I'm resentful at: My wife
The Cause: Misunderstands and nags. Likes Brown. Wants house put in her name.
Affects my: Pride–Personal sex relations–Security (fear).

We went back through our lives. Nothing counted but thoroughness and honesty. When we were finished we considered it carefully. The first thing apparent was that this world and its people were often quite wrong. To conclude that others were wrong was as far as most of us ever got. The usual outcome was that people continued to wrong us and we stayed sore. Sometimes it was remorse and then we were sore at ourselves. But the more we fought and tried to have our own way, the worse matters got. As in war, the victor only *seemed* to win. Our moments of triumph were short-lived.

It is plain that a life which includes deep resentment leads only to futility and unhappiness. To the precise extent that we permit these, do we squander the hours that might have been worth while. But with the alcoholic, whose hope is the maintenance and growth of a spiritual experience, this business of resentment is infinitely grave. We found that it is fatal. For when harboring such feeling we shut ourselves off from the sunlight of the Spirit. The insanity of alcohol returns and we drink again. And with us, to drink is to die.

If we were to live, we had to be free of anger. The grouch and the brainstorm were not for us. They may be the dubious luxury of normal men, but for alcoholics these things are poison.

We turned back to the list, for it held the key to the future. We were prepared to look for it from an entirely different angle. We began to see that the world and its people really dominated us. In that state, the wrong-doing of others, fancied or real, had power to actually kill. How could we escape? We saw that these resentments must be mastered, but how? We could not wish them away any more than alcohol.

This was our course: We realized that the people who wronged us were perhaps spiritually sick. Though we did not like their symptoms and the way these disturbed us, they, like ourselves, were sick too. We asked God to help us show them the same tolerance, pity, and patience that we would cheerfully grant a sick friend. When a person offended we said to ourselves, "This is a sick man. How can I be helpful to him? God save me from being angry. Thy will be done."

We avoid retaliation or argument. We wouldn't treat sick people that way. If we do, we destroy our chance of being helpful. We cannot be helpful to all people, but at least God will show us how to take a kindly and tolerant view of each and every one.

Referring to our list again. Putting out of our minds the wrongs others had done, we resolutely looked for our own mistakes. Where had we been selfish, dishonest, self-seeking and frightened? Though a situation had not been entirely our fault, we tried to disregard the other person involved entirely. Where were we to blame? The inventory was ours, not the other man's. When we saw our faults we listed them. We placed them before us in black and white. We admitted our wrongs honestly and were willing to set these matters straight.

Notice that the word "fear" is bracketed alongside the difficulties with Mr. Brown, Mrs. Jones, the employer, and the wife. This short word somehow touches about every aspect of our lives. It was an evil and corroding thread; the fabric of our existence was shot through with it. It set in motion trains of circumstances which brought us misfortune we felt we didn't deserve. But did not we, ourselves, set the ball rolling? Sometimes we think fear ought to be classed with stealing. It seems to cause more trouble.

We reviewed our fears thoroughly. We put them on paper, even though we had no resentment in connection with them. We asked ourselves why we had them. Wasn't it because self-reliance failed us? Self-reliance was good as far as it went, but it didn't go far enough. Some of us once had great self-confidence, but it didn't fully solve the fear problem, or any other. When it made us cocky, it was worse.

Perhaps there is a better way–we think so. For we are now on a different basis; the basis of trusting and relying upon God. We trust infinite God rather than our finite selves. We are in the world to play the role He assigns. Just to the extent that we do as we think He would have us, and humbly rely on Him, does He enable us to match calamity with serenity.

We never apologize to anyone for depending upon our Creator. We can laugh at those who think spirituality the way of weakness. Paradoxically, it is the way of strength. The verdict of the ages is that faith means courage. All men of faith have courage. They trust their God. We never apologize for

God. Instead we let Him demonstrate, through us, what He can do. We ask Him to remove our fear and direct our attention to what He would have us be. At once, we commence to outgrow fear.

Now about sex. Many of us needed an overhauling there. But above all, we tried to be sensible on this question. It's so easy to get way off the track. Here we find human opinions running to extremes–absurd extremes, perhaps. One set of voices cry that sex is a lust of our lower nature, a base necessity of procreation. Then we have the voices who cry for sex and more sex; who bewail the institution of marriage; who think that most of the troubles of the race are traceable to sex causes. They think we do not have enough of it, or that it isn't the right kind. They see its significance everywhere. One school would allow man no flavor for his fare and the other would have us all on a straight pepper diet. We want to stay out of this controversy. We do not want to be the arbiter of anyone's sex conduct. We all have sex problems. We'd hardly be human if we didn't. What can we do about them?

We reviewed our own conduct over the years past. Where had we been selfish, dishonest, or inconsiderate? Whom had we hurt? Did we unjustifiably arouse jealousy, suspicion or bitterness? Where were we at fault, what should we have done instead? We got this all down on paper and looked at it.

In this way we tried to shape a sane and sound ideal for our future sex life. We subjected each relation to this test–was it selfish or not? We asked God to mold our ideals and help us to live up to them. We remembered always that our sex powers were God-given and therefore good, neither to be used lightly or selfishly nor to be despised and loathed.

Whatever our ideal turns out to be, we must be willing to grow toward it. We must be willing to make amends where we have done harm, provided that we do not bring about still more harm in so doing. In other words, we treat sex as we would any other problem. In meditation, we ask God what we should do about each specific matter. The right answer will come, if we want it.

God alone can judge our sex situation. Counsel with persons is often desirable, but we let God be the final judge. We realize that some people are as fanatical about sex as others are loose. We avoid hysterical thinking or advice.

Suppose we fall short of the chosen ideal and stumble? Does this mean we are going to get drunk. Some people tell us so. But this is only a half-truth. It depends on us and on our motives. If we are sorry for what we have done, and have the honest desire to let God take us to better things, we believe we will be forgiven and will have learned our lesson. If we are not sorry, and our conduct continues to harm others, we are quite sure to drink. We are not theorizing. These are facts out of our experience.

To sum up about sex: We earnestly pray for the right ideal, for guidance in each questionable situation, for sanity, and for the strength to do the right thing. If sex is very troublesome, we throw ourselves the harder into helping others. We think of their needs and work for them. This takes us out of ourselves. It quiets the imperious urge, when to yield would mean heartache.

If we have been thorough about our personal inventory, we have written down a lot. We have listed and analyzed our resentments. We have begun to comprehend their futility and their fatality. We have commenced to see their terrible destructiveness. We have begun to learn tolerance, patience and good will toward all men, even our enemies, for we look on them as sick people. We have listed the people we have hurt by our conduct, and are willing to straighten out the past if we can.

In this book you read again and again that faith did for us what we could not do for ourselves. We hope you are convinced now that God can remove whatever self-will has blocked you off from Him. If you have already made a decision, and an inventory of your grosser handicaps, you have made a good beginning. That being so you have swallowed and digested some big chunks of truth about yourself.

Chapter VI

INTO ACTION

HAVING MADE our personal inventory, what shall we do about it? We have been trying to get a new attitude, a new relationship with our Creator, and to discover the obstacles in our path. We have admitted certain defects; we have ascertained in a rough way what the trouble is; we have put our finger on the weak items in our personal inventory. Now these are about to be cast out. This requires action on our part, which, when completed, will mean that we have admitted to God, to ourselves, and to another human being, the exact nature of our defects. This brings us to *the Fifth Step* in the program of recovery mentioned in the preceding chapter.

This is perhaps difficult–especially discussing our defects with another person. We think we have done well enough in admitting these things to ourselves. There is doubt about that. In actual practice, we usually find a solitary self-appraisal insufficient. Many of us thought it necessary to go much further. We will be more reconciled to discussing ourselves with another person when we see good reasons why we should do so. The best reason first: If we skip this vital step, we may not overcome drinking. Time after time newcomers have tried to keep to themselves certain facts about their lives. Trying to avoid this humbling experience, they have turned to easier methods. Almost invariably they got drunk. Having persevered with the rest of the program, they wondered why they fell. We think the reason is that they never completed their housecleaning. They took inventory all right, but hung on to some of the worst items in stock. They only *thought* they had lost their egoism and fear; they only *thought* they had humbled themselves. But they had not learned enough of humility, fearlessness and honesty, in the sense we find it necessary, until they told someone else *all* their life story.

More than most people, the alcoholic leads a double life. He is very much the actor. To the outer world he presents his stage character. This is the one he likes his fellows to see. He wants to enjoy a certain reputation, but knows in his heart he doesn't deserve it.

The inconsistency is made worse by the things he does on his sprees. Coming to his sense, he is revolted at certain episodes he vaguely remembers. These memories are a nightmare. He trembles to think someone might have observed him. As fast as he can, he pushes these memories far inside himself.

He hopes they will never see the light of day. He is under constant fear and tension–that makes for more drinking.

Psychologists are inclined to agree with us. We have spent thousands of dollars for examinations. We know but few instances where we have given these doctors a fair break. We have seldom told them the whole truth nor have we followed their advice. Unwilling to be honest with these sympathetic men, we were honest with no one else. Small wonder many in the medical profession have a low opinion of alcoholics and their chance for recovery!

We must be entirely honest with somebody if we expect to live long or happily in this world. Rightly and naturally, we think well before we choose the person or persons with whom to take this intimate and confidential step. Those of us belonging to a religious denomination which requires confession must, and of course, will want to go to the properly appointed authority whose duty it is to receive it. Though we have no religious connection, we may still do well to talk with someone ordained by an established religion. We often find such a person quick to see and understand our problem. Of course, we sometimes encounter people who do not understand alcoholics.

If we cannot or would rather not do this, we search our acquaintance for a close-mouthed, understanding friend. Perhaps our doctor or psychologist will be the person. It may be one of our own family, but we cannot disclose anything to our wives or our parents which will hurt them and make them unhappy. We have no right to save our own skin at another person's expense. Such parts of our story we tell to someone who will understand, yet be unaffected. The rule is we must be hard on ourself, but always considerate of others.

Notwithstanding the great necessity for discussing ourselves with someone, it may be one is so situated that there is no suitable person available. If that is so, this step may be postponed, only, however, if we hold ourselves in complete readiness to go through with it at the first opportunity. We say this because we are very anxious that we talk to the right person. It is important that he be able to keep a confidence; that he fully understand and approve what we are driving at; that he will not try to change our plan. But we must not use this as a mere excuse to postpone.

When we decide who is to hear our story, we waste no time. We have a written inventory and we are prepared for a long talk. We explain to our partner what we are about to do and why we have to do it. He should realize that we are engaged upon a life-and-death errand. Most people approached in this way will be glad to help; they will be honored by our confidence.

We pocket our pride and go to it, illuminating every twist of character, every dark cranny of the past. Once we have taken this step, withholding nothing, we are delighted. We can look the world in the eye. We can be alone at perfect peace and ease. Our fears fall from us. We begin to feel the nearness of our Creator. We may have had certain spiritual beliefs, but now we begin to have a spiritual experience. The feeling that the drink problem has disappeared will often come strongly. We feel we are on the Broad Highway, walking hand in hand with the Spirit of the Universe.

Returning home we find a place where we can be quiet for an hour, carefully reviewing what we have done. We thank God from the bottom of our heart that we know Him better. Taking this book down from our shelf we turn to the page which contains the twelve steps. Carefully reading the first five proposals we ask if we have omitted anything, for we are building an arch through which we shall walk a free man at last. Is our work solid so far? Are the stones properly in place? Have we skimped on the cement put into the foundation? Have we tried to make mortar without sand?

If we can answer to our satisfaction, we then look at *Step Six.* We have emphasized willingness as being indispensable. Are we now ready to let God remove from us all the things which we have admitted are objectionable? Can He now take them all–every one? If we still cling to something we will not let go, we ask God to help us be willing.

When ready, we say something like this: "My Creator, I am now willing that you should have all of me, good and bad. I pray that you now remove from me every single defect of character which stands in the way of my usefulness to you and my fellows. Grant me strength, as I go out from here, to do your bidding. Amen." We have then completed *Step Seven.*

Now we need more action, without which we find that "Faith without works is dead." Let's look at *Steps Eight and Nine.* We have a list of all persons we have harmed and to whom we are willing to make amends. We made it when we took inventory. We subjected ourselves to a drastic self-appraisal. Now we go out to our fellows and repair the damage done in the past. We attempt to sweep away the debris which has accumulated out of our effort to live on self-will and run the show ourselves. If we haven't the will to do this, we ask until it comes. Remember it was agreed at the beginning *we would go to any lengths for victory over alcohol.*

Probably there are still some misgivings. As we look over the list of business acquaintances and friends we have hurt, we may feel diffident about going to some of them on a spiritual basis. Let us be reassured. To some people we need not, and probably should not emphasize the spiritual feature on our first approach. We might prejudice them. At the moment we are trying to put our lives in order. But this is not an end in itself. Our real purpose is to fit ourselves to be of maximum service to God and the people about us. It is seldom wise to approach an individual, who still smarts from our injustice to him, and announce that we have gone religious. In the prize ring, this would be called leading with the chin. Why lay ourselves open to being branded fanatics or religious bores? We may kill a future opportunity to carry a beneficial message. But our man is sure to be impressed with a sincere desire to set right the wrong. He is going to be more interested in a demonstration of good will than in our talk of spiritual discoveries.

We don't use this as an excuse for shying away from the subject of God. When it will serve any good purpose, we are willing to announce our convictions with tact and common sense. The question of how to approach the man we hated will arise. It may be he has done us more harm than we have done him and, though we may have acquired a better attitude toward him, we are still not too keen about admitting our faults. Nevertheless, with a person we dislike, we take the bit in our teeth. It is harder to go to an enemy than to a friend, but we find it much more beneficial to us. We go to him in a helpful and forgiving spirit, confessing our former ill feeling and expressing our regret.

Under no condition do we criticize such a person or argue. Simply tell him that we will never get over drinking until we have done our utmost to straighten out the past. We are there to sweep off our side of the street, realizing that nothing worth while can be accomplished until we do so, never trying to tell him what he should do. His faults are not discussed. We stick to our own. If our manner is calm, frank, and open, we will be gratified with the result.

In nine cases out of ten the unexpected happens. Sometimes the man we are calling upon admits his own fault, so feuds of years' standing melt away in an hour. Rarely do we fail to make satisfactory progress. Our former enemies sometimes praise what we are doing and wish us well. Occasionally, they will offer assistance. It should not matter, however, if someone does throw us out of his office. We have made our demonstration, done our part. It's water over the dam.

Most alcoholics owe money. We do not dodge our creditors. Telling them what we are trying to do, we make no bones about our drinking; they usually know it anyway, whether we think so or not. Nor are we afraid of disclosing our alcoholism on the theory it may cause financial harm. Approached in this way, the most ruthless creditor will sometimes surprise us. Arranging the best deal we can we let these people know we are sorry. Our drinking has made us slow to pay. We must lose our fear of creditors no matter how far we have to go, for we are liable to drink if we are afraid to face them.

Perhaps we have committed a criminal offense which might land us in jail if it were known to the authorities. We may be short in our accounts and unable to make good. We have already admitted this in confidence to another person, but we are sure we would be imprisoned or lose our job if it were known. Maybe it's only a petty offense such as padding the expense account. Most of us have done that sort of thing. Maybe we are divorced, and have remarried but haven't kept up the alimony to number one. She is indignant about it, and has a warrant out for our arrest. That's a common form of trouble too.

Although these reparations take innumerable forms, there are some general principles which we find guiding. Reminding ourselves that we have decided to go to any lengths to find a spiritual experience, we ask that we be given strength and direction to do the right thing, no matter what the personal consequences may be. We may lose our position or reputation or face jail, but we are willing. We have to be. We must not shrink at anything.

Usually, however, other people are involved. Therefore, we are not to be the hasty and foolish martyr who would needlessly sacrifice others to save himself from the alcoholic pit. A man we know had remarried. Because of resentment and drinking, he had not paid alimony to his first wife. She was furious. She went to court and got an order for his arrest. He had commenced our way of life, had secured a position, and was getting his head above water. It would have been impressive heroics if he had walked up to the Judge and said, "Here I am."

We thought he ought to be willing to do that if necessary, but if he were in jail he could provide nothing for either family. We suggested he write his first wife admitting his faults and asking forgiveness. He did, and also sent a small amount of money. He told her what he would try to do in the future. He said he was perfectly willing to go to jail is she insisted. Of course she did not, and the whole situation has only since been adjusted.

Before taking drastic action which might implicate other people we secure their consent. If we have obtained permission, have consulted with others, asked God to help and the drastic step is indicated we must not shrink.

This brings to mind a story about one of our friends. While drinking, he accepted a sum of money from a bitterly-hated business rival, giving him no receipt for it. He subsequently denied having received the money and used the incident as a basis for discrediting the man. He thus used his own wrong-doing as a means of destroying the reputation of another. In fact, his rival was ruined.

He felt that he had done a wrong he could not possibly make right. If he opened that old affair, he was afraid it would destroy the reputation of his partner, disgrace his family and take away his means of livelihood. What right had he to involve those dependent upon him? How could he possibly make a public statement exonerating his rival?

After consulting with his wife and partner he came to the conclusion that it was better to take those risks than to stand before his Creator guilty of such ruinous slander. He saw that he had to place the outcome in God's hands or he would soon start drinking again, and all would be lost anyhow. He attended church for the first time in many years. After the sermon, he quietly got up and made an explanation. His action met widespread approval, and today he is one of the most trusted citizens of his town. This all happened years ago.

The chances are that we have domestic troubles. Perhaps we are mixed up with women in a fashion we wouldn't care to have advertised. We doubt if, in this respect, alcoholics are fundamentally much worse than other people. But drinking does complicate sex relations in the home. After a few years with an alcoholic, a wife gets worn out, resentful and uncommunicative. How could she be anything else? The husband begins to feel lonely, sorry for himself. He commences to look around in the night clubs, or their equivalent, for something besides liquor. Perhaps he is having a secret and exciting affair with "the girl who understands." In fairness we must say that she may understand, but what are we going to do about a thing like that? A man so involved often feels very remorseful at times, especially if he is married to a loyal and courageous girl who has literally gone through hell for him.

Whatever the situation, we usually have to do something about it. If we are sure our wife does not know, should we tell her? Not always, we think. If she knows in a general way that we have been wild, should we tell her in detail? Undoubtedly we should admit our fault. She may insist on knowing all the particulars. She will want to know who the woman is and where she is. We feel we ought to say to her that we have no right to involve another person. We are sorry for what we have done and, God willing, it shall not be repeated. More than that we cannot do; we have no right to go further. Though there may be justifiable exceptions, and though we wish to lay down no rule of any sort, we have often found this the best course to take.

Our design for living is not a one-way street. It is as good for the wife as for the husband. If we can forget, so can she. It is better, however, that one does not needlessly name a person upon whom she can vent jealousy.

Perhaps there are some cases where the utmost frankness is demanded. No outsider can appraise such an intimate situation. It may be that both will decide that the way of good sense and loving kindness is to let by-gones be by-gones. Each might pray about it, having the other one's happiness uppermost in mind. Keep it always in sight that we are dealing with that most terrible human emotion–jealousy. Good generalship may decide that the problem be attacked on the flank rather than risk a face-to-face combat.

If we have no such complication, there is plenty we should do at home. Sometimes we hear an alcoholic say that the only thing he needs to do is to keep sober. Certainly he must keep sober, for there will be no home if he doesn't. But he is yet a long way from making good to the wife or parents whom for years he has so shockingly treated. Passing all understanding is the patience mothers and wives have had with alcoholics. Had this not been so, many of us would have no homes today, would perhaps be dead.

The alcoholic is like a tornado roaring his way through the lives of others. Hearts are broken. Sweet relationships are dead. Affections have been uprooted. Selfish and inconsiderate habits have kept the home in turmoil. We feel a man is unthinking when he says that sobriety is enough. He is like the farmer who came up out of his cyclone cellar to find his home ruined. To his wife, he remarked, "Don't see anything the matter here, Ma. Ain't it grand the wind stopped blowin'?"

Yes, there is a long period of reconstruction ahead. We must take the lead. A remorseful mumbling that we are sorry won't fill the bill at all. We ought to sit down with the family and frankly analyze the past as we now see it, being very careful not to criticize them. Their defects may be glaring, but the chances are that our own actions are partly responsible. So we clean house with the family, asking each morning in meditation that our Creator show us the way of patience, tolerance, kindliness and love.

The spiritual life is not a theory. *We have to live it.* Unless one's family expresses a desire to live upon spiritual principles we think we ought not to urge them. We should not talk incessantly to them about spiritual matters. They will change in time. Our behavior will convince them more than our words. We must remember that ten or twenty years of drunkenness would make a skeptic out of anyone.

There may be some wrongs we can never fully right. We don't worry about them if we can honestly say to ourselves that we would right them if we could. Some people cannot be seen–we send them an honest letter. And there may be a valid reason for postponement in some cases. But we don't delay if it can be avoided. We should be sensible, tactful, considerate and humble without being servile or scraping. As God's people we stand on our feet; we don't crawl before anyone.

If we are painstaking about this phase of our development, we will be amazed before we are half way through. We are going to know a new freedom and a new happiness. We will not regret the past nor wish to shut the door on it. We will comprehend the word serenity and we will know peace. No matter how far down the scale we have gone, we will see how our experience can benefit others. That feeling of uselessness and self-pity will disappear. We will lose interest in selfish things and gain interest in our fellows. Self-seeking will slip away. Our whole attitude and outlook upon life will change. Fear of people and of economic insecurity will leave us. We will intuitively know how to handle situations which used to baffle us. We will suddenly realize that God is doing for us what we could not do for ourselves.

Are these extravagant promises? We think not. They are being fulfilled among us–sometimes quickly, sometimes slowly. They will always materialize if we work for them.

This thought brings us to *Step Ten*, which suggests we continue to take personal inventory and continue to set right any new mistakes as we go along. We vigorously commenced this way of living as we cleaned up the past. We have entered the world of the Spirit. Our next function is to grow in understanding and effectiveness. This is not an overnight matter. It should continue for our lifetime. Continue to watch for selfishness, dishonesty, resentment, and fear. When these crop up, we ask God at once to remove them. We discuss them with someone immediately and make amends quickly if we have harmed anyone. Then we resolutely turn our thoughts to someone we can help. Love and tolerance of others is our code.

And we have ceased fighting anything or anyone–even alcohol. For by this time sanity will have returned. We will seldom be interested in liquor. If tempted, we recoil from it as from a hot flame. We react sanely and normally, and we will find that this has happened automatically. We will see that our new attitude toward liquor has been given us without any thought or effort on our part. It just comes! That is the miracle of it. We are not fighting it, neither are we avoiding temptation. We feel as though we had been placed in a position of neutrality–safe and protected. We have not even sworn off. Instead, the problem has been removed. It does not exist for us. We are neither cocky nor are we afraid. That is how we react so long as we keep in fit spiritual condition.

It is easy to let up on the spiritual program of action and rest on our laurels. We are headed for trouble if we do, for alcohol is a subtle foe. We are not cured of alcoholism. What we really have is a daily reprieve contingent on the maintenance of our spiritual condition. Every day is a day when we must carry the vision of God's will into all of our activities. "How can I best serve Thee–Thy will (not mine) be done." These are thoughts which must go with us constantly. We can exercise our will power along this line all we wish. It is the proper use of the will.

Much has already been said about receiving strength, inspiration, and direction from Him who has all knowledge and power. If we have carefully followed directions, we have begun to sense the flow of His Spirit into us. To some extent we have become God-conscious. We have begun to develop this vital sixth sense. But we must go further and that means more action.

Step Eleven suggests prayer and meditation. We shouldn't be shy on this matter of prayer. Better men than we are using it constantly. It works, if we have the proper attitude and work at it. It would be easy to be vague about this matter. Yet, we believe we can make some definite and valuable suggestions.

When we retire at night, we constructively review our day. Were we resentful, selfish, dishonest or afraid? Do we owe an apology? Have we kept something to ourselves which should be discussed with another person at once? Were we kind and loving toward all? What could we have done better? Were we thinking of ourselves most of the time? Or were we thinking of what we could do for others, of what we could pack into the stream of life? But we must be careful not to drift into worry, remorse or morbid reflection, for that would diminish our usefulness to others. After making our review we ask God's forgiveness and inquire what corrective measures should be taken.

On awakening let us think about the twenty-four hours ahead. We consider our plans for the day. Before we begin, we ask God to direct our thinking, especially asking that it be divorced from self-pity, dishonest or self-seeking motives. Under these conditions we can employ our mental faculties with assurance, for after all God gave us brains to use. Our thought-life will be placed on a much higher plane when our thinking is cleared of wrong motives.

In thinking about our day we may face indecision. We may not be able to determine which course to take. Here we ask God for inspiration, an intuitive thought or a decision. We relax and take it easy. We don't struggle. We are often surprised how the right answers come after we have tried this for a while. What used to be the hunch or the occasional inspiration gradually becomes a working part of the mind. Being still inexperienced and having just made conscious contact with God, it is not probable that we are going to be inspired at all times. We might pay for this presumption in all sorts of absurd actions and ideas. Nevertheless, we find that our thinking will, as time passes, be more and more on the plane of inspiration. We come to rely upon it.

We usually conclude the period of meditation with a prayer that we be shown all through the day what our next step is to be, that we be given whatever we need to take care of such problems. We ask especially for freedom from self-will, and are careful to make no request for ourselves only. We may ask for ourselves, however, if others will be helped. We are careful never to pray for our own selfish ends. Many of us have wasted a lot of time doing that and it doesn't work. You can easily see why.

If circumstances warrant, we ask our wives or friends to join us in morning meditation. If we belong to a religious denomination which requires a definite morning devotion, we attend to that also. If not members of religious bodies, we sometimes select and memorize a few set prayers which emphasize the principles we have been discussing. There are many helpful books also. Suggestions about these may be obtained from one's priest, minister, or rabbi. Be quick to see where religious people are right. Make use of what they offer.

As we go through the day we pause, when agitated or doubtful, and ask for the right thought or action. We constantly remind ourselves we are no longer running the show, humbly saying to ourselves many times each day "Thy will be done." We are then in much less danger of excitement, fear, anger, worry, self-pity, or foolish decisions. We become much more efficient. We do not tire so easily, for we are not burning up energy foolishly as we did when we were trying to arrange life to suit ourselves.

It works–it really does.

We alcoholics are undisciplined. So we let God discipline us in the simple way we have just outlined.

But this is not all. There is action and more action. "Faith without works is dead." The next chapter is entirely devoted to *Step Twelve*.

Chapter VII

WORKING WITH OTHERS

PRACTICAL EXPERIENCE shows that nothing will so much insure immunity from drinking as intensive work with other alcoholics. It works when other activities fail. This is our *twelfth suggestion:* Carry this message to other alcoholics! You can help when no one else can. You can secure their confidence when others fail. Remember they are very ill.

Life will take on new meaning. To watch people recover, to see them help others, to watch loneliness vanish, to see a fellowship grow up about you, to have a host of friends–this is an experience you must not miss. We know you will not want to miss it. Frequent contact with newcomers and with each other is the bright spot of our lives.

Perhaps you are not acquainted with any drinkers who want to recover. You can easily find some by asking a few doctors, ministers, priests or hospitals. They will be only too glad to assist you. Don't start out as an evangelist or reformer. Unfortunately a lot of prejudice exists. You will be handicapped if you arouse it. Ministers and doctors are competent and you can learn much from them if you wish, but it happens that because of your own drinking experience you can be uniquely useful to other alcoholics. So cooperate; never criticize. To be helpful is our only aim.

When you discover a prospect for Alcoholics Anonymous, find out all you can about him. If he does not want to stop drinking, don't waste time trying to persuade him. You may spoil a later opportunity. This advice is given for his family also. They should be patient, realizing they are dealing with a sick person.

If there is any indication that he wants to stop, have a good talk with the person most interested in him–usually his wife. Get an idea of his behavior, his problems, his background, the seriousness of his condition, and his religious leanings. You need this information to put yourself in his place, to see how you would like him to approach you if the tables were turned.

Sometimes it is wise to wait till he goes on a binge. The family may object to this, but unless he is in a dangerous physical condition, it is better to risk it. Don't deal with him when he is very drunk, unless he is ugly and the family needs your help. Wait for the end of the spree, or at least for a lucid interval. Then let his family or a friend ask him if he wants to quit for good and if he would go to any extreme to do so. If he says yes, then his attention should be drawn to you as a person who has recovered. You should be described to him as one of a fellowship who, as part of their own recovery, try to help others and who will be glad to talk to him if he cares to see you.

If he does not want to see you, never force yourself upon him. Neither should the family hysterically plead with him to do anything, nor should they tell him much about you. They should wait for the end of his next drinking bout. You might place this book where he can see it in the interval. Here no specific rule can be given. The family must decide these things. But urge them not to be over-anxious, for that might spoil matters.

Usually the family should not try to tell your story. When possible, avoid meeting a man through his family. Approach through a doctor or an institution is a better bet. If your man needs hospitalization, he should have it, but not forcibly unless he is violent. Let the doctor, if he will, tell him he has something in the way of a solution.

When your man is better, the doctor might suggest a visit from you. Though you have talked with the family, leave them out of the first discussion. Under these conditions your prospect will see he is under no pressure. He will feel he can deal with you without being nagged by his family. Call on him while he is still jittery. He may be more receptive when depressed.

See your man alone, if possible. At first engage in general conversation. After a while, turn the talk to some phase of drinking. Tell him enough about your drinking habits, symptoms, and experiences to encourage him to speak of himself. If he wishes to talk, let him do so. You will thus get a better idea of how you ought to proceed. If he is not communicative, give him a sketch of your drinking career up to the time you quit. But say nothing, for the moment, of how that was accomplished. If he is in a serious mood dwell on the troubles liquor has caused you, being careful not to moralize or lecture. If his mood is light, tell him humorous stories of your escapades. Get him to tell some of his.

When he sees you know all about the drinking game, commence to describe yourself as an alcoholic. Tell him how baffled you were, how you finally learned that you were sick. Give him an account of the struggles you made to stop. Show him the mental twist which leads to the first drink of a spree. We suggest you do this as we have done it in the chapter on alcoholism. If he is alcoholic, he will understand you at once. He will match your mental inconsistencies with some of his own.

If you are satisfied that he is a real alcoholic, begin to dwell on the hopeless feature of the malady. Show him, from your own experience, how the queer mental condition surrounding that first drink prevents normal functioning of the will power. Don't, at this stage, refer to this book, unless he has seen it and wishes to discuss it. And be careful not to brand him as an alcoholic. Let him draw his own conclusion. If he sticks to the idea that he can still control his drinking, tell him that possibly he can–if he is not too alcoholic. But insist that if he is severely afflicted, there may be little chance he can recover by himself.

Continue to speak of alcoholism as an illness, a fatal malady. Talk about the conditions of body and mind which accompany it. Keep his attention focused mainly on your personal experience. Explain that many are doomed who never realize their predicament. Doctors are rightly loath to tell alcoholic patients the whole story unless it will serve some good purpose. But you may talk to him about the hopelessness of alcoholism because you offer a solution. You will soon have your friend admitting he has many, if not all, of the traits of the alcoholic. If his own doctor is willing to tell him that he is alcoholic, so much the better. Even though your protégé may not have entirely admitted his condition, he has become very curious to know how you got well. Let him ask you that question, if he will. *Tell him exactly what happened to you.* Stress the spiritual feature freely. If the man be agnostic or atheist, make it emphatic that *he does not have to agree with your conception of God.* He can choose any conception he likes, provided it makes sense to him. *The main thing is that he be willing to believe in a Power greater than himself and that he live by spiritual principles.*

When dealing with such a person, you had better use everyday language to describe spiritual principles. There is no use arousing any prejudice he may have against certain theological terms and conceptions about which he may already be confused. Don't raise such issues, no matter what your own convictions are.

Your prospect may belong to a religious denomination. His religious education and training may be far superior to yours. In that case he is going to wonder how you can add anything to what he already knows. But he will be curious to learn why his own convictions have not worked and why yours seem to work so well. He may be an example of the truth that faith alone is insufficient. To be vital, faith must be accompanied by self sacrifice and unselfish, constructive action. Let him see that you are not there to instruct him in religion. Admit that he probably knows more about it than you do, but call to his attention the fact that however deep his faith and knowledge, he could not have applied it or he would not drink. Perhaps your story will help him see where he has failed to practice the very precepts he knows so well. We represent no particular faith or denomination. We are dealing only with general principles common to most denominations.

Outline the program of action, explaining how you made a self-appraisal, how you straightened out your past and why you are now endeavoring to be helpful to him. It is important for him to realize that your attempt to pass this on to him plays a vital part in your recovery. Actually, he may be helping you more than you are helping him. Make it plain he is under no obligation to you, that you hope only that he will try to help other alcoholics when he escapes his own difficulties. Suggest how important it is that he places the welfare of other people ahead of his own. Make it clear that he is not under pressure, that he needn't see you again if he doesn't want to. You should not be offended if he wants to call it off, for he has helped you more than you have helped him. If your talk has been sane, quiet and full of human understanding, you have perhaps made a friend. Maybe you have disturbed him about the question of alcoholism. This is all to the good. The more hopeless he feels, the better. He will be more likely to follow your suggestions.

Your candidate may give reasons why he need not follow all of the program. He may rebel at the thought of a drastic housecleaning which requires discussion with other people. Do not contradict such views. Tell him you once felt as he does, but you doubt whether you would have made much progress had you not taken action. On your first visit tell him about the Fellowship of Alcoholics Anonymous. If he shows interest, lend him your copy of this book.

Unless your friend wants to talk further about himself, do not wear out your welcome. Give him a chance to think it over. If you do stay, let him steer the conversation in any direction he likes. Sometimes a new man is anxious to proceed at once, and you may be tempted to let him do so. This is sometimes a mistake. If he has trouble later, he is likely to say you rushed him. You will be most successful with alcoholics if you do not exhibit any passion for crusade or reform. Never talk down to an alcoholic from any moral or spiritual hilltop; simply lay out the kit of spiritual tools for his inspection. Show him how they worked with you. Offer him friendship and fellowship. Tell him that if he wants to get well you will do anything to help.

If he is not interested in your solution, if he expects you to act only as a banker for his financial difficulties or a nurse for his sprees, you may have to drop him until he changes his mind. This he may do after he gets hurt some more.

If he is sincerely interested and wants to see you again, ask him to read this book in the interval. After doing that, he must decide for himself whether he wants to go on. He should not be pushed or prodded by you, his wife, or his friends. If he is to find God, the desire must come from within.

If he thinks he can do the job in some other way, or prefers some other spiritual approach, encourage him to follow his own conscience. We have no monopoly on God; we merely have an approach that worked with us. But point out that we alcoholics have much in common and that you would like, in any case, to be friendly. Let it go at that.

Do not be discouraged if your prospect does not respond at once. Search out another alcoholic and try again. You are sure to find someone desperate enough to accept with eagerness what you offer. We find it a waste of time to keep chasing a man who cannot or will not work with you. If you leave such a person alone, he may soon become convinced that he cannot recover by himself. To spend too much time on any one situation is to deny some other alcoholic an opportunity to live and be happy. One of our Fellowship failed entirely with his first half dozen prospects. He often says that if he had continued to work on them, he might have deprived many others, who have since recovered, of their chance.

Suppose now you are making your second visit to a man. He has read this volume and says he is prepared to go through with the Twelve Steps of the program of recovery. Having had the experience yourself, you can give him much practical advice. Let him know you are available if he wishes to make a decision and tell his story, but do not insist upon it if he prefers to consult someone else.

He may be broke and homeless. If he is, you might try to help him about getting a job, or give him a little financial assistance. But you should not deprive your family or creditors of money they should have. Perhaps you will want to take the man into your home for a few days. But be sure you use discretion. Be certain he will be welcomed by your family, and that he is not trying to impose upon you for money, connections, or shelter. Permit that and you only harm him. You will be making it possible for him to be insincere. You may be aiding in his destruction rather than his recovery.

Never avoid these responsibilities, but be sure you are doing the right thing if you assume them. Helping others is the foundation stone of your recovery. A kindly act once in a while isn't enough. You have to act the Good Samaritan every day, if need be. It may mean the loss of many nights' sleep, great interference with your pleasures, interruptions to your business. It may mean sharing your money and your home, counseling frantic wives and relatives, innumerable trips to police courts, sanitariums, hospitals, jails and asylums. Your telephone may jangle at any time of the day or night. Your wife may sometimes say she is neglected. A drunk may smash the furniture in your home, or burn a mattress. You may have to fight with him if he is violent. Sometimes you will have to call a doctor and administer sedatives under his direction. Another time you may have to send for the police or an ambulance. Occasionally you will have to meet such conditions.

We seldom allow an alcoholic to live in our homes for long at a time. It is not good for him, and it sometimes creates serious complications in a family.

Though an alcoholic does not respond, there is no reason why you should neglect his family. You should continue to be friendly to them. The family should be offered your way of life. Should they accept and practice spiritual principles, there is a much better chance that the head of the family will recover. And even though he continues to drink, the family will find life more bearable.

For the type of alcoholic who is able and willing to get well, little charity, in the ordinary sense of the word, is need or wanted. The men who cry for money and shelter before conquering alcohol, are on the wrong track. Yet we do go to great extremes to provide each other with these very things, when such action is warranted. This may seem inconsistent, but we think it is not.

It is not the matter of giving that is in question, but when and how to give. That often makes the difference between failure and success. The minute we put our work on a service plane, the alcoholic commences to rely upon our assistance rather than upon God. He clamors for this or that, claiming he cannot master alcohol until his material needs are cared for. Nonsense. Some of us have taken very hard knocks to learn this truth: Job or no job–wife or no wife–we simply do not stop drinking so long as we place dependence upon other people ahead of dependence on God.

Burn the idea into the consciousness of every man that he can get well regardless of anyone. The only condition is that he trusts in God and cleans his house.

Now, the domestic problem: There may be divorce, separation, or just strained relations. When your prospect has made such reparation as he can to his family, and has thoroughly explained to them the new principles by which he is living, he should proceed to put those principles into action at home. That is, if he is lucky enough to have a home. Though his family be at fault in many respects, he should not be concerned about that. He should concentrate on his own spiritual demonstration. Argument and fault-finding are to be avoided like the plague. In many homes this is a difficult thing to do, but it must be done if any results are to be expected. If persisted in for a few months, the effect on a man's family is sure to be great. The most incompatible people discover they have a basis upon which they can meet. Little by little the family may see their own defects and admit them. These can then be discussed in an atmosphere of helpfulness and friendliness.

After they have seen tangible results, the family will perhaps want to go along. These things will come to pass naturally and in good time provided, however, the alcoholic continues to demonstrate that he can be sober, considerate, and helpful, regardless of what anyone says or does. Of course, we all fall much below this standard many times. But we must try to repair the damage immediately lest we pay the penalty by a spree.

If there be divorce or separation, there should be no undue haste for the couple to get together. The man should be sure of his recovery. The wife should fully understand his new way of life. If their old relationship is to be resumed it must be on a better basis, since the former did not work. This means a new attitude and spirit all around. Sometimes it is to the best interests of all concerned that a couple remains apart. Obviously, no rule can be laid down. Let the alcoholic continue his program day by day. When the time for living together has come, it will be apparent to both parties.

Let no alcoholic say he cannot recover unless he has his family back. This just isn't so. In some cases the wife will never come back for one reason or another. Remind the prospect that his recovery is not dependent upon people. It is dependent upon his relationship with God. We have seen men get well whose families have not returned at all. We have seen others slip when the family came back too soon.

Both you and the new man must walk day by day in the path of spiritual progress. If you persist, remarkable things will happen. When we look back, we realize that the things which came to us when we put ourselves in God's hands were better than anything we could have planned. Follow the dictates of a Higher Power and you will presently live in a new and wonderful world, no matter what your present circumstances!

When working with a man and his family, you should take care not to participate in their quarrels. You may spoil your chance of being helpful if you do. But urge upon a man's family that he has been a very sick person and should be treated accordingly. You should warn against arousing resentment or jealousy. You should point out that his defects of character are not going to disappear overnight. Show them that he has entered upon a period of growth. Ask them to remember, when they are impatient, the blessed fact of his sobriety.

If you have been successful in solving your own domestic problems, tell the newcomer's family how that was accomplished. In this way you can set them on the right track without becoming critical of them. The story of how you and your wife settled your difficulties is worth any amount of criticism.

Assuming we are spiritually fit, we can do all sorts of things alcoholics are not supposed to do. People have said we must not go where liquor is served; we must not have it in our homes; we must shun friends who drink; we must avoid moving pictures which show drinking scenes; we must not go into bars; our friends must hide their bottles if we go to their houses; we mustn't think or be reminded about alcohol at all. Our experience shows that this is not necessarily so.

We meet these conditions every day. An alcoholic who cannot meet them, still has an alcoholic mind; there is something the matter with his spiritual status. His only chance for sobriety would be some place like the Greenland Ice Cap, and even there an Eskimo might turn up with a bottle of scotch and ruin everything! Ask any woman who has sent her husband to distant places on the theory he would escape the alcohol problem.

In our belief any scheme of combating alcoholism which proposes to shield the sick man from temptation is doomed to failure. If the alcoholic tries to shield himself he may succeed for a time, but he usually winds up with a bigger explosion than ever. We have tried these methods. These attempts to do the impossible have always failed.

So our rule is not to avoid a place where there is drinking, *if we have a legitimate reason for being there.* That includes bars, nightclubs, dances, receptions, weddings, even plain ordinary whoopee parties. To a person who has had experience with an alcoholic, this may seem like tempting Providence, but it isn't.

You will note that we made an important qualification. Therefore, ask yourself on each occasion, "Have I any good social, business, or personal reason for going to this place? Or am I expecting to steal a little vicarious pleasure from the atmosphere of such places?" If you answer these questions satisfactorily, you need have no apprehension. Go or stay away, whichever seems best. But be sure you are on solid spiritual ground before you start and that your motive in going is thoroughly good. Do not think of what you will get out of the occasion. Think of what you can bring to it. But if you are shaky, you had better work with another alcoholic instead!

Why sit with a long face in places where there is drinking, sighing about the good old days. If it is a happy occasion, try to increase the pleasure of those there; if a business occasion, go and attend to your business enthusiastically. If you are with a person who wants to eat in a bar, by all means go along. Let your friends know they are not to change their habits on your account. At a proper time and place explain to all your friends why alcohol disagrees with you. If you do this thoroughly, few people will ask you to drink. While you were drinking, you were withdrawing from life little by little. Now you are getting back into the social life of this world. Don't start to withdraw again just because your friends drink liquor.

Your job now is to be at the place where you may be of maximum helpfulness to others, so never hesitate to go anywhere if you can be helpful. You should not hesitate to visit the most sordid spot on earth on such an errand. Keep on the firing line of life with these motives and God will keep you unharmed.

Many of us keep liquor in our homes. We often need it to carry green recruits through a severe hangover. Some of us still serve it to our friends provided they are not alcoholic. But some of us think we should not serve liquor to anyone. We never argue this question. We feel that each family, in the light of their own circumstances, ought to decide for themselves.

We are careful never to show intolerance or hatred of drinking as an institution. Experience shows that such an attitude is not helpful to anyone. Every new alcoholic looks for this spirit among us and is immensely relieved when he finds we are not witch-burners. A spirit of intolerance might repel alcoholics whose lives could have been saved, had it not been for such stupidity. We would not even do the cause of temperate drinking any good, for not one drinker in a thousand likes to be told anything about alcohol by one who hates it.

Some day we hope that Alcoholics Anonymous will help the public to a better realization of the gravity of the alcoholic problem, but we shall be of little use if our attitude is one of bitterness or hostility. Drinkers will not stand for it.

After all, our problems were of our own making. Bottles were only a symbol. Besides, we have stopped fighting anybody or anything. We have to!

Chapter VIII

TO WIVES

[Written in 1939, when there were few women in A.A., this chapter assumes that the alcoholic in the home is likely to be the husband. But many of the suggestions given here may be adapted to help the person who lives with a woman alcoholic–whether she is still drinking or is recovering in A.A.]

WITH FEW EXCEPTIONS, our book thus far has spoken of men. But what we have said applies quite as much to women. Our activities in behalf of women who drink are on the increase. There is every evidence that women regain their health as readily as men if they try our suggestions.

But for every man who drinks others are involved–the wife who trembles in fear of the next debauch; the mother and father who see their son wasting away.

Among us are wives, relatives and friends whose problem has been solved, as well as some who have not yet found a happy solution. We want the wives of Alcoholics Anonymous to address the wives of men who drink too much. What they say will apply to nearly everyone bound by ties of blood or affection to an alcoholic.

As wives of Alcoholics Anonymous, we would like you to feel that we understand as perhaps few can. We want to analyze mistakes we have made. We want to leave you with the feeling that no situation is too difficult and no unhappiness too great to be overcome.

We have traveled a rocky road, there is no mistake about that. We have had long rendezvous with hurt pride, frustration, self-pity, misunderstanding and fear. These are not pleasant companions. We have been driven to maudlin sympathy, to bitter resentment. Some of us veered from extreme to extreme, ever hoping that one day our loved ones would be themselves once more.

Our loyalty and the desire that our husbands hold up their heads and be like other men have begotten all sorts of predicaments. We have been unselfish and self-sacrificing. We have told innumerable lies to protect our pride and our husbands' reputations. We have prayed, we have begged, we have been patient. We have struck out viciously. We have run away. We have been hysterical. We have been terror stricken. We have sought sympathy. We have had retaliatory love affairs with other men.

Our homes have been battle-grounds many an evening. In the morning we have kissed and made up. Our friends have counseled chucking the men and we have done so with finality, only to be back in a little while hoping, always hoping. Our men have sworn great solemn oaths that they were through drinking forever. We have believed them when no one else could or would. Then, in days, weeks, or months, a fresh outburst.

We seldom had friends at our homes, never knowing how or when the men of the house would appear. We could make few social engagements. We came to live almost alone. When we were invited out, our husbands sneaked so many drinks that they spoiled the occasion. If, on the other hand, they took nothing, their self-pity made them killjoys.

There was never financial security. Positions were always in jeopardy or gone. An armored car could not have brought the pay envelopes home. The checking account melted like snow in June.

Sometimes there were other women. How heartbreaking was this discovery; how cruel to be told they understood our men as we did not!

The bill collectors, the sheriffs, the angry taxi drivers, the policemen, the bums, the pals, and even the ladies they sometimes brought home–our husbands thought we were so inhospitable. "Joykiller, nag, wet blanket"–that's what they said. Next day they would be themselves again and we would forgive and try to forget.

We have tried to hold the love of our children for their father. We have told small tots that father was sick, which was much nearer the truth than we realized. They struck the children, kicked out door panels, smashed treasured crockery, and ripped the keys out of pianos. In the midst of such pandemonium they may have rushed out threatening to live with the other woman forever. In desperation, we have even got tight ourselves–the drunk to end all drunks. The unexpected result was that our husbands seemed to like it.

Perhaps at this point we got a divorce and took the children home to father and mother. Then we were severely criticized by our husband's parents for desertion. Usually we did not leave. We stayed on and on. We finally sought employment ourselves as destitution faced us and our families.

We began to ask medical advice as the sprees got closer together. The alarming physical and mental symptoms, the deepening pall of remorse, depression and inferiority that settled down on our loved ones–these things terrified and distracted us. As animals on a treadmill, we have patiently and wearily climbed, falling back in exhaustion after each futile effort to reach solid ground. Most of us have entered the final stage with its commitment to health resorts, sanitariums, hospitals, and jails. Sometimes there were screaming delirium and insanity. Death was often near.

Under these conditions we naturally make mistakes. Some of them rose out of ignorance of alcoholism. Sometimes we sensed dimly that we were dealing with sick men. Had we fully understood the nature of the alcoholic illness, we might have behaved differently.

How could men who loved their wives and children be so unthinking, so callous, so cruel? There could be no love in such persons, we thought. And just as we were being convinced of their heartlessness, they would surprise us with fresh resolves and new attentions. For a while they would be their old sweet selves, only to dash the new structure of affection to pieces once more. Asked why they commenced to drink again, they would reply with some silly excuse, or none. It was so baffling, so heartbreaking. Could we have been so mistaken in the men we married? When drinking, they were strangers. Sometimes they were so inaccessible that it seemed as though a great wall had been built around them.

And even if they did not love their families, how could they be so blind about themselves? What had become of their judgment, their common sense, their will power? Why could they not see that drink meant ruin to them? Why was it, when these dangers were pointed out that they agreed, and then got drunk again immediately?

These are some of the questions which race through the mind of every woman who has an alcoholic husband. We hope this book has answered some of them. Perhaps your husband has been living in that strange world of alcoholism where everything is distorted and exaggerated. You can see that he really does love with his better self. Of course, there is such a thing as incompatibility, but in nearly every instance the alcoholic only seems to be unloving and inconsiderate; it is usually because he is warped and sickened that he says and does these appalling things. Today most of our men are better husbands and fathers than ever before.

Try not to condemn your alcoholic husband no matter what he says or does. He is just another very sick, unreasonable person. Treat him, when you can, as though he had pneumonia. When he angers you, remember that he is very ill.

There is an important exception to the foregoing. We realize some men are thoroughly bad-intentioned, that no amount of patience will make any difference. An alcoholic of this temperament may be quick to use this chapter as a club over your head. Don't let him get away with it. If you are positive he is one of this type you may feel you had better leave him. Is it right to let him ruin your life and the lives of your children? Especially when he has before him a way to stop his drinking and abuse if he really wants to pay the price.

The problem with which you struggle usually falls within one of four categories:

One: Your husband may be only a heavy drinker. His drinking may be constant or it may be heavy only on certain occasions. Perhaps he spends too much money for liquor. It may be slowing him up mentally and physically, but he does not see it. Sometimes he is a source of embarrassment to you and his friends. He is positive he can handle his liquor, that it does him no harm, that drinking is necessary in his business. He would probably be insulted if he were called an alcoholic. This world is full of people like him. Some will moderate or stop altogether, and some will not. Of those who keep on, a good number will become true alcoholics after a while.

Two: Your husband is showing lack of control, for he is unable to stay on the water wagon even when he wants to. He often gets entirely out of hand when drinking. He admits this is true, but is positive that he will do better. He has begun to try, with or without your cooperation, various means of moderating or staying dry. Maybe he is beginning to lose his friends. His business may suffer somewhat. He is worried at times, and is becoming aware that he cannot drink like other people. He sometimes drinks in the morning and through the day also, to hold his nervousness in check. He is remorseful after serious drinking bouts and tells you he wants to stop. But when he gets over the spree, he begins to think once more how he can drink moderately next time. We think this person is in danger. These are the earmarks of a real alcoholic. Perhaps he can still tend to business fairly well. He has by no means ruined everything. As we say among ourselves, "*He wants to want to stop.*"

Three: This husband has gone much further than husband number two. Though once like number two he became worse. His friends have slipped away, his home is a near-wreck and he cannot hold a position. Maybe the doctor has been called in, and the weary round of sanitariums and hospitals has begun. He admits he cannot drink like other people, but does not see why. He clings to the notion that he will yet find a way to do so. He may have come to the point where he desperately wants to stop but cannot. His case presents additional questions which we shall try to answer for you. You can be quite hopeful of a situation like this.

Four: You may have a husband of whom you completely despair. He has been placed in one institution after another. He is violent, or appears definitely insane when drunk. Sometimes he drinks on the way home from the hospital. Perhaps he has had delirium tremens. Doctors may shake their heads and advise you to have him committed. Maybe you have already been obliged to put him away. This picture may not be as dark as it looks. Many of our husbands were just as far gone. Yet they got well.

Let's now go back to number one. Oddly enough, he is often difficult to deal with. He enjoys drinking. It stirs his imagination. His friends feel closer over a highball. Perhaps you enjoy drinking with him yourself when he doesn't go too far. You have passed happy evenings together chatting and drinking before your fire. Perhaps you both like parties which would be dull without liquor. We have enjoyed such evenings ourselves; we had a good time. We know all about liquor as a social lubricant. Some, but not all of us, think it has its advantages when reasonably used.

The first principle of success is that you should never be angry. Even though your husband becomes unbearable and you have to leave him temporarily, you should, if you can, go without rancor. Patience and good temper are most necessary.

Our next thought is that you should never tell him what he must do about his drinking. If he gets the idea that you are a nag or a killjoy, your chance of accomplishing anything useful may be zero. He will use that as an excuse to drink more. He will tell you he is misunderstood. This may lead to lonely evenings for you. He may seek someone else to console him–not always another man.

Be determined that your husband's drinking is not going to spoil your relations with your children or your friends. They need your companionship and your help. It is possible to have a full and useful life, though your husband continues to drink. We know women who are unafraid, even happy under these conditions. Do not set your heart on reforming your husband. You may be unable to do so, no matter how hard you try.

We know these suggestions are sometimes difficult to follow, but you will save many a heartbreak if you can succeed in observing them. Your husband may come to appreciate your reasonableness and patience. This may lay the groundwork for a friendly talk about his alcoholic problem. Try to have him bring up the subject himself. Be sure you are not critical during such a discussion. Attempt instead, to put yourself in his place. Let him see that you want to be helpful rather than critical.

When a discussion does arise, you might suggest he read this book or at least the chapter on alcoholism. Tell him you have been worried, though perhaps needlessly. You think he ought to know the subject better, as everyone should have a clear understanding of the risk he takes if he drinks too much. Show him you have confidence in his power to stop or moderate. Say you do not want to be a wet blanket; that you only want him to take care of his health. Thus you may succeed in interesting him in alcoholism.

He probably has several alcoholics among his own acquaintances. You might suggest that you both take an interest in them. Drinkers like to help other drinkers. Your husband may be willing to talk to one of them.

If this kind of approach does not catch your husband's interest, it may be best to drop the subject, but after a friendly talk your husband will usually revive the topic himself. This may take patient waiting, but it will be worth it. Meanwhile you might try to help the wife of another serious drinker. If you act upon these principles, your husband may stop or moderate.

Suppose, however, that your husband fits the description of number two. The same principles which apply to husband number one should be practiced. But after his next binge, ask him if he would really like to get over drinking for good. Do not ask that he do it for you or anyone else. Just would he *like* to?

The chances are he would. Show him your copy of this book and tell him what you have found out about alcoholism. Show him that as alcoholics, the writers of the book understand. Tell him some of the interesting stories you have read. If you think he will be shy of a spiritual remedy, ask him to look at the chapter on alcoholism. Then perhaps he will be interested enough to continue.

If he is enthusiastic your cooperation will mean a great deal. If he is lukewarm or thinks he is not an alcoholic, we suggest you leave him alone. Avoid urging him to follow our program. The seed has been planted in his mind. He knows that thousands of men, much like himself, have recovered. But don't remind him of this after he has been drinking, for he may be angry. Sooner or later, you are likely to find him reading the book once more. Wait until repeated stumbling convinces him he must act, for the more you hurry him the longer his recovery may be delayed.

If you have a number three husband, you may be in luck. Being certain he wants to stop, you can go to him with this volume as joyfully as though you had struck oil. He may not share your enthusiasm, but he is practically sure to read the book and he may go for the program at once. If he does not, you will probably not have long to wait. Again, you should not crowd him. Let him decide for himself. Cheerfully see him through more sprees. Talk about his condition or this book only when he raises the issue. In some cases it may be better to let someone outside the family urge action without arousing hostility. If your husband is otherwise a normal individual, your chances are good at this stage.

You would suppose that men in the fourth classification would be quite hopeless, but that is not so. Many of Alcoholics Anonymous were like that. Everybody had given them up. Defeat seemed certain. Yet often such men had spectacular and powerful recoveries.

There are exceptions. Some men have been so impaired by alcohol that they cannot stop. Sometimes there are cases where alcoholism is complicated by other disorders. A good doctor or psychiatrist can tell you whether these complications are serious. In any event, try to have your husband read this book. His reaction may be one of enthusiasm. If he is already committed to an institution, but can convince you and your doctor that he means business, give him a chance to try our method, unless the doctor thinks his mental condition too abnormal or dangerous. We make this recommendation with some confidence. For years we have been working with alcoholics committed to institutions. Since this book was first published, A.A. has released thousands of alcoholics from asylums and hospitals of every kind. The majority have never returned. The power of God goes deep!

You may have the reverse situation on your hands. Perhaps you have a husband who is at large, but who should be committed. Some men cannot or will not get over alcoholism. When they become too dangerous, we think the kind thing is to lock them up, but of course a good doctor should always be consulted. The wives and children of such men suffer horrible, but not more than the men themselves.

But sometimes you must start life anew. We know women who have done it. If such women adopt a spiritual way of life their road will be smoother.

If your husband is a drinker, you probably worry over what other people are thinking and you hate to meet your friends. You draw more and more into yourself and you think everyone is talking about conditions at your home. You avoid the subject of drinking, even with your own parents. You do not know what to tell your children. When your husband is bad, you become a trembling recluse, wishing the telephone had never been invented.

We find that most of this embarrassment is unnecessary. While you need not discuss your husband at length, you can quietly let your friends know the nature of his illness. But you must be on guard not to embarrass or harm your husband.

When you have carefully explained to such people that he is a sick person, you will have created a new atmosphere. Barriers which have sprung up between you and your friends will disappear with the growth of sympathetic understanding. You will no longer be self-conscious or feel that you must apologize as though your husband were a weak character. He may be anything but that. Your new courage, good nature and lack of self-consciousness will do wonders for you socially.

The same principle applies in dealing with the children. Unless they actually need protection from their father, it is best not to take sides in any argument he has with them while drinking. Use your energies to promote a better understanding all around. Then that terrible tension which grips the home of every problem drinker will be lessened.

Frequently, you have felt obliged to tell your husband's employer and his friends that he was sick, when as a matter of fact he was tight. Avoid answering these inquiries as much as you can. Whenever possible, let your husband explain. Your desire to protect him should not cause you to lie to people when they have a right to know where he is and what he is doing. Discuss this with him when he is sober and in good spirits. Ask him what you should do if he places you in such a position again. But be careful not to be resentful about the last time he did so.

There is another paralyzing fear. You may be afraid your husband will lose his position; you are thinking of the disgrace and hard times which will befall you and the children. This experience may come to you. Or you may already have had it several times. Should it happen again, regard it in a different light. Maybe it will prove a blessing! It may convince your husband he wants to stop drinking forever. And now you know that he can stop if he will! Time after time, this apparent calamity has been a boon to us, for it opened up a path which led to the discovery of God.

We have elsewhere remarked how much better life is when lived on a spiritual plane. If God can solve the age-old riddle of alcoholism, He can solve your problems too. We wives found that, like everybody else, we were afflicted with pride, self-pity, vanity and all the things which go to make up the self-centered person; and we were not above selfishness or dishonesty. As our husbands began to apply spiritual principles in their lives, we began to see the desirability of doing so too.

At first, some of us did not believe we needed this help. We thought, on the whole, we were pretty good women, capable of being nicer if our husbands stopped drinking. But it was a silly idea that we were too good to need God. Now we try to put spiritual principles to work in every department of our lives. When we do that, we find it solves our problems too; the ensuing lack of fear, worry and hurt feelings is a wonderful thing. We urge you to try our program, for nothing will be so helpful to your husband as the radically changed attitude toward him which God will show you how to have. Go along with your husband if you possibly can.

If you and your husband find a solution for the pressing problem of drink you are, of course, going to be very happy. But all problems will not be solved at once. Seed has started to sprout in a new soil, but growth has only begun. In spite of your new-found happiness, there will be ups and downs. Many of the old problems will still be with you. This is as it should be.

The faith and sincerity of both you and your husband will be put to the test. These work-outs should be regarded as part of your education, for thus you will be learning to live. You will make mistakes, but if you are in earnest they will not drag you down. Instead, you will capitalize them. A better way of life will emerge when they are overcome.

Some of the snags you will encounter are irritation, hurt feelings and resentments. Your husband will sometimes be unreasonable and you will want to criticize. Starting from a speck on the domestic horizon, great thunderclouds of dispute may gather. These family dissensions are very dangerous, especially to your husband. Often you must carry the burden of avoiding them or keeping them under control. Never forget that resentment is a deadly hazard to an alcoholic. We do not mean that you have to agree with you husband whenever there is an honest difference of opinion. Just be careful not to disagree in a resentful or critical spirit.

You and your husband will find that you can dispose of serious problems easier than you can the trivial ones. Next time you and he have a heated discussion, no matter what the subject, it should be the privilege of either to smile and say, "This is getting serious. I'm sorry I got disturbed. Let's talk about it later." If your husband is trying to live on a spiritual basis, he will also be doing everything in his power to avoid disagreement or contention.

Your husband knows he owes you more than sobriety. He wants to make good. Yet you must not expect too much. His ways of thinking and doing are the habits of years. Patience, tolerance, understanding and love are the watchwords. Show him these things in yourself and they will be reflected back to you from him. Live and let live is the rule. If you both show a willingness to remedy your own defects, there will be little need to criticize each other.

We women carry with us a picture of the ideal man, the sort of chap we would like our husbands to be. It is the most natural thing in the world, once his liquor problem is solved, to feel that he will now measure up to that cherished vision. The chances are he will not for, like yourself, he is just beginning his development. Be patient.

Another feeling we are very likely to entertain is one of resentment that love and loyalty could not cure our husbands of alcoholism. We do not like the thought that the contents of a book or the work of another alcoholic has accomplished in a few weeks that for which we struggled for years. At such moments we forget that alcoholism is an illness over which we could not possibly have had any power. Your husband will be the first to say it was your devotion and care which brought him to the point where he could have a spiritual experience. Without you he would have gone to pieces long ago.

When resentful thoughts come, try to pause and count your blessings. After all, your family is reunited, alcohol is no longer a problem and you and your husband are working together toward an undreamed-of future.

Still another difficulty is that you may become jealous of the attention he bestows on other people, especially alcoholics. You have been starving for his companionship, yet he spends long hours helping other men and their families. You feel he should now be yours. It will do little good if you point that out and urge more attention for yourself. We find it a real mistake to dampen his enthusiasm for alcoholic work. You should join in his efforts as much as you possibly can. We suggest that you direct some of your thought to the wives of his new alcoholic friends. They need the counsel and love of a woman who has gone through what you have.

It is probably true that you and your husband have been living too much alone, for drinking many times isolates the wife of an alcoholic. Therefore, you probably need fresh interests and a great cause to live for as much as your husband. If you cooperate, rather than complain, you will find that his excess enthusiasm will tone down. Both of you will awaken to a new sense of responsibility for others. You, as well as your husband, ought to think of what you can put into life instead of how much you can take out. Inevitably your lives will be fuller for doing so. You will lose the old life to find one much better.

Perhaps your husband will make a fair start on the new basis, but just as things are going beautifully he dismays you be coming home drunk. If you are satisfied he really wants to get over drinking, you need not be alarmed. Though it is infinitely better that he have no relapse at all, as has been true with many of our men, it is by no means a bad thing in some cases. Your husband will see at once that he must redouble his spiritual activities if he expects to survive. You need not remind him of his spiritual deficiency–he will know of it. Cheer him up and ask him how you can be still more helpful.

The slightest sign of fear or intolerance may lessen your husband's chance or recovery. In a weak moment he may take your dislike of his high-stepping friends as one of those insanely trivial excuses to drink.

We never, never try to arrange a man's life so as to shield him from temptation. The slightest disposition on your part to guide his appointments or his affairs so he will not be tempted will be noticed. Make him feel absolutely free to come and go as he likes. This is important. If he gets drunk, don't blame yourself. God has either removed your husband's liquor problem or He has not. If not, it had better be found out right away. Then you and your husband can get right down to fundamentals. If a repetition is to be prevented, place the problem, along with everything else, in God's hands.

We realize that we have been giving you much direction and advice. We may have seemed to lecture. If that is so we are sorry, for we ourselves don't always care for people who lecture us. But what we have related is based upon experience, some of it painful. We had to learn these things the hard way. That is why we are anxious that you understand, and that you avoid these unnecessary difficulties.

So to you out there who may soon be with us–we say "Good luck and God bless you!"

Chapter IX

THE FAMILY AFTERWARD

OUR WOMEN FOLK have suggested certain attitudes a wife may take with the husband who is recovering. Perhaps they created the impression that he is to be wrapped in cotton wool and placed on a pedestal. Successful readjustment means the opposite. All members of the family should meet upon the common ground of tolerance, understanding and love. This involves a process of deflation. The alcoholic, his wife, his children, his "in-laws," each one is likely to have fixed ideas about the family's attitude towards himself or herself. Each is interested in having his or her wishes respected. We find the more one member of the family demands that the others concede to him, the more resentful they become. This makes for discord and unhappiness.

And why? Is it not because each wants to play the lead? Is not each trying to arrange the family show to his liking? Is he not unconsciously trying to see what he can take from the family life rather than give?

Cessation of drinking is but the first step away from a highly strained, abnormal condition. A doctor said to us, "Years of living with an alcoholic is almost sure to make any wife or child neurotic. The entire family is, to some extent, ill." Let families realize, as they start their journey, that all will not be fair-weather. Each in his turn may be footsore and may straggle. There will be alluring shortcuts and by-paths down which they may wander and lose their way.

Suppose we tell you some of the obstacles a family will meet; suppose we suggest how they may be avoided–even converted to good use for others. The family of an alcoholic longs for the return of happiness and security. They remember when father was romantic, thoughtful and successful. Today's life is measured against that of other years and, when it falls short, the family may be unhappy.

Family confidence in dad is rising high. The good old days will soon be back, they think. Sometimes they demand that dad bring them back instantly! God, they believe, almost owes this recompense on a long overdue account. But the head of the house has spent years in pulling down the structures of business, romance, friendship, health–these things are now ruined or damaged. It will take time to clear away the wreck. Though the old buildings will eventually be replaced by finer ones, the new structures will take years to complete.

Father knows he is to blame; it may take him many seasons of hard work to be restored financially, but he shouldn't be reproached. Perhaps he will never have much money again. But the wise family will admire him for what he is trying to be, rather than for what he is trying to get.

Now and then the family will be plagued by spectres from the past, for the drinking career of almost every alcoholic has been marked by escapades, funny, humiliating, shameful or tragic. The first impulse will be to bury these skeletons in a dark closet and padlock the door. The family may be possessed by the idea that future happiness can be based only upon forgetfulness of the past. We think that such a view is self-centered and in direct conflict with the new way of living.

Henry Ford once made a wise remark to the effect that experience is the thing of supreme value in life. That is true only if one is willing to turn the past to good account. We grow by our willingness to face and rectify errors and convert them into assets. The alcoholic's past thus becomes the principal asset of the family and frequently it is almost the only one!

This painful past may be of infinite value to other families still struggling with their problem. We think each family which has been relieved owes something to those who have not, and when the occasion requires, each member of it should be only too willing to bring former mistakes, no matter how grievous, out of their hiding places. Showing others who suffer how we were given help is the very thing which makes life seem so worth while to us now. Cling to the thought that, in God's hands, the dark past is the greatest possession you have–the key to life and happiness for others. With it you can avert death and misery for them.

It is possible to dig up past misdeeds so they become a blight, a veritable plague. For example, we know of situations in which the alcoholic or his wife have had love affairs. In the first flush of spiritual experience they forgave each other and drew closer together. The miracle of reconciliation was at hand. Then, under one provocation or another, the aggrieved one would unearth the old affair and angrily cast its ashes about. A few of us have had these growing pains and they hurt a great deal. Husbands and wives have sometimes been obliged to separate for a time until new perspective, new victory over hurt pride could be re-won. In most cases, the alcoholic survived this ordeal without relapse, but not always. So we think that unless some good and useful purpose is to be served, past occurrences should not be discussed.

We families of Alcoholics Anonymous keep few skeletons in the closet. Everyone knows about the others' alcoholic troubles. This is a condition which, in ordinary life, would produce untold grief; there might be scandalous gossip, laughter at the expense of other people, and a tendency to take advantage of intimate information. Among us, these are rare occurrences. We do talk about each other a great deal, but we almost invariably temper such talk by a spirit of love and tolerance.

Another principle we observe carefully is that we do not relate intimate experiences of another person unless we are sure he would approve. We find it better, when possible, to stick to our own stories. A man may criticize or laugh at himself and it will affect others favorably, but criticism or ridicule coming from another often produces the contrary effect. Members of a family should watch such matters carefully, for one careless, inconsiderate remark has been known to raise the very devil. We alcoholics are sensitive people. It takes some of us a long time to outgrow that serious handicap.

Many alcoholics are enthusiasts. They run to extremes. At the beginning of recovery a man will take, as a rule, one of two directions. He may either plunge into a frantic attempt to get on his feet in business, or he may be so enthralled by his new life that he talks or thinks of little else. In either case certain family problems will arise. With these we have had experience galore.

We think it dangerous if he rushes headlong at his economic problem. The family will be affected also, pleasantly at first, as they feel their money troubles are about to be solved, then not so pleasantly as they find themselves neglected. Dad may be tired at night and preoccupied by day. He may take small interest in the children and may show irritation when reproved for his delinquencies. If not irritable, he may seem dull and boring, not gay and affectionate as the family would like him to be. Mother may complain of inattention. They are all disappointed, and often let him feel it. Beginning with such complaints, a barrier arises. He is straining every nerve to make up for lost time. He is striving to recover fortune and reputation and feels he is doing very well.

Sometimes mother and children don't think so. Having been neglected and misused in the past, they think father owes them more than they are getting. They want him to make a fuss over them. They expect him to give them the nice times they used to have before he drank so much, and to show his contrition for what they suffered. But dad doesn't give freely of himself. Resentment grows. He becomes still less communicative. Sometimes he explodes over a trifle. The family is mystified. They criticize, pointing out how he is falling down on his spiritual program.

This sort of thing can be avoided. Both father and the family are mistaken, though each side may have some justification. It is of little use to argue and only makes the impasse worse. The family must realize that dad, though marvelously improved, is still convalescing. They should be thankful he is sober and able to be of this world once more. Let them praise his progress. Let them remember that his drinking wrought all kinds of damage that may take long to repair. If they sense these things, they will not take so seriously his periods of crankiness, depression, or apathy, which will disappear when there is tolerance, love, and spiritual understanding.

The head of the house ought to remember that he is mainly to blame for what befell his home. He can scarcely square the account in his lifetime. But he must see the danger of over-concentration on financial success. Although financial recovery is on the way for many of us, we found we could not place money first. For us, material well-being always followed spiritual progress; it never preceded.

Since the home has suffered more than anything else, it is well that a man exert himself there. He is not likely to get far in any direction if he fails to show unselfishness and love under his own roof. We know there are difficult wives and families, but the man who is getting over alcoholism must remember he did much to make them so.

As each member of a resentful family begins to see his shortcomings and admits them to the others, he lays a basis for helpful discussion. These family talks will be constructive if they can be carried on without heated argument, self-pity, self-justification or resentful criticism. Little by little, mother and children will see they ask too much, and father will see he gives too little. Giving, rather than getting, will become the guiding principle.

Assume on the other hand that father has, at the outset, a stirring spiritual experience. Overnight, as it were, he is a different man. He becomes a religious enthusiast. He is unable to focus on anything else. As soon as his sobriety begins to be taken as a matter of course, the family may look at their strange new dad with apprehension, then with irritation. There is talk about spiritual matters morning, noon and night. He may demand that the family find God in a hurry, or exhibit amazing indifference to them and say he is above worldly considerations. He may tell mother, who has been religious all her life, that she doesn't know what it's all about, and that she had better get his brand of spirituality while there is yet time.

When father takes this tack, the family may react unfavorably. They may be jealous of a God who has stolen dad's affections. While grateful that he drinks no more, they may not like the idea that God has accomplished the miracle where they failed. They often forget father was beyond human aid. They may not see why their love and devotion did not straighten him out. Dad is not so spiritual after all, they say. If he means to right his past wrongs, why all this concern for everyone in the world but his family? What about his talk that God will take care of them? They suspect father is a bit balmy!

He is not so unbalanced as they might think. Many of us have experienced dad's elation. We have indulged in spiritual intoxication. Like a gaunt prospector, belt drawn in over the last ounce of food, our pick struck gold. Joy at our release from a lifetime of frustration knew no bounds. Father feels he has struck something better than gold. For a time he may try to hug the new treasure to himself. He may not see at once that he has barely scratched a limitless lode which will pay dividends only if he mines it for the rest of his life and insists on giving away the entire product.

If the family cooperates, dad will soon see that he is suffering from a distortion of values. He will perceive that his spiritual growth is lopsided, that for an average man like himself, a spiritual life which does not include his family obligations may not be so perfect after all. If the family will appreciated that dad's current behavior is but a phase of his development, all will be well. In the midst of an understanding and sympathetic family, these vagaries of dad's spiritual infancy will quickly disappear.

The opposite may happen should the family condemn and criticize. Dad may feel that for years his drinking has placed him on the wrong side of every argument, but that now he has become a superior person with God on his side. If the family persists in criticism, this fallacy may take a still greater hold on father. Instead of treating the family as he should, he may retreat further into himself and feel he has spiritual justification for so doing.

Though the family does not fully agree with dad's spiritual activities, they should let him have his head. Even if he displays a certain amount of neglect and irresponsibility towards the family, it is well to let him go as far as he likes in helping other alcoholics. During those first days of convalescence, this will do more to insure his sobriety than anything else. Though some of his manifestations are alarming and disagreeable, we think dad will be on a firmer foundation than the man who is placing business or professional success ahead of spiritual development. He will be less likely to drink again, and anything is preferable to that.

Those of us who have spent much time in the world of spiritual make-believe have eventually seen the childishness of it. This dream world has been replaced by a great sense of purpose, accompanied by a growing consciousness of the power of God in our lives. We have come to believe He would like us to keep our heads in the clouds with Him, but that our feet ought to be firmly planted on earth. That is where our fellow travelers are, and that is where our work must be done. These are the realities for us. We have found nothing incompatible between a powerful spiritual experience and a life of sane and happy usefulness.

One more suggestion: Whether the family has spiritual convictions or not, they may do well to examine the principles by which the alcoholic member is trying to live. They can hardly fail to approve these simple principles, though the head of the house still fails somewhat in practicing them. Nothing will help the man who is off on a spiritual tangent so much as the wife who adopts a sane spiritual program, making a better practical use of it.

There will be other profound changes in the household. Liquor incapacitated father for so many years that mother became head of the house. She met these responsibilities gallantly. By force of circumstances, she was often obliged to treat father as a sick or wayward child. Even when he wanted to assert himself he could not, for his drinking placed him constantly in the wrong. Mother made all the plans and gave the directions. When sober, father usually obeyed. Thus mother, through no fault of her own, became accustomed to wearing the family trousers. Father, coming suddenly to life again, often begins to assert himself. This means trouble, unless the family watches for these tendencies in each other and comes to a friendly agreement about them.

Drinking isolates most homes from the outside world. Father may have laid aside for years all normal activities–clubs, civic duties, sports. When he renews interest in such things, a feeling of jealousy may arise. The family may feel they hold a mortgage on dad, so big that no equity should be left for outsiders. Instead of developing new channels of activity for themselves, mother and children demand that he stay home and make up the deficiency.

At the very beginning, the couple ought to frankly face the fact that each will have to yield here and there if the family is going to play an effective part in the new life. Father will necessarily spend much time with other alcoholics, but this activity should be balanced. New acquaintances who know nothing of alcoholism might be made and thoughtful consideration given their needs. The problems of the community might engage attention. Though the family has no religious connections, they may wish to make contact with or take membership in a religious body.

Alcoholics who have derided religious people will be helped by such contacts. Being possessed of a spiritual experience, the alcoholic will find he has much in common with these people, though he may differ with them on many matters. If he does not argue about religion, he will make new friends and is sure to find new avenues of usefulness and pleasure. He and his family can be a bright spot in such congregations. He may bring new hope and new courage to many a priest, minister, or rabbi, who gives his all to minister to our troubled world. We intend the foregoing as a helpful suggestion only. So far as we are concerned, there is nothing obligatory about it. As non-denominational people, we cannot make up others' minds for them. Each individual should consult his own conscience.

We have been speaking to you of serious, sometimes tragic things. We have been dealing with alcohol in its worst aspect. But we aren't a glum lot. If newcomers could see no joy or fun in our existence, they wouldn't want it. We absolutely insist on enjoying life. We try not to indulge in cynicism over the state of the nations, nor do we carry the world's troubles on our shoulders. When we see a man sinking into the mire that is alcoholism, we give him first aid and place what we have at his disposal. For his sake, we do recount and almost relive the horrors of our past. But those of us who have tried to shoulder the entire burden and trouble of others find we are soon overcome by them.

So we think cheerfulness and laughter make for usefulness. Outsiders are sometimes shocked when we burst into merriment over a seemingly tragic experience out of the past. But why shouldn't we laugh? We have recovered, and have been given the power to help others.

Everybody knows that those in bad health, and those who seldom play, do not laugh much. So let each family play together or separately as much as their circumstances warrant. We are sure God wants us to be happy, joyous, and free. We cannot subscribe to the belief that his life is a vale of tears, though it once was just that for many of us. But it is clear that we made our own misery. God didn't do it. Avoid then, the deliberate manufacture of misery, but if trouble comes, cheerfully capitalize it as an opportunity to demonstrate His omnipotence.

Now about health: A body badly burned by alcohol does not often recover overnight nor do twisted thinking and depression vanish in a twinkling. We are convinced that a spiritual mode of living is a most powerful health restorative. We, who have recovered from serious drinking, are miracles of mental health. But we have seen remarkable transformations in our bodies. Hardly one of our crowd now shows any dissipation.

But this does not mean that we disregard human health measures. God has abundantly supplied this world with fine doctors, psychologists, and practitioners of various kinds. Do not hesitate to take your health problems to such persons. Most of them give freely of themselves, that their fellows may enjoy sound minds and bodies. Try to remember that though God has wrought miracles among us, we should never belittle a good doctor or psychiatrist. Their services are often indispensable in treating a newcomer and in following his case afterward.

One of the many doctors who had the opportunity of reading this book in manuscript form told us that the use of sweets was often helpful, of course depending upon a doctor's advice. He thought all alcoholics should constantly have chocolate available for its quick energy value at times of fatigue. He added that occasionally in the night a vague craving arose which would be satisfied by candy. Many of us have noticed a tendency to eat sweets and have found this practice beneficial.

A word about sex relations. Alcohol is so sexually stimulating to some men that they have over-indulged. Couples are occasionally dismayed to find that when drinking is stopped the man tends to be impotent. Unless the reason is understood, there may be an emotional upset. Some of us had this experience, only to enjoy, in a few months, a finer intimacy than ever. There should be no hesitancy in consulting a doctor or psychologist if the condition persists. We do not know of many cases where this difficulty lasted long.

The alcoholic may find it hard to re-establish friendly relations with his children. Their young minds were impressionable while he was drinking. Without saying so, they may cordially hate him for what he has done to them and to their mother. The children are sometimes dominated by a pathetic hardness and cynicism. They cannot seem to forgive and forget. This may hang on for months, long after their mother has accepted dad's new way of living and thinking.

In time they will see that he is a new man and in their own way they will let him know it. When this happens, they can be invited to join in morning meditation and then they can take part in the daily discussion without rancor or bias. From that point on, progress will be rapid. Marvelous results often follow such a reunion.

Whether the family goes on a spiritual basis or not, the alcoholic member has to if he would recover. The others must be convinced of his new status beyond the shadow of a doubt. Seeing is believing to most families who have lived with a drinker.

Here is a case in point: One of our friends is a heavy smoker and coffee drinker. There was no doubt he over-indulged. Seeing this, and meaning to be helpful, his wife commenced to admonish him about it. He admitted he was overdosing these things, but frankly said that he was not ready to stop. His wife is one of those persons who really feels there is something rather sinful about these commodities, so she nagged, and her intolerance finally threw him into a fit of anger. He got drunk.

Of course our friend was wrong–dead wrong. He had to painfully admit that and mend his spiritual fences. Though he is now a most effective member of Alcoholics Anonymous, he still smokes and drinks coffee, but neither his wife nor anyone else stands in judgment. She sees she was wrong to make a burning issue out of such a matter when his more serious ailments were being rapidly cured.

We have three little mottoes which are apropos. Here they are:

First Things First
Live and Let Live
Easy Does It.

Chapter X

TO EMPLOYERS

AMONG MANY employers nowadays, we think of one member who has spent much of his life in the world of big business. He has hired and fired hundreds of men. He knows the alcoholic as the employer sees him. His present views ought to prove exceptionally useful to business men everywhere.

But let him tell you:

I was at one time assistant manager of a corporation department employing sixty-six hundred men. One day my secretary came in saying Mr. B– insisted on speaking with me. I told her to say that I was not interested. I had warned him several times that he had but one more chance. Not long afterward he had called me from Hartford on two successive days, so drunk he could hardly speak. I told him he was through–finally and forever.

My secretary returned to say that it was not Mr. B– on the phone; it was Mr. B–'s brother, and he wished to give me a message. I still expected a plea for clemency, but these words came through the receiver: "I just wanted to tell you Paul jumped from a hotel window in Hartford last Saturday. He left us a note saying you were the best boss he ever had, and that you were not to blame in any way."

Another time, as I opened a letter which lay on my desk, a newspaper clipping fell out. It was the obituary of one of the best salesmen I ever had. After two weeks of drinking, he had placed his toe on the trigger of a loaded shotgun–the barrel was in his mouth. I had discharged him for drinking six weeks before.

Still another experience: A woman's voice came faintly over long distance from Virginia. She wanted to know if her husband's company insurance was still in force. Four days before he had hanged himself in his woodshed. I had been obliged to discharge him for drinking, though he was brilliant, alert, and one of the best organizers I have ever known.

Here were three exceptional men lost to this world because I did not understand alcoholism as I do now. What irony–I became an alcoholic myself! And but for the intervention of an understanding person, I might have followed in their footsteps. My downfall cost the business community unknown thousands of dollars, for it takes real money to train a man for an executive position. This kind of waste goes on unabated. We think the business fabric is shot through with a situation which might be helped by better understanding all around.

Nearly every modern employer feels a moral responsibility for the well-being of his help, and he tries to meet these responsibilities. That he has not always done so for the alcoholic is easily understood. To him the alcoholic has often seemed a fool of the first magnitude. Because of the employee's special ability, or of his own strong personal attachment to him, the employer has sometimes kept such a man at work long beyond a reasonable period. Some employers have tried every known remedy. In only a few instances has there been a lack of patience and tolerance. And we, who have imposed on the best of employers, can scarcely blame them if they have been short with us.

Here, for instance, is a typical example: An officer of one of the largest banking institutions in America knows I no longer drink. One day he told me about an executive of the same bank who, from his description, was undoubtedly alcoholic. This seemed to me like an opportunity to be helpful, so I spent two hours talking about alcoholism, the malady, and described the symptoms and results as well as I could. His comment was, "Very interesting. But I'm sure this man is done drinking. He has just returned from a three months' leave of absence, has taken a cure, looks fine, and to clinch the matter, the board of directors told him this was his last chance."

The only answer I could make was that if the man followed the usual pattern, he would go on a bigger bust than ever. I felt this was inevitable and wondered if the bank was doing the man an injustice. Why not bring him into contact with some of our alcoholic crowd? He might have a chance. I pointed out that I had had nothing to drink whatever for three years, and this in the face of difficulties that would have made nine out of ten men drink their heads off. Why not at least afford him an opportunity to hear my story? "Oh no," said my friend, "this chap is either through with liquor, or he is minus a job. If he has your will power and guts, he will make the grade."

I wanted to throw up my hands in discouragement, for I saw that I had failed to help my banker friend understand. He simply could not believe that his brother-executive suffered from a serious illness. There was nothing to do but wait.

Presently the man did slip and was fired. Following his discharge, we contacted him. Without much ado, he accepted the principles and procedure that had helped us. To me, this incident illustrates lack of understanding as to what really ails the alcoholic, and lack of knowledge as to what part employers might profitably take in salvaging their sick employees.

If you desire to help it might be well to disregard your own drinking, or lack of it. Whether you are a hard drinker, a moderate drinker or a teetotaler, you may have some pretty strong opinions, perhaps prejudices. Those who drink moderately may be more annoyed with an alcoholic than a total abstainer would be. Drinking occasionally, and understanding your own reactions, it is possible for you to become quite sure of many things which, so far as the alcoholic is concerned, are not always so. As a moderate drinker, you can take your liquor or leave it alone. Whenever you want to, you control your drinking. Of an evening, you can go on a mild bender, get up in the morning, shake your head and go to business. To you, liquor is no real problem. You cannot see why it should be to anyone else, save the spineless and stupid.

When dealing with an alcoholic, there may be a natural annoyance that a man could be so weak, stupid and irresponsible. Even when you understand the malady better, you may feel this feeling rising.

A look at the alcoholic in your organization is many times illuminating. Is he not usually brilliant, fast-thinking, imaginative and likable? When sober, does he not work hard and have a knack of getting things done? If he had these qualities and did not drink would he be worth retaining? Should he have the same consideration as other ailing employees? Is he worth salvaging? If your decision is yes, whether the reason be humanitarian or business or both, then the following suggestions may be helpful.

Can you discard the feeling that you are dealing only with habit, with stubbornness, or a weak will? If this presents difficulty, re-reading chapters two and three, where alcoholic sickness is discussed at length, might be worth while. You, as a business man, want to know the necessities before considering the result. If you concede that your employee is ill, can he be forgiven for what he has done in the past? Can his past absurdities be forgotten? Can it be appreciated that he has been a victim of crooked thinking, directly caused by the action of alcohol on his brain?

I well remember the shock I received when a prominent doctor in Chicago told me of cases where pressure of the spinal fluid actually ruptured the brain. No wonder an alcoholic is strangely irrational. Who wouldn't be, with such a fevered brain? Normal drinkers are not so affected, nor can they understand the aberrations of the alcoholic.

Your man has probably been trying to conceal a number of scrapes, perhaps pretty messy ones. They may be disgusting. You may be at a loss to understand how such a seemingly above-board chap could be so involved. But these scrapes can generally be charged, no matter how bad, to the abnormal action of alcohol on his mind. When drinking, or getting over a bout, an alcoholic, sometimes the model of honesty when normal, will do incredible things. Afterward, his revulsion will be terrible. Nearly always, these antics indicate nothing more than temporary conditions.

This is not to say that all alcoholics are honest and upright when not drinking. Of course that isn't so, and such people may often impose on you. Seeing your attempt to understand and help, some men will try to take advantage of your kindness. If you are sure your man does not want to stop, he may as well be discharged, the sooner the better. You are not doing him a favor by keeping him on. Firing such an individual may prove a blessing to him. It may be just the jolt he needs. I know, in my own particular case, that nothing my company could have done would have stopped me for, so long as

I was able to hold my position, I could not possibly realize how serious my situation was. Had they fired me first, and had they then taken steps to see that I was presented with the solution contained in this book, I might have returned to them six months later, a well man.

But there are many men who want to stop, and with them you can go far. Your understanding treatment of their cases will pay dividends.

Perhaps you have such a man in mind. He wants to quit drinking and you want to help him, even if it be only a matter of good business. You now know more about alcoholism. You can see that he is mentally and physically sick. You are willing to overlook his past performances. Suppose an approach is made something like this:

State that you know about his drinking, and that it must stop. You might say you appreciate his abilities, would like to keep him, but cannot if he continues to drink. A firm attitude at this point has helped many of us.

Next he can be assured that you do not intend to lecture, moralize, or condemn; that if this was done formerly, it was because of misunderstanding. If possible express a lack of hard feeling toward him. At this point, it might be well to explain alcoholism, the illness. Say that you believe he is a gravely-ill person, with this qualification–being perhaps fatally ill, does he want to get well? You ask, because many alcoholics, being warped and drugged, do not want to quit. But does he? Will he take every necessary step, submit to anything to get well, to stop drinking forever?

If he says yes, does he really mean it, or down inside does he think he is fooling you, and that after rest and treatment he will be able to get away with a few drinks now and then? We believe a man should be thoroughly probed on these points. Be satisfied he is not deceiving himself or you.

Whether you mention this book is a matter for your discretion. If he temporizes and still thinks he can ever drink again, even beer, he might as well be discharged after the next bender which, if an alcoholic, he is almost certain to have. He should understand that emphatically. Either you are dealing with a man who can and will get well or you are not. If not, why waste time with him? This may seem severe, but it is usually the best course.

After satisfying yourself that your man wants to recover and that he will go to any extreme to do so, you may suggest a definite course of action. For most alcoholics who are drinking, or who are just getting over a spree, a certain amount of physical treatment is desirable, even imperative. The matter of physical treatment should, of course, be referred to your own doctor. Whatever the method, its object is to thoroughly clear mind and body of the effects of alcohol. In competent hands, this seldom takes long nor is it very expensive. Your man will fare better if placed in such physical condition that he can think straight and no longer craves liquor. If you propose such a procedure to him, it may be necessary to advance the cost of the treatment, but we believe it should be made plain that any expense will later be deducted from his pay. It is better for him to feel fully responsible.

If your man accepts your offer, it should be pointed out that physical treatment is but a small part of the picture. Though you are providing him with the best possible medical attention, he should understand that he must undergo a change of heart. To get over drinking will require a transformation of thought and attitude. We all had to place recovery above everything, for without recovery we would have lost both home and business.

Can you have every confidence in his ability to recover? While on the subject of confidence, can you adopt the attitude that so far as you are concerned this will be a strictly personal matter, that his alcoholic derelictions, the treatment about to be undertaken, will never be discussed without his consent? It might be well to have a long chat with him on his return.

To return to the subject matter of this book: It contains full suggestions by which the employee may solve his problem. To you, some of the ideas which it contains are novel. Perhaps you are not quite in sympathy with the approach we suggest. By no means do we offer it as the last word on this subject, but so far as we are concerned, it has worked with us. After all, are you not looking for results rather than methods? Whether your employee likes it or not, he will learn the grim truth about alcoholism. That won't hurt him a bit, even though he does not go for this remedy.

We suggest you draw the book to the attention of the doctor who is to attend your patient during treatment. If the book is read the moment the patient is able, while acutely depressed, realization of his condition may come to him.

We hope the doctor will tell the patient the truth about his condition, whatever that happens to be. When the man is presented with this volume it is best that no one tell him he must abide by its suggestions. The man must decide for himself.

You are betting, or course, that your changed attitude plus the contents of this book will turn the trick. In some case it will, and in others it may not. But we think that if you persevere, the percentage of successes will gratify you. As our work spreads and our numbers increase, we hope your employees may be put in personal contact with some of us. Meanwhile, we are sure a great deal can be accomplished by the use of the book alone.

On your employee's return, talk with him. Ask him if he thinks he has the answer. If he feels free to discuss his problems with you, if he knows you understand and will not be upset by anything he wishes to say, he will probably be off to a fast start.

In this connection, can you remain undisturbed if the man proceeds to tell you shocking things? He may, for example, reveal that he has padded his expense account or that he has planned to take your best customers away from you. In fact, he may say almost anything if he has accepted our solution which, as you know, demands rigorous honesty. Can you charge this off as you would a bad account and start fresh with him? If he owes you money you may wish to make terms.

If he speaks of his home situation, you can undoubtedly make helpful suggestions. Can he talk frankly with you so long as he does not bear business tales or criticize his associate? With this kind of employee such an attitude will command undying loyalty.

The greatest enemies of us alcoholics are resentment, jealousy, envy, frustration, and fear. Wherever men are gathered together in business there will be rivalries and, arising out of these, a certain amount of office politics. Sometimes we alcoholics have an idea that people are trying to pull us down. Often this is not so at all. But sometimes our drinking will be used politically.

One instance comes to mind in which a malicious individual was always making friendly little jokes about an alcoholic's drinking exploits. In this way he was slyly carrying tales. In another case, an alcoholic was sent to a hospital for treatment. Only a few knew of it at first but, within a short time, it was billboarded throughout the entire company. Naturally this sort of thing decreased the man's chance of recovery. The employer can many times protect the victim from this kind of talk. The employer cannot play favorites, but he can always defend a man from needless provocation and unfair criticism.

As a class, alcoholics are energetic people. They work hard and they play hard. Your man should be on his mettle to make good. Being somewhat weakened, and faced with physical and mental readjustment to a life which knows no alcohol, he may overdo. You may have to curb his desire to work sixteen hours a day. You may need to encourage him to play once in a while. He may wish to do a lot for other alcoholics and something of the sort may come up during business hours. A reasonable amount of latitude will be helpful. This work is necessary to maintain his sobriety.

After your man has gone along without drinking for a few months, you may be able to make use of his services with other employees who are giving you the alcoholic run-around–provided, of course, they are willing to have a third party in the picture. An alcoholic who has recovered, but holds a relatively unimportant job, can talk to a man with a better position. Being on a radically different basis of life, he will never take advantage of the situation.

Your man may be trusted. Long experience with alcoholic excuses naturally arouses suspicion. When his wife next calls saying he is sick, you may jump to the conclusion he is drunk. If he is, and is still trying to recover, he will tell you about it even if it means the loss of his job. For he knows he must be honest if he would live at all. He will appreciated knowing you are not bothering your head about him, that you are not suspicious nor are you trying to run his life so he will be shielded from temptation to drink. If he is conscientiously following the program of recovery he can go anywhere your business may call him.

In case he does stumble, even once, you will have to decide whether to let him go. If you are sure he doesn't mean business, there is no doubt you should discharge him. If, on the contrary, you are sure he is doing his utmost, you may wish to give him another chance. But you should feel under no obligation to keep him on, for your obligation has been well discharged already.

There is another thing you might wish to do. If your organization is a large one, your junior executives might be provided with this book. You might let them know you have no quarrel with alcoholics of your organization. These juniors are often in a difficult position. Men under them are frequently their friends. So, for one reason or another, they cover these men, hoping matters will take a turn for the better. They often jeopardize their own positions by trying to help serious drinkers who should have been fired long ago, or else given an opportunity to get well.

After reading this book, a junior executive can go to such a man and say approximately this, "Look here, Ed. Do you want to stop drinking or not? You put me on the spot every time you get drunk. It isn't fair to me or the firm. I have been learning something about alcoholism. If you are an alcoholic, you are a mighty sick man. You act like one. The firm wants to help you get over it, and if you are interested, there is a way out. If you take it, your past will be forgotten and the fact that you went away for treatment will not be mentioned. But if you cannot or will not stop drinking, I think you ought to resign."

Your junior executive may not agree with the contents of our book. He need not, and often should not show it to his alcoholic prospect. But at least he will understand the problem and will no longer be misled by ordinary promises. He will be able to take a position with such a man which is eminently fair and square. He will have no further reason for covering up an alcoholic employee.

It boils right down to this: No man should be fired just because he is alcoholic. If he wants to stop, he should be afforded a real chance. If he cannot or does not want to stop, he should be discharged. The exceptions are few.

We think this method of approach will accomplish several things. It will permit the rehabilitation of good men. At the same time you will feel no reluctance to rid yourself of those who cannot or will not stop. Alcoholism may be causing your organization considerable damage in its waste of time, men and reputation. We hope our suggestions will help you plug up this sometimes serious leak. We think we are sensible when we urge that you stop this waste and give your worthwhile man a chance.

The other day an approach was made to the vice president of a large industrial concern. He remarked: "I'm glad you fellows got over your drinking. But the policy of this company is not to interfere with the habits of our employees. If a man drinks so much that his job suffers, we fire him. I don't see how you can be of any help to us for, as you see, we don't have any alcoholic problem." This same company spends millions for research every year. Their cost of production is figured to a fine decimal point. They have recreational facilities. There is company insurance. There is a real interest, both humanitarian and business, in the well-being of employees. But alcoholism–well, they just don't believe they have it.

Perhaps this is a typical attitude. We, who have collectively seen a great deal of business life, at least from the alcoholic angle, had to smile at this gentleman's sincere opinion. He might be shocked if he knew how much alcoholism is costing his organization a year. That company may harbor many actual or potential alcoholics. We believe that managers of large enterprises often have little idea how prevalent this problem is. Even if you feel your organization has no alcoholic problem, it may pay to take another look down the line. You may make some interesting discoveries.

Of course, this chapter refers to alcoholics, sick people, deranged men. What our friend, the vice president, had in mind was the habitual or whoopee drinker. As to them, his policy is undoubtedly sound, but he did not distinguish between such people and the alcoholic.

It is not to be expected that an alcoholic employee will receive a disproportionate amount of time and attention. He should not be made a favorite. The right kind of man, the kind who recovers, will not want this sort of thing. He will not impose. Far from it. He will work like the devil and thank you to his dying day.

Today I own a little company. There are two alcoholic employees, who produce as much as five normal salesmen. But why not? They have a new attitude, and they have been saved from a living death. I have enjoyed every moment spent in getting them straightened out. [*See Appendix VI–We shall be happy to hear from you if we can be of help.*]

Chapter XI

A VISION FOR YOU

FOR MOST normal folks, drinking means conviviality, companionship and colorful imagination.

It means release from care, boredom and worry. It is joyous intimacy with friends and a feeling that life is good. But not so with us in those last days of heavy drinking. The old pleasures were gone. They were but memories. Never could we recapture the great moments of the past. There was an insistent yearning to enjoy life as we once did and a heartbreaking obsession that some new miracle of control would enable us to do it. There was always one more attempt–and one more failure.

The less people tolerated us, the more we withdrew from society, from life itself. As we became subjects of King Alcohol, shivering denizens of his mad realm, the chilling vapor that is loneliness settled down. It thickened, ever becoming blacker. Some of us sought out sordid places, hoping to find understanding companionship and approval. Momentarily we did–then would come oblivion and the awful awakening to face the hideous Four Horsemen–Terror, Bewilderment, Frustration, Despair. Unhappy drinkers who read this page will understand!

Now and then a serious drinker, being dry at the moment says, "I don't miss it at all. Feel better. Work better. Having a better time." As ex-problem drinkers, we smile at such a sally. We know our friend is like a boy whistling in the dark to keep up his spirits. He fools himself. Inwardly he would give anything to take half a dozen drinks and get away with them. He will presently try the old game again, for he isn't happy about his sobriety. He cannot picture life without alcohol. Some day he will be unable to imagine life either with alcohol or without it. Then he will know loneliness such as few do. He will be at the jumping-off place. He will wish for the end.

We have shown how we got out from under. You say, "Yes, I'm willing. But am I to be consigned to a life where I shall be stupid, boring and glum, like some righteous people I see? I know I must get along without liquor, but how can I? Have you a sufficient substitute?"

Yes, there is a substitute and it is vastly more than that. It is a fellowship in Alcoholics Anonymous. There you will find release from care, boredom and worry. Your imagination will be fired. Life will mean something at last.

The most satisfactory years of your existence lie ahead. Thus we find the fellowship, and so will you.

"How is that to come about?" you ask. "Where am I to find these people?"

You are going to meet these new friends in your own community. Near you, alcoholics are dying helplessly like people in a sinking ship. If you live in a large place, there are hundreds. High and low, rich and poor, these are future fellows of Alcoholics Anonymous. Among them you will make lifelong friends. You will be bound to them with new and wonderful ties, for you will escape disaster together and you will commence shoulder to shoulder your common journey. Then you will know what it means to give of yourself that others may survive and rediscover life. You will learn the full meaning of "Love thy neighbor as thyself."

It may seem incredible that these men are to become happy, respected, and useful once more. How can they rise out of such misery, bad repute and hopelessness? The practical answer is that since these things have happened among us, they can happen with you. Should you wish them above all else, and be willing to make use of our experience, we are sure they will come. The age of miracles is still with us. Our own recovery proves that!

Our hope is that when this chip of a book is launched on the world tide of alcoholism, defeated drinkers will seize upon it, to follow its suggestions. Many, we are sure, will rise to their feet and march on. They will approach still other sick ones and fellowships of Alcoholics Anonymous may spring up in each city and hamlet, havens for those who must find a way out.

In the chapter "Working With Others" you gathered an idea of how we approach and aid others to health. Suppose now that through you several families have adopted this way of life. You will want to know more of how to proceed from that point. Perhaps the best way of treating you to a glimpse of your future will be to describe the growth or the fellowship among us. Here is a brief account:

Years ago, in 1935, one of our number made a journey to a certain western city. From a business standpoint, his trip came off badly. Had he been successful in his enterprise, he would have been set on his feet financially which, at the time, seemed vitally important. But his venture wound up in a law suit and bogged down completely. The proceeding was shot through with much hard feeling and controversy.

Bitterly discouraged, he found himself in a strange place, discredited and almost broke. Still physically weak, and sober but a few months, he saw that his predicament was dangerous. He wanted so much to talk with someone, but whom?

One dismal afternoon he paced a hotel lobby wondering how his bill was to be paid. At the end of the room stood a glass covered directory of local churches. Down the lobby a door opened into an attractive bar. He could see the gay crowd inside. In there he would find companionship and release. Unless he took some drinks, he might not have the courage to scrape an acquaintance and would have a lonely weekend.

Of course he couldn't drink, but why not sit hopefully at a table, a bottle of ginger ale before him? After all, had he not been sober six months now? Perhaps he could handle, say, three drinks–no more! Fear gripped him. He was on thin ice. Again it was the old, insidious insanity–that first drink. With a shiver, he turned away and walked down the lobby to the church directory. Music and gay chatter still floated to him from the bar.

But what about his responsibilities–his family and the men who would die because they would not know how to get well, ah–yes, those other alcoholics? There must be many such in this town. He would phone a clergyman. His sanity returned and he thanked God. Selecting a church at random from the directory, he stepped into a booth and lifted the receiver.

His call to the clergyman led him presently to a certain resident of the town, who, though formerly able and respected, was then nearing the nadir of alcoholic despair. It was the usual situation: home in jeopardy, wife ill, children distracted, bills in arrears and standing damaged. He had a desperate desire to stop, but saw no way out, for he had earnestly tried many avenues of escape. Painfully aware of being somehow abnormal, the man did not fully realize what it meant to be alcoholic.

When our friend related his experience, the man agreed that no amount of will power he might muster could stop his drinking for long. A spiritual experience, he conceded, was absolutely necessary, but the price seemed high upon the basis suggested. He told how he lived in constant worry about those who might find out about his alcoholism. He had, of course, the familiar alcoholic obsession that few knew of his drinking. Why, he argued, should he lose the remainder of his business, only to bring still more suffering to his family by foolishly admitting his plight to people from whom he made his livelihood? He would do anything, he said, but that.

Being intrigued, however, he invited our friend to his home. Some time later, and just as he thought he was getting control of his liquor situation, he went on a roaring bender. For him, this was the spree that ended all sprees. He saw that he would have to face his problems squarely that God might give him mastery.

One morning he took the bull by the horns and set out to tell those he feared what his trouble had been. He found himself surprisingly well received, and learned that many knew of his drinking. Stepping into his car, he made the rounds of people he had hurt. He trembled as he went about, for this might mean ruin, particularly to a person in his line of business.

At midnight he came home exhausted, but very happy. He has not had a drink since. As we shall see, he now means a great deal to his community, and the major liabilities of thirty years of hard drinking have been repaired in four.

But life was not easy for the two friends. Plenty of difficulties presented themselves. Both saw that they must keep spiritually active. One day they called up the head nurse of a local hospital. They explained their need and inquired if she had a first class alcoholic prospect.

She replied, "Yes, we've got a corker. He's just beaten up a couple of nurses. Goes off his head completely when he's drinking. But he's a grand chap when he's sober, though he's been in here eight times in the last six months. Understand he was once a well-known lawyer in town, but just now we've got him strapped down tight."

Here was a prospect all right but, by the description, none too promising. The use of spiritual principles in such case was not so well understood as it is now. But one of the friends said, "Put him in a private room. We'll be down."

Two days later, a future fellow of Alcoholics Anonymous stared glassily at the strangers beside his bed. "Who are you fellows, and why this private room? I was always in a ward before."

Said one of the visitors, "We're giving you a treatment for alcoholism."

Hopelessness was written large on the man's face as he replied, "Oh, but that's no use. Nothing would fix me. I'm a goner. The last three times, I got drunk on the way home from here. I'm afraid to go out the door. I can't understand it."

For an hour, the two friends told him about their drinking experiences. Over and over, he would say: "That's me. That's me. I drink like that."

The man in the bed was told of the acute poisoning from which he suffered, how it deteriorates the body of an alcoholic and warps his mind. There was much talk about the mental state preceding the first drink.

"Yes, that's me," said the sick man, "the very image. You fellows know your stuff all right, but I don't see what good it'll do. You fellows are somebody. I was once, but I'm a nobody now. From what you tell me, I know more than ever I can't stop." At this both the visitors burst into a laugh. Said the future Fellow Anonymous: "Damn little to laugh about that I can see."

The two friends spoke of their spiritual experience and told him about the course of action they carried out.

He interrupted: "I used to be strong for the church, but that won't fix it. I've prayed to God on hangover mornings and sworn that I'd never touch another drop but by nine o'clock I'd be boiled as an owl."

Next day found the prospect more receptive. He had been thinking it over. "Maybe you're right," he said. "God ought to be able to do anything." Then he added, "He sure didn't do much for me when I was trying to fight this booze racket alone."

On the third day the lawyer gave his life to the care and direction of his Creator, and said he was perfectly willing to do anything necessary. His wife came, scarcely daring to be hopeful, though she thought she saw something different about her husband already. He had begun to have a spiritual experience.

That afternoon he put on his clothes and walked from the hospital a free man. He entered a political campaign, making speeches, frequenting men's gathering places of all sorts, often staying up all night. He lost the race by only a narrow margin. But he had found God–and in finding God had found himself.

That was in June, 1935. He never drank again. He too, has become a respected and useful member of his community. He has helped other men recover, and is a power in the church from which he was long absent.

So, you see, there were three alcoholics in that town, who now felt they had to give to others what they had found, or be sunk. After several failures to find others, a fourth turned up. He came through an acquaintance who had heard the good news. He proved to be a devil-may-care young fellow whose parents could not make out whether he wanted to stop drinking or not. They were deeply religious people, much shocked by their son's refusal to have anything to do with the church. He suffered horribly from his sprees, but it seemed as if nothing could be done for him. He consented, however, to go to the hospital, where he occupied the very room recently vacated by the lawyer.

He had three visitors. After a bit, he said, "The way you fellows put this spiritual stuff makes sense. I'm ready to do business. I guess the old folks were right after all." So one more was added to the Fellowship.

All this time our friend of the hotel lobby incident remained in that town. He was there three months. He now returned home, leaving behind his first acquaintances, the lawyer and the devil-may-care chap. These men had found something brand new in life. Though they knew they must help other alcoholics if they would remain sober, that motive became secondary. It was transcended by the happiness they found in giving themselves for others. They shared their homes, their slender resources, and gladly devoted their spare hours to fellow-sufferers. They were willing, by day or night, to place a new man in the hospital and visit him afterward. They grew in numbers. They experienced a few distressing failures, but in those cases they made an effort to bring the man's family into a spiritual way of living, thus relieving much worry and suffering.

A year and six months later these three had succeeded with seven more. Seeing much of each other, scarce an evening passed that someone's home did not shelter a little gathering of men and women, happy in their release, and constantly thinking how they might present their discovery to some newcomer. In addition to these casual get-togethers, it became customary to set apart one night a week for a meeting to be attended by anyone or everyone interested in a spiritual way of life. Aside from fellowship and sociability, the prime object was to provide a time and place where new people might bring their problems.

Outsiders became interested. One man and his wife placed their large home at the disposal of this strangely assorted crowd. This couple has since become so fascinated that they have dedicated their home to the work. Many a distracted wife has visited this house to find loving and understanding companionship among women who knew her problem, to hear from the lips of their husbands what had happened to them, to be advised how her own wayward mate might be hospitalized and approached when next he stumbled.

Many a man, yet dazed from his hospital experience, has stepped over the threshold of that home into freedom. Many an alcoholic who entered there came away with an answer. He succumbed to that gay crowd inside, who laughed at their own misfortunes and understood his. Impressed by those who visited him at the hospital, he capitulated entirely when, later, in an upper room of this house, he heard the story of some man whose experience closely tallied with his own. The expression on the faces of the women, that indefinable something in the eyes of the men, the stimulating and electric atmosphere of the place, conspired to let him know that here was haven at last.

The very practical approach to his problems, the absence of intolerance of any kind, the informality, the genuine democracy, the uncanny understanding which these people had were irresistible. He and his wife would leave elated by the thought of what they could now do for some stricken acquaintance and his family. They knew they had a host of new friends; it seemed they had known these strangers always. They had seen miracles, and one was to come to them. They had visioned the Great Reality–their loving and All Powerful Creator.

Now, this house will hardly accommodate its weekly visitors, for they number sixty or eighty as a rule. Alcoholics are being attracted from far and near. From surrounding towns, families drive long distances to be present. A community thirty miles away has fifteen fellows of Alcoholics Anonymous. Being a large place, we think that someday its Fellowship will number many hundreds. [*Written in 1939.*]

But life among Alcoholics Anonymous is more than attending gatherings and visiting hospitals. Cleaning up old scrapes, helping to settle family differences, explaining the disinherited son to his irate parents, lending money and securing jobs for each other, when justified–these are everyday occurrences. No one is too discredited or has sunk too low to be welcomed cordially–if he means business. Social distinctions, petty rivalries and jealousies–these are laughed out of countenance. Being wrecked in the same vessel, being restored and united under one God, with hearts and minds attuned to the welfare of others, the things which matter so much to some people no longer signify much to them. How could they?

Under only slightly different conditions, the same thing is taking place in many eastern cities. In one of these there is a well-known hospital for the treatment of alcoholic and drug addiction. Six years ago one of our number was a patient there. Many of us have felt, for the first time, the Presence and Power of God within its walls. We are greatly indebted to the doctor in attendance there, for he, although it might prejudice his own work, has told us of his belief in ours.

Every few days this doctor suggests our approach to one of his patients. Understanding our work, he can do this with an eye to selecting those who are willing and able to recover on a spiritual basis. Many of us, former patients, go there to help. Then, in this eastern city, there are informal meetings such as we have described to you, where you may now see scores of members. There are the same fast friendships, there is the same helpfulness to one another as you find among our western friends. There is a good bit of travel between East and West and we foresee a great increase in this helpful interchange.

Some day we hope that every alcoholic who journeys will find a

Fellowship of Alcoholics Anonymous at his destination. To some extent this is already true. Some of us are salesmen and go about. Little clusters of twos and threes and fives of us have sprung up in other communities, through contact with our two larger centers. Those of us who travel drop in as often as we can. This practice enables us to lend a hand, at the same time avoiding certain alluring distractions of the road, about which any travelling man can inform you.

Thus we grow. And so can you, though you be but one man with this book in your hand. We believe and hope it contains all you will need to begin.

We know what you are thinking. You are saying to yourself: "I'm jittery and alone. I couldn't do that." But you can. You forget that you have just now tapped a source of power much greater than yourself. To duplicate, with such backing, what we have accomplished is only a matter of willingness, patience and labor.

We know of an A.A. member who was living in a large community. He had lived there but a few weeks when he found that the place probably contained more alcoholics per square mile than any city in the country. This was only a few days ago at this writing (1939). The authorities were much concerned. He got in touch with a prominent psychiatrist who had undertaken certain responsibilities for the mental health of the community. The doctor proved to be able and exceedingly anxious to adopt any workable method of handling the situation. So he inquired, what did our friend have on the ball?

Our friend proceeded to tell him. And with such good effect that the doctor agreed to a test among his patients and certain other alcoholics from a clinic which he attends. Arrangements were also made with the chief psychiatrist of a large public hospital to select still others from the stream of misery which flows through that institution.

So our fellow worker will soon have friends galore. Some of them may sink and perhaps never get up, but if our experience is a criterion, more than half of those approached will become fellows of Alcoholics Anonymous. When a few men in this city have found themselves, and have discovered the joy of helping others to face life again, there will be no stopping until everyone in that town has had his opportunity to recover–if he can and will.

Still you may say: "But I will not have the benefit of contact with you who write this book." We cannot be sure. God will determine that, so you must remember that your real reliance is always upon Him. He will show you how to create the fellowship you crave. [*Alcoholics Anonymous will be glad to hear from you. Address: P.O. Box 459, Grand Central Station, New York, NY 10163.*]

Our book is meant to be suggestive only. We realize we know only a little. God will constantly disclose more to you and to us. Ask Him in your morning meditation what you can do each day for the man who is still sick. The answers will come, if your own house is in order. But obviously you cannot transmit something you haven't got. See to it that your relationship with Him is right, and great events will come to pass for you and countless others. This is the Great Fact for us.

Abandon yourself to God as you understand God. Admit your faults to Him and to your fellows. Clear away the wreckage of your past. Give freely of what you find and join us. We shall be with you in the Fellowship of the Spirit, and you will surely meet some of us as you trudge the Road of Happy Destiny.

May God bless you and keep you–until then.

PERSONAL STORIES

*How Thirty-Seven Alcoholics
Recovered From Their Malady*

Beginning with the story of "Dr. Bob," a co-founder of A.A., there are here presented three groups of personal histories, twelve stories each.

PART I

PIONEERS OF A.A.

This group of ten stories shows that sobriety in A.A. can be lasting.

PART II

THEY STOPPED IN TIME

Twelve stories which may help you decide whether you are alcoholic; also, whether A.A. is for you.

PART III

THEY LOST NEARLY ALL

Those who believe their drinking to be hopeless may again find hope in these twelve impressive tales.

PART I: PIONEERS OF A.A.

Dr. Bob and the twelve men and women who here tell their stories were among the early members of A.A.'s first groups.

All ten have now passed away of natural causes, having maintained complete sobriety.

Today, hundreds of additional A.A. members can be found who have had no relapse for more than thirty years.

All of these, then, are the pioneers of A.A. They bear witness that release from alcoholism can really be permanent.

DOCTOR BOB'S NIGHTMARE

A co-founder of Alcoholics Anonymous. The birth of our Society dates from his first day of permanent sobriety, June 10, 1935.

To 1950, the year of his death, he carried the A.A. messages to more than 5,000 alcoholic men and women, and to all these he gave his medical services without thought of charge.

In this prodigy of service, he was well assisted by Sister Ignatia at St. Thomas Hospital in Akron, Ohio, one of the greatest friends our Fellowship will ever know.

I WAS BORN in a small New England village of about seven thousand souls. The general moral standard was, as I recall it, far above the average. No beer or liquor was sold in the neighborhood, except at the State liquor agency where perhaps one might procure a pint if he could convince the agent that he really needed it. Without this proof the expectant purchaser would be forced to depart empty handed with none of what I later came to believe was the great panacea for all human ills. Men who had liquor shipped in from Boston or New York by express were looked upon with great distrust and disfavor by most of the good townspeople. The town was well supplied with churches and schools in which I pursued my early educational activities.

My father was a professional man of recognized ability and both my father and mother were most active in church affairs. Both father and mother were considerably above the average in intelligence.

Unfortunately for me, I was the only child, which perhaps engendered the selfishness which played such an important part in bringing on my alcoholism.

From childhood through high school I was more or less forced to go to church, Sunday School and evening service, Monday night Christian Endeavor and sometimes to Wednesday evening prayer meeting. This had the effect of making me resolve that when I was free from parental domination, I would never again darken the doors of a church. This resolution I kept steadfastly for the next forty years, except when circumstances made it seem unwise to absent myself.

After high school came four years in one of the best colleges in the country where drinking seemed to be a major extra-curricular activity. Almost everyone seemed to do it. I did it more and more, and had lots of fun without much grief, either physical or financial. I seemed to be able to snap back the next morning better than most of my fellow drinkers, who were cursed (or perhaps blessed) with a great deal of morning-after nausea. Never once in my life have I had a headache, which fact leads me to believe that I was an alcoholic almost from the start. My whole life seemed to be centered around doing what I wanted to do, without regard for the rights, wishes, or privileges of anyone else; a state of mind which became more and more predominant as the years passed. I was graduated with "summa cum laude" in the eyes of the drinking fraternity, but not in the eyes of the Dean.

The next three years I spent in Boston, Chicago, and Montreal in the employ of a large manufacturing concern, selling railway supplies, gas engines of all sorts, and many other items of heavy hardware. During these years, I drank as much as my purse permitted, still without paying too great a penalty, although I was beginning to have morning jitters at times. I lost only a half-day's work during these three years.

My next move was to take up the study of medicine, entering one of the largest universities in the country. There I took up the business of drinking with much greater earnestness than I had previously shown. On account of my enormous capacity for beer, I was elected to membership in one of the drinking societies, and soon became one of the leading spirits. Many mornings I have gone to classes, and even though fully prepared, would turn and walk back to the fraternity house because of my jitters, not daring to enter the classroom for fear of making a scene should I be called on for recitation.

This went from bad to worse until Sophomore spring when, after a prolonged period of drinking, I made up my mind that I could not complete my course, so I packed my grip and went South to spend a month on a large farm owned by a friend of mine. When I got the fog out of my brain, I decided that quitting school was very foolish and that I had better return and continue my work. When I reached school, I discovered the faculty had other ideas on the subject. After much argument they allowed me to return and take my exams, all of which I passed creditably. But they were much disgusted and told me they would attempt to struggle along without my presence. After many painful discussions, they finally gave me my credits and I migrated to another of the leading universities of the country and entered as a Junior that fall.

There my drinking became so much worse that the boys in the fraternity house where I lived felt forced to send for my father, who made a long journey in the vain endeavor to get me straightened around. This had little effect however for I kept on drinking and used a great deal more hard liquor than in former years.

Coming up to final exams I went on a particularly strenuous spree. When I went in to write the examinations, my hand trembled so I could not hold a pencil. I passed in at least three absolutely blank books. I was, of course, soon on the carpet and the upshot was that I had to go back for two more quarters and remain absolutely dry, if I wished to graduate. This I did, and proved myself satisfactory to the faculty, both in deportment and scholastically.

I conducted myself so creditably that I was able to secure a much coveted internship in a western city, where I spent two years. During these two years I was kept so busy that I hardly left the hospital at all. Consequently, I could not get into any trouble.

When those two years were up, I opened an office downtown. I had some money, all the time in the world, and considerable stomach trouble. I soon discovered that a couple of drinks would alleviate my gastric distress, at least for a few hours at a time, so it was not at all difficult for me to return to my former excessive indulgence.

By this time I was beginning to pay very dearly physically and, in hope of relief, voluntarily incarcerated myself at least a dozen times in one of the local sanitariums. I was between Scylla and Charybdis now, because if I did not drink my stomach tortured me, and if I did my nerves did the same thing. After three years of this, I wound up in the local hospital where they attempted to help me, but I would get my friends to smuggle me a quart, or I would steal the alcohol about the building, so that I got rapidly worse.

Finally, my father had to send a doctor out from my home town who managed to get me back there in some way, and I was in bed about two months before I could venture out of the house. I stayed about town a couple of months more and returned to resume my practice. I think I must have been thoroughly scared by what had happened, or by the doctor, or probably both, so that I did not touch a drink again until the country went dry.

With the passing of the Eighteenth Amendment I felt quite safe. I knew everyone would buy a few bottles, or cases, of liquor as their exchequers permitted, and that it would soon be gone. Therefore it would make no great difference, even if I should do some drinking. At that time I was not aware of the almost unlimited supply the government made it possible for us doctors to obtain, neither had I any knowledge of the bootlegger who soon appeared on the horizon. I drank with moderation at first, but it took me only a relatively short time to drift back into the old habits which had wound up so disastrously before.

During the next few years, I developed two distinct phobias. One was the fear of not sleeping, and the other was the fear of running out of liquor. Not being a man of means, I knew that if I did not stay sober enough to earn money, I would run out of liquor. Most of the time, therefore, I did not take the morning drink which I craved so badly, but instead would fill up on large doses of sedatives to quiet the jitters, which distressed me terribly. Occasionally, I would yield to the morning craving, but if I did, it would be only a few hours before I would be quite unfit for work. This would lessen my chances of smuggling some home that evening, which in turn would mean a night of futile tossing around in bed followed by a morning of unbearable jitters. During the subsequent fifteen years I had sense enough never to go to the hospital if I had been drinking, and very seldom did I receive patients. I would sometimes hide out in one of the clubs of which I was a member, and had the habit at times of registering at a hotel under a fictitious name. But my friends usually found me and I would go home if they promised that I should not be scolded.

If my wife were planning to go out in the afternoon, I would get a large supply of liquor and smuggle it home and hide it in the coal bin, the clothes chute, over door jambs, over beams in the cellar and in cracks in the cellar tile. I also made use of old trunks and chests, the old can container, and even the ash container. The water tank on the toilet I never used, because that looked too easy. I found out later that my wife inspected it frequently. I used to put eight or twelve ounce bottles of alcohol in a fur lined glove and toss it onto the back airing porch when winter days got dark enough. My bootlegger had hidden alcohol at the back steps where I could get it at my convenience. Sometimes I would bring it in my pockets, but they were inspected, and that became too risky. I used also to put it up in four ounce bottles and stick several in my stocking tops. This worked nicely until my wife and I went to see Wallace Beery in "Tugboat Annie," after which the pant-leg and stocking racket were out!

I will not take space to relate all my hospital or sanitarium experiences.

During all this time we became more or less ostracized by our friends. We could not be invited out because I would surely get tight, and my wife dared not invite people in for the same reason. My phobia for sleeplessness demanded that I get drunk every night, but in order to get more liquor for the next night, I had to stay sober during the day, at least up to four o'clock. This routine went on with few interruptions for seventeen years. It was really a horrible nightmare, this earning money, getting liquor, smuggling it home, getting drunk, morning jitters, taking large doses of sedatives to make it possible for me to earn more money, and so on ad nauseam. I used to promise my wife, my friends, and my children that I would drink no more–promises which seldom kept me sober even through the day, though I was very sincere when I made them.

For the benefit of those experimentally inclined, I should mention the so-called beer experiment. When beer first came back, I thought that I was safe. I could drink all I wanted of that. It was harmless; nobody ever got drunk on beer. So I filled the cellar full, with the permission of my good wife. It was not long before I was drinking at least a case and a half a day. I put on thirty pounds weight in about two months, looked like a pig, and was uncomfortable from shortness of breath. It then occurred to me that after one was all smelled up with beer nobody could tell what had been drunk, so I began to fortify my beer with straight alcohol. Of course, the result was very bad, and that ended the beer experiment.

About the time of the beer experiment I was thrown in with a crowd of people who attracted me because of their seeming poise, health, and happiness. They spoke with great freedom from embarrassment, which I could never do, and they seemed very much at ease on all occasions and appeared very healthy. More than these attributes, they seemed to be happy. I was self conscious and ill at ease most of the time, my health was at the breaking point, and I was thoroughly miserable. I sensed they had something I did not have, from which I might readily profit. I learned that it was something of a spiritual nature, which did not appeal to me very much, but I thought it could do no harm. I gave the matter much time and study for the next two and a half years, but I still got tight every night nevertheless. I read everything I could find, and talked to everyone who I thought knew anything about it.

My wife became deeply interested, and it was her interest that sustained mine, though I at no time sensed that it might be an answer to my liquor problem. How my wife kept her faith and courage during all those years, I'll never know, but she did. If she had not, I know I would have been dead a long time ago. For some reason, we alcoholics seem to have the gift of picking out the world's finest women. Why they should be subjected to the tortures we inflict upon them, I cannot explain.

About this time a lady called up my wife one Saturday afternoon saying she wanted me to come over that evening to meet a friend of hers who might help me. It was the day before Mother's Day and I had come home plastered, carrying a big potted plant which I set down on the table and forthwith went upstairs and passed out. The next day she called again. Wishing to be polite, though I felt very badly, I said, "Let's make the call," and extracted from my wife a promise that we would not stay over fifteen minutes.

We entered her house at exactly five o'clock and it was eleven fifteen when we left. I had a couple of shorter talks with this man afterward, and stopped drinking abruptly. This dry spell lasted for about three weeks; then I went to Atlantic City to attend several days' meeting of a national society of which I was a member. I drank all the scotch they had on the train and bought several quarts on my way to the hotel. This was on Sunday. I got tight that night, stayed sober Monday till after the dinner and then proceeded to get tight again. I drank all I dared in the bar, and then went to my room to finish the job. Tuesday I started in the morning, getting well organized by noon. I did not want to disgrace myself so I then checked out. I bought some more liquor on the way to the depot. I had to wait some time for the train. I remember nothing from then on until I woke up at a friend's house, in a town near home. These good people notified my wife, who sent my newly made friend over to get me. He came and got me home and to bed, gave me a few drinks that night, and one bottle of beer the next morning.

That was June 10, 1935, and that was my last drink. As I write, nearly four years have passed.

The question which might naturally come into your mind would be: "What did the man do or say that was different from what others had done or said?" It must be remembered that I had read a great deal and talked to everyone who knew, or thought they knew anything about the subject of alcoholism. But this was a man who had experienced many years of frightful drinking, who had had most all the drunkard's experiences known to man, but who had been cured by the very means I had been trying to employ, that is to say the spiritual approach. He gave me information about the subject of alcoholism which was undoubtedly helpful. *Of far more importance was the fact that he was the first living human with whom I had ever talked, who knew what he was talking about in regard to alcoholism from actual experience. In other words, he talked my language.* He knew all the answers, and certainly not because he had picked them up in his reading.

It is a most wonderful blessing to be relieved of the terrible curse with which I was afflicted. My health is good and I have regained my self-respect and the respect of my colleagues. My home life is ideal and my business is as good as can be expected in these uncertain times.

I spend a great deal of time passing on what I learned to others who want and need it badly. I do it for four reasons:

1. Sense of duty.
2. It is a pleasure.
3. Because in so doing I am paying my debt to the man who took time to pass it on to me.
4. Because every time I do it I take out a little more insurance for myself against a possible slip.

Unlike most of our crowd, I did not get over my craving for liquor much during the first two and a half years of abstinence. It was almost always with me. But at no time have I been anywhere near yielding. I used to get terribly upset when I saw my friends drink and knew I could not, but I schooled myself to believe that though I once had the same privilege, I had abused it so frightfully that it was withdrawn. So it doesn't behoove me to squawk about it, for, after all, nobody ever had to throw me down and pour any liquor down my throat.

If you think you are an atheist, an agnostic, a skeptic, or have any other form of intellectual pride which keeps you from accepting what is in this book, I feel sorry for you. If you still think you are strong enough to beat the game alone, that is your affair. But if you really and truly want to quit drinking liquor for good and all, and sincerely feel that you must have some help, we know that we have an answer for you. It never fails, if you go about it with one half the zeal you have been in the habit of showing when you were getting another drink.

Your Heavenly Father will never let you down!

(1) ALCOHOLIC ANONYMOUS NUMBER THREE

Pioneer member of Akron's Group No. 1, the first A.A. group in the world. He kept the faith; therefore, he and countless others found a new life.

ONE OF FIVE children, I was born on a Kentucky farm in Carlyle County. My parents were well-to-do people and their marriage was a happy one. My wife, a Kentucky girl, came with me to Akron where I completed my course in law at the Akron Law School.

My case is rather unusual in one respect. There were no childhood episodes of unhappiness to account for my alcoholism. I had, seemingly, just a natural affinity for grog. My marriage was happy and, as I have said, I never had any of the reasons, conscious or unconscious, which are often given for drinking. Yet, as my record shows, I did become an extremely serious case.

Before my drinking had cut me down completely, I achieved a considerable measure of success, having been a city councilman for five years and a financial director of Kenmore, a suburb later taken into the city itself. But, of course, this all went down the drain with my increased drinking. So, at the time Dr. Bob and Bill came along, I had about run out my strength.

The first time that I became intoxicated I was eight years old. This was no fault of my father or my mother, as they were both very much opposed to drinking. A couple of hired hands were cleaning out the barn on the farm, and I was riding to and fro on the sled, and while they were loading, I drank hard cider out of a barrel in the barn. On the return trip, after two or three loads, I passed out and had to be carried to the house. I remember that my father kept whiskey around the house for medical purposes and entertainment, and I would drink from this when no one was about and then water it to keep my parents from knowing I was drinking.

This continued until I enrolled in our state university and, at the end of the four years, I realized that I was a drunk. Morning after morning I would awake sick and with terrible jitters, but there was always a flask of liquor sitting on the table beside my bed. I would reach over and get this and take a shot and in a few moments get up and take another, shave and eat my breakfast, slip a half pint of liquor in my hip pocket, and go on to school. Between classes I would run down to the washroom, take enough to steady my nerves and then go on to the next class. This was in 1917.

I left the university in the latter part of my senior year and enlisted in the army. At the time, I called it patriotism. Later I realized that I was running from alcohol. It did help to a certain extent, since I got in places where I could not obtain anything to drink and so broke the habitual drinking.

Then Prohibition came into effect, and the facts that the stuff obtainable was so horrible and sometimes deadly, and that I had married and had a job which I had to look after, helped me for a period of some three or four years, although I would get drunk every time I could get hold of enough to drink to get started. My wife and I belonged to some bridge clubs, and they began to make wine and serve it. However, after two or three trials, I found this was not satisfactory because they did not serve enough to satisfy me. So I would refuse to drink. This problem was soon solved, however, as I began to take my bottle along with me and hide it in the bathroom or in the shrubbery outside.

As time went on, my drinking became progressively worse. I would be away from my office two or three weeks at a time, horrible days and nights when I would lie on the floor of my home and reach over to get the bottle, take a drink, and then go back into oblivion.

During the first six months of 1935, I was hospitalized eight times for intoxication and shackled to the bed two or three days before I even knew where I was.

On June 26, 1935, I came to in the hospital and to say I was discouraged is to put it mildly. Each of the seven times that I had left this hospital in the last six months, I had come out fully determined in my own mind that I would not get drunk again–for at least six or eight months. It hadn't worked out that way and I didn't know what the matter was and did not know what to do.

I was moved into another room that morning and there was my wife. I thought to myself, "Well, she is going to tell me this is the end," and I certainly couldn't blame her and did not intend to try to justify myself. She told me that she had been talking to a couple of fellows about drinking. I resented this very much, until she informed me that they were a couple of drunks just as I was. That wasn't so bad, to tell it to another drunk.

She said, "You are going to quit." That was worth a lot even though I did not believe it. Then she told me that these two drunks she had been talking to had a plan whereby they thought they could quit drinking, and part of that plan was that they tell it to another drunk. This was going to help them stay sober. All the other people that had talked to me wanted to help *me*, and my pride prevented me from listening to them and caused only resentment on my part, but I felt as if I would be a real stinker if I did not listen to a couple of fellows for a short time, if that would cure *them*. My wife also told me that I could not pay them even if I wanted to and had the money, which I did not.

They came in and began to give me instruction in the program which later became known as Alcoholics Anonymous. There was not much of it at that time.

I looked up and there were two great big fellows over six foot tall, very likable looking. (I knew afterwards that the two who came in were Bill W. and Doctor Bob.) Before very long we began to relate some incidents of our drinking, and pretty soon I realized that both of them knew what they were talking about, because you can see things and smell things when you're drunk that you can't other times. If I had thought they didn't know what they were talking about, I wouldn't have been willing to talk to them at all.

After a while, Bill said, "Well, now, you've been talking a good long time, let me talk a minute or two." So, after hearing some more of my story, he turned around and said to Doc–I don't think he knew I heard him, but I did–he said, "Well, I believe he's worth saving and working on." They said to me, "Do you want to quit drinking? It's none of our business about your drinking. We're not up here trying to take any of your rights or privileges away from you, but we have a program whereby we think we can stay sober. Part of that program is that we take it to someone else who needs it and wants it. Now, if you don't want it, we'll not take up your time, and we'll be going and looking for someone else."

The next thing they wanted to know was if I thought I could quit of my own accord, without any help, if I could just walk out of the hospital and never take another drink. If I could, that was wonderful, that was just fine, and they would very much appreciate a person who had that kind of power, but they were looking for a man that knew he had a problem and knew that he couldn't handle it himself and needed outside help. The next thing they wanted to know was if I believed in a Higher Power. I had no trouble there because I had never actually ceased to believe in God and had tried lots of times to get help but hadn't succeeded. Next they wanted to know would I be willing to go to this Higher Power and ask for help, calmly and without any reservations.

They left this with me to think over, and I lay there on that hospital bed and went back over and reviewed my life. I thought of what liquor had done to me, the opportunities that I had discarded, the abilities that had been given to me and how I had wasted them, and I finally came to the conclusion that if I didn't want to quit, I certainly ought to want to, and that I was willing to do anything in the world to stop drinking.

I was willing to admit to myself that I had hit bottom, that I had gotten hold of something that I didn't know how to handle by myself. So after reviewing these things and realizing what liquor had cost me, I went to this Higher Power that, to me, was God, without any reservation, and admitted that I was completely powerless over alcohol and that I was willing to do anything in the world to get rid of the problem. In fact, I admitted that from now on I was willing to let God take over instead of me. Each day I would try to find out what His will was and try to follow that, rather than trying to get Him to always agree that the things I thought up for myself were the things best for me. So, when they came back, I told them.

One of the fellows, I think it was Doc, said, "Well, you want to quit?" I said, "Yes, Doc, I would like to quit, at least for five, six, or eight months, until I get things straightened up, and begin to get the respect of my wife and some other people back, and get my finances fixed up and so on." And they both laughed very heartily and said, "That's better than you've been doing, isn't it?" Which of course was true. They said, "We've got some bad news for you. It was bad news for us, and it will probably be bad news for you. Weather you quit six days, months, or years, if you go out and take a drink or two, you'll end up in this hospital tied down, just like you have been in these past six months. You are an alcoholic." As far as I know that was the first time I had ever paid any attention to that word. I figured I was just a drunk. And they said, "No, you have a disease, and it doesn't make any difference how long you do without it, after a drink or two you'll end up just like you are now." That certainly was real disheartening news, at the time.

The next question they asked was, "You can quit twenty-four hours, can't you?" I said, "Sure, yes, anybody can do that, for twenty-four hours." They said, "That's what we're talking about. Just twenty-four hours at a time." That sure did take a load off of my mind. Every time I'd start thinking about drinking, I would think of the long, dry years ahead without having a drink; but this idea of twenty-four hours, that it was up to me from then on, was a lot of help.

(At this point, the Editors intrude just long enough to supplement Bill D.'s account, that of the man on the bed, with that of Bill W., the man who sat by the side of the bed.) Says Bill W.:

Nineteen years ago last summer, Dr. Bob and I saw him (Bill D.) for the first time. Bill lay on his hospital bed and looked at us in wonder.

Two days before this, Dr. Bob had said to me, "If you and I are going to stay sober, we had better get busy." Straightway, Bob called Akron's City Hospital and asked for the nurse on the receiving ward. He explained that he and a man from New York had a cure for alcoholism. Did she have an alcoholic customer on whom it could be tried? Knowing Bob of old, she jokingly replied, "Well, Doctor, I suppose you've already tried it yourself?"

Yes, she did have a customer–a dandy. He had just arrived in D.T.'s., had blacked the eyes of two nurses, and now they had him strapped down tight. Would this one do? After prescribing medicines, Dr. Bob ordered, "Put him in a private room. We'll be down as soon as he clears up."

Bill didn't seem too impressed. Looking sadder than ever, he wearily ventured, "Well, this is wonderful for you fellows, but it can't be for me. My case is so terrible that I'm scared to go out of this hospital at all. You don't have to sell me religion, either. I was at one time a deacon in the church, and I still believe in God. But I guess He doesn't believe much in me."

Then Dr. Bob said, "Well, Bill, maybe you'll feel better tomorrow. Wouldn't you like to see us again?"

"Sure I would," replied Bill, "Maybe it won't do any good, but I'd like to see you both, anyhow. You certainly know what you are talking about."

Looking in later we found Bill with his wife, Henrietta. Eagerly he pointed to us saying, "These are the fellows I told you about; they are the ones who understand."

Bill then related how he had lain awake nearly all night. Down in the pit of his depression, new hope had somehow been born. The thought flashed through his mind, "If they can do it, I can do it!" Over and over he said this to himself. Finally, out of his hope, there burst conviction. Now he was sure. Then came a great joy. At length, peace stole over him and he slept.

Before our visit was over, Bill suddenly turned to his wife and said, "Go fetch my clothes, dear. We're going to get up and get out of here." Bill D. walked out of that hospital a free man, never to drink again.

A.A.'s Number One Group dates from that very day.

(Bill D. now continues his story.)

It was in the next two or three days after I had first met Doc and Bill that I finally came to a decision to turn my will over to God and to go along with this program the best that I could. Their talk and action had instilled in me a certain amount of confidence, although I was not too absolutely certain. I wasn't afraid that the program wouldn't work, but I still was doubtful whether I would be able to hang on to the program, but I did come to the conclusion that I was willing to put everything I had into it, with God's power, and that I wanted to do just that. As soon as I had done that, I did feel a great release. I knew that I had a helper whom I could rely upon, who wouldn't fail me. If I could stick to Him and listen, I would make it. I remember when the boys came back, I told them, "I have gone to this Higher Power and I have told Him that I am willing to put His world first, above everything. I have already done it, and I am willing to do it again here in the presence of you, or I am willing to say it any place, anywhere in the world from now on and not be ashamed of it." And this certainly gave me a lot of confidence and seemed to take a lot of the burden off me.

I remember telling them too that it was going to be awfully tough, because I did some other things, smoked cigarettes and played penny ante poker and sometimes bet on the horse races, and they said, "Don't you think you're having more trouble with this drinking than with anything else at the present time? Don't you believe you are going to have all you can do to get rid of that?" "Yes," I said reluctantly, "I probably will." They said, "Let's forget about those other things, that is, trying to eliminate them all at once, and concentrate on the drink." Of course, we had talked over quite a number of the failings that I had and made a sort of an inventory, which wasn't too difficult, because I had an awful lot of things wrong that were very apparent to me. Then they said, "There is one other thing. You should go out and take this program to somebody else who needs it and wants it."

Of course, by this time, my business was practically nonexistent. I didn't have any. Naturally, for quite a time, I wasn't too well physically, either. It took me a year, or a year and a half, to get to feeling physically well, and it was rather tough, but I soon found folks whose friendship I had once had, and I found, after I had been sober for quite some little time, that these people began to act like they had in previous years, before I had gotten so bad, so that I didn't pay too awful much attention to financial gains. I spent most of my time trying to get back these friendships and to make some recompense towards my wife, whom I had hurt a lot.

It would be hard to estimate how much A.A. has done for me. I really wanted the program, and I wanted to go along with it. I noticed that the others seemed to have such a release, a happiness, a something that I thought a person ought to have. I was trying to find the answer. I knew there was even more, something that I hadn't got, and I remember one day, a week or two after I had come out of the hospital, Bill was at my house talking to my wife and me. We were eating lunch, and I was listening and trying to find out why they had this release that they seemed to have. Bill looked across at my wife and said to her, "Henrietta, the Lord has been so wonderful to me, curing me of this terrible disease, that I just want to keep talking about it and telling people."

I thought, "I think I have the answer." Bill was very, very grateful that he had been released from this terrible thing and he had given God the credit for having done it, and he's so grateful about it he wants to tell other people about it. That sentence, "The Lord has been so wonderful to me, curing me of this terrible disease, that I just want to keep telling people about it," has been a sort of a golden text for the A.A. program and for me.

Of course, as time went on, I began to get my health back and began to be so I didn't have to hide from people all the time–it's just been wonderful. I still go to meetings, because I like to go. I meet the people that I like to talk to. Another reason that I go is that I'm still grateful for the good years that I've had. I'm so grateful for both the program and the people in it that I still want to go. And then probably the most wonderful thing that I have learned from the program–I've seen this in the A.A. Grapevine a lot of times, and I've had people say it to me personally, and I've heard people get up in meetings and say it–"I came into A.A. solely for the purpose of sobriety, but it has been through A.A. that I have found God."

I feel that is about the most wonderful thing that a person can do.

(2) HE HAD TO BE SHOWN

"Who is convinced against his will is of the same opinion still." But not this man.

I WAS THE OLDEST of three children, and my father was an alcoholic. One of the earliest memories that I have is of a bottle sitting on his desk with a skull and crossbones and marked "Poison." At that time, as I remember, he had promised never to take another drink. Of course he did. I can also remember that he was a salesman and a very good one. When he was uptown–we were living in the little town of Moscow–I went up to try to get some money from him to buy groceries. He wouldn't give me any money for the groceries, but he did take me across the street and buy me a bag of candy, which I later took back and traded for a loaf of bread. I was not more than six at that time.

My father died in 1901 when I was eight years old and I was in the second or third grade at school. I immediately quit school and went to work, and from that time until I was high school age there was never a return to school. I always built up in my own mind the great things that I was going to do, and in fact I accomplished about 50 percent of them and then lost interest. That continued through my entire life. When I was sixteen years old, my mother remarried and I was given the opportunity of going back to school. I went into the high school grades, but having missed all the intermediate grades, I didn't get along too well, so I developed the habit of going back to school just long enough for the football season and then quitting.

There was always a tremendous drive and ambition to become a great guy, because I think I recognized inwardly that I didn't have any special talents. At a comparatively early age, I can remember being jealous of my brother. He did things much better than I did because he applied himself and learned how to do them, and I never applied myself. Whether I could have done as well as he, I don't know.

I was married at the age of nineteen to a grand girl and had good business prospects. I had bought a piece of ground in Cuyahoga Falls and cut it into lots and had a profit of approximately $40,000 and that was a lot of money in those days. With that profit, I built a number of houses, but then I neglected them. I wouldn't put sufficient time on them. Consequently, my labor bills ran up. I lost money, and then just fooled away a large part of that profit.

When I was eighteen, at the end of high school, the high school team had a banquet at a well-known roadhouse outside of Akron. We boys drove out in somebody's car and went to the bar on the way to the dining room and I, in an effort to impress the other boys that I was city-bred, having lived in Scranton and Cleveland, asked them if they didn't want to drink. They looked at one another queerly and, finally, one of them allowed he'd have a beer and they all followed him, each of them saying he'd have a beer too. I ordered a martini, extra dry. I didn't even know what a martini looked like, but I had heard a man down the bar order one. That was my first drink. I kept watching the man down the bar to see what he did with a contraption like that, and he just smelled of his drink and set it down again, so I did the same. He took a couple of puffs of a cigarette and I took a couple of puffs of my cigarette. He tossed off half of his martini; I tossed off half of mine and it nearly blew the top of my head off. It irritated my nostrils; I choked, I didn't like it. There was nothing about that drink that I liked. But I watched him, and he tossed off the rest of his, so I tossed off the rest of mine. He ate his olive and I ate mine. I didn't even like the olive. It was repulsive to me from every standpoint. I drank nine martinis in less than an hour.

Twenty-two years later, Doctor Bob told me that what I had done was like turning a switch and setting up a demand for more alcohol in my system. I didn't know that then. I had no more reason to drink those martinis than a jackrabbit. At that particular time, the boys put me on a shutter and took me out to the shed, and I lay in the car while they enjoyed their banquet. That was the first time I ever drank hard liquor. Blackout drinking at once. I had no pleasure out of the drinking at all. All of a sudden I found myself guzzling. Right then I determined that never so long as I lived would I have anything more to do with martinis. They acted on me like the beating of a club.

I think it was probably more than a year before I had anything more to do with liquor. I was opening up these lots that I spoke of. I had a crew of men working there and I wanted them to work Sunday afternoons so that I could sell lots on Sunday. I went over and bought a jug of hard cider and a gallon of wine that I gave these fellows to drink. When they got through the day's work, part was left which I proceeded to drink. During the day, looking over the contracts and money in my pocket, I found that I had sold six lots that I couldn't even remember, and didn't even know the people I had sold them to. I had to look in the telephone book later to find out who these people were. Another blackout. Wine and hard cider.

I early discovered that if I drank anything, I was not accountable for what happened. I decided that I couldn't drink. Anyhow, I recognized the fact that I couldn't drink like normal people, but I tried hard and kept on trying for twenty-two years.

I sold three lots to an elderly lady in Cleveland. I came to Cleveland with the deeds to these lots and to pick up my money. She paid me in cash. The next morning I woke up in jail in Cleveland and the jailor had $1,175 of my money in an envelope. I didn't remember anything that had happened. This was six or eight months after the last drinking episode.

Then I got married. (As I've said, I was nineteen). I felt having gotten married, I was an adult and one of the first things I did was to buy two cases of whiskey with no idea of drinking it. (I might say right here that never in my life did I ever *intend* to get drunk. I never had any desire to get drunk. So I consciously thought). I was a very young married man, having his whiskey in the cupboard over the sink, and when I helped my wife with the dishes at night I would take a cup of tea and spike it with whiskey. I could get through an evening with just a couple of snorts.

This was a regular occurrence for a little while. Eventually, there would be a ball game, or a show, or some sort of special occasion to celebrate and I would turn up drunk. About that period, too, came increasing procrastination and the avoidance of responsibilities. I would put off doing anything that I could until the next day and, consequently, everything would pile up and then there would be the blackout.

At the end of this selling of lots, just prior to World War I, I got into the crude rubber business, and six months later there was only one broker and myself left in Akron. So in spite of anything that I might do, I prospered, being one of only two brokers in the rubber center of the world.

I found, however, that when I would leave Akron to go to Chicago, I would get drunk. As long as there was everyday business, I could drink occasionally and didn't always get drunk. I was a periodic. A big event of any kind precipitated heavy drinking. It had long since become a serious problem. I was prone to do everything on a big scale. I can well remember sitting with seven dollars in my pocket, planning on giving my family a hundred or two hundred dollars, when I made it next year. But I didn't do a thing about giving them any part of the seven bucks I had in my pocket.

The rubber prosperity went on for about six years–1916 to 1922. It fell apart in the twenties. Every company in the country, except Firestone, was reorganized at that time. I was always able to skate along the fringe of big money. I made a point of knowing important people. I could work a deal up to where all I had to do was to go ahead with it; all the planning had been done, all the financing had been done, but then I'd say, "Nuts to it!" and walk away. Near success, only near. I figured the only difference between me and a millionaire was that I hadn't the strength, or that he got the breaks and I didn't.

Akron was really on the boom in those days, 1919-1920; expansion was terrific. I optioned a piece of land just off East Market Street to put up a three-hundred suite apartment. One hundred for unmarried women at one end, one hundred for men at the other, and one hundred for married couples in the middle. In the basement were to be dry-cleaning facilities, a barbershop, a pool room, a grocery shop and everything. I had contracted for half of it, at least verbally, and the contractors were taking half of the second mortgage bond. At that particular stage, I lost interest in it, sold the option for $5,000 and forgot the whole deal. Another time, I had a rubber pool project. My idea was to have all the companies pool their funds and buy rubber when rubber was cheap and then put it in a pool. When rubber reached a certain low point, they would draw on the rubber out of the pool and buy. With the big companies, and with the amount of money we could have gotten and the promises I had, it could have been done. I worked along until I had really big names in rubber on a tentative contract, and then I neglected to go through with it.

To my mind, drinking didn't have anything to do with not going through with things. I don't know whether I drank to cover up being a failure, or whether I drank and then missed the deals. I was able to rationalize it anyway. I can well remember over a long period of years when I thought I was the only person in the world who knew that sooner or later I was going to get drunk. I can remember occasions when friends recommended me for positions or business opportunities that I wouldn't take because I felt that at some future date I'd get drunk and they would be hurt.

In the meantime, the domestic situation was not getting along too well. We had two children, a boy and a girl, and when the boy was about twelve, we broke up the marriage. That was at my suggestion. I can remember telling the poor little soul that I could probably quit drinking if I wasn't married to her, and told her that, after all, I didn't like restraint! I didn't like having to come home at a certain time; I didn't like this, I didn't like that, and I think the poor girl actually divorced me to help me stop drinking! Naturally, what little restraint I had exercised before was gone now, and my drinking became worse.

Long since I had come to believe I was insane because I did so many things I didn't want to do. I didn't want to neglect my children. I loved them, I think, as much as any parent. But I did neglect them. I didn't want to get into fights, but I did get into fights. I didn't want to get arrested, but I did get arrested. I didn't want to jeopardize the lives of innocent people by driving an automobile while intoxicated, but I did. I quite naturally came to the conclusion that I must be insane. My big job was to keep other people from finding it out. I can remember well thinking that I would quit drinking, really go to work hard, apply myself eight hours a day, five days a week, make a lot of money, and then I could start drinking again. That was the reverse of my former pattern of fearing to go to work because I might drink! Always at the end of these dreams was drinking. Now I attempted to quit. I think this was about 1927. I was divorced in 1925 or 1926. I determined that I wouldn't drink. I remember one occasion when I did not drink for three hundred and sixty-four days, but I didn't quite make the year.

Another time, I had gone around to Max R. trying to get a job driving one of his trucks. He had known something of my drinking pattern, and he asked me what I was doing about it. I told him that I had not had a drink for ninety days and that I had come to the conclusion that I was one of those individuals who couldn't drink. So, knowing that, I had determined that so long as I lived I would never take another drink. On that statement and the fact that I had been sober for ninety days, he gave me a job selling lots in an allotment he had. I was moved in as Sales Manager and had four men working under me. At the end of about four months, I not only had good looking clothes–and I might say that at the time I first talked to Max I didn't have a suit of clothes I could bend over in real sudden; now I had six suits of clothes. I had an automobile. Everything in the world a man could possibly want, and I was driving from Akron to Cleveland, having just been to the bank and discovered that I had approximately $5,000. I drove towards Cleveland wondering why I found myself in such a changed set of conditions as compared with those of six months before. I came to the conclusion it was because I hadn't been drunk. And I hadn't been drunk because I hadn't taken a drink. And I then and there said a prayer, if you please. An offer of appreciation for not having had a drink for those few months and then and there, without anybody promising me anything or threatening me, I made a solemn vow that never so long as I live would I take another drink.

(My mother and father were Catholics and I had been baptized, but at the end of my instructions for Confirmation I had not gone to church, and then when my mother remarried, she married a Protestant and the whole religious angle was forgotten. So I had never had any lasting contact with any kind of religion.)

So I was driving to Cleveland when I made this solemn promise never to drink again. That was at three-thirty in the afternoon. At three-thirty the next morning, I was in Champlain Street Station, in jail for driving while intoxicated and insulting an officer; and the suit of which I was so proud was in such shape that the turnkey had to get me a pair of trousers to go into court in the next morning. I had run into a man I always drank with. Whenever this man and I met–I didn't know his name then nor do I know it now–we would always get drunk. I had run into him, and he looked real prosperous; his face and eyes looked clear and he started to compliment me on my good front and how well I looked, and I said, "I haven't had a drink for nine months." He said, "Well, I haven't had a drink for three months." And we stood there for twenty minutes, telling each other how much better we were, how much better we looked, how much better off we were financially, mentally, physically, morally, and in every way, shape and manner. And then we both realized we should go. We shook hands, and he hung onto my hand for a moment and said, "Tell you what I'll do for old time's sake. I'll buy you one drink, and if you suggest a second one, I'll poke you right in the nose." And I think we calculated, or I did, that there wasn't anybody who knew that I wasn't drinking. I could take one drink and get right back on the wagon. Nobody would know it, so I agreed to have the one drink. We went into a bootleg joint and I don't remember leaving that place. I was picked up at two-thirty that morning with my car smashed up by a street-car because I had run into a big concrete safety zone, and the street-car had run into me, and they took me out through the roof–there's where I lost the suit. I had lost a hundred dollars I had in my pocket, and lost a wristwatch too. I lost the car, of course. But more important, I lost my sobriety. And I continued to drink, on and off then, until every dollar I had in the world was gone again and I was right back living at my sister's, getting my cigarettes by calling her grocer and telling him to put in a couple of cartons with her order, exactly as I had before I started to work at Max's.

In 1932, some friends of mine advised me that I might try Christian Science, which had done a lot for some of their friends. So I started to investigate Science through some friends of mine who were Readers in the church. I accepted their help, and it was helpful. I quit drinking immediately. The circumstances under which I reached these people were very odd because I was led there through things that I said when I couldn't even remember speaking. I told somebody that I was going down to get Christian Science and they took me down, but I don't remember saying that. Yet I wound up at this place. I attended their meetings every Sunday and Wednesday for about nine months. If there was a lecture on the subject within a hundred miles of Akron, I attended. Then I started to miss meetings because it was raining or snowing or something else. Pretty soon, I wasn't going at all, and was avoiding those people who had been so kind to me. I avoided them rather than explain why they weren't seeing me. My sobriety continued for another six months.

At the end of fifteen months, I tried the beer experiment. After drinking one glass of beer at the end of my work period for about five days, I thought I'd better find out whether I really had the stuff licked. So I didn't have a beer one night, and as I drove home I was breaking my arm patting myself on the back because I had proved I could lick liquor. I had proved that liquor was not my master. I had avoided a drink this time. So having licked it, there was no reason why I shouldn't have a drink, and I stopped in before I got home and had one. Then I got into the habit of having beers, and decided that a drink of whiskey was not any worse; so I would get the one drink of whiskey but, on second thought, I decided that as long as I was only going to have one, I might as well make it a double-header. So I had one double-header every night for about two or three weeks. I didn't drink very long at a time. I think the longest drunk I was ever on was eleven days, but usually only two days with a complete blackout for a day, and then backing off by drinking as long as I could get anything.

This Christian Science experience with a sobriety of fifteen months was in 1932. Then I started drinking again, with possibly a little more restraint, periods a little bit longer than they had been before, but substantially the same pattern. During the latter part of the Christian Science experience I had gotten a job and was working at Firestone. I was bouncing along and not doing too badly. There were times when I got to drinking, and I had been warned by Firestone that they wouldn't stand for this much longer, so, clearly, they were conscious of the fact that I drank too much and too often.

To show you the point to which this obsession went, there came an occasion when I had spent a most delightful weekend, and at nine o'clock on Sunday night I was on my way home, and I thought I would get a drink. I went into a bar, and there I got into a fight. I was arrested and taken to jail where I was beaten up by two or three fellows who were already in there and whom I tried to boss. I was badly beaten. I tried to conduct a kangaroo court and hit them with a broomstick. I had a broken nose, a fractured cheekbone, and was black from the lower part of my face up into my hair. I was black and blue, with my lips all swollen, when they roused us to go into court in the morning. I looked so terrible in the court that the judge suggested that I get a continuance and let me sign all the papers to go to a hospital and to a doctor. I went downstairs and there was the grizzly old veteran police officer in charge of the property desk, and as he gave me the stuff, he asked, "Are you going out in the street that way?" I said, "I'm certainly not going to stay here!" I had white trousers on, white shoes and a white shirt that was streaked with blood. He said, "Well, why don't you take a cab?" I said, "All right, call me a cab," as though I was talking to a bellboy. He did call me a cab and when I got into the cab, I said, "Drive me to a liquor store." We drove to a store in North Hill and I sent him in with what money I had to get a quart. He brought the quart out and I took a good swig. When I got home I had to give him a check for the taxi fare. I drank some more and slept through the day. At night, I woke up and the folks with whom I roomed were home by then. I offered them a drink, and they came to the bottom of the stairs and I stuck my face around the top of the stairs and the good woman fainted, just looking at me. So they decided that I should have a doctor. They called a doctor and it happened that they called one I knew. He came in and took a look at me and sent me to the hospital.

When I had been in the hospital ten days, Sister Ignatia, who has played such a part in the development of A.A. in this area, stuck her head in the door one morning and announced, looking at me quizzically, that they might be able to make something human out of my face after all. And at the end of fourteen days, they let me out. Three days later I went to work. The next day, they called me in for an examination, and the doctor wouldn't let me continue working and pardoned me from the plant for ten days because he said my eye had been injured. So I was barred from the plant for ten days, and during that ten day period I was drunk twice, showing how little control these restraints had on me.

Shortly after that, my brother, who had then become associated with a group of people and had stopped drinking, urged me to attend meetings with him. Naturally, I wanted no part of any meetings. I explained to my sister that some of the people he was meeting with had been in hospitals. I couldn't afford to be found with those people, but I said I would certainly pay his dues if it would keep him from drinking. But me, I wanted no part of it! I didn't have any need of such an association!

One morning, after I had been on a binge for a couple of days, I awoke to find my brother and Doctor Bob in my room talking to me about not drinking. My only thought that day was getting a drink, and how to get rid of those clowns was my big problem. They asked me if I would take some medicine, and I promised that I would if they got me a drink. So Paul was dispatched and brought back a pint. I got two drinks, each of them a quarter of that pint, in me, and was talking along with these people, but I felt that sooner or later they were going to have me cornered because they were smarter than I was and the drink was beginning to take effect; but as I reached for the third drink Bob said, "Listen, Buster, you promised to take some medicine if we got you a drink. Now we got you the drink, but you haven't taken the medicine." I agreed with him and told him in no uncertain terms that I never broke my word in my life. I told him I'd take the medicine and I would take it, but I hadn't told him when, and thereupon I got away with the third drink. I then began asking a lot of questions of both my brother and Dr. Bob about how this thing worked, and I suppose I was becoming more glassy-eyed all the while, for eventually I said to Bob, "You're all dried up. You're never going to want another drink, are you?"; and this answer of his is very important to those of us who are victims of alcoholism. He said, "So long as I'm thinking as I'm thinking now, and so long as I'm doing the things I'm doing now, I don't believe I'll ever take another drink." And I said, "Well, what about Paul, have you got him all dried up?" He said Paul would have to answer for himself. So Paul repeated substantially what Dr. Bob had said. And I said, "Now you want to dry me up. I'm not going to want another drink?" "Well," the doctor said, "we have hopes in that direction." I said, "In that case, there's no use of wasting this," and I got the last of that pint. A few minutes later, Dr. Bob left, leaving with my brother some medicine I should get. Paul measured the medicine out, but he figured that with my track record that little bit wouldn't be enough, so he doubled it and added a few drops more and then gave it to me. I immediately became unconscious. This was on Thursday. I regained consciousness on Sunday. I had taken five and a half ounces of paraldehyde. Because it effected so strenuously, they felt that hospitalization was indicated and I awoke in a hospital.

On Sunday when I came to, it was a bad, wet, snowy day in February, 1937, and Paul and Doc and a lot of the other fellows were in Cleveland on business. The people in the group hadn't been around that day; part of my family was in Florida and the rest of them weren't speaking to me, so I spent a very lonesome day and by evening I was feeling very sorry for myself. It was getting pretty dark and I hadn't turned on any lights, when some big fellow stepped inside the door and flipped on the light switch. I said, "Look, Bub, if I want those lights on, I'll turn them on." I'll never forget, he never even hesitated and I had never seen him before in my life. He took off his hat and his overcoat, and he said, "You don't look very good. How are you feeling?" I said, "How do you suppose? I'm feeling terrible." He said, "Maybe you need a little drink." That was the smartest man I'd met in months. I thought he had it in his pocket, so I said, "You got some?" He said, "No, call the nurse." And he got me a drink. Then he started to talk to me about his drinking experiences, what his drinking had cost him, how much he had drunk and where, things like that, and I remember I was quite bored because I had never seen the guy before and had no interest at all in what, where and when he drank. The man turned out to be Bill D., a very early member of A.A., and I couldn't tell you a word of what he said. Not one experience registered with me. When he left, I realized from his story that as a drinker I was just a panty-waist. I knew I could quit because he had quit; he hadn't had a drink for over a year. The important thing was that he was happy. He was released, relieved from his alcoholism and was happy and contented because of it. That I shall never forget.

The next day, others from the group came in to see me. I remember well one fellow, Joe, walking nearly three miles through slush, wet and snow to come to the hospital to see a man that he had never seen before in his life, and that impressed me very much. He walked to the hospital to save bus fare and did it gladly in order to be helpful to an individual he had never even seen. There were only seven or eight people in the group before me and they all visited me during my period in the hospital. The very simple program they advised me to follow was that I should ask to know God's will for me for that one day, and then, to the best of my ability, to follow that, and at night to express my gratefulness to God for the things that had happened to me during the day. When I left the hospital I tried this for a day and it worked, for a week and it worked, and for a month, and it worked–and then for a year and it still worked. It has continued to work now for nearly eighteen years.

(3) HE THOUGHT HE COULD DRINK LIKE A GENTLEMAN

But he discovered that there are some gentlemen who can't drink.

I WAS BORN in Cleveland, Ohio, in 1889, the last child of a family of eight children. My parents were hard working people. My father was a railroad man and a Civil War veteran. I can remember that in my childhood, he was ill at ease with the children because he attempted to assert an army discipline that had been ground into him during his three and a half years of army service. The differences between my father and my sisters, who were school teachers, made an excellent environment for the type of child I was–that is, slick and cute enough to take advantage of any adult quarrel. In other words, I was always safe from the discipline of my father, and, having developed along that line, I had considerable difficulty in school. Rules were made for others, but not for me. Of course, it was always my aim to have my own way without being caught.

My mother was eighty-nine years old when she died, and I was a full-blown alcoholic at the time of her death. She was a woman devoted to her family and loyal to her husband, but quarrels did not make a happy environment for her. I had four brothers and three sisters. As I look back, all the brothers developed personality problems. The sisters seemed to remain unaffected. I seemed to react by developing a streak of varying meanness, which would cause me to do things to create excitement and to get attention. I very early sampled the effects of alcohol. In fact, on one occasion, I was picked up by the police and brought home. I was then about sixteen years old. I didn't go to high school. I went to five grade schools, primarily because I was expelled for my conduct, but I eventually graduated from the eighth grade.

I was always interested in mechanics and after having about twenty miscellaneous jobs, lasting from one day to two weeks, I obtained a job as a toolmaker apprentice. Being intensely interested in the work, I changed my conduct sufficiently to master the job. I finished my apprenticeship and was moved into the drafting department. That was in Cleveland. As a draftsman, I worked for several large companies and gained a variety of experience. Not far from where I lived they built a new technical high school and one of the teachers sold me on the idea that I needed a little mechanical drawing if I were going to be a good toolmaker. I proceeded to take up the drawing and advanced rapidly in it. The school then obtained a job for me in the drafting department of another company. After I was on the drafting board about two years I decided I wanted a technical education. I was then about eighteen. I did not have a high school education so I went to night school to take the full high school course, which I finished in two years and nine months. I apparently was willing to subdue these personality disturbances in a tremendous drive to succeed. I had an objective. I could discipline myself but along the way there would be festivities and occasions when I got drunk. Although, during this period I was not addicted to any pattern of alcohol consumption, when I did drink the drinking was pretty wild.

I then entered Case School and worked while I went to school and finished there. This was an engineering college. Following graduation, I was offered a pretty good job which I took. In the fall of the graduating year, I became involved in some litigation over the ownership of inventions and patents. This experience sent me to law school where I went at night and which course I completed in less than three years, taking the highest state bar examinations and passing them. The law school experience was not inspired by a desire to follow patent law, which has been my profession since: I went to law school primarily to learn the law of contracts following my own experience with litigation. A year later, after I completed the course in contracts, I quit the law school, and undertook some engineering work for a patent law firm on behalf of clients who were in difficulties and who desired to keep their troubles from their own engineering department. This work consumed a period of about two-thirds of a year, and worked out successfully so I decided to follow patent law. I went back to law school, and doubled up on the courses because I was then approaching thirty years of age and I wanted to get through as quickly as possible. I was supporting myself through all this education by being a toolmaker and a draftsman.

I married when I was twenty-eight years old, and started in law school after I was married. As a matter of fact, I had two children at the time I was admitted to the bar.

I kept myself so busy that, outside of some school and group parties, I didn't go overboard on drinking very much between the ages of twenty-five and thirty. My life was fairly well crowded and I didn't seem to need any stimulants to keep me going. By the time I had completed law school I had picked up some experience in patent law, for I remained with the patent law firm and worked too in Washington where they found that I was a capable infringement investigator. In 1924, I had acquired enough clients of my own so that the firm made me a junior partner. My drinking career began about four years after I had moved up into partnership and had joined certain clubs, societies and so forth, and during which period we had Prohibition. I was then about thirty-seven or thirty-eight.

All during Prohibition, every alcoholic felt that he made the best hooch, regardless of how bad it was. I became a specialist in making elderberry blossom wine.

There had been some occasions–there was an automobile wreck, for instance–when I had police escort home but not to jail, all of which, instead of doing me a favor, did me harm because I was then full of self-esteem as to the progress I had made both professionally and financially. The first definite indications of an alcoholic pattern began to arise when I would go to New York on business and disappear, and wind up in Philadelphia or Boston for two or three day periods. I would have to return to New York and pick up my bills and bags. These periods became more frequent and I resolved that when I became forty, which was very shortly, I was going on the wagon. Forty came and went and then the resolution was advanced to forty-one, forty-two, and so on in the usual pattern. I realized that I had a problem, although my realization was not very deep because my own conceit wouldn't admit that I had any personality problems. I could not see why I couldn't drink like a gentleman, and that was my primary ambition–until I landed in A.A. This pattern deepened and became worse. I became a constant drinker with a terrific fight to control the amount of my consumption each day.

My practice had advanced to the point where it could stand a lot of abuse and it got it. Whenever a situation arose that fast talk wouldn't explain away, I simply withdrew. In other words, I fired the client before the client fired me. I was willful, full of will to do things I wanted to do and to get the things that I wanted to have.

Insofar as religion was concerned, I had Catholic training in my youth. I went to both Catholic and public schools. I never left the church, but I was a fringe member, and the thought simply never occurred to me that through the exercise of what I had I might find the answer to my problem, simply because I wouldn't admit that I had a problem. The successful demonstration I had made of my life problems in other respects convinced me that someday I was going to be able to drink like a gentleman.

When I was about forty-seven, after indulging in all kinds of self-deception to control my drinking, I arrived at a period when I felt convinced I had to have so much alcohol every day and that the real problem was to control how much. After two or three years of effort along this line, I reached the point of actual despair that I ever would be able to drink only a harmless amount each day. And then my thinking became calculation as to how much longer I had to live, how long the assets would last. By that time, I had one boy in college, another a senior in high school, and a daughter about twelve years old. My efficiency as a professional man was probably reduced to 25 percent of what it should have been.

I had two partners. They suffered from my conduct without saying anything, but the reason for this was that I still managed to hang onto a very substantial practice. They probably felt that it was useless, that surely I had enough intelligence to know what I was doing. They were wrong. They never raised the issue. In fact, as I look back, I have often thought that they probably concluded that they would put up with me for a couple of years, that I couldn't live much longer, and that they would inherit whatever was left of the practice. That is not unusual.

As far as my home was concerned, I did not see then, though of course I can see now, that it was anything but a happy situation for my wife. My children had lost respect for me and, in fact, it was only after three or four years of sobriety that any of them ever said anything to me to indicate that I had recouped even a little of their respect.

I was forty-nine and a half years old when I was first approached about the Akron Group. It was not known to me as a group, but I later learned that my wife had known about it for nine months and had prayed constantly that I would stumble into Akron some way or another. She knew that at that time any suggestion she made about my drinking would only build up a barrier, a consideration for which I am ever grateful. Had anyone undertaken to explain to me what the A.A. movement was, what it's real function was, I probably would have been set back several years and I doubt if I would have survived at all.

So the story of my introduction into A.A. begins with the activities of my wife. She had a hairdresser who used to tell her about a brother-in-law who had been quite a drinker and about some doctor in Akron who had straightened him out. My wife didn't tell me this, but one Sunday afternoon when Mary was trying to get the cobwebs out of my mind, Clarence and his sister-in-law, the hairdresser, called at the house. I was introduced to them and Clarence proceeded to put on his Twelve Step work. I was kind of shocked about anybody talking about themselves the way he did, and my impression was that the guy was a little "touched." However, on a couple of other occasions, Clarence seemed to bob up at the last saloon that I would stop at on the way home every day. I resented it of course, and I offered Clarence his commission, whatever it might be, if he would please not bother me because I had arrived at the conclusion that he was a solicitor for some alcoholic institute. One evening I had gone out after dinner to take on a couple of double-headers and stayed a little later than usual, and when I came home Clarence was sitting on the davenport with Bill W. I do not recollect the specific conversation that went on but I believe I did challenge Bill to tell me something about A.A. and I do recall one other thing: I wanted to know what this was that worked so many wonders, and hanging over the mantel was a picture of Gethsemane and Bill pointed to it and said, "There it is," which didn't make much sense to me. There was also some conversation about Dr. Bob and I must have said that I would go down to Akron with Bill in the morning.

The next morning, my wife came into my room and wakened me and said, "That man is downstairs and he said you said you'd go to Akron." I said, "Did I say that?" She said. "Well, he wouldn't be here if you didn't say so." And being a big-shot man of my word, I said, "Well, if I said so, then I'll go." That's about the spirit in which I went to Akron. Bill bought me a drink or two on the way, and Dorothy S. came with us, and the three of us went over to the City Hospital. We drove my car and I left it down in the yard. Bill left me at the elevator and said, "Your room is so and so," and I didn't see him again for six months. The interne came along with a glassful of bleached lightning that put me away for about fifteen hours. I went into the hospital in April, 1939.

My experience in the hospital I considered to be terrific because Dr. Bob told me very quickly that medicine would have very little to do with it, outside of trying to restore my appetite for food. I had had no hospitalization up to this time because I would not call doctors when I was getting over a bad one. I would use barbiturates. In fact, the last three years of my drinking was a routine of barbiturates in the morning, so that I could stop shaking enough to shave, and then alcohol beginning about four-thirty or five o'clock, with a struggle not to take a drink at noon or during the day, because I had the idea that if I took one drink, I would smell as though I had a pint.

Dr. Bob did not lay out the whole program. He startled me by informing that he was an alcoholic, that he had found a way which so far enabled him to live without taking a drink, and that the main idea was to find a way how not to take that first drink. He told me that there were some other fellows that had tried this with success, and if I cared to see any of them he'd have them come in to see me. I believe every member of the Akron Group did come to see me, which impressed me terrifically, not so much because of the stories they told, but because they would take the time to come and talk to me without even knowing who I was. I did not know there was such a thing as group activity until I left the hospital. I left on a Wednesday afternoon, had dinner in Akron and then went to a house where I encountered my first meeting. I had attended several of these meetings before I discovered that all those who were there were not alcoholics. That is, it was sort of a mixed bunch of Oxford Groupers, who were interested in the alcoholic problem, and of alcoholics themselves. My reaction to those meetings was good. In fact, I never lost my faith, since I had been prepared by some conversations toward the end of my sojourn in the hospital with Dr. Bob, conversations pretty much along spiritual lines. There was one experience with Doc which made a terrific impression upon me. The afternoon that I was to leave the hospital, he came in to see me and asked me if I were willing to attempt to follow the program. I told him that I had no other intention. That was at the end of eight days in which I had had no liquor. He then pulled up his chair with one of his knees touching mine and said, "Will you pray with me for your success?" And he then said a beautiful prayer. That was an experience that I have never forgotten, and many times in my own work with A.A. newcomers I feel kind of guilty because I haven't done the same thing.

One of the things that came up repeatedly in the stories they told me was that once they had accepted the program, they never had a desire to take a drink. That was skeptically received by me when I first heard it, but after some twenty-eight or thirty fellows had come to see me, and pretty nearly all of them had said the same thing, I began to believe it. In my own experience I was so jubilant at finding myself sober, and I had so many things to catch up on, that a month went by before the thought even occurred to me. I had a genuine release right from the start. I've never had a desire to take a drink.

Doc dwelt on the idea that this was an illness, but Doc was pretty frank with me. He found that I had enough faith in the Almighty to be fairly frank. He pointed out to me that probably it was more of a moral or spiritual illness than it was a physical one.

We went to Akron for about six weeks and we did a lot of visiting among the people in Akron. There were, at that time, in the neighborhood of twelve or thirteen Cleveland members who had been sober anywhere from a year and a half to a couple of months. They had all been to Akron. It was finally decided to undertake the organization of a Cleveland group and toward the end of May, 1939, the first meeting was held in Cleveland in my home. At that meeting, there were a number of Akron people and all the Cleveland people.

Professionally, after I was sober for a month or so I realized that I should school myself to dissolve the partnership I was in because I felt that I would never regain the respect of my partners no matter how long I was sober, and that I would be at a disadvantage. I still had enough practice to earn a good living if I would only work, so I resolved that in January of 1940 I would launch a patent law firm of my own.

Shortly after I came to this conclusion, I was importuned by another well-known patent law firm to help them out on some trial work because their trial man had had a heart attack and had been forbidden to go into the courtroom. Somewhere in one of the conversations, I mentioned that I was contemplating forming a new firm. On hearing that, these people induced me to make the move immediately and join them as a senior partner, which I did. I found in the fall of 1939, that I was not mentally impaired, so far as trial work was concerned, and thereafter took up where I had left off when I was about forty-five years old. My physical health was badly shaken, but I began to pick up. In fact, after six months of living on food instead of on whiskey, I gained about thirty pounds.

I realized that there wasn't anything I could say to place myself in a more favorable light with my children, that it was going to be a matter of time; for I also understood the intolerance of young people towards deficiencies in their elders. I believe though that it helped my family tremendously to have the A.A. meetings every week in my own home. My oldest child sometimes sat in on the meetings.

I had accepted Catholicism somewhat as an inheritance. My education had been pretty much pagan–science. I resolved that if I were going to continue with the Catholic Church, I was going to know the roots of the doctrine, since those roots had caused me some confusion. So I enrolled at the university for night courses in religion, and I pursued those courses for a year. In summing up, I can say that A.A. has made me, I hope, a real Catholic.

(4) WOMEN SUFFER TOO

Despite great opportunities, alcohol nearly ended her life. An early member, she spread the word among women in our pioneering period.

WHAT WAS I saying... from far away, as if in a delirium, I heard my own voice–calling someone "Dorothy," talking of shops, of jobs... the words came clearer... this sound of my own voice frightened me as it got closer... and suddenly, there I was, talking of I knew not what, to someone I'd never seen before that very moment. Abruptly I stopped speaking. Where was I?

I'd waked up in strange rooms before, fully dressed on a bed or a couch; I'd waked up in my own room, in or on my own bed, not knowing what hour or day it was, afraid to ask... but this was different. This time I seemed to be already awake, sitting upright in a big easy chair, in the middle of an animated conversation with a perfectly strange young woman, who didn't appear to think it strange. *She* was chatting on, pleasantly and comfortably.

Terrified, I looked around. I was in a large, dark, rather poorly furnished room–the living room of a basement flat. Cold chills started chasing up and down my spine; my teeth were chattering; my hands were shaking so I tucked them under me to keep them from flying away. My fright was real enough, but it didn't account for these violent reactions. I knew what they were, all right–a drink would fix them. It must have been a long time since I had my last drink–but I didn't dare ask this stranger for one. I must get out of here. In any case I must get out of here before I let slip my abysmal ignorance of how I came to be here and she realized that I was stark, staring mad. I was mad–I must be.

The shakes grew worse, and I looked at my watch–six o'clock. It had been one o'clock when I last remembered looking. I'd been sitting comfortably in a restaurant with Rita, drinking my sixth martini and hoping the waiter would forget about the lunch order–at least long enough for me to have a couple more. I'd only had two with her, but I'd managed four in the fifteen minutes I'd waited for her, and of course I'd had the usual uncounted swigs from the bottle as I painfully got up and did my slow spasmodic dressing. In fact I had been in very good shape at one o'clock–feeling no pain. What *could* have happened? That had been in the center of New York, on noisy 42nd Street... this was obviously a quiet residential section. Why had "Dorothy" brought me here? Who was she? How had I met her? I had no answers, and I dared not ask. She gave no sign of recognizing anything wrong, but what had I been doing for those lost five hours? My brain whirled. I might have done terrible things, and I wouldn't even know it!

Somehow I got out of there and walked five blocks past brownstone houses. There wasn't a bar in sight, but I found the subway station. The name on it was unfamiliar and I had to ask the way to Grand Central. It took three-quarters of an hour and two changes to get there–back to my starting point. I had been in the remote reaches of Brooklyn.

That night I got very drunk, which was usual, but I remembered everything, which was very unusual. I remembered going through what my sister assured me was my nightly procedure of trying to find Willie Seabrook's name in the telephone book. I remembered my loud resolution to find him and ask him to help me get into that "Asylum" he had written about. I remembered asserting that I was going to *do* something about this, that I couldn't go on... I remembered looking longingly at the window as an easier solution and shuddering at the memory of that other window, three years before, and the six agonizing months in a London hospital ward. I remembered filling the peroxide bottle in my medicine chest with gin, in case my sister found the bottle I hid under the mattress. And I remembered the creeping horror of the interminable night, in which I slept for short spells and woke dripping with cold sweat and shaken with utter despair, to drink hastily from my bottle and mercifully pass out again. "You're mad, you're mad, you're mad!" pounded through my brain with each returning ray of consciousness, and I drowned the refrain with drink.

That went on for two more months before I landed in a hospital and started my slow fight back to normalcy. It had been going on like that for over a year. I was thirty-two years old.

When I look back on that last horrible year of constant drinking, I wonder how I survived it, either physically or mentally. For there were, of course, periods of clear realization of what I had become, attended by memories of what I had been, what I had expected to be. And the contrast was pretty shattering. Sitting in a Second Avenue bar, accepting drinks from anyone who offered, after my small stake was gone, or sitting at home alone, with the inevitable glass in my hand, I would remember, and remembering, I would drink faster, seeking speedy oblivion. It was hard to reconcile this ghastly present with the simple facts of the past.

My family had money–I had never known denial of any material desire. The best boarding schools and a finishing school in Europe had fitted me for the conventional role of debutante and young matron. The times in which I grew up (the Prohibition era immortalized by Scott Fitzgerald and John Held Jr.) had taught me to be gay with the gayest; my own inner urges led me to outdo them all. The year after coming out, I married. So far, so good–all according to plan, like thousands of others. But then the story became my own. My husband was an alcoholic, and since I had only contempt for those without my own amazing capacity, the outcome was inevitable. My divorce coincided with my father's bankruptcy, and I went to work, casting off all allegiances and responsibilities to any other than myself. For me, work was only a different means to the same end, to be able to do exactly what I wanted to do.

For the next ten years I did just that. For greater freedom and excitement I went abroad to live. I had my own business, successful enough for me to indulge most of my desires. I met all the people I wanted to meet; I saw all the places I wanted to see; I did all the things I wanted to do–and I was increasingly miserable.

Headstrong and willful, I rushed from pleasure to pleasure and found the returns diminishing to the vanishing point. Hangovers began to assume monstrous proportions, and the morning drink became an urgent necessity. "Blanks" were more frequent, and I seldom knew how I'd got home. When my friends suggested that I was drinking too much, they were no longer my friends. I moved from group to group–then from place to place–and went on drinking. With a creeping insidiousness, drink had become more important than anything else. It no longer gave me pleasure–it merely dulled the pain–but I *had* to have it. I was bitterly unhappy. No doubt I had been an exile too long–I should go home to America. I did. And to my surprise, my drinking grew worse.

When I entered a sanitarium for prolonged and intensive psychiatric treatment, I was convinced that I was having a serious mental breakdown. I wanted help, and I tried to cooperate. As the treatment progressed, I began to get a picture of myself, of the temperament that had caused me so much trouble. I had been hypersensitive, shy, idealistic. My inability to accept the harsh realities of life had resulted in a disillusioned cynic, clothed in a protective armor against the world's misunderstanding. That armor had turned into prison walls, locking me in loneliness–and fear. All I had left was an iron determination to live my own life in spite of the alien world–and here I was, an inwardly frightened, outwardly defiant woman, who desperately needed a prop to keep going.

Alcohol was that prop, and I didn't see how I could live without it. When my doctor told me I should never touch a drink again, I *couldn't afford* to believe him. I had to persist in my attempts to get straightened out enough to be able to use the drinks I needed, without their turning on me. Besides, how could *he* understand? He wasn't a drinking man; he didn't know what it was to *need* a drink, nor what a drink could do for one in a pinch. I wanted to *live*, not in a desert, but in a normal world; and my idea of a normal world was among people who drank–teetotalers were not included. And I was sure that I couldn't be with people who drank, without drinking. In that I was correct: I couldn't be comfortable with *any* kind of people without drinking. I never had been.

Naturally, in spite of my good intentions, in spite of my protected life behind sanitarium walls, I several times got drunk, and was astounded... and badly shaken.

That was the point at which my doctor gave me the book *Alcoholics Anonymous* to read. The first chapters were a revelation to me. I wasn't the only person in the world who felt and behaved like this! I wasn't mad or vicious–I was a sick person. I was suffering from an actual disease that had a name and symptoms like diabetes or cancer or TB–and a disease was respectable, not a moral stigma! But then I hit a snag. I couldn't stomach religion, and I didn't like the mention of God or any of the other capital letters. If that was the way out, it wasn't for me. I was an intellectual and I needed an intellectual answer, not an emotional one. I told my doctor so in no uncertain terms. I wanted to learn to stand on my own two feet, not to change one prop for another, and an intangible and dubious one at that. And so on and on, for several weeks, while I grudgingly plowed through some more of the offending book, and felt more and more hopeless about myself.

Then the miracle happened–to *me!* It isn't always so sudden with everyone, but I ran into a personal crisis which filled me with a raging and righteous anger. And as I fumed helplessly and planned to get good and drunk and *show them*, my eye caught a sentence in the book lying open on my bed: "We cannot live with anger." The walls crumpled–and the light streamed in. I wasn't trapped. I wasn't helpless. I was *free*, and I didn't have to drink to "show them." This wasn't "religion"–this was freedom! Freedom from anger and fear, freedom to know happiness and love.

I went to a meeting to see for myself this group of freaks or bums who had done this thing. To go into a gathering of people was the sort of thing that all my life, from the time I left my private world of books and dreams to meet the real world of people and parties and jobs, had left me feeling an uncomfortable outsider, needing the warming stimulus of drinks to join in. I went trembling into a house in Brooklyn filled with strangers... and I found I had come home at last, to my own kind. There is another meaning for the Hebrew word that in the King James version of the Bible is translated "salvation." It is: "to come home." I had found my salvation. I wasn't alone any more.

That was the beginning of a new life, a fuller life, a happier life than I had ever known or believed possible. I had found friends, understanding friends who often knew what I was thinking and feeling better than I knew myself, and who didn't allow me to retreat into my prison of loneliness and fear over a fancied slight or hurt. Talking things over with them, great floods of enlightenment showed me myself as I really was–and I was like them. We all had hundreds of character traits, fears and phobias, likes and dislikes, in common. Suddenly I could accept myself, faults and all, as I was–for weren't we all like that? And, accepting, I felt a new inner comfort and the willingness and strength to do something about the traits I couldn't live with.

It didn't stop there. They knew what to do about those black abysses that yawned, ready to swallow me, when I felt depressed or nervous. There was a concrete program, designed to secure the greatest possible inner security for us long-time escapists. The feeling of impending disaster that had haunted me for years began to dissolve as I put into practice more and more of the Twelve Steps. It worked!

An active member of A.A. since 1939, I feel myself a useful member of the human race at last. I have something to contribute to humanity, since I am peculiarly qualified, as a fellow-sufferer, to give aid and comfort to those who have stumbled and fallen over this business of meeting life. I get my greatest thrill of accomplishment from the knowledge that I have played a part in the new happiness achieved by countless others like myself. The fact that I can work again and earn my living is important but secondary. I believe that my once overweening self-will has finally found its proper place, for I can say many times daily, "Thy will be done, not mine"... and mean it.

(5) THE EUROPEAN DRINKER

Beer and wine were not the answer.

I WAS BORN in Europe, in Alsace to be exact, shortly after it had become German, and practically grew up with "good Rhine wine" of song and story. My parents had some vague ideas of making a priest out of me and for some years I attended the Franciscan school at Basle, Switzerland, just across the border, about six miles from my home. But, although I was a good Catholic, the monastic life had little appeal for me.

Very early I became apprenticed to harness-making and acquired considerable knowledge of upholstering. My daily consumption of wine was about a quart, but that was common where I lived. Everybody drank wine. And it is true that there was no great amount of drunkenness. But I can remember, in my teens, that there were a few characters who caused the village heads to nod pityingly and sometimes in anger as they paused to say, "That sot, Henri" and "Ce pauvre Jules," who drank too much. They were undoubtedly the alcoholics of our village.

Military service was compulsory and I did my stretch with the class of my age, goose-stepping in German barracks and taking part in the Boxer Rebellion in China, my first time at any great distance from home. In foreign parts many a soldier who has been abstemious at home learns to use new and potent drinks. So I indulged with my comrades in everything the Far East had to offer. I cannot say, however, that I acquired any craving for hard liquor as a result. When I got back to Germany I settled down to finish my apprenticeship, drinking the wine of the country as usual.

Many friends of my family had emigrated to America, so at twenty-four I decided that the United States offered me the opportunity I was never likely to find in my native land. I came directly to a growing industrial city in the middle west, where I have lived practically ever since. I was warmly welcomed by friends of my youth who had preceded me. For weeks after my arrival I was feted and entertained in the already large colony of Alsatians in the city, and among the Germans in their saloons and clubs. I early decided that the wine of America was very inferior stuff and took up beer instead.

Fond of singing, I joined a German singing society which had good club headquarters. There I sat in the evenings, enjoying with my friends our memories of the "old country," singing the old songs we all knew, playing simple card games for drinks and consuming great quantities of beer.

At that time I could go into any saloon, have one or two beers, walk out and forget about it. I had no desire whatever to sit down at a table and stay a whole morning or afternoon drinking. Certainly, at that time I was one of those who "can take it or leave it alone." There had never been any drunkards in my family. I came of good stock, of men and women who drank wine all their lives as a beverage, and while they occasionally got drunk at special celebrations, they were up and about their business the next day.

Prohibition came. Having regard for the law of the land, I resigned myself to the will of the national legislators and quit drinking altogether, not because I had found it harmful, but because I couldn't get what I was accustomed to drink. You can all remember that in the first few months after the change, a great many men, who had formerly been used to a few beers every day or an occasional drink of whiskey, simply quit all alcoholic drinks. For the great majority of us, however, that condition didn't last. We saw very early that prohibition wasn't going to work. It wasn't very long before home-brewing was an institution and men began to search feverishly for old recipe books on wine-making.

But I hardly tasted anything for two years and started in business for myself, founding a mattress factory which is today an important industrial enterprise in our city. I was doing very well with that and general upholstering work, and there was every indication that I would be financially independent by the time I reached middle age. By this time I was married and was paying for a home. Like most immigrants I wanted to be somebody and have something and I was very happy and contented as I felt success crown my efforts. I missed the old social times, of course, but had no definite craving even for beer.

Successful home-brewers among my friends began to invite me to their homes. I decided that if these fellows could make it I would try it myself, and so I did. It wasn't very long until I had developed a pretty good brew with uniformity and plenty of authority. I knew the stuff I was making was a lot stronger than I had been used to, but I never suspected that steady drinking of it might develop a taste for something even stronger.

It wasn't long before the bootlegger was an established institution in this, as in other towns. I was doing well in business, and in going around town I was frequently invited to have a drink in a speakeasy. I condoned my domestic brewing along with the bootleggers and their business. More and more I formed the habit of doing some of my business in the speakeasy, and after a time I did not need that as an excuse. The "speaks" usually sold whiskey. Beer was too bulky and it couldn't be kept in a jug under the counter ready to be dumped when John Law would came around. I was now forming an entirely new drinking technique. Before long I had a definite taste for hard liquor, knew nausea and headaches I had never known before, but as in the old days, I suffered them out. Gradually, however, I'd suffer so much that I simply had to have the morning-after drink.

I became a periodic drinker. I was eased out of the business I had founded and was reduced to doing general upholstery in a small shop at the back of my house. My wife upbraided me often and plenty when she saw that my "periodics" were gradually losing me what business I could get. I began to bring bottles in. I had them hidden away in the house and all over my shop in careful concealment. I had all the usual experiences of the alcoholic, for I was certainly one by this time. Sometimes, after sobering up after a bout of several weeks, I would righteously resolve to quit. With a great deal of determination, I would throw out full pints–pour them out and smash the bottles–firmly resolved never to take another drink of the stuff. I was going to straighten up.

In four or five days I would be hunting all over the place, at home and in my workshop, for the bottles I had destroyed, cursing myself for being a damned fool. My "periodics" became more frequent until I reached the point where I wanted to devote all my time to drinking, working as little as possible, and then only when the necessity of my family demanded it. As soon as I had satisfied that, what I earned as an upholsterer went for liquor. I would promise to have jobs done and never do them. My customers lost confidence in me to the point where I retained what business I had only because I was a well-trained and reputedly fine craftsman. "Best in the business, when he's sober," my customers would say, and I still had a following who would give me work though they deplored my habits, because they knew the job would be well done when they eventually got it.

I had always been a good Catholic, possibly not so devoted as I should have been, but fairly regular in my attendance at services. I had never doubted the existence of the Supreme Being, but now I began to absent myself from my church where I had formerly been a member of the choir. Unfortunately, I had no desire to consult my priest about my drinking. In fact I was scared to talk to him about it, for I feared the kind of talk he would give me. Unlike many other Catholics who frequently take pledges for definite periods–a year, two years or for good, I never had any desire to "take a pledge" before the priest. And yet, realizing at last that liquor really had me, I wanted to quit. My wife wrote away for advertised cures for the liquor habit and gave them to me in coffee. I even got them myself and tried them. None of the various cures of this kind were any good.

Then occurred the event that saved me. An alcoholic who was a doctor came to see me. He didn't talk like a preacher at all. In fact his language was perfectly suited to my understanding. He had no desire to know anything, except whether I was definite about my desire to quit drinking. I told him with all the sincerity at my command that I did. Even then he went into no great detail about how he and a crowd of alcoholics, with whom he associated, had mastered their difficulty. Instead he told me that some of them wanted to talk to me and would be over to see me.

This doctor had imparted his knowledge to just a few other men at that time–not more than four or five–they now number more than seventy persons. [*Written in 1939.*] And, because as I have discovered since, it is part of the "treatment" that these men be sent to see and talk with alcoholics who want to quit, he kept them busy. He had already imbued them with his own spirit until they were ready and willing at all times to go where sent, and as a doctor he well knew that this mission and duty would strengthen them as it later helped me. The visits from these men impressed me at once. Where preaching and prayers had touched me very little, I immediately desired further knowledge of these men.

I could see they were sober. The third man who came to see me had been one of the greatest business-getters his company had ever employed. From the top of the heap in a few years he had skidded to becoming a shuffling customer, still entering the better barrooms but welcomed by neither mine host nor his patrons. His own business was practically gone.

"You've been trying man's ways and they always fail," he told me. "You can't win unless you try God's way."

I had never heard of the remedy expressed in just this language. In a few sentences he made God seem personal to me, explained Him as a being who was interested in me, the alcoholic, and that all I needed to do was to be willing to follow His way; that as long as I followed it I would be able to overcome my desire for liquor.

Well, there I was, willing to try it, but I didn't know how, except in a vague way. I knew somehow that it meant more than just going to church and living a moral life. If that was all, then I was a little doubtful that it was the answer I was looking for.

He went on talking and told me that he had found the plan has a basis of love, and the practice of Christ's injunction, "Love thy neighbor as thyself." Taking that as a foundation, he reasoned that if a man followed that rule he could not be selfish. I could see that. And he further said that God could not accept me as a sincere follower of His Divine Law unless I was ready to be thoroughly honest about it.

That was perfectly logical. My church taught that. I had always known that in theory. We talked, too, about personal morals. Every man has his problem of this kind, but we didn't discuss it very much. My visitor well knew, that as I tried to follow God I would get to study these things out for myself.

That day I gave my will to God and asked to be directed. But I have never thought of that as something to do and then forget about. I very early came to see that there had to be a continual renewal of that simple deal with God; that I had perpetually to keep the bargain. So I began to pray; to place my problems in God's hands.

For a long time I kept on trying, in a pretty dumb way at first, I know, but very earnestly. I didn't want to be a fake. And I began putting into practice what I was learning every day. It wasn't very long until my doctor friend sent me to tell another alcoholic what my experience had been. This duty together with my weekly meetings with my fellow alcoholics, and my daily renewal of the contract I originally made with God, have kept me sober when nothing else ever did.

I have been sober for many years now. The first few months were hard. Many things happened; business trials, little worries, and feelings of general despondency came near driving me to the bottle, but I made progress. As I go along I seem to get strength daily to be able to resist more easily. And when I get upset, cross-grained and out of tune with my fellow man I know that I am out of tune with God. Searching where I have been at fault, it is not hard to discover and get right again, for I have proven to myself and to many others who know me that God can keep a man sober if he will let Him.

(6) THE VICIOUS CYCLE

How it finally broke a Southerner's obstinacy and destined this salesman to start A.A. at Philadelphia.

JANUARY 8, 1938–that was my D-Day; the place, Washington, D.C. This last real merry-go-round had started the day before Christmas, and I had really accomplished a lot in those fourteen days. First, my new wife had walked out, bag, baggage and furniture; then the apartment landlord had thrown me out of the empty apartment; and the finish was the loss of another job. After a couple of days in dollar hotels and one night in the pokey, I finally landed on my mother's doorstep–shaking apart, with several days' beard, and, of course, broke as usual. Many of these same things had happened to me many times before, but this time they had all descended together. For me, this was it.

Here I was, thirty-nine years old and a complete washout. Nothing had worked. Mother would take me in only if I stayed locked in a small storeroom and gave her my clothes and shoes. We had played this game before. That is the way Jackie found me, lying on a cot in my skivvies, with hot and cold sweats, pounding heart, and that awful itchy scratchiness all over. Somehow, I had always managed to avoid D.T.'s.

I seriously doubt I ever would have asked for help, but Fitz, an old school friend of mine, had persuaded Jackie to call on me. Had he come two or three days later, I think I would have thrown him out, but he hit when I was open for anything.

Jackie arrived about 7 in the evening and talked until 3 a.m. I don't remember much of what he said, but I did realize that here was another guy exactly like me; he had been in the same laughing academies and the same jails, known the same loss of jobs, same frustrations, same boredom and the same loneliness. If anything, he had known all of them even better and more often than I. Yet he was happy, relaxed, confident and laughing. That night, for the first time in my life, I really let down my hair and admitted my general loneliness. Jackie told me about a group of fellows in New York, of whom my old friend Fitz was one, who had the same problem I had, and who, by working together to help each other, were not now drinking and were happy like himself. He said something about God or a Higher Power, but I brushed that off–that was for the birds, not for me. Little more of our talk stayed in my memory, but I do know I slept the rest of that night, while before I had never known what a real night's sleep was.

This was my introduction to this "understanding fellowship," although it was to be more than a year later before our Society was to bear the name Alcoholics Anonymous. All of us in A.A. know the tremendous happiness that is in our sobriety, but there are also tragedies. My sponsor, Jackie, was one of these. He brought in many of our original members, yet he himself could not make it and died of alcoholism. The lesson of his death still remains with me, yet I often wonder what would have happened if somebody else had made that first call on me. So I always say that as long as I remember January 8, that is how long I will remain sober.

The age-old question in A.A. is which came first, the neurosis or the alcoholism. I like to think I was fairly normal before alcohol took over. My early life was spent in Baltimore, where my father was a physician and a grain merchant. My family lived in very prosperous circumstances, and while both my parents drank, sometimes too much, neither was an alcoholic. Father was a very well-integrated person, and while mother was high-strung and a bit selfish and demanding, our home life was reasonably harmonious. There were four of us children, and although both of my brothers later became alcoholic–one died of alcoholism–my sister has never taken a drink in her life.

Until I was thirteen I attended public schools, with regular promotions and average grades. I have never shown any particular talents, nor have I had any really frustrating ambitions. At thirteen I was packed off to a very fine Protestant boarding school in Virginia, where I stayed four years, graduating without any special achievements. In sports I made the track and tennis teams; I got along well with the other boys and had a fairly large circle of acquaintances but no intimate friends. I was never homesick and was always pretty self-sufficient.

However, here I probably took my first step towards my coming alcoholism by developing a terrific aversion to all churches and established religions. At this school we had Bible readings before each meal, and church services four times on Sunday, and I became so rebellious at this that I swore I would never join or go to any church, except for weddings or for funerals.

At seventeen I entered the university, really to satisfy my father, who wanted me to study medicine there as he had. That is where I had my first drink, and I still remember it, for every "first" drink afterwards did exactly the same trick–I could feel it go right through every bit of my body and down to my very toes. But each drink after the first seemed to become less effective, and after three or four, they all seemed like water. I was never a hilarious drunk; the more I drank, the quieter I got, and the drunker I got, the harder I fought to stay sober. So it is clear that I never had any fun out of drinking–I would be the soberest-seeming one in the crowd, and, all of a sudden, I was the drunkest. Even that first night I blacked out, which leads me to believe that I was an alcoholic from my very first drink. The first year in college I just got by in my studies. I majored in poker and drinking. I refused to join any fraternity, as I wanted to be a freelance, and that year my drinking was confined to one-night stands, once or twice a week. The second year my drinking was more or less restricted to weekends, but I was nearly kicked out for scholastic failure.

In the spring of 1917, in order to beat being fired from school, I became "patriotic" and joined the army. I am one of the lads who came out of the service with a lower rank than when I went in. I had been to OTC the previous summer, so I went into the army as a sergeant but I came out a private, and you really have to be unusual to do that. In the next two years, I washed more pans and peeled more potatoes than any other doughboy. In the army, I became a periodic alcoholic–the periods always coming whenever I could make the opportunity. However, I did manage to keep out of the guardhouse. My last bout in the army lasted from November 5 to 11, 1918. We heard by wireless on the fifth that the Armistice would be signed the next day (this was a premature report), so I had a couple of cognacs to celebrate; then I hopped a truck and went AWOL. My next conscious memory was in Bar le Duc, many miles from base. It was November 11, and bells were ringing and whistles blowing for the real Armistice. There I was, unshaven, clothes torn and dirty, with no recollection of wandering all over France but, of course, a hero to the local French. Back at camp, all was forgiven because it was the End, but in the light of what I have since learned, I know I was a confirmed alcoholic at nineteen.

With the war over and back in Baltimore with the folks, I had several small jobs for three years, and then I went to work soliciting as one of the first ten employees of a new national finance company. What an opportunity I shot to pieces there! This company now does a volume of over three billion dollars annually. Three years later, at twenty-five, I opened and operated their Philadelphia office and was earning more than I ever have since. I was the fair-haired boy all right, but two years later I was blacklisted as an irresponsible drunk. It doesn't take long.

My next job was in sales promotion for an oil company in Mississippi, where I promptly became high man and got lots of pats on the back. Then I turned two company cars over in a short time and bingo–fired again. Oddly enough, the big shot who fired me from this company was one of the first men I met when I later joined the New York A.A. Group. He had also gone all the way through the wringer and had been dry two years when I saw him again.

After the oil job blew up, I went back to Baltimore and Mother, my first wife having said a permanent goodbye. Then came a sales job with a national tire company. I reorganized their city sales policy and eighteen months later, when I was thirty, they offered me the branch managership. As part of this promotion, they sent me to their national convention in Atlantic City to tell the big wheels how I'd done it. At this time I was holding what drinking I did down to weekends, but I hadn't had a drink at all in a month. I checked into my hotel room and then noticed a placard tucked under the glass on the bureau stating "There will be positively NO drinking at this convention," signed by the president of the company. That did it! Who, me? The Big Shot? The only salesman invited to talk at the convention? The man who was going to take over one of the biggest branches come Monday? I'd show 'em who was boss! No one in that company saw me again–ten days later I wired my resignation.

As long as things were tough and the job a challenge, I could always manage to hold on pretty well, but as soon as I learned the combination, got the puzzle under control, and the boss to pat me on the back, I was gone again. Routine jobs bored me, but I would take on the toughest one I could find, work day and night until I had it under control; then it would become tedious, and I'd lose all interest in it. I could never be bothered with the follow-through and would invariably reward myself for my efforts with that "first" drink.

After the tire job came the thirties, the Depression, and the downhill road. In the eight years before A.A. found me, I had over forty jobs–selling and traveling–one thing after another, and the same old routine. I'd work like mad for three or four weeks without a single drink, save my money, pay a few bills and then "reward" myself with alcohol. Then I'd be broke again, hiding out in cheap hotels all over the country, having one-night jail stands here and there, and always that horrible feeling "What's the use–nothing is worthwhile." Every time I blacked out, and that was every time I drank, there was always that gnawing fear, "What did I do this time?" Once I found out. Many alcoholics have learned they can bring their bottle to a cheap movie theater and drink, sleep, wake up and drink again in the darkness. I had repaired to one of these one morning with my jug, and, when I left late in the afternoon, I picked up a newspaper on the way home. Imagine my surprise when I read in a page-one "box" that I had been taken from the theater unconscious around noon that day, removed by ambulance to a hospital and stomach-pumped, and then released. Evidently I had gone right back to the movie with a bottle, stayed there several hours, and started home with no recollection of what had happened.

The mental state of the sick alcoholic is beyond description. I had no resentments against individuals–the whole world was all wrong. My thoughts went round and round with "What's it all about anyhow? People have wars and kill each other; they struggle and cut each other's throats for success, and what does anyone get out of it? Haven't I been successful, haven't I accomplished extraordinary things in business? What do I get out of it? Everything's all wrong and the hell with it." For the last two years of my drinking I prayed on every drink that I wouldn't wake up again. Three months before I met Jackie I had made my second feeble try at suicide.

This was the background that made me willing to listen on January 8. After being dry two weeks and sticking close to Jackie, all of a sudden I found I had become the sponsor of my sponsor, for he was suddenly taken drunk. I was startled to learn he had only been off the booze a month or so himself when he brought me the message! However, I made an SOS call to the New York Group, whom I hadn't met yet, and they suggested we both come there. This we did the next day, and what a trip! I really had a chance to see myself from a nondrinking point of view. We checked into the home of Hank, the man who had fired me eleven years before in Mississippi, and there I met Bill, our founder. Bill had then been dry three years and Hank, two. At the time, I thought them just a swell pair of screwballs, for they were not only going to save all the drunks in the world but also all the so-called normal people! All they talked of that first weekend was God and how they were going to straighten out Jackie's and my life. In those days we really took each other's inventories firmly and often. Despite all this, I *did* like these new friends because, again, they were like me. They had also been periodic big shots who had goofed out repeatedly at the wrong time, and they also knew how to split one paper match into three separate matches. (This is very useful knowledge in places where matches are prohibited.) They, too, had taken a train to one town and had wakened hundreds of miles in the opposite direction, never knowing how they got there. The same old routines seemed to be common to us all. During that first weekend I decided to stay in New York and take all they gave out with, except the "God stuff." I knew they needed to straighten out *their* thinking and habits, but *I* was all right; *I* just drank too much. Just give me a good front and a couple of bucks, and I'd be right back in the big time. I'd been dry three weeks, had the wrinkles out, and had sobered up my sponsor all by myself!

Bill and Hank had just taken over a small automobile polish company, and they offered me a job–ten dollars a week and keep at Hank's house. We were all set to put DuPont out of business.

At that time the group in New York was composed of about twelve men who were working on the principle of every drunk for himself; we had no real formula and no name. We would follow one man's ideas for a while, decide he was wrong and switch to another's method. But we *were* staying sober as long as we kept and talked together. There was one meeting a week at Bill's home in Brooklyn, and we all took turns there spouting off about how we had changed our lives overnight, how many drunks we had saved and straightened out, and last, but not least, how God had touched each of us personally on the shoulder. Boy, what a circle of confused idealists! Yet we all had one really sincere purpose in our hearts, and that was not to drink. At our weekly meeting I was a menace to serenity those first few months, for I took every opportunity to lambaste that "spiritual angle," as we called it, or anything else that had any tinge of theology. Much later I discovered the elders held many prayer meetings hoping to find a way to give me the heave-ho but at the same time stay tolerant and spiritual. They did not seem to be getting an answer, for here I was staying sober and selling lots of auto polish, on which they were making 1,000 percent profit. So I rocked along my merry independent way until June, when I went out selling auto polish in New England. After a very good week, two of my customers took me to lunch on Saturday. We ordered sandwiches, and one man said, "Three beers." I let mine sit. After a bit, the other man said, "Three beers." I let mine sit too. Then it was my turn–I ordered "Three beers," but this time it was different; I had a cash investment of thirty cents, and, on a ten-dollar-a-week salary, that's a big thing. So I drank all three beers, one after the other, and said, "I'll be seeing you, boys," and went around the corner for a bottle. I never saw either of them again.

I had completely forgotten the January 8 when I found the fellowship, and I spent the next four days wandering around New England half drunk, by which I mean I couldn't get drunk and I couldn't get sober. I tried to contact the boys in New York, but telegrams bounced right back, and when I finally got Hank on the telephone he fired me right then. This was when I really took my first good look at myself. My loneliness was worse than it had ever been before, for now even my own kind had turned against me. This time it really hurt, more than any hangover ever had. My brilliant agnosticism vanished, and I saw for the first time that those who really believed, or at least honestly tried to find a Power greater than themselves, were much more composed and contented than I had ever been, and they seemed to have a degree of happiness I had never known.

Peddling off my polish samples for expenses, I crawled back to New York a few days later in a very chastened frame of mind. When the others saw my altered attitude, they took me back in, but for me they *had* to make it tough; if they hadn't, I don't think I ever would have stuck it out. Once again, there was the challenge of a tough job, but this time I was determined to follow through. For a long time the only Higher Power I could concede was the power of the group, but this was far more than I had ever recognized before, and it was at least a beginning. It was also an ending, for never since June 16, 1938, have I had to walk alone.

Around this time our big A.A. book was being written, and it all became much simpler; we had a definite formula which some sixty of us agreed was the middle course for all alcoholics who wanted sobriety, and that formula has not been changed one iota down through the years. I don't think the boys were completely convinced of my personality change, for they fought shy of including my story in the book, so my only contribution to their literary efforts was my firm conviction–since I was still a theological rebel–that the word *God* should be qualified with the phrase "as we understand Him"–for that was the only way I could accept spirituality.

After the book appeared, we all became very busy in our efforts to save all and sundry, but I was still actually on the fringes of A.A. While I went along with all that was done and attended the meetings, I never took an active job of leadership until February 1940. Then I got a very good position in Philadelphia and quickly found I would need a few fellow alcoholics around me if I was to stay sober. Thus I found myself in the middle of a brand-new group. When I started to tell the boys how we did it in New York and all about the spiritual part of the program, I found they would not believe me unless I was practicing what I preached. Then I found that as I gave in to this spiritual or personality change, I was getting a little more serenity. In telling newcomers how to change their lives and attitudes, all of a sudden I found I was doing a little changing myself. I had been too self-sufficient to write a moral inventory, but I discovered in pointing out to the new man his wrong attitudes and actions that I was really taking my own inventory, and that if I expected him to change, I would have to work on myself too. This change has been a long, slow process for me, but through these latter years the dividends have been tremendous.

In June 1945, with another member, I made my first–and only–Twelfth Step call on a female alcoholic, and a year later I married her. She has been sober all the way through, and for me that has been good. We can share in the laughter and tears of our many friends, and most important, we can share our A.A. way of life and are given a daily opportunity to help others.

In conclusion, I can only say that whatever growth or understanding has come to me, I have no wish to graduate. Very rarely do I miss the meetings of my neighborhood A.A. group, and my average has never been less than two meetings a week. I have served on only one committee in the past nine years, for I feel that I had my chance the first few years and that newer members should fill the jobs. They are far more alert and progressive than we floundering fathers were, and the future of our fellowship is in their hands. We now live in the West and are very fortunate in our area A.A.; it is good, simple and friendly, and our one desire is to stay *in* A.A. and not *on* it. Our pet slogan is "Easy Does It."

And I still say that as long as I remember that January 8 in Washington, that is how long, by the grace of God as I understand Him, I will retain a happy sobriety.

(7) THE NEWS HAWK

This newsman covered life from top to bottom; but he ended up, safely enough, in the middle.

WITH NOTHING but a liberal arts education, very definitely estranged from my family and already married, soon after graduation from college I became a bookmaker's clerk on the British racing circuits, far better off financially than the average professional man. I moved in a gay crowd in the various "pubs" and sporting clubs. My wife traveled with me, but with a baby coming I decided to settle in a large city where I got a job with a commission agent which is a polite term for a hand-book operator. My job was to collect bets and betting-slips in the business section, a lucrative spot. My boss, in his way, was "big business." Drinking was all in the day's work.

One evening, the book, after checking up, was very definitely in the red for plenty through a piece of studied carelessness on my part, and my boss, very shrewd and able, fired me with a parting statement to the effect that once was enough. With a good stake I sailed for New York. I knew I was through among the English "bookies."

Tom Sharkey's brawling bar in 14th Street and the famous wine-room at the back were headquarters for me. I soon ran through my stake. Some college friends got me jobs when I finally had to go to work, but I didn't stick to them. I wanted to travel. Making my way to Pittsburg, I met other former friends and got a job in a large factory where piece-makers were making good money. My fellow-workers were mostly good Saturday night drinkers and I was right with them. Young and able to travel with the best of them, I managed to hold my job and keep my end up in the barrooms.

I quit the factory and got a job on a small newspaper, going from that to a Pittsburgh daily, long ago defunct. Following a big drunk on that sheet, where I was doing leg-work and rewrite, a feeling of nostalgia made me buy a ticket for Liverpool and I returned to Britain.

During my visit there, renewing acquaintance with former friends, I soon spent most of my money. I wanted to roam again and through relatives got a supercargo job on an Australian packet which allowed me to visit my people in Australia where I was born. But I didn't stay long. I was soon back in Liverpool. Coming out of a pub near the Cunard pier I saw the Lusitania standing out in the middle of the Mersey. She had just come in and was scheduled to sail in two days.

In my mind's eye I saw Broadway again and Tom Sharkey's bar; the roar of the subway was in my ears. Saying goodbye to my wife and baby, I was treading Manhattan's streets in a little more than a week. Again I spent my bankroll, by no means as thick as the one I had when I first saw the skyline of Gotham. I was soon broke, this time without train fare to go anywhere. I got my first introduction to "riding the rods and making a blind."

In my early twenties the hardships of hobo life did not discourage me, but I had no wish to become just a tramp. Forced to detrain from an empty gondola on the other side of Chicago by a terrific rainstorm which drenched me to the skin, I hit the first factory building I saw for a job. That job began a series of brief working spells, each one ending in a "drunk" and the urge to travel. My migrations extended for over a year as far west as Omaha. Drifting back to Ohio, I landed on a small newspaper and later was impressed into the direction of boy-welfare work at the local "Y." I stayed sober for four years except for a one-night carousal in Chicago. I stayed so sober that I used to keep a quart of medicinal whiskey in my bureau which I used to taper off the occasional newspaper alcoholics who were sent to see me.

Lots of times, vain-gloriously, I used to take the bottle out, look at it and say, "I've got you licked."

The war was getting along. Curious about it, feeling I was missing something, absolutely without any illusions about the aftermath, with no pronounced feeling of patriotism, I joined up with a Canadian regiment, serving a little over two years. Slight casualties, complicated however by a long and serious illness, were my only mishaps. Remarkably enough, I was a very abstemious soldier. My four years of abstinence had something to do with it, but soldiering is a tough enough game for a sober man, and I had no yen for full-pack slogging through mud with a cognac or vin rouge hangover.

Discharged in 1919, I really made up for my dry spell. Quebec, Toronto, Buffalo, and finally Pittsburgh, were the scenes of man-sized drunks until I had gone through my readjusted discharge pay, a fair sum.

I again became a reporter on a Pittsburgh daily. I applied for a publicity job and got it. My wife came over from Scotland and we started housekeeping in a large Ohio city.

The new job lasted five years. Every encouragement was given me with frequent salary increases, but the sober times between "periods" became shorter. I myself could see deterioration in my work from being physically and mentally affected by liquor, although I had not yet reached the point where all I wanted was more to drink. Successive Monday morning hangovers, which despite mid-week resolutions to do better, came with unfailing regularity, eventually caused me to quit my job. Washington, D.C. and news-gathering agency work followed, along with many parties. I couldn't stand the pace. My drinking was never the spaced doses of the careful tippler; it was always gluttonous.

Returning to the town I had left three months before, I became editor of a monthly magazine, soon had additional publicity and advertising accounts and the money rolled in. The strain of overwork led me to the bottle again. My wife made several attempts to get me to stop and I had the usual visits from persons who would always ask me "Why?"–as if I knew! Offered the job of advertising manager for an eastern automotive company, I move to Philadelphia to begin life anew. In three months John Barleycorn had me kicked out.

I did six years of newspaper advertising, and trade journal work with many, many drunks of drab and dreary hue woven into the pattern of my life. I visited my family just once in that time. An old avocation, the collecting of first editions, rare books and Americana, fascinated me between times. I had some financial success through no ability of my own and, when jobless and almost wiped out in 1930, I began to trade and sell my collection; much of the proceeds went to keep my apartment stocked with liquor and almost every night saw me helpless to bed.

I tried to help myself. I even began to go the rounds of the churches. I listened to famous ministers–found nothing. I began to know the inside of jails and work-houses. My family would have nothing to do with me, in fact couldn't because I couldn't spare any of my money, which I needed for drink, to support them. My last venture, a book shop, was hastened to closed doors by my steady intoxication. Then I had an idea.

Loading a car with good old books to sell to collectors, librarians, universities and historical societies, I started out to travel the country. I stayed sober during the trip except for an occasional bottle of beer because funds barely met expenses. When I hit Houston, Texas, I found employment in a large bookstore. Need I say that in a very short time I was walking along a prairie highway with arm extended and thumb pointed? In the two succeeding years I held ten different jobs ranging from newspaper copy-desk and rewrite, to traffic director for an oil field equipment company. Always, in between, there were intervals of being broke, riding freights and hitch-hiking interminable distances from one big town to another in three states. Now on a new job I was always thinking about payday and how much liquor I could buy and the pleasure I could have.

I knew I was a drunkard. Enduring all hangover hells that every alcoholic experiences, I made the usual resolutions. My thoughts sometimes turned to the idea that three must be a remedy. I have stood listening to street-corner preachers tell how they beat the game. They seemed to be happy in their fashion, they and their little groups of supporters, but always pride of intellect stopped me from seeking what they evidently had. Sniffing at emotional religion, I walked away. I was an honest agnostic, but definitely not a hater of the church or its adherents. What philosophy I had was thoroughly paganistic–all my life was devoted to a search for pleasure. I wanted to do nothing except what it pleased me to do when I wanted to do it.

Federal Theatre in Texas gave me an administrative job which I held for a year, only because I worked hard and productively when I worked, and because my very tolerant chief ascribed my frequent lapses to a bohemian temperament. When it was closed through Washington edict I began with Federal Writers in San Antonio. In those days my system was always to drink up my last pay check and believe that necessity would bring the next job. A friend who knew I would soon be broke mounted guard over me when I left my job of writing the histories of Texas cities and put me aboard a bus for the town I had left almost five years before.

In five years a good many persons had forgotten that I had been somewhat notorious. I arrived drunk, but I promised my wife I would keep sober, and I knew I could get work if I did. Of course I didn't keep sober. My wife and family stood by me for ten weeks and then, quite justifiably, ejected me. I managed to maintain myself with odd jobs, did ten weeks in a social rescue institution, and at length wound up in a second-hand bookstore in an adjacent town as manager. While there I was called to the hospital in my home town to see a former partner who had insisted that I visit him. I found my friend was there for alcoholism and now he was insisting that he had found the only cure. I listened to him, rather tolerantly. I noticed a Bible on his table and it amazed me. I had never known him to be anything but a good healthy pagan with a propensity for getting into liquor jams and scrapes. As he talked I gathered vaguely, (because he was a faltering beginner then, just as I am now) that to be relieved of alcoholism I would have to be different.

Some days later, after he had been discharged, a stranger came into my shop in the nearby town. He introduced himself and began to tell me about a bunch of some sixty former drinkers and drunkards who met once a week, and he invited me to go with him to the next meeting. I thanked him, pleaded business engagements and promised I'd go with him at some future date.

"Anyhow, I'm on the wagon now," I said. "I'm doing a job I like and it's quiet where I live, practically no temptations. I don't feel bothered about liquor."

He looked at me quizzically. He knew too well that it didn't mean a thing, just as I knew in my heart that it would be only a question of time–a few days, a week, or even a month, it was inevitable–till I would be off on another bender. The time came just a week later. As I look back on the events of two months, I can clearly see that I had been circling around, half-afraid of encountering the remedy for my situation, half wanting it, deferring fulfillment of my promise to get in touch with the doctor I had heard about. An accident while drunk laid me low for about three weeks. As soon as I could get up and walk I started to drink again and kept it up until my friend of the hospital, who, in his first try at the new way of life had stubbed his toe in Chicago but had come back to the town to take counsel and make a new start, picked me up and got me into a hospital.

I had been drinking heavily from one state of semicoma to another and it was several days before I got "defogged," but subconsciously I was in earnest about wanting to quit liquor forever. It was no momentary emotionalism born of self-pity in a maudlin condition. I was seeking something and I was ready to learn. I did not need to be told that my efforts were and would be unavailing if I did not get help. The doctor who came to see me almost at once did not assail me with any new doctrines; he made sure that I had a need and that I wanted to have that need filled, and little by little I learned how my need could be met. The story of Alcoholics Anonymous fascinated me. Singly and in groups of two or three, they came to visit me. Some of them I had known for years, good two-fisted drinkers who had disappeared from their former haunts. I had missed them myself from the barrooms of the town.

There were business men, professional men, and factory workers. All sorts were represented and their relation of experiences and how they had found the only remedy, added to their human existence as sober men, laid the foundation of a very necessary faith. Indeed, I was beginning to see that I would require implicit faith, like a small child, if I was going to get anywhere. The big thing was that these men were all sober and evidently had something I didn't have. Whatever it was, I wanted it.

I left the hospital on a meeting night. I was greeted warmly, honestly, and with a true ring of sincerity by everyone present. That night I was taken home by a former alcoholic and his wife. They did not show me to my room and wish me a good night's rest. Instead, over coffee cups, this man and his wife told me what had been done for them. They were earnest and obviously trying to help me on the road I had chosen. They will never know how much their talk with me helped. The hospitality of their home and their fine fellowship were freely mine.

I had never, since the believing days of childhood, been able to conceive an authority directing the universe. But I had never been a flippant, wise-cracking sneerer at the few persons I had met who had impressed me as Christian men and women, or at any institution whose sincerity of purpose I could see. No conviction was necessary to establish my status as a miserable failure at managing my own life. I began to read the Bible daily and to go over a simple devotional exercise as a way to begin each day. Gradually I began to understand.

I cannot say that my taste for liquor has entirely disappeared. It has been that way with some, but it has not been with me and may never be. Neither can I honestly say that I have forgotten the "fleshpots of Egypt." I haven't. But I can remember the urge of the Prodigal Son to return to his Father.

Formerly, in the acute mental and physical pain during the remorseful periods succeeding each drunk, I found my recollection of the misery I had gone through a bolsterer of resolution and afterward, perhaps, a deterrent for a time. But in those days I had no one to whom I might take my troubles. Today I have. Today I have Someone who will always hear me; I have a warm fellowship among men who understand my problems; I have tasks to do and am glad to do them, to see others who are alcoholics and to help them in any way I can to become sober men. I took my last drink in 1937.

(8) FROM FARM TO CITY

She tells how A.A. works when the going is rough. A pioneer woman member of A.A.'s first Group.

I COME FROM a very poor family in material things, with a fine Christian mother, but with no religious background. I was the oldest in a family of seven, and my father was an alcoholic. I was deprived of many of the things that we feel are important in life, such as education particularly, because of my father's drinking. Mine was far from a happy childhood. I had none of those things that children should have to make them happy.

We moved in from the country at the age when girls want all sorts of nice things. I remember starting to city school, coming from a country school, and wanting so very, very much to be like the other girls and trying flour on my face for powder because I wasn't able to have any real powder. I remember feeling that they were all making fun of me. I feared that I wasn't dressed like the rest. I know that one of the outfits I had was a skirt and a very funny looking blouse that my mother had picked up at a rummage sale. I look back and remember these things because they made me very unhappy, and added to my feeling of inferiority at never being the same as other people.

At the age of sixteen, I was invited to spend the summer with an aunt and I, very delightedly, accepted the invitation. It was a small town–Liberty, Indiana. When I came to my aunt, she knew that I had had an unhappy childhood, and she said, "Now, Ethel, you're welcome to have boy friends in our home, but there are two boys in this town that I don't want you to date, and one of them comes from a very fine family, one of the best. But he's in all sorts of scrapes because he drinks too much." Four months later, I married this guy. I'm sure his family felt that it was a marriage that–well, I was a girl from the wrong side of the tracks–definitely!

I felt that his family were accepting me because it was good sense. I could do something for their Russ. But they didn't do anything for me to build up my ego. And Russ didn't tell me he'd stop drinking, and he certainly didn't stop. It went on and grew worse and worse. We had two daughters. I was sixteen when we were married and he was seven years older. I remember one instance when he took off and went down to Cincinnati and was gone for a week on a drunk.

Finally, it got so bad that I left him and went back home and took my two children with me. I didn't see him for a year, or even hear from him. That was seven or eight years after we were married. I was still bitter because I felt that drink had completely ruined my childhood and my married life, and I hated everything pertaining to it. I was about twenty-five then, and I had never touched a drop.

I got a job in the woolen mills in Ravena–very hard work. I looked much older than I was, I was always large, and I went back to work in this job. I kept my children with me. At the end of a year, the children got a card from their father, which I still have and cherish. He said, "Tell Mommy I still love her." I had gone to an attorney to see about getting a divorce during that year.

Then he came into town on the bum. He had taken up light work, and he had a safety valve and a pair of spurs and the clothes on his back, and that was all. I welcomed him with open arms. I didn't realize how I still felt about him. He told me that he would never drink again. And I believed him. As many times as he would tell me that, I still believed him. Partially so, anyway. He got a job and went back to work.

He stayed "dry" for thirteen years! Dr. Bob often said that it was a record for what he felt was a typical alcoholic.

We built up a splendid life. At the end of those thirteen years I never dreamed that he'd ever take another drink. I had never taken one. Our oldest daughter got married; they were living at our house. Our other daughter was in her last year of high school, and one night the new son-in-law and my husband went out to the prize fight. I never was concerned anymore, anywhere he went. He hardly ever went to anything like that without me. We were together all the time, but this night I got up and saw it was late. I heard my son-in-law coming upstairs, and I asked him where dad was. He had a very peculiar look on his face, and he said, "He's coming." He *was* coming, on his hands and knees, up the stairs. As I look back, I was very broken up about it. But I don't believe now that it was with any deep feeling of resentment that I said to him, "The children are raised, and if this is the way you want it, this is the way we'll have it. Where you go, I'll go, and what you drink, I'll drink." That's when I started drinking.

We were the most congenial drinkers you ever saw. We never rowed or fought. We had the grandest time ever. We just loved it. We'd start out on the craziest trips. He'd always say, "Take me for a ride, Ma." So, sometimes we'd end up in Charleston, West Virginia, or here or there, drinking all along the way. These vacations became quite something, and he always had two weeks vacation the first two weeks of every September.

One year we got as far as Bellaire, Ohio. We always started out on the Saturday before Labor Day. I'm pretty near afraid of Labor Day yet. One Sunday afternoon, the only time I ever got picked up for drunken driving, I got picked up in Bellaire. They threw us in the jail. I wasn't nearly in the condition I had been in many times to be picked up. I really wasn't very high. They called the Mayor in so we wouldn't have to stay in there over the holiday. He took his one hundred and seventeen dollars and let us go, and we proceeded. That to me was the greatest humiliation, to think that I'd finally landed in jail. My husband said that I said, "Can you imagine them giving us that jail fare?" And he said, "What jail fare?" And I said, "Well, they brought a pitcher of coffee, and a sandwich wrapped up for me." And he said, "That wasn't jail fare. They didn't give me anything to eat. Somebody must have taken pity on you and gone out and got it for you." And another thing, it's a wonder they didn't throw us back in because I could become very dignified and sarcastic. As we left, and they were escorting us across the bridge into Wheeling, I, with great dignity and sarcasm, told them if their wives were ever visiting in Akron, and they, too, were looking for their route signs as I was, that I hoped that I could extend to them the hospitality that had been shown to me in Bellaire.

The next time vacation time rolled around that was a bitter lesson to us. Of course, this year we were drinking heavier and heavier and we decided on staying home and being sensible, doing a little drinking, and painting the house. So, on that Saturday before Labor Day, I got drunk and set the house on fire–so we didn't have to paint it. I think that was the last vacation before sobriety.

I hated myself worse and worse, and as I hated myself I became more defiant towards everything and everybody. We drank with exactly the same accord that we finally accepted A.A. We comforted each other.

My defiant attitude became worse. There was a very religious family that lived down the road from us, and we were on the same party line. I'd hear them on the phone having prayer meetings and so forth, that sort of talk over the phone, and it completely burnt me up. They used a sound truck some. It would stop out in front of our house, and I still believe those people sent it! They'd sit out there and play hymns and I'd be lying in there with a terrific hangover. If I'd had a gun I'd have shot the horns right off the thing, because it made me raving mad.

It was just about this time, in 1940, that we met up with A.A. Russ read a piece in the paper, and he kind of snickered, and said, "See here, where John D. has found something to keep him from drinking!" "What's that?" I said. "Oh, some darn thing they've got here in the paper about it." We talked about it afterwards, and we felt that there might be some time we'd need it. It was a thought that there might be some hope for us.

One morning after a terrific drinking bout, I was in a little bar near our house, and I shook so that I was very much ashamed, because I was getting the shakes worse and worse. I sipped the drink off the bar because I couldn't hold it in my hand, but I was still a lady, believe it or not, and I was deeply ashamed. There was a man watching, and I turned to him and said, with a defiant air I carried with me all the time, "If I don't quit this I'm going to have to join that alcoholic business they're talking about." He said, "Sister, if you think you're a screwball now, all you have to do is join up with that. I'll get you the password, and I can find out where they meet because I know a guy that belongs. But they are the craziest bunch! They roll on the floor and holler, and pull their hair." "Well, I'm nuts enough now," I said to him. But right then the hope died that had been in my heart when we read about John D.

Time went on and the drinking got worse and worse, and I was in another barroom, down the road the other way, a small one, and I took my glass–that morning I'd been able to lift it from the bar–and I said to the woman behind the bar, "I wish I might never take another drop of that stuff. It's killing me." She said, "Do you really mean that?" I said, "Yes." She said, "Well, you better talk to Jack." (Jack was the owner of the place. We always tried to buy him a drink, and he always told us he had liquor trouble–couldn't drink.) She said to me, "You know, he used to own the Merry-Go-Round. He used to drink, and then he found something that started up in Akron that helped him quit drinking." Right away, I saw it was the same outfit this other guy told me about, and then again hope died.

Finally, one morning, I got up and got in the car and cried all the way down to the M.'s–the people who owned the bar–and told her I was licked and wanted help. I thought, "No matter how crazy they are I'll do anything they say to do." I drove these three or four miles down the road only to find that Jack was out. (This was funny. They owned this joint, she ran it, and he sold for a brewery. That was his job. And he'd been dry a year. I don't think Jack was hospitalized. I think his entry into A.A. was through spending some hours with Dr. Bob at his office. He brought many people into A.A. through his barroom.) Mrs. M. said she would send Jack over as quick as he came in.

He came with two cans of beer. He gave my husband one and me one about ten-thirty on the eighth day of May in 1941. He said, "There's a doctor here in Akron. I'm going in to see him, and see what can be done." Dr. Bob was in Florida, but Jack didn't know that.

That was our last drink of anything alcoholic. That nasty little can of beer! At two-forty-five that morning I thought I would die. I lay across the bed on my stomach with nothing but pain and sickness. I was scared to death to call a doctor. I thought when people did what we did that they just locked them up. I didn't know that anything was ever done for them in a medical way. So I stayed awake.

Men from A.A. started coming out to the house the next day. I paced the floor with a bath towel around my shoulders, the perspiration running off me. An attorney sat at the side of the bed where I was lying, and he sat on the edge of his chair and looked as innocent as a baby. I thought, "That guy never could have been drunk." He said, "This is my story,"–real prim. And I thought, "I bet he's a sissy. I bet he never drank." But he told a story of drinking that was amazing to me.

Jack brought the Saturday Post with Jack Alexander's story. He said, "Read this." Jack didn't seem to have too much of the spiritual understanding. He said, "I think this will tell you more. This is based, really, on the Sermon on the Mount. Now, if you've got a Bible around..." One of our gifts from the family was a very lovely Bible, but we'd let the bulldog chew it because we weren't too interested in it. I had a little Testament, which was very small print. When you have a hangover and can't even sit still, try to read small print! Russ said, "Mother, if this tells us how to do it, you'll have to read it." And I'd try, but I couldn't even see the letters. But it was so important that we do the things we were told to do! Jack said there was a meeting in Akron every Wednesday night and that it was very important that we go. Jack said, "Now you start and go to these meetings, and then you'll find out all about it." I don't think that there was anything said about religion. I didn't know anything about the Sermon on the Mount.

I had the Big Book (Alcoholics Anonymous) that had been brought to me. Paul S. had just called me, and I remember he stressed reading the Big Book. I was reading it for all that was in it, and I said to Russ, "We can't do this. We couldn't begin to." And Jim G. had such a wonderful sense of humor, and when he came I was in tears, and I told him, "I want to do this, but I can't. This is too much. I could never go and make up to all the people I've done wrong to." He said, "Let's put the Big Book away again, and when you read it again, turn to the back and read some of the stories. Have you read those?" No, I was all interested in this part that told you how to do it. That was the only part I was interested in. And then he got us to laugh, which was what we needed. When we went to bed my sides ached, and I said to my husband, "I thought I would never laugh again, but I have laughed."

"Well," I said to dad, when the A.A. people kept coming with these lovely cars and looked so nice, "I suppose the neighbors say, 'Now those old fools must have up and died, but where's the hearse?'"

On Wednesday night Jack M. said, "You meet me at the Ohio Edison Building, and I will take you to the meeting." And we went down through the valley, and I remembered reading about the Ku Klux Klan and how they burnt crosses, and I thought, "God alone knows what we are getting into this time!" I didn't know what they were going to do because he didn't tell us much. So we came to King's School. And they introduced me to Miriam and Annabelle. They told Annabelle to take me under her wing, and I shall never forget how she sort of curled up her nose and said, "They tell me you drink too." I often think how that could have turned some people away, because there were no other women alcoholics there then. And I said, "Why sure, that's what I'm here for." And I was glad, and I have been ever since, that I said that. And I wasn't resentful toward her, either.

There was a young fellow who led the meeting and that was a beautiful thing to me. He talked about his wife taking his little boy away from him because of his drinking, and how he got back together with them through A.A., and we began feeling grateful right then that all these things hadn't been taken from us. They opened with a little prayer, and I thought it was very fine that we stood, all of us together, and closed with the Lord's Prayer.

I'd like to say here how important it was to us then that we do all the little things that people said were important, because later when Russ was so sick that I had to hold him up, they had a meeting out at the house. When we closed the meeting with the Lord's Prayer, Russ said, "Mother, help me stand." This was after his illness. We were in A.A. three and a half years when he was taken from me. We had never missed a Wednesday night at King's School for a year. We had that record.

I always feel that our God consciousness was a steady growth after we became associated with A.A. And we loved every minute of that association. We had big picnics out at the house with A.A. We had meetings at each other's homes and, of course, that was a grand place for people to get together out there; they seemed to think so too.

I give a great deal of credit to Doc and Anne for changing our life. They spent at least an evening a week in our home out there for weeks and weeks. Sometimes saying very little, but letting us say. Russ used to be very much pleased because he'd say, "I think Dr. Bob thoroughly enjoys coming out here. He can relax and it's quiet."

At that time they didn't let us know that people ever had trouble. I mean slips. I remember sometime, it was possibly six months after we had been going steadily to King's School, that we were coming home from a meeting and saw a car along the way, and a fellow in back drinking a bottle of beer. And Russ said, "I would have sworn that was Jack M." The next morning his wife came dragging him in before Russ went to work, while I was getting breakfast. It had been Jack M. We wept and Russ didn't go to work.

Jack had been sober about a year and a half. His wife was cussing him, raving at him, "I just brought him over to show you what kind of a guy he is! He wants to go to the hospital, and I'm not paying for the hospital again!" We were so mad at her because she talked to him that way. Russ said, "Don't do another thing today but help him. *Do* something for him! If he thinks he needs to go to the hospital, I'll pay for him." She said, "He's not going to the hospital, whether you pay for it or I pay for it, he's not going!"

In the spiritual strength I had found, because of A.A., I finally felt that I had made a complete surrender, that I had really turned my life over that summer. I thought I had done that until Russ' second collapse, and the doctor told me very candidly that he wasn't long for this world. I knew then that I hadn't made a complete surrender, because I tried to bargain with the God I had found, and I said, "Anything but that! Don't do that to me!"

Russ lived a year longer than they expected him to live, and in that year he was in bed for at least six months. I can't express what A.A. meant to us during that year. Before the end finally came, I had, I guess, made the surrender because I finally had been able to say that I would not mind too much. And I realize that there was one salvation for me. Thank God I had no desire for a drink when he died.

There were two women in the St. Thomas Hospital at that time in a room. (Russ was buried on Friday, and on Sunday afternoon Hilda S. had invited me there to dinner Sunday night, and I didn't think I could do it. I knew Doc and Anne were going to be there, and all of them thought it would be good for me, but the first thing I did was to go to St. Thomas and try to talk to those women.) I sat down on the side of one of their beds, and I started to weep, and I couldn't stop, and I was startled, and I apologized again and again for it. And that woman told me long after that was the surest proof to her that this program could work. If, on Sunday, I could be there, trying to think of something that would help her with this problem, then we must have something that could work. I felt it certainly must be very depressing to her that I should sit there by her bedside and cry.

I feel that one of the things that I still have to guard against is that I used to be set in my way about what I considered the old-time A.A. I have to tell myself, "Other things are progressing and A.A. must too." We old-timers who get scattered and separated and then witness the construction of services to get in more people and to make this thing function, we think that A.A. has changed, but the root of it hasn't. We are older in A.A., and we're older in years. It's only natural that we don't have the capacity to change, but we ought not to criticize those who have.

There's another thing I would stress. I think it's awfully hard on people, especially if they're new people, to hear these long drawn out talks. I don't ever remember that I was bored myself when we first came in, and they came out to the house and talked to us about these things. I ate up every bit of it, because I wanted to find out how to stay sober.

Before I stop–I always was a great talker–I want to say that nobody will ever know how I miss Annie's advice about things. I would get in the biggest dither about something. I hadn't been in too long when one of the men's wives called me one Sunday and told me she didn't think I had any part of the program. Well, I wasn't sure I did, and it was awful foggy, and I wept and asked her what she thought I ought to do about it. She said she didn't know, but that I sure showed plain enough I didn't have any part of it. I didn't think I was going to get drunk right then, but I remember how comforting it was when I called Anne and told her. I was crying, and I said, "Alice says she knows I don't have any part of the program." She talked to me and laughed about it and got me all over it. Another thing that was helpful to me. I used to think I was cowardly because when things came out pertaining to the program that troubled me, I said to her many times, "Annie, am I being a coward because I lay those things away on the shelf and skip it?" She said, "I feel you're just being wise. If it isn't anything that's going to help you or anybody else, why should you become involved in it, and get all disturbed about it?"

So there you are. That's my story. I know I've talked too long, but I always do. And, anyhow, if I went on for ten or a hundred times as long I couldn't even begin to tell you all that A.A. has meant to me.

(9) THE MAN WHO MASTERED FEAR

He spent eighteen years in running away, and then found he didn't have to run. So he started A.A. in Detroit.

FOR EIGHTEEN YEARS, from the time I was twenty-one, fear governed my life. By the time I was thirty, I had found that alcohol dissolved fear–for a little while. In the end I had two problems instead of one: fear and alcohol.

I came from a good family. I believe the sociologists would call it upper middle class. By the time I was twenty-one, I had had six years of life in foreign countries, spoke three languages fluently, and had attended college for two years. A low ebb in the family fortunes necessitated my going to work when I was twenty. I entered the business world with every confidence that success lay ahead of me. I had been brought up to believe this, and I had shown during my teens considerable enterprise and imagination about earning money. To the best of my recollection, I was completely free from any abnormal fears. Vacations from school and from work spelled "travel" to me–and I traveled with gusto. During my first year out of college, I had endless dates and went to countless dances, balls, and dinner parties.

Suddenly all this changed. I underwent a shattering nervous breakdown. Three months in bed. Three more months of being up and around the house for brief periods and in bed the rest of the time. Visits from friends which lasted over fifteen minutes exhausted me. A complete checkup at one of the best hospitals revealed nothing. I heard for the first time an expression that I was to grow to loathe: "There is nothing organically wrong." Psychiatry might have helped, but psychiatrists had not penetrated the Middle West.

Spring came. I went for my first walk. Half a block from my house, I tried to turn the corner. Fear froze me in my tracks, but the instant I turned back toward home, this paralyzing fear left me. This was the beginning of an unending series of such experiences. I told our family doctor–an understanding man who gave hours of his time trying to help me–about this experience. He told me that it was imperative that I walk around the entire block, cost me what it might in mental agony. I carried out his instructions. When I reached a point directly back of our house, where I could have cut through a friend's garden, I was almost overpowered by the desire to get home, but I made the whole journey. Probably only a few readers of this story will be able, from personal experiences of their own, to understand the exhilaration and sense of accomplishment I felt after finishing this seemingly simple assignment.

The details of the long road back to something resembling normal living–the first short streetcar ride, the purchase of a used bike, which enabled me to widen the narrow horizon of life, the first trip downtown–I will not dwell on. I got an easy, part-time job selling printing for a small neighborhood printer. This widened the scope of my activities. A year later I was able to buy a Model T roadster and take a better job with a downtown printer. From this job and the next one with yet another printer, I was courteously dismissed. I simply did not have the pep to do hard, "cold-turkey" selling. I switched into real estate brokerage and property management work. Almost simultaneously, I discovered that cocktails in the late afternoon and highballs in the evening relieved the many tensions of the day. This happy combination of pleasant work and alcohol lasted for five years. Of course, the latter ultimately killed the former, but of this, more anon.

All this changed when I was thirty years old. My parents died, both in the same year, leaving me, a sheltered and somewhat immature man, on my own. I moved into a "bachelor hall." These men all drank on Saturday nights and enjoyed themselves. My pattern of drinking became very different from theirs. I had bad, nervous headaches, particularly at the base of my neck. Liquor relieved these. At last I discovered alcohol as a cure-all. I joined their Saturday night parties and enjoyed myself too. But I also stayed up week nights after they had retired and drank myself into bed. My thinking about drinking had undergone a great change. Liquor had become a crutch on the one hand and a means of retreat from life on the other.

The ensuing nine years were the Depression years, both nationally and personally. With the bravery born of desperation, and abetted by alcohol, I married a young and lovely girl. Our marriage lasted four years. At least three of those four years must have been a living hell for my wife, because she had to watch the man she loved disintegrate morally, mentally and financially. The birth of a baby boy did nothing toward staying the downward spiral. When she finally took the baby and left, I locked myself in the house and stayed drunk for a month.

The next two years were simply a long, drawn-out process of less and less work and more and more whiskey. I ended up homeless, jobless, penniless, and rudderless, as the problem guest of a close friend whose family was out of town. Haunting me through each day's stupor–and there were eighteen or nineteen such days in this man's home–was the thought: "Where do I go when his family comes home?" When the day of their return was almost upon me, and suicide was the only answer I had been able to think of, I went into Ralph's room one evening and told him the truth. He was a man of considerable means, and he might have done what many men would have done in such a case. He might have handed me fifty dollars and said that I ought to pull myself together and make a new start. I have thanked God many times in the last sixteen years that *that* was just what he did not do!

Instead, he got dressed, took me out, bought me three or four double shots, and put me to bed. The next day he turned me over to a couple who, although neither was an alcoholic, knew Dr. Bob and were willing to drive me to Akron where they would turn me over to his care. The only stipulation they made was this: I had to make the decision myself. What decision? The choice was limited. To go north into the empty pine country and shoot myself, or to go south in the faint hope that a bunch of strangers might help me with my drinking problem. Well, suicide was a last-straw matter, and I had not drawn the last straw yet. So I was driven to Akron the very next day by these Good Samaritans and turned over to Dr. Bob and the then tiny Akron Group.

Here, while in a hospital bed, men with clear eyes, happy faces, and a look of assurance and purposefulness about them came to see me and told me their stories. Some of these were hard to believe, but it did not require a giant brain to perceive that they had something I could use. How could I get it? It was simple, they said, and went on to explain to me in their own language the program of recovery and daily living which we know today as the Twelve Steps of A.A. Dr. Bob dwelt at length on how prayer had given him release, time and time again, from the nearly overpowering compulsion to take a drink. It was he who convinced me, because his own conviction was so real, that a Power greater than myself could help me in the crises of life and that the means of communicating with this Power was simple prayer. Here was a tall, rugged, highly educated Yankee talking in a matter-of-course way about God and prayer. If he and these other fellows could do it, so could I.

When I got out of the hospital, I was invited to stay with Dr. Bob and his dear wife, Anne. I was suddenly and uncontrollably seized with the old, paralyzing panic. The hospital had seemed so safe. Now I was in a strange house, in a strange city, and fear gripped me. I shut myself in my room, which began to go around in circles. Panic, confusion and chaos were supreme. Out of this maelstrom just two coherent thoughts came to the surface; one, a drink would mean homelessness and death; two, I could no longer relieve the pressure of fear by starting home, as was once my habitual solution to this problem, because I no longer had a home. Finally, and I shall never know how much later it was, one clear thought came to me: Try prayer. You can't lose, and maybe God will help you–just maybe, mind you. Having no one else to turn to, I was willing to give Him a chance, although with considerable doubt. I got down on my knees for the first time in thirty years. The prayer I said was simple. It went something like this: "God, for eighteen years I have been unable to handle this problem. Please let me turn it over to you."

Immediately a great feeling of peace descended upon me, intermingled with a feeling of being suffused with a quiet strength. I lay down on the bed and slept like a child. An hour later I awoke to a new world. *Nothing had changed and yet everything had changed.* The scales had dropped from my eyes, and I could see life in its proper perspective. I had tried to be the center of my own little world, whereas God was the center of a vast universe of which I was perhaps an essential, but a very tiny, part.

It is well over sixteen years since I came back to life. I have never had a drink since. This alone is a miracle. It is, however, only the first of a series of miracles which have followed one another as a result of my trying to apply to my daily life the principles embodied in our Twelve Steps. I would like to sketch for you the highlights of these sixteen years of a slow but steady and satisfying upward climb.

Poor health and a complete lack of money necessitated my remaining with Dr. Bob and Anne for very close to a year. It would be impossible for me to pass over this year without mentioning my love for, and my indebtedness to, these two wonderful people who are no longer with us. They made me feel as if I were a part of their family, and so did their children. The example which they and Bill W., whose visits to Akron were fairly frequent, set me of service to their fellow men imbued me with a great desire to emulate them. Sometimes during that year I rebelled inwardly at what seemed like lost time and at having to be a burden to these good people whose means were limited. Long before I had any real opportunity to give, I had to learn the equally important lesson of receiving graciously.

During my first few months in Akron, I was quite sure that I never wanted to see my hometown again. Too many economic and social problems would beset me there. I would make a fresh start somewhere else. After six months of sobriety, I saw the picture in a different light: Detroit was the place I had to return to, not only because I must face the mess I had made there, but because it was there that I could be of the most service to A.A. In the spring of 1939, Bill stopped off in Akron on his way to Detroit on business. I jumped at the suggestion that I accompany him. We spent two days there together before he returned to New York. Friends invited me to stay on for as long as I cared to. I remained with them for three weeks, using part of the time in making many amends, which I had had no earlier opportunity of making.

The rest of my time was devoted to A.A. spadework. I wanted "ripe" prospects, and I didn't feel that I would get very far chasing individual drunks in and out of bars. So I spent much of my time calling on the people who I felt would logically come in contact with alcoholic cases–doctors, ministers, lawyers, and the personnel men in industry. I also talked A.A. to every friend who would listen, at lunch, at dinner, on street corners. A doctor tipped me off to my first prospect. I landed him and shipped him by train to Akron, with a pint of whiskey in his pocket to keep him from wanting to get off the train in Toledo! Nothing has ever to this day equaled the thrill of that first case.

Those three weeks left me completely exhausted, and I had to return to Akron for three more months of rest. While there, two or three more "cash customers" (as Dr. Bob used to call them–probably because they had so little cash) were shipped in to us from Detroit. When I finally returned to Detroit to find work and to learn to stand on my own feet, the ball was already rolling, however slowly. But it took six more months of work and disappointments before a group of three men got together in my rooming-house bedroom for their first A.A. meeting.

It sounds simple, but there were obstacles and doubts to overcome. I well remember a session I had with myself soon after I returned. It ran something like this: If I go around shouting from the rooftops about my alcoholism, it might very possibly prevent me from getting a good job. But *supposing that just one man died* because I had, for selfish reasons, kept my mouth shut? No. I was supposed to be doing God's will, not mine. His road lay clear before me, and I'd better quit rationalizing myself into any detours. I could not expect to keep what I had gained unless I gave it away.

The Depression was still on and jobs were scarce. My health was still uncertain. So I created a job for myself selling women's hosiery and men's made-to-order shirts. This gave me the freedom to do A.A. work and to rest for periods of two or three days when I became too exhausted to carry on. There was more than one occasion when I got up in the morning with just enough money for coffee and toast and the bus fare to carry me to my first appointment. No sale–no lunch. During that first year, however, I managed to make both ends meet and to avoid ever going back to my old habit-pattern of borrowing money when I could not earn it. Here by itself was a great step forward.

During the first three months, I carried on all these activities without a car, depending entirely on buses and streetcars–I, who had always to have a car at my immediate command. I, who had never made a speech in my life and who would have been frightened sick at the prospect, stood up in front of Rotary groups in different parts of the city and talked about Alcoholics Anonymous. I, carried away with the desire to serve A.A., gave what was probably one of the first radio broadcasts about A.A., living through a case of mike fright and feeling like a million dollars when it was all over. I lived through a week of the fidgets because I had agreed to address a group of alcoholic inmates in one of our state mental hospitals. There was the same reward–exhilaration at a mission accomplished. Do I have to tell you who gained the most out of all this?

Within a year of my return to Detroit, A.A. was a definitely established little group of about a dozen members, and I too was established in a modest but steady job handling an independent dry-cleaning route of my own. I was my own boss. It took five years of A.A. living, and a substantial improvement in my health, before I could take a full-time office job where someone else was boss.

This office job brought me face to face with a problem that I had sidestepped all my adult life, lack of training. This time I did something about it. I enrolled in a correspondence school that taught nothing but accounting. With this specialized training, and a liberal business education in the school of hard knocks, I was able to set up a shop some two years later as an independent accountant. Seven years of work in this field brought an opportunity to affiliate myself actively with one of my clients, a fellow A.A. We complement each other beautifully, as he is a born salesman and my taste is for finance and management. At long last I am doing the kind of work I have always wanted to do but never had the patience and emotional stability to train myself for. The A.A. program showed me the way to come down to earth, start from the bottom, and work up. This represents another great change for me. In the long ago past I used to start at the top as president or treasurer and end up with the sheriff breathing down my neck.

So much for my business life. Obviously I have overcome fear to a sufficient degree to think in terms of success in business. With God's help I am able, for one day at a time, to carry business responsibilities that, not many years ago, I would not have dreamed of assuming. But what about my social life? What about those fears which once paralyzed me to the point of my becoming a semi-hermit? What about my fear of travel?

It would be wonderful were I able to tell you that my confidence in God and my application of the Twelve Steps to my daily living have utterly banished fear. But this would not be the truth. The most accurate answer I *can* give you is this: Fear has never again ruled my life since that day in September 1938, when I found that a Power greater than myself could not only restore me to sanity but could keep me both sober and sane. Never in sixteen years have I dodged anything because I was afraid of it. I have faced life instead of running away from it.

Some of the things that used to stop me in my tracks from fear still make me nervous in the anticipation of their doing, but once I kick myself into doing them, nervousness disappears and I enjoy myself. In recent years I have had the happy combination of time and money to travel occasionally. I am very apt to get into quite an uproar for a day or two before starting, but I *do* start, and once started, I have a swell time.

Have I ever wanted a drink during these years? Only once did I suffer from a nearly overpowering compulsion to take a drink. Oddly enough, the circumstances and surroundings were pleasant. I was at a beautifully set dinner table. I was in a perfectly happy frame of mind. I had been in A.A. a year, and the last thing in my mind was a drink. There was a glass of sherry at my place. I was seized with an almost uncontrollable desire to reach out for it. I shut my eyes and asked for help. In fifteen seconds or less, the feeling passed. There have also been numerous times when I have thought about taking a drink. Such thinking usually began with thoughts of the pleasant drinking of my youth. I learned early in my A.A. life that I could not afford to fondle such thoughts, as you might fondle a pet, because this particular pet could grow into a monster. Instead, I quickly substitute one or another vivid scene from the nightmare of my later drinking.

Twenty-odd years ago I made a mess out of my one and only marriage. It was therefore not extraordinary that I should shy away from any serious thought of marriage for a great many years after joining A.A. Here was something requiring a greater willingness to assume responsibility and a larger degree of cooperation and "give and take" than even business requires of one. However, I must have felt, deep down inside myself, that living the selfish life of a bachelor was only half living. By living alone you can pretty much eliminate grief from your life, but you also eliminate joy. At any rate the last great step toward a well-rounded life still lay ahead of me. So six months ago I acquired a ready-made family consisting of one charming wife, four grown children to whom I am devoted, and three grandchildren. Being an alcoholic, I couldn't dream of doing anything by halves! My wife, a sister member in A.A., had been a widow nine years and I had been single eighteen years. The adjustments in such a case are difficult and take time, but we both feel that they are certainly worth it. We are both depending upon God and our use of the A.A. program to help us make a success of this joint undertaking.

It is undoubtedly too soon for me to say how much of a success I shall be as a husband in time to come. I do feel, though, that the fact that I finally *grew up* to a point where I could even tackle such a job is the apex of the story of a man who spent eighteen years running away from life.

(10) HE SOLD HIMSELF SHORT

But he found that there was a Higher Power that had more faith in him than he had in himself. Thus, A.A. was born in Chicago.

I GREW UP in a small town outside Akron, Ohio, where the life was typical of any average small town. I was very much interested in athletics, and because of this and parental influence, I didn't drink or smoke in either grade or high school.

All of this changed when I went to college. I had to adapt to new associations and associates, and it seemed to be the smart thing to drink and smoke. I confined drinking to weekends, and drank normally in college and for several years thereafter.

After I left school, I went to work in Akron, living at home with my parents. Home life was again a restraining influence. When I drank, I hid it from my folks out of respect for their feelings. This continued until I was twenty-seven. Then I started traveling, with the United States and Canada as my territory, and with so much freedom and with an unlimited expense account, I was soon drinking every night and kidding myself that it was all part of the job. I know now that 60 percent of the time I drank alone without benefit of customers.

In 1930, I moved to Chicago. Shortly thereafter, aided by the Depression, I found that I had a great deal of spare time and that a little drink in the morning helped. By 1932, I was going on two or three day benders. That same year, my wife became fed up with my drinking around the house and called my Dad in Akron to come and pick me up. She asked him to do something about me because she couldn't. She was thoroughly disgusted.

This was the beginning of five years of bouncing back and forth between my home in Chicago and Akron to sober up. It was a period of binges coming closer and closer together and being of longer duration. Once Dad came all the way to Florida to sober me up after a hotel manager called him and said that if he wanted to see me alive he better get there fast. My wife could not understand why I would sober up for Dad but not for her. They went into a huddle, and Dad explained that he simply took my pants, shoes, and money away so that I could get no liquor and had to sober up.

One time my wife decided to try this too. After finding every bottle that I had hidden around the apartment, she took away my pants, my shoes, my money, and my keys, threw them under the bed in the back bedroom, and slip-locked our door. By 1 a.m. I was desperate. I found some wool stockings, some white flannels that had shrunk to my knees, and an old jacket. I jimmied the front door so that I could get back in, and walked out. I was hit by an icy blast. It was February with snow and ice on the ground and I had a four-block walk to the nearest cab stand, but I made it. On my ride to the nearest bar, I sold the driver on how misunderstood I was by my wife and what an unreasonable person she was. By the time we reached the bar, he was willing to buy me a quart with his own money. Then when we got back to the apartment, he was willing to wait two or three days until I got my health back to be paid off for the liquor and fare. I was a good salesman. My wife could not understand the next morning why I was drunker than the night before, when she took my bottles.

After a particularly bad Christmas and New Year's holiday, Dad picked me up again early in January 1937 to go through the usual sobering up routine. This consisted of walking the floor for three or four days and nights until I could take nourishment. This time he had a suggestion to offer. He waited until I was completely sober, and on the day before I was to head back for Chicago, he told me of a small group of men in Akron who apparently had the same problem that I had but were doing something about it. He said they were sober, happy, and had their self-respect back, as well as the respect of their neighbors. He mentioned two of them whom I had known through the years and suggested that I talk with them. But I had my health back, and, besides, I reasoned, they were much worse than I would ever be. Why, even a year ago I had seen Howard, an ex-doctor, mooching a dime for a drink. I could not possibly be that bad. I would at least have asked for a quarter! So I told Dad that I would lick it on my own, that I would drink nothing for a month and after that only beer.

Several months later Dad was back in Chicago to pick me up again, but this time my attitude was entirely different. I could not wait to tell him that I wanted help, that if these men in Akron had anything, I wanted it and would do anything to get it. I was completely licked by alcohol.

I can still remember very distinctly getting into Akron at 11 p.m. and routing this same Howard out of bed to do something about me. He spent two hours with me that night telling me his story. He said he had finally learned that drinking was a fatal illness made up of an allergy plus an obsession, and once the drinking had passed from habit to obsession, we were completely hopeless and could look forward only to spending the balance of our lives in mental institutions –or to death.

He laid great stress on the progression of his attitude toward life and people, and most of his attitudes had been very similar to mine. I thought at times that he was telling my story! I had thought that I was completely different from other people, that I was beginning to become a little balmy, even to the point of withdrawing more and more from society and wanting to be alone with my bottle.

Here was a man with essentially the same outlook on life, except that he had done something about it. He was happy, getting a kick out of life and people, and beginning to get his medical practice back again. As I look back on that first evening, I realize that I began to hope, then, for the first time; and I felt that if he could regain these things, perhaps it would be possible for me too.

The next afternoon and evening, two other men visited me and each told me his story and the things that they were doing to try to recover from this tragic illness. They had that certain something that seemed to glow, a peace, a serenity combined with happiness. In the next two or three days the balance of this handful of men contacted me, encouraged me, and told me how they were trying to live this program of recovery and the fun they were having doing it.

Then and then only, after a thorough indoctrination by eight or nine individuals, was I allowed to attend my first meeting. This first meeting was held in the living room of a home and was led by Bill D., the first man that Bill W. and Dr. Bob had worked with successfully.

The meeting consisted of perhaps eight or nine alcoholics and seven or eight wives. It was different from the meetings now held. The big A.A. book had not been written, and there was no literature except various religious pamphlets. The program was carried on entirely by word of mouth.

The meeting lasted an hour and closed with the Lord's Prayer. After it was closed, we all retired to the kitchen and had coffee and doughnuts and more discussion until the small hours of the morning.

I was terribly impressed by this meeting and the quality of happiness these men displayed, despite their lack of material means. In this small group, during the Depression, there was no one who was not hard up.

I stayed in Akron two or three weeks on my initial trip trying to absorb as much of the program and philosophy as possible. I spent a great deal of time with Dr. Bob, whenever he had the time to spare, and in the homes of two or three other people, trying to see how the family lived the program. Every evening we would meet at the home of one of the members and have coffee and doughnuts and spend a social evening.

The day before I was due to go back to Chicago–I was Dr. Bob's afternoon off–he had me down to the office and we spent three or four hours formally going through the Six-Step program as it was at that time. The six steps were:

1. Complete deflation.
2. Dependence and guidance from a Higher Power.
3. Moral inventory.
4. Confession.
5. Restitution.
6. Continued work with other alcoholics.

Dr. Bob led me through all of these steps. At the moral inventory, he brought up some of my bad personality traits or character defects, such as selfishness, conceit, jealousy, carelessness, intolerance, ill-temper, sarcasm, and resentments. We went over these at great length and then he finally asked me if I wanted these defects of character removed. When I said yes, we both knelt at his desk and prayed, each of us asking to have these defects taken away.

This picture is still vivid. If I live to be a hundred, it will always stand out in my mind. It was very impressive, and I wish that every A.A. could have the benefit of this type of sponsorship today. Dr. Bob always emphasized the religious angle very strongly, and I think it helped. I know it helped me. Dr. Bob then led me through the restitution step, in which I made a list of all of the persons I had harmed and worked out ways and means of slowly making restitution.

I made several decisions at that time. One of them was that I would try to get a group started in Chicago; the second was that I would have to return to Akron to attend meetings at least every two months until I did get a group started in Chicago; third, I decided I must place this program above everything else, even my family, because if I did not maintain my sobriety, I would lose my family anyway. If I did not maintain my sobriety, I would not have a job. If I did not maintain my sobriety, I would have no friends left. I had few enough at that time.

The next day I went back to Chicago and started a vigorous campaign among my so-called friends or drinking companions. Their answer was always the same: If they should need it at any time, they would surely get in touch with me. I went to a minister and a doctor whom I still knew, and they, in turn, asked me how long I had been sober. When I told them six weeks, they were polite and said that they would contact me in case they had anyone with an alcoholic problem.

Needless to say, it was a year or more before they did contact me. On my trips back to Akron to get my spirits recharged and to work with other alcoholics, I would ask Dr. Bob about this delay and wonder just what was wrong with me. He would invariably reply, "When you are right and the time is right, Providence will provide. You must always be willing and continue to make contacts."

A few months after I made my original trip to Akron, I was feeling pretty cocky, and I didn't think my wife was treating me with proper respect, now that I was an outstanding citizen. So I set out to get drunk deliberately, just to teach her what she was missing. A week later I had to get an old friend from Akron to spend two days sobering me up. That was my lesson, that one could not take the moral inventory and then file it away; that the alcoholic has to continue to take inventory every day if he expects to get well and stay well. That was my only slip. It taught me a valuable lesson. In the summer of 1938, almost a year from the time I made my original contact with Akron, the man for whom I was working, and who knew about the program, approached me and asked if I could do anything about one of his salesmen who was drinking very heavily. I went to the sanitarium where this chap was incarcerated and found to my surprise that he was interested. He had been wanting to do something about his drinking for a long time but did not know how. I spent several days with him, but I did not feel adequate to pass the program on to him by myself. So I suggested that he take a trip to Akron for a couple of weeks, which he did, living with one of the A.A. families there. When he returned, we had practically daily meetings from that time on.

A few months later one of the men who had been in touch with the group in Akron came to Chicago to live, and then there were three of us who continued to have informal meetings quite regularly.

In the spring of 1939, the Big Book was printed, and we had two inquiries from the New York office because of a fifteen-minute radio talk that was made. Neither one of the two was interested for himself, one being a mother who wanted to do something for her son. I suggested to her that she should see the son's minister or doctor, and that perhaps he would recommend the A.A. program.

The doctor, a young man, immediately took fire with the idea, and while he did not convince the son, he turned over two prospects who were anxious for the program. The three of us did not feel up to the job, and after a few meetings we convinced the prospects that they, too, should go to Akron where they could see an older group in action.

In the meantime, another doctor in Evanston became convinced that the program had possibilities and turned over a woman to us to do something about. She was full of enthusiasm and she made the trip to Akron too. Immediately on her return we began to have formal meetings once a week, in the autumn of 1939, and we have continued to do this and to expand ever since.

Occasionally, it is accorded to a few of us to watch something fine grow from a tiny kernel into something of gigantic goodness. Such has been my privilege, both nationally and in my home city. From a mere handful in Akron, we have spread throughout the world. From a single member in the Chicago area, commuting to Akron, we now exceed six thousand.

These last eighteen years have been the happiest of my life, trite though that statement may seem. Fifteen of those years I would not have enjoyed had I continued drinking. Doctors told me before I stopped that I had only three years at the outside to live.

This latest part of my life has had a purpose, not in great things accomplished but in daily living. Courage to face each day has replaced the fears and uncertainties of earlier years. Acceptance of things as they are has replaced the old impatient champing at the bit to conquer the world. I have stopped tilting at windmills and, instead, have tried to accomplish the little daily tasks, unimportant in themselves, but tasks that are an integral part of living fully.

Where derision, contempt, and pity were once shown me, I now enjoy the respect of many people. Where once I had casual acquaintances, all of whom were fair-weather friends, I now have a host of friends who accept me for what I am. And over my A.A. years I have made many real, honest, sincere friendships that I shall always cherish.

I'm rated as a modestly successful man. My stock of material goods isn't great. But I have a fortune in friendships, courage, self-assurance, and honest appraisal of my own abilities. Above all, I have gained the greatest thing accorded to any man, the love and understanding of a gracious God, who has lifted me from the alcoholic scrap heap to a position of trust, where I have been able to reap the rich rewards that come from showing a little love for others and from serving them as I can.

(11) HOME BREWMEISTER

An originator of Cleveland's Group No. 3, this one fought Prohibition in vain.

STRANGELY ENOUGH, I became acquainted with the "hilarious life" just at the time in my life when I was beginning to really settle down to a common-sense, sane, domestic life. My wife became pregnant and the doctor recommended the use of port or ale... so... I bought a six gallon crock and a few bottles, listened to advice from amateur brewmeisters, and was off on my beer manufacturing career on a small scale (for the time being). Somehow or other, I must have misunderstood the doctor's instructions, for I not only made beer for my wife, I also drank it for her.

As time went on, I found that it was customary to open a few bottles whenever visitors dropped in. That being the case, it didn't take long to figure out that my meager manufacturing facilities were entirely inadequate to the manufacture of beer for social and domestic consumption. From that point on, I secured crocks of ten gallon capacity and really took quite an active interest in the manufacture of home brew.

We were having card parties with limburger and beer quite regularly. Eventually, of course, what with all the hilarity that could be provoked with a few gallons of beer, there seemed to be no need of bridge or poker playing for entertainment. The parties waxed more liquid and hilarious as time went on, and eventually I discovered that a little shot of liquor now and then between beers had the tendency to put me in a whacky mood much quicker than having to down several quarts of beer to obtain the same results. The inevitable result of this discovery was that I soon learned that beer made a very good chaser for whiskey. That discovery so intrigued me that I stayed on that diet almost entirely for the balance of my extended drinking life. The last day of my drinking career, I drank twenty-two of them between 10 and 12 a.m. and I shall never know how many more followed them until I was poured into bed that night.

I was getting along fairly well with my party drinking for quite some time, but eventually I began to visit beer joints in between parties. A night or so a week in a joint, and a party or so a week at home or with friends, along with a little lone drinking, soon had me preparing for the existence of a top flight drunkard.

Three years after I started on my drinking career, I lost my first job. At the time, I was living out of town, so I moved back to the home town and made a connection in a responsible position with one of the larger companies in the finance business. Up to this point I had spent six years in the business and had enjoyed the reputation of being very successful.

My new duties were extremely confining and my liquor consumption began to increase at this time. Upon leaving the office in the evening, my first stop would be a saloon about a block from the office. However, as there happened to be several saloons within that distance, I didn't find it necessary to patronize the same place each evening. It doesn't pay to be seen in the same place at the same hour every day.

The general procedure was to take four or five shots in the first place I stopped at. This would get me feeling fit, and then I would start for home and fireside, thirteen miles away. On the way home numerous places must be passed. If I were alone I would stop at four or five of them, but only one or two in the event I had my mistrusting wife with me.

Eventually I would arrive home for a late supper for which, of course, I had absolutely no relish. I would make a feeble attempt at eating supper, but I never met with any howling success. I never enjoyed any meal, but I ate my lunch at noon for two reasons: first, to help get me out of the fog of the night before, and second, to furnish some measure of nourishment. Eventually, the noon meal was also dispensed with.

I cannot remember just when I became the victim of insomnia, but I do know that the last year and a half I never went to bed sober a single night. I couldn't sleep. I had a mortal fear of going to bed and tossing all night. Evenings at home were an ordeal. As a result, I would fall off in a drunken stupor every night.

How was I able to discharge my duties at the office during those horrible mornings, I will never be able to explain. Handling customers, dealers, insurance people, dictation, telephoning, directing new employees, answering to superiors, etc. However, it finally caught up with me, and when it did, I was a mental, physical, and nervous wreck.

I arrived at the stage where I couldn't quite make it to the office some mornings. Then I would send an excuse of illness. But the firm became violently ill with my drunkenness and their course of treatment was to remove their ulcer, in the form of me, from their payroll, amid much fanfare and very personal and slighting remarks and insinuations.

During this time, I had been threatened, beaten, kissed, praised and damned alternately by relatives, family, friends and strangers, but of course it all went for naught. How many times I swore off in the morning and got drunk before sunset I don't know. I was on the toboggan and really making time.

After being fired, I lined up with a new finance company that was just starting in business, and took the position of business promotion man, contacting automobile dealers. While working in an office, there was some semblance of restraint, but, oh boy, when I got on the outside with this new company without supervision, did I go to town!

I really worked for several weeks, and having had a fairly wide acceptance with the dealer trade, it was not difficult for me to line enough of them up to give me a very substantial volume of business with a minimum of effort.

Now I was getting drunk all the time. It wasn't necessary to report to the office in person every day, and when I did go in, it was just to make an appearance and bounce right out again.

Finally this company also became involved and I was once more looking for a job. Then I learned something else. I learned that a person just can't find a job hanging in a dive or barroom all day and all night, as jobs don't seem to turn up in those places. I became convinced of that because I spent most of my time there and nary a job turned up. By this time, my chances of getting lined up in my chosen business were shot. Everyone had my number and wouldn't hire me at any price.

I have omitted details of transgressions that I made when drunk for several reasons. One is that I don't remember too many of them, as I was one of those drunks who could be on his feet and attend a meeting or a party, engage in a conversation with people and do things that any nearly normal person would do, and the next day not remember a thing about where I was, what I did, whom I saw, or how I got home. (That condition was a distinct handicap to me in trying to vindicate myself with the not so patient wife).

Things eventually came to the point where I had no friends. I didn't care to go visiting unless the parties we might visit had plenty of liquor on hand and I could get stinking drunk. Fact is, that I was always well on my way before I would undertake to go visiting at all.

After holding good positions, making better than average income for over ten years, I was in debt, had no clothes to speak of, no money, no friends, and no one any longer tolerating me but my wife. My son had absolutely no use for me. Even some of the saloon-keepers where I had spent so much time and money, requested that I stay away from their places. Finally, an old business acquaintance of mine, whom I hadn't seen for several years offered me a job. I was on that job a month and drunk most of the time.

Just at this time my wife heard of a doctor in another city who had been very successful with drunks. She offered me the alternative of going to see him or her leaving me for good and all. Well... I had a job, and I really wanted desperately to stop drinking, but I couldn't, so I readily agreed to visit the doctor she recommended.

That was the turning point of my life. My wife accompanied me on my visit and the doctor really told me some things that in my state of jitters nearly knocked me out of the chair. He talked about himself, but I was sure it was me. He mentioned lies, deceptions, etc. in the course of his story in the presence of the one person in the world I wouldn't want to know such things. How did he know all this? I had never seen him before, and at the time hoped I would never see him again. However, he explained to me that he had been just such a rummy as I, only for a much longer period of time.

He advised me to enter the particular hospital with which he was connected and I readily agreed. In all honesty though, I was skeptical, but I wanted so definitely to quit drinking that I would have welcomed any sort of physical torture or pain to accomplish the result.

I made arrangements to enter the hospital three days later and promptly went out and got stiff for three days. It was with grim foreboding and advanced jitters that I checked in at the hospital. Of course, I had no hint or intimation as to what the treatment was to consist of. Was I to be surprised!

After being in the hospital for several days, a plan of living was outlined to me. A very simple plan that I find much joy and happiness in following. It is impossible to put on paper all the benefits I have derived... physical, mental, domestic, spiritual, and monetary. This is no idle talk. It is the truth.

From a physical standpoint, I gained sixteen pounds in the first two months I was off liquor. I eat three good meals a day now, and really enjoy them. I sleep like a baby, and never give a thought to such a thing as insomnia. I feel as I did when I was fifteen years younger.

Mentally... I know where I was last night, the night before, and the nights before that. Also, I have no fear of anything. I have self-confidence and assurance that cannot be confused with the cockiness or noise-making I once possessed. I can think clearly and am helped much in my thinking and judgment by my spiritual development which grows daily.

From a domestic standpoint, we really have a home now. I am anxious to get home after dark. My wife is ever glad to see me come in. My youngster had adopted me. Our home is always full of friends and visitors. (No home brew as an inducement).

Spiritually... I have found a Friend who never lets me down and is ever eager to help. I can actually take my problems to Him and He does give me comfort, peace, and radiant happiness.

From a monetary standpoint... in the last few years, I have reduced my reckless debts to almost nothing, and have had money to get along comfortably. I still have my job, and just prior to the writing of this narrative, I received an advancement.

For all of these blessings, I thank Him.

(12) THE KEYS OF THE KINGDOM

This worldly lady helped to develop A.A. in Chicago and thus passed her keys to many.

A LITTLE MORE than fifteen years ago, through a long and calamitous series of shattering experiences, I found myself being helplessly propelled toward total destruction. I was without power to change the course my life had taken. How I had arrived at this tragic impasse, I could not have explained to anyone. I was thirty-three years old and my life was spent. I was caught in a cycle of alcohol and sedation that was proving inescapable, and consciousness had become intolerable.

I was a product of the post-war prohibition era of the roaring '20s. That age of the flapper and the "It" girl, speakeasies and the hip flask, the boyish bob and the drugstore cowboy, John Held Jr. and F. Scott Fitzgerald, all generously sprinkled with a patent pseudo-sophistication. To be sure, this had been a dizzy and confused interval, but most everyone else I knew had emerged from it with both feet on the ground and a fair amount of adult maturity.

Nor could I blame my dilemma on my childhood environment. I couldn't have chosen more loving and conscientious parents. I was given every advantage in a well-ordered home. I had the best schools, summer camps, resort vacations and travel. Every reasonable desire was possible of attainment for me. I was strong and healthy and quite athletic.

I experienced some of the pleasure of social drinking when I was sixteen. I definitely liked it, everything about it, the taste, the effects; and I realize now that a drink did something for me or to me that was different from the way it affected others. It wasn't long before any party without drinks was a dud for me.

I was married at twenty, had two children, and was divorced at twenty-three. My broken home and broken heart fanned my smoldering self-pity into a fair-sized bonfire, and this kept me well supplied with reasons for having another drink, and then another.

At twenty-five I had developed an alcoholic problem. I began making the rounds of the doctors in the hope that one of them might find some cure for my accumulating ailments, preferably something that could be removed surgically.

Of course the doctors found nothing. Just an unstable woman, undisciplined, poorly adjusted, and filled with nameless fears. Most of them prescribed sedatives and advised rest and moderation.

Between the ages of twenty-five and thirty I tried everything. I moved a thousand miles away from home to Chicago and a new environment. I studied art; I desperately endeavored to create an interest in many things, in a new place among new people. Nothing worked. My drinking habits increased in spite of my struggle for control. I tried the beer diet, the wine diet, timing, measuring, and spacing of drinks. I tried them mixed, unmixed, drinking only when happy, only when depressed. And still, by the time I was thirty years old, I was being pushed around with a compulsion to drink that was completely beyond my control. I couldn't stop drinking. I would hang on to sobriety for short intervals, but always there would come the tide of an overpowering *necessity* to drink, and, as I was engulfed in it, I felt such a sense of panic that I really believed I would die if I didn't get that drink inside.

Needless to say, this was not pleasurable drinking. I had long since given up any pretense of the social cocktail hour. This was drinking in sheer desperation, alone and locked behind my own door. Alone in the relative safety of my home because I knew I dare not risk the danger of blacking out in some public place or at the wheel of a car. I could no longer gauge my capacity, and it might be the second or the tenth drink that would erase my consciousness.

The next three years saw me in sanitariums, once in a ten-day coma, from which I very nearly did not recover, in and out of hospitals or confined at home with day and night nurses. By now I wanted to die but had lost the courage even to take my life. I was trapped, and for the life of me I did not know how or why this had happened to me. And all the while my fear fed a growing conviction that before long it would be necessary for me to be put away in some institution. People didn't behave this way outside of an asylum. I had heartsickness, shame, and fear bordering on panic, and no complete escape any longer except in oblivion. Certainly, now, anyone would have agreed that only a miracle could prevent my final breakdown. But how does one get a prescription for a miracle?

For about one year prior to this time, there was one doctor who had continued to struggle with me. He had tried everything from having me attend daily mass at 6 a.m. to performing the most menial labor for his charity patients. Why he bothered with me as long as he did I shall never know, for he knew there was no answer for me in medicine, and he, like all doctors of his day, had been taught that the alcoholic was incurable and should be ignored. Doctors were advised to attend patients who could be benefited by medicine. With the alcoholic, they could only give temporary relief and in the last stages not even that. It was a waste of the doctors' time and the patients' money. Nevertheless, there were a few doctors who saw alcoholism as a disease and felt that the alcoholic was a victim of something over which he had no control. They had a hunch that there must be an answer for these apparently hopeless ones, somewhere. Fortunately for me, my doctor was one of the enlightened.

And then, in the spring of 1939, a very remarkable book was rolled off a

New York press with the title *Alcoholics Anonymous*. However, due to financial difficulties the whole printing was, for a while, held up and the book received no publicity nor, of course, was it available in the stores, even if one knew it existed. But somehow my good doctor heard of this book and also he learned a little about the people responsible for its publication. He sent to New York for a copy, and after reading it, he tucked it under his arm and called on me. That call marked the turning point in my life.

Until now, I had never been told that I was an alcoholic. Few doctors will tell a hopeless patient that there is no answer for him or for her. But this day my doctor gave it to me straight and said, "People like you are pretty well known to the medical profession. Every doctor gets his quota of alcoholic patients. Some of us struggle with these people because we know that they are really very sick, but we also know that, short of some miracle, we are not going to help them except temporarily and that they will inevitably get worse and worse until one of two things happens. Either they die of acute alcoholism or they develop wet brains and have to be put away permanently."

He further explained that alcohol was no respecter of sex or background but that most of the alcoholics he had encountered had better-than-average minds and abilities. He said the alcoholics seemed to possess a native acuteness and usually excelled in their fields, regardless of environmental or educational advantages.

"We watch the alcoholic performing in a position of responsibility, and we know that because he is drinking heavily and daily, he has cut his capacities by 50 percent, and still he seems able to do a satisfactory job. And we wonder how much further this man could go if his alcoholic problem could be removed and he could throw 100 percent of his abilities into action.

"But, of course," he continued, "eventually the alcoholic loses all of his capacities as his disease gets progressively worse, and this is a tragedy that is painful to watch: the disintegration of a sound mind and body."

Then he told me there was a handful of people in Akron and New York who had worked out a technique for arresting their alcoholism. He asked me to read the book *Alcoholics Anonymous*, and then he wanted me to talk with a man who was experiencing success with his own arrestment. This man could tell me more. I stayed up all night reading that book. For me it was a wonderful experience. It explained so much I had not understood about myself, and, best of all, it promised recovery if I would do a few simple things and be willing to have the desire to drink removed. Here was hope. Maybe I could find my way out of this agonizing existence. Perhaps I could find freedom and peace, and be able once again to call my soul my own.

The next day I received a visit from Mr. T., a recovered alcoholic. I don't know what sort of person I was expecting, but I was very agreeably surprised to find Mr. T. a poised, intelligent, well-groomed, and mannered gentleman. I was immediately impressed with his graciousness and charm. He put me at ease with his first few words. Looking at him, it was hard to believe he had ever been as I was then.

However, as he unfolded his story for me, I could not help but believe him. In describing his suffering, his fears, his many years of groping for some answer to that which always seemed to remain unanswerable, he could have been describing me, and nothing short of experience and knowledge could have afforded him that much insight! He had been dry for two and a half years and had been maintaining his contact with a group of recovered alcoholics in Akron. Contact with this group was extremely important to him. He told me that eventually he hoped such a group would develop in the Chicago area but that so far this had not been started. He thought it would be helpful for me to visit the Akron group and meet many like himself.

By this time, with the doctor's explanation, the revelations contained in the book, and the hope-inspiring interview with Mr. T., I was ready and willing to go into the interior of the African jungles, if that was what it took, for me to find what these people had.

So I went to Akron, and also to Cleveland, and I met more recovered alcoholics. I saw in these people a quality of peace and serenity that I knew I must have for myself. Not only were they at peace with themselves, but they were getting a kick out of life such as one seldom encounters, except in the very young. They seemed to have all the ingredients for successful living: philosophy, faith, a sense of humor (they could laugh at themselves), clear-cut objectives, appreciation–and most especially appreciation and sympathetic understanding for their fellow man.

Nothing in their lives took precedence over their response to a call for help from some alcoholic in need. They would travel miles and stay up all night with someone they had never laid eyes on before and think nothing of it. Far from expecting praise for their deeds, they claimed the performance a privilege and insisted that they invariably received more than they gave. Extraordinary people!

I didn't dare hope I might find for myself all that these people had found, but if I could acquire some small part of their intriguing quality of living–and sobriety–that would be enough.

Shortly after I returned to Chicago, my doctor, encouraged by the results of my contact with A.A., sent us two more of his alcoholic patients. By the latter part of September 1939, we had a nucleus of six and held our first official group meeting.

I had a tough pull back to normal good health. It has been so many years since I had not relied on some artificial crutch, either alcohol or sedatives. Letting go of everything at once was both painful and terrifying. I could never have accomplished this alone. It took the help, understanding, and wonderful companionship that was given so freely to me by my ex-alkie friends–this and the program of recovery embodied in the Twelve Steps. In learning to practice these steps in my daily living, I began to acquire faith and a philosophy to live by. Whole new vistas were opened up for me, new avenues of experience to be explored, and life began to take on color and interest. In time, I found myself looking forward to each new day with pleasurable anticipation.

A.A. is not a plan for recovery that can be finished and done with. It is a way of life, and the challenge contained in its principles is great enough to keep any human being striving for as long as he lives. We do not, cannot, outgrow this plan. As arrested alcoholics, we must have a program for living that allows for limitless expansion. Keeping one foot in front of the other is essential for maintaining our arrestment. Others may idle in a retrogressive groove without too much danger, but retrogression can spell death for us. However, this isn't as rough as it sounds, as we do become grateful for the necessity that makes us toe the line, and we find that we are compensated for a consistent effort by the countless dividends we receive.

A complete change takes place in our approach to life. Where we used to run from responsibility, we find ourselves accepting it with gratitude that we can successfully shoulder it. Instead of wanting to escape some perplexing problem, we experience the thrill of challenge in the opportunity it affords for another application of A.A. techniques, and we find ourselves tackling it with surprising vigor.

The last fifteen years of my life have been rich and meaningful. I have had my share of problems, heartaches, and disappointments because that is life, but also I have known a great deal of joy and a peace that is the handmaiden of an inner freedom. I have a wealth of friends and, with my A.A. friends, an unusual quality of fellowship. For, to these people, I am truly related. First, through mutual pain and despair, and later through mutual objectives and newfound faith and hope. And, as the years go by, working together, sharing our experiences with one another, and also sharing a mutual trust, understanding, and love–without strings, without obligation–we acquire relationships that are unique and priceless.

There is no more aloneness, with that awful ache, so deep in the heart of every alcoholic that nothing, before, could ever reach it. That ache is gone and never need return again.

Now there is a sense of belonging, of being wanted and needed and loved. In return for a bottle and a hangover, we have been given the Keys of the Kingdom.

PART II: THEY STOPPED IN TIME

We think that about one-half of today's incoming A.A. members were never advanced stages of alcoholism; though given time all might have.

Most of these fortunate ones have had little or no acquaintance with delirium, with hospitals, asylums, and jails. Some were drinking heavily, and there had been occasional serious episodes. But with many, drinking had been little more than a sometimes uncontrollable nuisance. Seldom had any of these lost either health, business, family, or friends.

Why do men and women like these join A.A.?

The twelve who now tell their experiences answer that question. They saw that they had become actual or potential alcoholics, even though no serious harm had yet been done.

They realized that repeated lack of drinking control, when they really wanted control, was the fatal symptom that spelled problem drinking. This, plus mounting emotional disturbances, convinced them that compulsive alcoholism already had them; that complete ruin would be only a question of time.

Seeing this danger, they came to A.A. They realized that in the end alcoholism could be as mortal as cancer; certainly no sane man would wait for a malignant growth to become fatal before seeking help.

Therefore, these twelve A.A.'s, and thousands like them, have been saved years of infinite suffering. They sum it up like this: "We didn't wait to hit bottom because, thank God, we could see the bottom. Actually, the bottom came up and hit us. That sold us on Alcoholics Anonymous."

(1) RUM, RADIO AND REBELLION

This man faced the last ditch when his wife's voice from 1300 miles away sent him to A.A.

"YOU AN ALCOHOLIC! I don't believe it."

"Sure, I've seen you tight several times, but you're no alcoholic!"

"You kidding–you an alcoholic?"

Many times have I heard the above expressions since I have been in A.A., and many times I have had to reply "Definitely I am an alcoholic, and while it may be hard for you to believe, it is not hard for me, for I have learned many things about alcohol and myself that would, perhaps, be difficult for you to understand."

As these words are written at fifty-three years of age, with over nine years in A.A. behind me, with all its wonderful teachings, I haven't the slightest doubt about being an alcoholic.

I have always considered myself one of the lucky members of our fraternity. Lucky because my excessive drinking never got me in jail, or hospitalized, nor did it ever cost me a job. As a matter of fact, when I came into Alcoholics Anonymous I was close to being at the peak of my career. I certainly was, as far as my living standard was concerned. However, what I had gained materially on the credit side of my ledger, I have since learned was more than offset on the debit side by egotism, resentment, and dishonesty.

I was born in Cleveland, Ohio, the only child of a prominent dentist, and a very proud mother. They were neither poor nor wealthy, but far better off than the average couple. I had every advantage a child could have, private schools (several of them), dancing schools, two colleges, coon skin coats, automobiles, a listing in the social register and all the rest. All of which could turn out but one thing–a very popular, but spoiled, brat.

In the various schools I attended, it was always a case of just getting by. Too many outside activities to do much studying. I was active and did well, however, in school publications, dramatics (which came in handy during my drinking career), and Greek letter societies. I had no trouble at all in being elected to the two drinking societies at my college.

I had run away from school to join the army in World War I, but missed it by one day since the Armistice was signed the very day I landed in Atlanta to sign up with Uncle Sam. As usual, I ran out of money, and, as usual, I wired my father for funds to come home. He answered by wiring that I could stay there until I learned enough to get home. It was a terrible blow at the time and I thought he was pretty much of a heel, but of course it was the finest thing he could have done for me under the circumstances. It took me a year to make it home. I went to work in Birmingham for a newspaper at fifteen dollars a week. Prohibition came along, and with it my first taste of moonshine. I didn't particularly like it, but I loved the effects, and managed for the next twenty-five years to drink anything and everything, either handed to me or purchased, at the slightest excuse.

When I did make it home in 1920, I re-entered school and caught up with my class in a few short months–I actually did a year's work in three months, proving much to the disgust of my Dad that I could do it when I wanted to.

All I can remember about the Roaring Twenties is that I drank a great deal, though I was having a grand time, managed to get to Europe for a few weeks, was very proud of the dozens of speak-easy cards entitling me to an entrée in the better joints between Cleveland and New York, took on a wife, and built a home in a fashionable suburb of Cleveland.

High living, a great many fair-weather friends, the 1929 stock market crash, and a couple of years of Depression, soon relieved me one by one of my worldly goods, including my wife. In this I was greatly aided and abetted by one John Barleycorn. Like all alcoholics endeavoring to run away from themselves and their environment, I decided to go to New York. This was at the height of the Depression and the end of Prohibition. Neither of these circumstances was very helpful to my type, since I had not learned to face realities.

The next few years in New York can be described in a very few words. Drinking–and more drinking. I got behind in my rent, but never in my drinking. Looking back, it is surprising to me now that I managed to keep working and have enough money to squander at the various spots in the big city. By this time I had become associated with the fast growing and fascinating business of broadcasting. I was working for a Chicago firm that represented several large radio stations. It was my job to sell time on these stations to advertising agencies in New York. It was also my job to entertain the owners of these stations when they came East on business–or the pretense of business. This phase was right down my alley; I had my master's degree in the art of making "whoopee."

I was living in a small room on West 53rd Street right off Fifth Avenue, when I met a young lady who eventually was responsible for altering my entire way of living. She was studying fashion design, was living in the same rooming house, and was from my home town of Cleveland. I made little headway in my first few meetings with her. She was intent on her studies, and kept her distance. By persistence and salesmanship I managed to see more and more of my new friend, and because of her sympathetic nature she tolerated my company. Her influence and companionship managed to lessen my drinking to some degree. After several months of acquaintance I asked her to marry me, but was politely refused. I asked this question weekly for the next couple of years.

In January 1938, I had the opportunity to go to northern Vermont to manage a small daytime radio station that was up against it financially, and was about to fold its antenna. The challenge intrigued me; also it was another opportunity to run away from myself and the "fast life of the big city." Once again I asked my girl to marry me and join me in this new venture. At this time, however, she had an opportunity to go to Salt Lake City on a new project for the government, but she did promise me that if I would curtail my drinking and buckle down to hard work she would give serious consideration to my latest proposal and maybe join me at a later date when I got settled. With new hope in my heart and new resolutions I set off for Vermont.

My work kept me busy the first few months on the new job. It was strictly a one man operation and I knew I had to tend to my knitting to make a go of it. Furthermore, I knew that I was looked upon as a city slicker from New York, and I had to be pretty cautious among small town, conservative Yankees. One of the things I needed badly was business for the station. New programming was beginning to build an audience, but sponsors were pretty scarce. I got around this by joining the local Rotary Club, and through this association with the business men of the community my little station began to grow. It also was the beginning of another cycle in my drinking. It started when I joined a few of the men for cocktails before the noonday Rotary luncheon. Before long I was at the luncheon meetings an hour before the others, that old and familiar trademark of every alcoholic. Since the radio station was getting on its feet, it didn't require so many nights of evening work, and that permitted leisure time for drinking. After all–wasn't I entitled to it? I sure had been working awfully hard of late. It wasn't long before I became a five o'clock alcoholic. During this time I faithfully was writing my girl in Utah. Of course I kept her posted on how well the station was doing and wrote convincing letters of how well I was doing with the liquor problem. My salesmanship was still good, for in the fall of 1938 she called me from Salt Lake and finally agreed to take me on for better or for worse. We were married in Montreal in November.

Proud of my little station and of my new bride I settled down to a happy married life. It was to be short lived, for on the day before Christmas I completely disillusioned my wife and ruined our first Christmas by coming home from the Rotary lunch dead drunk. It was the first of many such experiences that became the only cause of harsh words, tears and heartaches in an otherwise truly beautiful marriage.

In 1940 another good opportunity came up and we moved to Pittsburgh where I was to manage two radio stations under the same ownership. My business reputation had reached from Vermont to Pennsylvania, but, thank goodness, my drinking reputation had not. Once again I was back in big time operations, and along with them, big shot complexes. It didn't take long for me to fall in with a fast crowd who had their lunch in the men's bar of a leading hotel. I graduated there from a five o'clock alcoholic to a noon-day one. By hook or crook I usually managed to sober up before I reached home, but always "terribly tired" from a "hard day's work," and just having to have one or two before dinner. My wonderful wife did everything to play along with me. She was tolerant beyond all belief. I did everything to make her an alcoholic too. She tried reasoning with me, endeavored to work out various drinking schedules, in fact all the tricks were practiced faithfully for a short time somewhere along my shaky road to unhappiness. The inevitable always happened. I would follow certain drinking schedules or diets faithfully for a few days, and then somewhere along the line would over-train and upset the applecart. On more than one occasion my wife would threaten to leave me. Time after time, I would beg forgiveness on bended knees, with tears rolling down my cheeks, and promise I would never again drink too much. And deep in my heart I really meant what I said because I loved her more than anything else in the world, yes–even more than liquor. It was hard for her to believe in my love by my actions. Even I couldn't understand it, because I did love her so. How could I continually break my promises? Soon I was to discover the answer.

In the very early spring of 1944, my frustrated wife couldn't take it any longer. After another of my "never again episodes" she packed up and left for her parents' home in Florida. Her parting words were "I am not leaving you because I don't love you; it's because I do love you. I can't bear to be here when you lose the respect of others, and above all–when you lose your own self-respect."

For a few weeks I toed the line. I was going to prove to her that liquor wasn't necessary in my life, and above all that I still loved her more than anything else in the world and that I wanted her back. This routine was short lived too. I began hitting the bottle again, and with it self-pity, resentment, loneliness and remorse set in deeply. Why should this happen to me–hadn't I provided a good home–wasn't I making a good living–didn't I just get a substantial raise that had put me in the upper bracket class? Sure I still loved her, but hang it all, she was unreasonable! I had given her everything a wife could ask for. The more I thought like this the more I drank to submerge my sorrows. One Saturday noon I staggered home with every intention of showing her. I would end it all, and then, by George, she'd be sorry!

I entered the house, opened a new bottle of whiskey and sat down to drink myself into the right frame of mind to get in my car, start the motor and close the garage door behind me. A few hours later I came out of a complete stupor in our living room with a flash of sanity. Looking directly at me was a large oil painting of my wife, and her very words seemed to shout at me–"I am not leaving you because I don't love you; it's because I do love you. I can't bear to be here when you lose the respect of others, and above all–when you lose your own self-respect." This was about 10 p.m., and the time here is important.

It had happened to me and I had to do something about it. Thank God that in spite of my heavy drinking my mind was clear enough to make a decision then and there. I had read and heard a little about A.A. and so, groping for the phone book, I found the A.A. number and with hope in my heart eagerly telephoned. I heard a lovely voice, and a sympathetic ear listened to my plea. I was told that someone would call on me shortly, to sit tight and not take another drink. Sure enough in a couple of hours two men were at my door and for the first time I heard some facts about liquor and my problem that sounded sensible to me. They told me their stories, which were much more rugged than mine–yet what they said made sense, and the way they put it was easy for me to understand, with an understanding I had never had before. I promised my two sponsors that I would attend their meeting the next Tuesday evening. I kept away from liquor and eagerly waited.

My first meeting gave me a great deal of hope and lots of willing ears for my tale of woe and for my questions. After a few meetings I decided to drive to Florida unannounced to see my wife and tell her about my new found friends and association. I was certainly a complete surprise when I arrived at her family's home, but because I arrived on the wings of a tropical hurricane there wasn't much she could do but let me in. That night she too had new hope because I had made sure she would know what I was doing about my drinking by packing every bit of A.A. literature I could put my hands on right on top so she couldn't help but see it when she opened my bag.

I stayed on in Florida for three weeks, enjoying our reunion, a new found health and a deeper love than I had ever experienced before. We came back to Pittsburgh as happy as a bride and groom. We attended meetings together, and mutually enjoyed our new found friends. In September of this same year I went to New York alone. I thought this was a good time to experiment with liquor. Of course, it didn't work. I tried a few drinks my last night in the city before coming home. Luck was with me for I made my train, but I arrived home the next morning with a new kind of hangover. I had done something terrible! I had not only let my wife down but also a lot of other wonderful people who had helped me. Of course, more than anything else I had let myself down, but I didn't realize how much then–as I do now. I didn't say a word to anyone about my lapse. I went back to my group meetings, but not whole-heartedly, and I often skipped them with the excuse that I was too tired. It was worrying my wife a little, but she had the good sense not to take me to task about it or goad me into going. I got through the holidays all right until New Year's Day. We had some people in, and I was making drinks in the kitchen, when I suddenly decided to hoist the bottle for a quick one. I had just raised the bottle to my lips when my wife opened the door and froze me completely in my tracks with "Happy New Year, dear." I didn't take the drink. I was scared–would she leave me again? Later I told her I had not taken the drink and that I was all right. When our meeting night came around the next evening, I went–"for her sake" I told her. I said I was okay, but if it would make her feel better I would go "as tired as I was after the strenuous holidays." She told me not to bother going "for her sake"; she told me in a nice way that it didn't make any difference to her–and that really scared me–so I went.

A lucky break, at least some will call it lucky, was in store for me at my group that night. Attending his fourth or fifth meeting was an old friend I had not seen for twenty years. He was full of his new found life of happiness and sobriety. His enthusiasm and keen interest in A.A. fired my spirits again. I attended my weekly meetings with regularity, re-read the Big Book, attended other group meetings, gave leads when asked to and did some Twelve Step work whenever I was called upon to do so. In other words, I began contributing, and so, naturally, I began to get something more. A whole new world of happiness and love began to unfold before my eyes, a truly new way of living.

One night at the dinner table my wife said that tonight was my first birthday in A.A., and that the group would have the usual ice cream and cake for the "one year man." Now I was on the spot. I had never told a soul about my lapse in New York. For the next couple of hours a terrible battle went on between the good gremlins and the bad ones, one faction urging me to tell the truth, the other telling me to sit tight and say nothing. I had no trouble making the right decision when I saw my wife open her purse at the meeting that night and deposit a cute little angel in the middle of my birthday cake. When I was called upon for a few words I had to tell my friends that I wasn't one year old in A.A. that evening but only a "nine month baby." With that utterance I again made a wonderful discovery. I had thrown off a big lie that had been burdening me down for months. What a wonderful new feeling, what a wonderful relief!

I could end my story here, but for the new man I would like to add a few words. You'll read and hear a great deal about the spiritual part of our program. I haven't written anything about that part of my story, but I believe in a Greater Power which I call God and I ask for His wisdom and guidance daily. My first spiritual experience in A.A. came quite early to me. You will recall that I said the time that I got the idea out of a clear sky to call A.A. on a certain night was at about 10. While I was in Florida trying to convince my wife with all the A.A. literature that she should come back to me, she went over to her desk and picked up a clipping she had taken from the St. Petersburg Times about A.A. It was the first she had heard or read about it and she said she had considered sending it to me or trying to have someone in Pittsburgh send it to me so I wouldn't know where it came from. However, knowing me, she thought it was a foolish idea, that I wouldn't be interested. But for some reason–she just didn't know why–she just had to hold onto that clipping, with its thin hope. She said she cut this clipping from the paper at about 10 on the same night, and at the same time as I called A.A. in Pittsburgh–some 1,300 miles away.

To the new man I would also like to say that this program is not for sissies for, in my humble opinion, it takes a man to make the grade. It is not too difficult nor too easy to grasp. I have had many more reasons to drink since I have been in A.A. than I had in all the years of my drinking. I've had more problems but, thank God, I have had the teachings of A.A. with which to face them. And, believe me, I thank God that I found out about A.A. before I had to beat my brains out–before I had been hospitalized, jailed or lost a job. When I hear the more rugged stories of the alcoholics who became sicker than I did with this affliction, I humbly thank God for showing me "the handwriting on the wall."

In meeting me casually, I don't think my strong belief in "The Man Upstairs" shows, but I have no other explanation for the many good things that have happened to me since I have been in A.A.–they came to me from a Greater Power. These words may be difficult for you to understand now, but be patient and you'll know what I mean.

If I were asked what in my opinion was the most important factor in being successful in this program, besides following the Twelve Steps, I would say Honesty. And the most important person to be honest with is Yourself. If there is something in my story that rings a bell with you, then *do* something–now! I repeat, I am one of the fortunate members of A.A.–a lucky guy who is very grateful.

(2) FEAR OF FEAR

This lady was cautious. She decided she wouldn't let herself go in her drinking. And she would never, never take that morning drink!

I DIDN'T THINK I was an alcoholic. I thought my problem was that I had been married to a drunk for twenty-seven years. And when my husband found A.A., I came to the second meeting with him. I thought it was wonderful, simply marvelous, for him. But not for me. Then I went to another meeting, and I still thought it was wonderful–for him, but not for me.

It was a hot summer night in 1949, down in the Greenwich Village Group, and there was a little porch out there in the old meeting place on Sullivan Street, and after the meeting I went out on the steps for some air. In the doorway stood a lovely young girl who said, "Are you one of us souses too?" I said, "Oh, goodness, no! My husband is. He's in there." She told me her name, and I said, "I know you from somewhere." It turned out that she had been in high school with my daughter. I said, "Eileen, are you one of those people?" And she said, "Oh, yes. I'm in this."

As we walked back through the hall, I, for the first time in my life, said to another human being, "I'm having trouble with my drinking too." She took me by the hand and introduced me to the woman that I'm very proud to call my sponsor. This woman and her husband are both in A.A., and she said to me, "Oh, but you're not the alcoholic; it's your husband." I said, "Yes." She said, "How long have you been married?" I said, "Twenty-seven years." She said, "Twenty-seven years to an alcoholic! How did you ever stand it?" I thought, now here's a nice, sympathetic soul! This is for me. I said, "Well, I stood it to keep the home together, and for the children's sake." She said, "Yes, I know. You're just a martyr, aren't you?" I walked away from that woman grinding my teeth and cursing under my breath. Fortunately, I didn't say a word to George on the way home. But that night I tried to go to sleep. And I thought, "You're some martyr, Jane! Let's look at the record." And when I looked at it, I knew I was just as much a drunk as George was, if not worse. I nudged George next morning, and I said, "I'm in," and he said, "Oh, I knew you'd make it."

I started drinking nearly thirty years ago–right after I was married. My first drinking spree was on corn liquor and I was allergic to it, believe me. I was deathly sick every time I took a drink. But we had to do a lot of entertaining. My husband liked to have a good time; I was very young, and I wanted to have a good time too. The only way I knew to do it was to drink right along with him.

I got into terrific trouble with my drinking. I was afraid, and I had made my mind up that I would never get drunk, so I was watchful and careful. We had a small child, and I loved her dearly, so that held me back quite a bit in my drinking career. Even so, every time I drank, I seemed to get in trouble. I always wanted to drink too much, so I was watchful, always watchful, counting my drinks. If we were invited to a formal party and I knew they were only going to have one or two drinks, I wouldn't have any. I was being very cagey, because I knew that if I did take one or two, I might want to take five or six or seven or eight.

I did stay fairly good for a few years. But I wasn't happy, and I didn't ever let myself go in my drinking. As my son, our second child, came along, and as he became school age and was away at school most of the time, something happened. I really started drinking with a bang.

I never went to a hospital. I never lost a job. I was never in jail. And, unlike many others, I never took a drink in the morning. I needed a drink, but I was afraid to take a morning drink, because I didn't want to be a drunk. I became a drunk anyway, but I was scared to death to take that morning drink. I was accused of it many times when I went to play bridge in the afternoon, but I really never did take a morning drink. I was still woozy from the night before.

I should have lost my husband, and I think that only the fact that he was an alcoholic too kept us together. No one else could have stayed with me. Many women who have reached the stage that I had reached in my drinking have lost husbands, children, homes, everything they hold dear. I have been very fortunate in many ways. The important thing I lost was my own self-respect. I could feel fear coming into my life. I couldn't face people. I couldn't look them straight in the eyes, although I was always a self-possessed, brazen sort of person. I'd brazen anything out. I lied like a trooper to get out of many scrapes.

But I felt a fear coming into my life, and I couldn't cope with it. I got so that I hid quite a bit of the time, wouldn't answer the phone, and stayed by myself as much as I could. I noticed that I was avoiding all my social friends, except for my bridge. I couldn't keep up with any of my other friends, and I wouldn't go to anyone's house unless I knew they drank as heavily as I did. I never knew it was the first drink that did it. I thought I was losing my mind when I realized that I couldn't stop drinking. That frightened me terribly.

George tried many times to go on the wagon. If I had been sincere in what I thought I wanted more than anything else in life–a sober husband and a happy, contented home–I would have gone on the wagon with him. I did try, for a day or two, but something always would come up that would throw me. It would be a little thing–the rugs being crooked, or any silly little thing that I'd think was wrong–and off I'd go, drinking. And sneaking my drinks. I had bottles hidden all over the apartment. I didn't think my children knew about it, but I found out they did. It's surprising, how we think we fool everybody in our drinking.

I reached a stage where I couldn't go into my apartment without a drink. It didn't bother me any more whether George was drinking or not. I had to have liquor. Sometimes I would lie on the bathroom floor, deathly sick, praying I would die, and praying to God as I always had prayed to Him when I was drinking: "Dear God, get me out of this one and I'll never do it again." And then I'd say, "God, don't pay any attention to me. You know I'll do it tomorrow, the very same thing."

I used to make excuses to try and get George off the wagon. I'd get so fed up with drinking all alone and bearing the burden of guilt all by myself, that I'd egg him on to drink, to get started again. And then I'd fight with him because he had started! And the whole merry-go-round would be on again. And he, poor dear, didn't know what was going on. He used to wonder when he'd spot one of my bottles around the house just how he could have overlooked that particular bottle. I myself didn't know all the places I had them hidden.

We have only been in A.A. a few years, but now we're trying to make up for lost time. Twenty-seven years of confusion is what my early married life was. Now the picture has changed completely. We have faith in each other, trust in each other, and understanding. A.A. has given us that. It has taught me so many things. It has changed my thinking entirely, about everything I do. I can't afford resentments against anyone, because they are the build-up of another drunk. I must live and let live. And "think"–that one important word means so much to me. My life was always act and react. I never stopped to think. I just didn't give a whoop about myself or anyone else.

I try to live our program as it has been outlined to me, one day at a time. I try to live today so that tomorrow I won't be ashamed when I wake up in the morning. In the old days I hated to wake up and look back at what last night had been like. I never could face it the next morning. And unless I had some rosy picture of what was going to happen that day, I wouldn't even feel like getting up in the morning at all. It really wasn't living. Now I feel so very grateful not only for my sobriety, which I try to maintain day by day, but I'm grateful also for the ability to help other people. I never thought I could be useful to anyone except my husband and my children and perhaps a few friends. But A.A. has shown me that I can help other alcoholics.

Many of my neighbors devoted time to volunteer work during the war. There was one woman especially, and I'd watch her from my window every morning, leaving faithfully to go to the hospital in the neighborhood. I said to her one day when I met her on the street, "What sort of volunteer work do you do?" She told me; it was simple; I could have done it very easily. She said, "Why don't you do it too?" I said, "I'd love to." She said, "Suppose I put your name down as a volunteer. We need them so badly even if you can only give one or two days?" But then I thought, well, now wait, how will I feel next Tuesday? How will I feel next Friday, if I make it a Friday? How will I feel next Saturday morning? I never knew. I was afraid to set even one day. I could never be sure I'd have a clear head and hands that were willing to do some work. So I never did any volunteer work. And I felt depleted, whipped.

I had the time, I certainly had the capability, but I never did a thing.

I am trying now, each day, to make up for all those selfish, thoughtless, foolish things I did in my drinking days. I hope that I never forget to be grateful.

(3) THE PROFESSOR AND THE PARADOX

Says he, "We A.A.'s surrender to win; we give away to keep; we suffer to get well, and we die to live."

I AM IN the public information business. I use that phrase or designation because if I say I am a college professor everybody always has a tendency to run the other way. And when they learn that I am a specialist in English, they have looks of horror for fear they are going to slip up and say "ain't". I often wish I sold shoes or insurance or fixed automobiles or plumbed pipes. I would have more friends.

My story is not a great deal different from others–except in a few specific details. All the roads of alcoholism lead to the same place and condition. I suppose I have always been shy, sensitive, fearful, envious, and resentful, which in turn leads one to be arrogantly independent, a defiant personality. I believe I got a Ph.D. degree principally because I wanted to either outdo or defy everybody else. I have published a great deal of scholarly research–I think for the same reason. Such determination, such striving for perfection, is undoubtedly an admirable and practical quality to have, for a while; but when a person mixes such a quality with alcohol, that quality can eventually cut him almost to pieces. At least it did so to me.

I began drinking as a social drinker, in my early twenties. Drinking constituted no problem for me until well after I finished graduate school at the age of thirty. But as the tensions and anxieties of my life began to mount, and the set-backs from perfection began to increase, I finally slipped over the line between moderate drinking and alcoholism. No longer would I drink a few beers or a cocktail or two and let it go at that. No longer did I let months or even weeks go by without liquor. And when drinking, I entered what I now know was the dream-world of alcoholic fantasy. Then for about five years of progressively worse alcoholic drinking, of filling my life and home with more and more wreckage, it looked as if I were going to ride this toboggan of destruction to the bitter end.

Maybe I didn't get as bad as some of the others. I must confess that I never went to teach one of my classes drunk or drinking–but I've been awfully hung-over. My pattern was to be drunk at night, boil myself out to creep to work in the morning, drunk the next night, boil myself out in the morning, drunk again the next night, boil myself out the next morning. I may not have drunk as much whiskey as some, but there isn't anybody whose drunk any more Sal Hepatica than I have!

Now there are all kinds of drunks: melancholy drunks, weeping drunks, travelling drunks, slap-happy and stupid drunks, and a number of other varieties. I was a self-aggrandizing and occasionally violent drunk. You wouldn't think a little fellow like me could do much damage, but when I'm drunk I'm pure dynamite. I'm not going into any of the details–the University can fire me yet!

I came to believe actually that life was not worth living unless I could drink. I was utterly miserable and sometimes desperate, living always with a feeling of impending calamity (I knew something was bound to "break loose"). And to do away with such a fear, I would try a little more drinking, with the inevitable result–for by this time one drink would set up in me that irresistible urge to take another and another until I was down or hungover and in trouble. In the hungover stage I would vow never to touch another drop, and then be drunk the next night.

I knew at least that there had to be some changes made. I tried to change the time and place and amount of my drinking. I tried to change my environment, my place of living–like most of us who at one time or another think that our trouble is geography rather than whiskey. I even entertained the idea of changing wives. I tried to change everything and everybody, *except myself*–the only thing I *could* change.

I did not know that it was physically impossible for me to drink moderately. I did not know that my body's drinking machinery had worn out, and that the parts could not be replaced. I did not know that just one drink made it impossible for me to control my behavior and conduct and my future drinking. I did not know, in short, that I was powerless over alcohol. My family and my friends sensed or knew these things about me long before I did.

Finally, as with most of us in A.A., the crisis came. I realized I had a drinking problem which had to be solved. My wife and a close friend tried to persuade me to contact the only member of Alcoholics Anonymous we knew of in town. This I refused to do. But I agreed that I would stop drinking altogether, maintaining stoutly and sincerely that I could and would solve this problem "on my own." I would feel much better doing it that way, I insisted. I stayed sober for two entire weeks! Then I pitched a "lulu"–a terrific drunken affair in which I became violently insane. I also landed in the City Jail.

I don't know exactly what happened on this bender, but here are some things that did happen which I was told about subsequently. First, the officers who had come out to my house did not want to take me in–but I insisted! Also, I insisted that they wait in the living room while I went back to the bedroom and changed into my best and newest suit (with socks and tie to match), so that I would look nice in jail! I don't remember the ride downtown, but when I "came to" in the jail corridor, I didn't like the looks of the little cage they were shoving me into, so I took issue about that with three officers and indulged in some fisticuffs with all three of them at once–each one of them twice my size and armed with a gun and a blackjack. Now what kind of thinking and acting is that? If that isn't insanity, or absurd grandiosity, or some sort of mental illness, what is it? Because I yelled so loud and made so much noise, I ended up downstairs under the concrete in a place they call "solitary." (That's a fine place–now isn't it?–for a college professor to spend the night!) Two days later I was willing to try A.A., which I had only vaguely heard of a few months before. I called at the home of the man who started the A.A. group in my town, and I went humbly with him to an A.A. meeting the following night.

As I look back, something must have happened to me during those two days. Some forces must have been at work which I do not understand. But on those two days–between jail and A.A.–something happened to me that had never happened before. I repeat, I don't know what it was. Maybe I had made a "decision "–just a part of Step Three (I had made lots of promises but never a decision)–though it seems to me that I was at the time too confused and fogged up to make much of one. Maybe it was the guiding hand of God, or (as we Baptists say) the Holy Spirit. I like to think that it was just that, followed by my own attempt to take the Twelve Steps to recovery. Whatever it was, I have been in A.A. and I have been dry ever since. That was more than six years ago.

A.A. does not function in a way which people normally expect it to. For example, instead of using our "will power," as everyone outside A.A. seems to think we do, we give up our wills to a Higher Power, place our lives in hands–invisible hands–stronger than ours. Another example: If twenty or thirty of us real drunks get away from home and meet in a clubroom downtown on Saturday night, the normal expectation is that all thirty of us will surely get roaring drunk, but it doesn't work out that way, does it? Or talking about whiskey and old drinking days (one would normally think) is sure to raise a thirst, but it doesn't work that way either, does it? Our program and procedures seem to be in many ways contrary to normal opinion. And so, in connection with this idea, let me pass on what I consider the four paradoxes of how A.A. works. (A paradox, you probably already know, is a statement which is seemingly self-contradictory; a statement which appears to be false, but which, upon careful examination, in certain instances proves to be true.)

1. We SURRENDER TO WIN. On the face of it, *surrendering* certainly does not seem like *winning*. But it is in A.A. Only after we have come to the end of our rope, hit a stone wall in some aspect of our lives beyond which we can go no further; only when we hit "bottom" in despair and surrender, can we accomplish sobriety which we could never accomplish before. We must, and we do, surrender in order to win.

2. We GIVE AWAY TO KEEP. That seems absurd and untrue. How can you keep anything if you give it away? But in order to keep whatever it is we get in A.A., we must go about giving it away to others, for no fees or rewards of any kind. When we cannot afford to give away what we have received so freely in A.A., we had better get ready for our next "drunk." It

will happen every time. We've got to continue to give it away in order to keep it.

3. We SUFFER TO GET WELL. There is no way to escape the terrible *suffering* of remorse and regret and shame and embarrassment which starts us on the road to getting well from our affliction. There is no new way to shake out a hangover. It's painful. And for us, necessarily so. I told this to a friend of mine as he sat weaving to and fro on the side of the bed, in terrible shape, about to die for some paraldehyde. I said, "Lost John"–that's his nickname–"Lost John, you *know* you're going to have to do a certain amount of shaking sooner or later." "Well," he said, "for God's sake let's make it later!" We suffer to get well.

4. We DIE TO LIVE. That is a beautiful paradox straight out of the Biblical idea of being "born again" or "in losing one's life to find it." When we work at our Twelve Steps, the old life of guzzling and fuzzy thinking, and all that goes with it, gradually dies, and we acquire a different and a better way of life. As our shortcomings are removed, one life of us dies, and another life of us lives. We in A.A. die to live.

(4) A FLOWER OF THE SOUTH

Somewhat faded, she nevertheless bloomed afresh. She still had her husband, her home, and a chance to help start A.A. in Texas.

I KNOW THAT if I do daily what I have done for these last thirteen and a half years, I will stay sober. I didn't know that when I came into A.A. I knew that I wanted to try A.A. and if that didn't work, I didn't think anything would. I wish I could tell you how and why A.A. works, but I don't know. I only know that it does–if you desire it with your whole heart and without reservation. I think that no one comes to A.A. until he's tried everything else. As I grow in A.A., I realize that a person with as much self-will as I had, as hard a head and as diseased an ego, had to try everything that I could think of, butting my head against every stone wall before I was ready to come in. The only thing I have really to offer you is my own story, telling you just what sort of a drunk I was.

I came from a family where alcohol was socially acceptable. I lived in New Orleans where, in the twenties, cocktail parties, dances and night spots were almost the order of the day–or rather the night. I can't remember a dinner at home that we didn't have a white wine or claret on the table. We always had cordials after dinner and I know my sister and my brother and I loved creme de menthe. So I was used to it, but I didn't know what the effect of alcohol was because I always had wine, usually with dinner, but always with a lot of ice and about two tablespoons of sugar in it. Drinking it with your meals, you didn't feel it.

I believe the first time I ever realized what alcohol would do for me was at my own wedding. I was an extremely sensitive person and so self-conscious that I hurt all over.

The night that I was married I had a big church wedding. But I couldn't enjoy anything; I was scared to death. Scared that my dress wasn't going to fit right, that the church wasn't going to be filled, that I'd fall flat on my face walking up the aisle; in fact, I was afraid I wasn't going to be a prima donna in the place where I should be. You didn't carry a little orchid up the aisle in those days; you carried a great big bouquet, like a funeral spray, and you didn't have your picture taken until just before you went to the church. As self-conscious as I was, I had to pose for those pictures, holding this huge bouquet. By the time all this was over, I was really in a terrific state, and my father taking in things said, "Miss Esther is about to faint. Get her something to drink." The servant he turned to was our old cook, and she liked to drink. Emma ran out to the kitchen and came back with a water glass full of bourbon and made me drink it down. The church was just three blocks from our home. I got right into the car and they drove me over, and just as soon as I got to the church they started the wedding. As I started down the aisle, that bourbon went right through me. I walked up that aisle just like Mae West in her prime. I wanted to do it all over again.

I don't think that I was conscious of what had happened to me, but I think that it registered sub-consciously. It was really medicinal that night, that whiskey, and it was a medication after that. As long as it eased situations socially, it helped just fine, but somewhere along the line, it backfired. When I crossed that line, I don't know. Something went haywire and I got to depend on it so I could do nothing without it.

I think that it was about 1931 that it first dawned on me that I had a problem, and yet nobody was very critical about it except my family, and that was only because I decided, after seven years of marriage, that I would divorce my husband. I did divorce him in July. It only took a month to get a divorce in Texas. Then I went home. I was free, white and twenty-one and I had a time for myself. I put my poor mother and father through agonies but, finally, I couldn't stand living with them and having them watch everything I did. I had no feeling of security, and I knew that I had done a very stupid thing, so I went back to Texas and remarried my ex-husband. Then we moved up to Oklahoma. That was when all the boys and Esther got drunk and the wives didn't. They would talk about it. That went on for about three years, and then we moved back to Texas again. I really started drinking then.

Frank, my husband, would come home day after day and find me passed out. Or he would leave on a trip and by the time he came home, I'd be passed out. So finally, he said to me one morning, "Esther, why do you do this?" I said, "Well, I don't know why." I had been reading a lot about psychiatry and I thought, "Maybe if I talk to a psychiatrist he can find out what is happening, and then I can drink like a lady." Frank said, "If you'd like to talk to a psychiatrist, I'll see a doctor and find out who to go to here." Frank left to find the doctor and I got drunk.

Frank found the doctor, but the doctor didn't want to take an alcoholic. He called me that because I was drinking too much. So I got drunker and drunker, and then, suddenly, I woke up in the booby-hatch.

I had never been inside of an insane asylum and I really thought I was going to a private hospital. I woke up in this bare room with nothing around me but bars; they wouldn't let me smoke and treated me, well, like I was nuts. I knew this, and right away I got furious and would not even talk to the doctor in the place. I wanted to go home. But they kept me there–I was supposed to stay a month, but they only kept me there seventeen days. I know that I was terribly screwed up inside, but I came out much worse. I could not identify myself with the people with whom I found myself and there was no understanding, and I can't stand confinement anyhow. Because of this state of confusion and frustration I had hysterics on the seventeenth day for the first and only time in my life. So the doctor let me go home on one condition. He asked if I would cooperate with him after I went home, and if I would have a trained nurse stay with me for at least two weeks.

I was so happy over getting home that I changed overnight, but not enough!

This was in 1936 or 1937. I was crazy about my doctor. I cooperated with that man 100 percent! That is how dishonest I was with myself. I know now that I asked questions and told him that I wanted to learn, but I told him only what I wanted to believe about myself. The questions he asked me that I didn't answer honestly, I thought were none of his business. I could see no reason why they should have any relationship to this problem of getting drunk every now and then. So it drove me deeper into the psychosis or neurosis that I had, and that I hated deep down in my heart. I resented the fact that Frank had done this to me, and I just didn't know what was going on. Life was pretty miserable.

About this time, at Christmas, after being under this doctor's care, we decided that there wasn't anything more to do. Every time I got drunk, my husband would send me to a nursing home. He hesitated to send me back to that hospital. I think I disrupted the hospital.

Anyhow, after Christmas my husband gave me a cocker spaniel who is, I think, just as notorious in A.A. as I am. Frank had to go to New York, but because I had a dog, we had a duplex, and I thought–if only we had a house! A duplex apartment isn't any place to raise a dog. So I located a house, and I thought we ought to move into it immediately, but Frank was horrified, because he never knew what was going to happen to me. He always thought that maybe I was safer in a building where there were other people. He said that because of my drinking, he shouldn't leave, but that he had to go to New York for two weeks. Then he said I couldn't possibly move on the first of February because I couldn't stay in that place by myself.

He said, "If your father will come out and stay with you, you can have the house." So I called my father and he said, "Yes," he'd come out and stay with me for that time. I loved my father dearly and I adored my dog, and I'd gotten this new house and Frank had just given me a new fur coat and I was thrilled to death. So Frank went to New York and despite all these things, I got drunk.

My father, as I have said, was very indulgent and loved me dearly, and knew how to get around me. He talked me into taking the Samaritan Treatment. He even had the people come out, and tell me what kind of a room I was going to have, and that he could come and see me, and that the dog could come and see me. So I took the Samaritan Treatment. I guess there are plenty of other graduates of this treatment around. There are no easy ways to sober up, but that's the most excruciating. I took that treatment three times and it didn't work–at least, for me.

There was a doctor in our church congregation who was interested in my case, and he thought it was a vitamin deficiency. So I went down to him quite a few times a month and had him shoot me full of the stuff; and then I went across the street to a little drug store to take a glass of beer or two beers, and then stopped at the liquor store to get myself a pint and go home. You know those vitamins just don't keep you sober!

In 1940, we moved once more, to Houston; my husband thought maybe a change of environment would help and I'd be all right. There was nothing else left to try. We had tried everything. The only thing that I could do would be to call the doctor to help sober me up.

I wouldn't go to hospitals because I wanted my dog there, so I had to have a trained nurse. The only time my dog would have anything to do with me was when I had a hangover, and when I was so sick he was the only one who would have anything to do with me at all.

I have told you some of the funny things, but not much of the shame and degradation. I fell down and knocked out my front teeth. I dropped a two-quart water bottle on my big toe. I couldn't walk, having it in a cast, and the doctor left the cast on three weeks longer than was necessary because he never found me sober enough to take it off. It was one bang after another, so finally, one afternoon in April of 1941, I got as drunk as a skunk, and while I do not walk very straight sober, you should see me when I'm drunk! I was just as drunk as I could be, getting ready to take an afternoon walk. I got into slacks and out I went, weaving with the dog. A patrol car passed. The cop must have seen the condition that I was in because he decided to take me home. When he picked me up, I must have gotten sassy and told him that he couldn't do that, so he took my dog home and took me to jail! As I said before, I don't like to be fenced in, and with those bars you don't get hotel service. They phoned my husband that I was in jail and in such terrible shape that they didn't know what I would do to myself; and they realized that jail was no place for me, but that he was to wait a while before he got me, because at the time they called him to come over for me I was beating a tin cup against the wall. I wanted a cigarette and room service, which I didn't get. So I was in just a few hours. But somewhere during that time, I remembered going back on the bunk and crying my eyes out. I think that is when I hit bottom.

My husband couldn't tell whether I wanted to do something about my drinking. I was as defiant as anybody could be because I was scared. I didn't know which way to turn. So when he came for me, as he walked down the stairs, I could see him through the bars, and he was signing for me; I looked at him and said, "Don't you sign anything in this place!" I was going to sue the city for what they did to me. But Frank turned around and looked at me and said, "Esther, remember you're in jail and not at home." I don't want anybody ever to look at me like that again. The contempt and disgust that was in his face and thoughts! I think I actually read more contempt than was really there because just a week before someone had sent him the Saturday Evening Post article on A.A., and there was a glimmer of hope in it for him.

There was something else that I could try–A.A. But Frank was frightened to death to give it to me, because I resented everything he said and did. So he waited another week or two and I don't think I stayed sober hardly at all.

Frank was out of town, and I remember that he'd gotten in this one night and found me drunk. The next morning he came into my room and said, "Esther, I'm not going to lecture you anymore, but I want you to read this article. If you will try this thing, I'll go along with you. If you don't, you will have to go home. I cannot sit by and watch you destroy yourself."

When he left I thought, what is this crack-pot thing? I took two or three drinks so my eyes could focus, and I could see that horrible picture of the awful drunk on the first page; he couldn't get the drink to his mouth, he had a towel around his hand and he needed a shave. But, from the very first paragraph on, something happened to me. I realized that there were other people in this world who behaved and acted as I did, and that I was a sick person, that I was suffering from an actual disease. It had a name and symptoms, just like diabetes or T.B. I wasn't entirely immoral; I wasn't bad; I wasn't vicious. It was such a feeling of relief that I wanted to know more about it and with that, I think for the first time, came the realization that there was something horribly, horribly wrong with me. Up to that time, I was so completely baffled by my behavior that I had never really stopped to think at all.

So, as I have said, I don't know how or why A.A. works. I only know that it first reached me through that Saturday Evening Post article. There was no one I could call. I know that when Frank came home, I said, "I want to try this thing," and he said, "There's a box to write to in New York." It was the A.A. General Service Office in New York that I wrote to, and that office has always meant a lot to me. Today, because of A.A.'s growth during the intervening years, it is of course much bigger than it was then.

I wrote on a Saturday. I was shaking so, I asked my husband to write the letter for me, but he said no. This was something I had to do all by myself. So I wrote this letter in very shaky handwriting, and in just one week came back a letter with A.A. literature from New York. They sent me the regular letter they send to everybody else, but along with it, Ruth Hock, the nonalcoholic secretary, wrote a little note in long-hand because she could see from the letter that I really needed help badly. That personal touch did help me too.

That was on Saturday and my husband was leaving town Sunday night. He said, "Wait until I get back and I will go with you to see this man." (That was the man the A.A. office had referred me to.) So Frank left town, and by Monday morning I had been sober for that whole week. I wanted to try A.A. with my whole heart and soul. I had learned an awful lot about myself in that one little article. Monday morning I was feeling just like a million dollars–all I needed was half a pint! So I got a half pint and at midnight that night, I called the number I had been given, but the man who had started the group was in the hospital so I didn't know what to do. The letter from A.A. had said this man would see me–there weren't any women.

I stayed drunk from Monday until Friday, and I call that my spill into A.A. I'm glad I had it then. In spite of knowing that my drunkenness was a symptom of the things that were wrong with me, and that I could never drink again, I thought I couldn't yet give it up, although I was going to try. I never want to forget that last drunk as long as I live. It was one of the worst I ever had. It was the first time in my life that I could not get a lift out of what I was drinking; and so one Friday night, May 16, 1941, at five minutes to six, I had half a water glass of warm gin, and that is when I first asked God to help me.

There are so many to whom I feel deeply grateful; to my husband (and best critic), whose generous love, compassion and understanding have helped me along the way; to those before me in A.A. who inspired the first article I read, and the friend who sent that article to Frank; to Ruth for her personal note, and the first A.A. to talk to me; to my Bishop, whose loving and believing spirit inspired me; and to all the members of the Houston Group who were so patient, kind and helpful–and to countless others.

In my second year in A.A. we were transferred to Dallas. However, I threw myself into Twelve Step work, and what I feared would be a calamity turned out to be the most blessed of blessings. My work with other alcoholics has led me, day by day, into ever wider and richer experiences.

I wish I could tell you all that A.A. has done for me, all that I think and feel about A.A., but it's something that I have experienced and have never been able to put into words. I know that I must work at it as long as I live; I know that it is only by working at it that I can stay sober and have a happy life. It is an endless career.

It has changed not simply one department of my life–it has changed my whole life. It has been a fellowship with God and man that has held good wherever I've turned and whatever I've done. It is a way of life that pays as it goes, every step of the way, in compensations that have been wonderfully rich and rewarding. It has made life a thousand times easier and simpler than did the endless compromises and conflicts by which I lived before. It pays daily in more harmonious relations with my fellow men, in ever clearer insight into the true meaning of life, and in the answering love and gratitude wherever and whenever I have been the instrument of God's will in the lives of others. In all these ways I've experienced, in ever growing measure and beyond all expectations and rewards, a joy which I had never before imagined.

The words of Dr. Bob and Bill are with me all the time. Dr. Bob said, "Love and service keep us dry," and Bill says, "Always we must remember that our first duty is face-to-face help for the alcoholic who still suffers." Dr. Bob tells about keeping it simple and not to louse it up. It's the last thing I ever heard him say, and I think there are some of us who, at times, try to read extra messages and complexities into the Steps. To me, A.A. is within the reach of every alcoholic, because it can be achieved in any walk of life and because the achievement is not ours but God's. I feel that there is no situation too difficult, none too desperate, no unhappiness too great to be overcome in this great fellowship–Alcoholics Anonymous.

(5) UNTO THE SECOND GENERATION

A young veteran tells how a few rough experiences pushed him into A.A.–and how he was therefore spared years of suffering.

MY EYES OPENED onto a hazy world. Two fuzzy objects came into focus. Slowly I realized I was in bed and that the objects were my feet, encased in a harness affair. I blinked slowly as I shifted my gaze to my arms. They also were held in some sort of strap arrangement.

Gradually consciousness returned enough to let me know I was in a hospital. I looked about the room. At one end of the bed, near the foot, was a printed card, and beneath that was a charted graph. I couldn't focus enough to make out the chart, but the card contained two words–"ACUTE ALCOHOLISM." Then it came to me. I was in a hospital. The place–Hawaii. The year–1948. I closed my eyes and tried to think.

I remembered having had a little drink of whiskey with a can of warm beer as a chaser. Then something happened. What was it? I couldn't recall. I opened my eyes again and a shadow fell across the bed. Standing there was a gray haired man–tall, trim and in uniform. There were gold bars on his shoulders.

Now I know. I'm in the U.S. Navy. This must be the doctor. He asked how I felt. I didn't reply. A corpsman stood beside him. The doctor motioned to the corpsman to undo my straightjacket and leg restraints. I moved about a little. The doctor sat down beside the bed and asked me how I felt.

"Do you know why you're in here?" he queried.

I could tell him a lot of reasons why I am here in an alky ward at the age of twenty. I don't know how I got here this trip, but it doesn't matter very much. I'm an alcoholic. Don't mince words. I'm a rummy. I can't control my drinking any more. It controls me.

I remembered back to high school when I was fifteen. We all had lockers. The other pupils kept books, pencils, paper, gym equipment and such stuff in their lockers. I did, too. I also kept beer. At fifteen I was strictly a beer drinker. I didn't graduate to the hard stuff until I was sixteen. The other kids would light out for the hamburger huts or ice cream parlors, the pizza joints or bowling alleys, after football games and dances. I didn't. I went to saloons where I could get drinks.

I didn't give a whoop about anything scholastic. I got a job after school pumping gas and worked until ten or eleven at night. I was the kid of the crew. I tried to mimic the talk, ideas, moods and even the drinking of the older men. It hurt to be considered a kid. I talked out of the side of my mouth, as they did. I smoked as much, tried to drink as much, and do everything they did, only more so.

I found I could boost my income by selling gas coupons (rationing was in effect then) that I'd taken in earlier from other customers, by filching nickels from the Coke machine, by short-sticking customers on oil, and by selling oil I'd drained out of other cars.

School was getting to be one big bore. I was skipping classes about two days a week and doing no book work whatever. I was failing in everything. The principal had no alternative but to expel me. I beat him to it. I quit, when I was just past sixteen.

I had a drinking problem on my hands even at that time. So did my parents. They both drank like fish. They had been drinking for many years and were getting progressively worse. Home life didn't mean much to me. They were kind when they thought about it, but that wasn't often. I wanted love and affection but I didn't get it. I did as I pleased most of the time.

I wasn't burdened with parental guidance and I didn't want any. I ran away for the second time, with another lad. We got to Omaha, from my home in Chicago. We headed out of town walking–no money, cold and hungry. It was late at night. We spotted a church in a small town. We broke open a window and got inside. We started to light matches to see, but the draft blew them out. So we rolled old newspapers together and made torches to find a good soft pew and get some sleep. My torch blazed madly and the pew caught fire.

We heard some yells outside. A busload of basketball players had been passing and saw the flames. They summoned the fire department and the sheriff. I spent the next three days in a cell. My Dad, who was a newspaper man and had some connections, had meantime put a stop on me, and I guess that report went all over the country. We were identified and I was put on a train for Chicago. The sheriff bade us goodbye very happily. I still think Dad paid him something to let me go.

Back home again! Drinking conditions at home were even worse than before. I would rather have stayed in jail except I didn't like the bologna and cold potatoes for breakfast. I got a job with the newspaper my Dad worked for. I liked it and soon moved into the photo department, which was what I wanted to do. "Ace crime photographer," that's me.

About this time I got my first crush on a girl. I teamed up with a cute little blonde with whom I was working at the office, and for about a year we were inseparable. Beaches, parties, dances, movies–everything. Here was the lost love I'd missed at home. I was drinking quite a bit of whiskey now. She didn't like it, but I thought it made a man of me. Once in a while I stayed home for a night, to see how my folks were doing. They were doing very well–at least a fifth apiece a day, except on Dad's days off when they did some serious drinking.

I was now nearly eighteen. I enlisted in the Navy to escape the army draft. It looked as if the war would be over any day, but I had to go anyhow. I planned to stay home the night before I left, but my folks got so drunk I walked off early in the evening and spent the night with my girl, getting very drunk myself. Next morning I was sworn in, feeling no pain. I went into the Navy in fine style. I was drunk. Three years later I was discharged in the same way.

At Great Lakes Boot Camp I latched onto a soft billet. My job was to make out the guard schedules and thus I was exempt from ordinary recruit training activities. This went on for thirteen weeks, the first eight of which I wasn't allowed visitors. But my Dad pulled some strings and got in to see me after three weeks. He and Mom smuggled in a couple of pints to me. This was fine, but it was just an extra dividend, for I'd made connections by this time and was buying a bottle a day from the cook. I stayed in the barracks all day, "making out guard schedules," and getting mildly plastered from the jug under my desk. I applied for photo school at Pensacola Air Base and made it. While waiting to depart I was selected–by giving a CPO five dollars–to be bartender in the Navy Chief's Club. At night I tended bar.

While I was at Pensacola my Dad became dangerously ill and almost died of pneumonia plus a heart attack. I got emergency leave for twenty days. Mom and I drank every waking moment because we felt so sorry for Dad. I tried to control her drinking by pouring her whiskey down the sink before I'd leave for the night, to get drunker myself.

I don't know why I didn't fall out of the open cockpit of some of those planes I flew in while taking aerial pictures. I didn't. And when this six month school was over I applied for duty in Hawaii and pulled it. I wanted to get as far away from home as possible.

Pearl Harbor was a breeze of nine months, a gay Hawaiian paradise, drinking under the palms, listening to the surf beat on the shore, a bottle of whiskey near at hand. I was becoming a solitary drinker, but I didn't care. I was transferred to Kaneohe Bay, across the hump to the windward side of Oahu, to the aviation base. This was wonderful. I talked the Old Man into letting me live in the photo lab instead of the barracks, and for eighteen months nothing interfered with my drinking. The boys at the Post Office used to bring me my jugs; mail couldn't be opened for inspection at the gate. This was an ideal set-up.

I was only twenty now, but I was a man. Wasn't I drinking more than a quart every day? I knew I was hitting the skids, but what of it? Didn't I come from a family of drinkers? There wasn't much I could do about it, and I didn't want to do anything anyway.

About this time my folks found A.A. It solved their problems and they started living a sane life again. They wrote me many long letters about it. I thought it was fine for them. They really needed it. But I knew I'd never get that way.

I seldom left the base anymore except once in a while when I felt the need of talking to some girl. Then I'd get a pass to Honolulu. Meanwhile the letters from home were telling about how much my folks wanted to make up to me for some of the things I'd missed. I hadn't told them about my drinking, but I guess they knew. I'd reply and some of my letters they saved. To this day I haven't been able to decipher what I wrote to them.

One night I was sitting in the lab alone with a fifth and a case of beer listening to dreamy Hawaiian music on the radio. Slowly a pile of pineapples started to build up on the table. They got bigger and bigger and nearer and nearer, as if they were going to fall and crush me. Two of them leaped from the table and crashed into my head. I was knocked to the floor, swinging madly at the faces on those pineapples. I swung, I swore, I started throwing beer cans at the advancing hordes of pineapple faces. I cut my hands, my face, my legs. Then I collapsed. I had D.T.'s.

The doctor was still sitting beside my bed. My past had slipped before me in a twinkling. The doctor said I'd been brought into the hospital like a madman, crying, raving, ranting, swearing, completely in the throes of Delirium Tremens.

I was released in a week, a week of hell with no drinks. I told the doctor my parents' drinking history and blamed them. He was interested and said he'd help me all he could. He even went to bat for me before the court martial that inevitably followed and, as a result, I drew only thirty days–fifteen in solitary.

Two months later I was discharged. I was supposed to come home on a troop ship, but I talked the base commander into flying home. We were supposed to take off at noon, but were delayed until 6 p.m. I spent the time in a nearby tavern, was loaded on the ship, went to sleep before take-off, and the next thing I knew someone was shaking me and telling me we were over San Diego.

I went to Tijuana that night and landed in jail. Drunk and causing a brawl, they said. Heck. All I'd wanted was one more drink. I was escorted back to San Diego next morning–by the Shore Patrol, but I was discharged on schedule.

I headed home for the most wonderful experience of all time–meeting my "new" parents–Mom and Dad looked different than I had pictured them. They had color in their faces, sparkle in their eyes and love in their hearts. It was a glorious homecoming. Dad got out a jug for me and poured welcome home drinks. I took it easy, because they didn't know about me. But I was soon drinking as heavily as I had been.

I would drink all night in bars, come home about 5 a.m., down a good big glass of whiskey straight, and tumble into bed. Or maybe I'd come home wild drunk, singing and raving about what a fine place home was and what grand parents I had since they joined A.A.

Sometimes I'd make it home and go to sleep at the wheel of my car, for all the neighbors to see next morning as they left for work. I paid nine hundred dollars for a second hand car on my return. I lost it many times and Mom and Dad would drive me around until I found it. I spent eighteen hundred dollars fixing up that car in the first year I was home, after four bad smashups. Why I wasn't killed or how I got home I don't know.

The end came early in 1950. I'd lost my car again, pawned my wallet and all identification papers for a bottle, and gotten home somehow. Again I went into a mild form of D.T.'s, but with no pineapples this time. The folks called a doctor and he knocked me out with sedatives. I'd heard a lot about A.A. and met a great many A.A.'s during that year at home, but I hadn't thought of it for myself. I'd thought of it in an offhand way, of course. But I didn't want to stop drinking–not at twenty-two. I merely wanted to cut down. And the folks said A.A. was for people who wanted to quit, otherwise it wouldn't work.

But as I came out of this second bout with D.T.'s, I knew I was licked. I'd packed more drinking into seven years than many a heavy drinker does in a lifetime. And I'd proved I couldn't handle it, time and again. That doctor in the Navy hospital told me I wouldn't live five years if I didn't quit. I'd fooled him thus far. But for how long? "I've got to stop if I want to live," I told myself, and if I don't want to break my parents' hearts and maybe jeopardize their own carefully built up and hard fought-for sobriety.

"I'll do it," I told myself. "I'll do it. I'll join A.A. if it kills me. Mom has said the only requisite to start is willingness. Well, I'm willing, if it will curb this awful desire to drink, this fear of not having a drink, this feeling of always being alone, scared, deserted, sick. Dear God, I'll do anything! Only show me how."

That is how I came into A.A. There was a red plush carpet to welcome me, but even so it wasn't easy. I'd acquired a new girl, a lovely girl who knew of my problem and had tried to help me. A week after my decision to join A.A., she called it quits. Three days later I lost my job. This combination nearly threw me. I thought, "If this is A.A. why not go back to drinking, kill myself with booze in the next three years the doctor had given me, and call it a bad job?"

But I didn't. I attended meetings, I talked to my folks, I talked to younger people they had gotten in contact with to sponsor me. And somehow or other I stayed sober.

I joined A.A. at twenty-two. I'm twenty-six now and I haven't had a drink since I made my decision. At that time life to me was spelled "w-h-i-s-k-e-y." Today I think of life in terms of happiness, contentment, freedom from fear and despair, sane thinking, ability to face problems as they occur, the opportunity to help other alcoholics and to be decent.

Were I to revert to drinking, even now, I wouldn't give anything for these four years in A.A. They have been the happiest of my life. I have been helped morally, spiritually, mentally and materially through A.A. I used to think, "Why live without whiskey?" Now I know I can't live without A.A.

Four years ago I had nothing but a jumbled, mad existence. Today I have all that anyone could ask. I have a lovely wife who understands my problem and helps me with it. I have two wonderful little boys. I have a good job. I have kind and sympathetic parents. I'm buying a home. I owe no one–except A.A.

(6) HIS CONSCIENCE

It was the only part of him that was soluble in alcohol.

HOW WAS I to know that I was an alcoholic? No one ever told me that I was or even hinted that I had passed the point of no return.

Some years ago my thinking was that alcoholics just did not live in my world. Yes, I had seen them on my infrequent visits to the seamy side of town. I had been panhandled by them in almost every city in Canada. In my estimation an alcoholic was a down-and-out, a badly dressed bum who much preferred drinking to working.

If I had been asked I would have said that I did not even know an alcoholic. As for being one, it was the very farthest thing from my mind. I would have bitterly resented any such suggestion. Besides, I thought that any alcoholic was a misfit with a mental quirk of some kind. It was my opinion that they were all introverts and on tests I had twice been classified as an extrovert.

Certainly I did not know that alcoholism was an illness. Furthermore, I had no idea that it was a progressive illness.

I come from a family of five children and I had a very happy childhood in a small Canadian town. Both my mother and father were religious, without over emphasizing it. In due time, I went through grade and high school and entered college as a little better than average student.

The First War had broken out before I got around to taking my first drink. I joined the army fairly early in that war.

Oddly enough, I drank very little while in the service for the very good reason that every time I took a drink something disagreeable happened to me. My first drink was scotch undiluted. It put me temporarily out of business through strangulation. The second drink made me sick at my stomach. After the third trial I went to sleep in the summer sun and was painfully sunburned. In France I gave away my rum ration far more often than I drank it.

With the War half over I was sent back to Canada for my discharge from wounds and shock. During the period of waiting for my final papers, along with friends, I spent a good deal of time in a neighboring speakeasy enjoying a few social drinks.

Out of the army, my drinking dropped away to a drink or two on very special occasions, two or three times a year. So it went for the next ten years, no pattern, no problem.

Toward the end of the twenties the company by which I was employed went through a merger. I was given a more responsible position which entailed a great deal of traveling from coast to coast. I found that a few drinks with agreeable companions, in sleeping cars or hotels, helped while away the time. Frankly, I preferred the company of those who took a drink or two to those who did not.

For the next few years I had a lot of fun with alcohol. I liked the taste of it; I liked the effect of it.

I conducted myself properly and no harm came of it. Without realizing it, I came to look forward to several drinks before dinner and then to some during the evening. I gradually developed into a heavy drinker with the result that I didn't feel so well in the mornings.

I would like to make it clear at this point that neither business pressure nor added responsibility had anything to do with my drinking. I had the capacity for handling business without any fear of criticism. I enjoyed the companionship of drinking friends, but I began to notice that there was this difference between us; they were still satisfied with one or two drinks, but alcohol was having a different effect on me. My system seemed to need more alcohol than theirs. In retrospect, my only conclusion is that at that time I was becoming more physically sensitive to and losing my tolerance for alcohol.

But obviously my illness was progressing because it wasn't very long until I started experiencing blackouts. There were times when I would lose my car. At this distance it seems funny, but in those days it was a serious business. With some serious drinking in mind, I would take great care to park my car in some inconspicuous place, some distance from where I intended to do this drinking. After several hours, I would return only to find that it wasn't there. At least it wasn't where I thought I had left it. Then I would start walking up blocks one way and down blocks the other way until I would finally locate it, usually in an entirely different direction than where I was sure I had parked it. On those occasions, I would always end up with a feeling of remorse not far removed from a loathing of myself and the condition I was in. And, of course, I was always terribly afraid of being seen by someone who knew me.

It wasn't long until travelling even by train became a hazard. I could somehow manage to catch a train, but all too often it was not the train which I intended to catch. Sometimes it would be going in the wrong direction, and I would end up in a town or city where I had no intention of being and, therefore, had no business to transact.

Having blackouts also meant that I couldn't clearly remember all of what had transpired the night before, and then it was only a short step to not being able to remember any of it. This became very embarrassing to me. I began to avoid discussing the happenings of the night before. In fact, I no longer wanted to talk about my drinking. I took to drinking alone.

Up to this point, my rise in the business world had been steady. I had become vice-president of the Canadian end of a large company known the world over. Now I found myself delaying making decisions, putting off appointments because my eyes were blood-shot and I didn't feel so well. It was difficult for me to concentrate and even to follow closely a business conversation.

Time and time again I went on the wagon; I said I was through with drink, and at the time actually meant what I said. The end result was always the same. Sooner or later, I started in all over again and binges came closer and closer together.

From time to time friends and relatives spoke to me about my drinking. My wife and family asked me to control it, to pull myself together, to use my will power, to drink like a gentleman. I made dozens of promises and at the time of making them, I sincerely meant to keep every one. I became two different people, one person when I was sober and an entirely different one when I was drinking.

I discovered the morning drink and soon it took two, three or four to straighten me out. I had the shakes so badly that shaving became a task that I feared and dreaded because my hand was so unsteady. I discovered that the shakes came only when I allowed the alcoholic content of my system to drop too low. All too often when I brought it up with some stiff jolts, I went into a blackout. Striking an even balance seemed beyond my power.

I will never forget the first time I became conscious of that overpowering compulsion. No matter what happened–I simply had to have a drink. This compulsion soon became part of my make-up.

One Monday morning when the compulsion was on me, I met an old drinking friend. Our meeting was generally the signal for a bender of some proportions. I always thought that he was the one who should watch his drinking habits–not me. On this particular morning, he was clear-eyed and sober, truly a minor miracle for Monday. He looked well and he looked happy. He said he felt fine and that he had stopped drinking. I asked him whether he had got religion. He said no, but that he had joined A.A. That was the first time I had ever heard of such an organization. Since he couldn't produce a drink, I went on my way and forgot about it.

From this time on, my drinking progressed rapidly. My family life deteriorated. My friends no longer wanted to drink with me. Business trips always became benders. One bender ended by starting another. I discovered that the conscience was the only part of a human being that was soluble in alcohol. I lied about my drinking. I lied about everything else–even things that didn't matter. I thought that everyone was watching me.

The company for which I worked told me politely but firmly that, unless I controlled my drinking, we would have to part. I promised to do better and mend my ways. I was drunk within the hour. Two months later I appeared drunk at a meeting and the next day I was on my own.

I promptly went on the wagon, got another good position and stayed sober for a year. Although this new position offered many opportunities, I did not take advantage of them. I'm sure that this was because I found out that being on the wagon was the most miserable of all existences. I was moody and irritable. My mind was never at rest. I imagined all sorts of things. I worried about the past and I could see no hope for the future. On occasions,

I attended parties where there was some drinking and good natured fun. I hated every minute of it because I just could not join in with this fun. I sat morosely by myself, wondering how soon the endless evening would be over. In short, I was just plain sorry for myself. After several evenings like this, I did everything I could to avoid social engagements and felt more lonely than ever before. I had lost the art of being friendly. The people I had liked best irritated me most.

At the end of the year I fell off the wagon, promising myself that I would stop after just a drink or two. Within two weeks I was drinking harder than I ever had before. The only way I knew to drive away remorse was to drink more and more.

After nine months of mental suffering and physical torture, I sat at home one night alone with a bottle beside me. I had been drinking hard all day, but no matter how much I drank the shakes did not even diminish. My mind was clear, but the bottle on which I depended did not do anything for me. My way of life passed before me as on a screen. I saw how I had slipped and how rapidly I was deteriorating. The cure of the bottle on which I had grown to depend no longer worked. I broke out in a cold sweat. I was without hope. I could not stop drinking. The ceiling came down. The walls pressed in. The floor came up. I could think of no answer. There seemed no way out. Was it too late?

There just wasn't any use of taking another drink; even that didn't help. Then across my mind came the picture of my drinking friend whom I had met three years before–clear-eyed and sober. Then and there I decided to try A.A. I put the bottle away.

Next morning, I made my first contact with A.A. I was asked some questions, one of which was, "Do you turn to lower companionship and inferior environment while drinking?" Ashamed, I felt as if they had been reading my mail. This, and other questions, convinced me that here were people who understood my problem.

One thing my A.A friend said to me that morning was, "Today could be the most important day in your life." It was and still is, for nothing but good has come to me through A.A.

After admitting and accepting the fact that I was powerless over alcohol, my first great feeling of relief was that I was no longer alone. I was in a fellowship of people who had the same problem that I had; indeed, most of them had been very much worse off than I.

Having enjoyed good companionship for many years, my loneliness near the end of my drinking had become a real hell to me, but this new fellowship of understanding people gave me new life and new strength. I now realize that an alcoholic cannot get along alone, any more than anyone else can. I, like all men, was a social being who desperately needed fellowship and acceptance. These I found in A.A. where hands were reached out to me. I was not condemned. On the contrary, I was greatly encouraged by these people who spoke my language and, what was so important, offered me hope.

When I became a member of A.A., I immediately went to the president of the company for which I worked and told him about it. His hearty handshake and unmistakable look of approval were all that passed between us. That was enough. I knew I was on my way up again–as long as I remembered to stay away from the first drink.

As sober days passed into sober weeks, I was soon back in the confidence of men who once again respected my judgment in business. I no longer had any fear of interviews with fellow executives because my eyes were clear and my hand was steady. My home life improved and today is happier than ever before.

Certainly, I still have my ups and downs in my new life without alcohol, but during my years in A.A., I have been and am continually learning to accept the things I cannot change, being given courage to change the things I can, and the wisdom to know the difference.

How has all this happened to me? I have already mentioned how important was this new-found fellowship, but I am sure there is more to it than that alone. Right from the start of my attending A.A. meetings, I heard various speakers give all credit to a Power greater than themselves. One morning as I was walking to work, from seemingly nowhere at all, there came a thought that there was a possibility that I might never drink again. I have had no desire to drink since that time. It was certainly nothing that I myself could have done that brought this new-found peace. There was only one answer. This Power greater than myself had, as to so many others, restored me to sanity.

Finally, let me say that I am sure that I could not have in the past seven years, nor can I in the future, enjoy my happy and contented sobriety unless I try to share it with others. Therefore, my earnest hope in relating my experience here is that it will help someone, anyone with a drinking problem, but particularly that person who may still be hanging on to his job or business, or may still be holding his home together.

It has often occurred to me that, if I had been a baseball player and had lost an arm, I would soon have reconciled myself to the fact that I could no longer play baseball. Similarly, with the great help of this fellowship, I have reconciled myself to the fact that I can no longer handle alcohol even to the extent of taking a single drink.

A.A. has given me a happy and contented way of living, and I am very deeply grateful to the founders and early members of A.A. who plotted the course and who kept the faith.

(7) THE HOUSEWIFE WHO DRANK AT HOME

She hid her bottles in the clothes hampers and dresser drawers. In A.A., she discovered she had lost nothing and had found everything.

MY STORY HAPPENS to be a particular kind of woman's story: the story of the woman who drinks at home. I had to be at home –I had two babies. When alcohol took me over, my bar was my kitchen, my living room, my bedroom, the back bathroom, and the two laundry hampers.

At one time the admission that I was and am an alcoholic meant shame, defeat, and failure to me. But in the light of the new understanding that I have found in A.A., I have been able to interpret that defeat and that failure and that shame as seeds of victory. Because it was only through feeling defeat and feeling failure, the inability to cope with my life and with alcohol, that I was able to surrender and accept the fact that I had this disease and that I had to learn to live again without alcohol.

I was never a very heavy social drinker. But during a period of particular stress and strain about thirteen years ago, I resorted to alcohol in my home, alone, as a means of temporary release and of getting a little extra sleep.

I had problems. We all have them, and I thought a little brandy or a little wine now and then could certainly hurt no one. I don't believe, when I started, that I even had in mind the thought that I was drinking. I *had* to sleep, I *had* to clear my mind and free it from worry, and I *had* to relax. But from one or two drinks of an afternoon or evening, my intake mounted, and mounted fast. It wasn't long before I was drinking all day. I had to have that wine. The only incentive that I had, toward the end, for getting dressed in the morning was to get out and get "supplies" to help me get my day started. But the only thing that got started was my drinking.

I should have realized that alcohol was getting hold of me when I started to become secretive in my drinking. I began to have to have supplies on hand for the people who "might come in." And of course a half-empty bottle wasn't worth keeping, so I finished it up and naturally had to get more in right away for the people who "might come in unexpectedly." But I was always the unexpected person who had to finish the bottle. I couldn't go to one wine store and look the man honestly in the face and buy a bottle, as I used to do when I had parties and entertained and did normal drinking. I had to give him a story and ask him the same question over and over again, "Well, now, how many will that bottle serve?" I wanted him to be sure that I wasn't the one who was going to drink the whole bottle.

I had to hide, as a great many people in A.A. have had to do. I did my hiding in the hampers and in my dresser drawers. When we begin to do things like that with alcohol, something's gone wrong. I needed it, and I knew I was drinking too much, but I wasn't conscious of the fact that I should stop. I kept on. My home at that time was a place to mill around in. I wandered from room to room, thinking, drinking, drinking, thinking. And the mops would come out, the vacuum would come out, everything would come out, but nothing would get done. Toward five o'clock, helter-skelter, I'd get everything put away and try to get supper on the table, and after supper I'd finish the job up and knock myself out.

I never knew which came first, the thinking or the drinking. If I could only stop thinking, I wouldn't drink. If I could only stop drinking, maybe I wouldn't think. But they were all mixed up together, and I was all mixed up inside. And yet I had to have that drink. You know the deteriorating effects, the disintegrating effects of chronic wine-drinking. I cared nothing about my personal appearance. I didn't care what I looked like; I didn't care what I did. To me, taking a bath was just being in a place with a bottle where I could drink in privacy. I had to have it with me at night, in case I woke up and needed that drink.

How I ran my home, I don't know. I went on, realizing what I was becoming, hating myself for it, bitter, blaming life, blaming everything else but the fact that I should turn about and do something about my drinking. Finally I didn't care; I was beyond caring. I just wanted to live to a certain age, carry through with what I felt was my job with the children, and after that–no matter. Half a mother was better than no mother at all.

I needed that alcohol. I couldn't live without it. I couldn't do anything without it. But there came a point when I could no longer live with it. And that came after a three-weeks' illness of my son. The doctor prescribed a teaspoon of brandy for the boy to help him through the night when he coughed. Well, of course, that was all I needed–to switch from wine to brandy for three weeks. I knew nothing about alcoholism or the D.T.'s, but when I woke up on this last morning of my son's illness, I taped the keyhole on my door because "everyone was out there." I paced back and forth in the apartment with the cold sweats. I screamed on the telephone for my mother to get up there; something was going to happen; I didn't know what, but if she didn't get there quick, I'd split wide open. I called my husband up and told him to come home.

After that I sat for a week, a body in a chair, a mind off in space. I thought the two would never get together. I knew that alcohol and I had to part. I couldn't live with it any more. And yet, how was I going to live without it? I didn't know. I was bitter, living in hate. The very person who stood with me through it all and has been my greatest help was the person that I turned against, my husband. I also turned against my family, my mother. The people who would have come to help me were just the people I would have nothing to do with.

Nevertheless, I began to try to live without alcohol. But I only succeeded in fighting it. And believe me, an alcoholic cannot fight alcohol. I had all kinds of reasons for my drinking. I had problems. I was a woman, tied to my home. What I needed was a change, mental relaxation, getting out and doing something. I thought that was my answer. I said to my husband, "I'm going to try to get interested in something outside, get myself out of this rut I'm in." I thought I was going out of my mind. If I didn't have a drink, I had to do something.

I became one of the most active women in the community, what with P.T.A., other community organizations, and drives. I'd go into an organization, and it wasn't long before I was on the committee, then I was chairman of the committee; and if I was in a group, I'd soon be treasurer or secretary of the group. But I wasn't happy. I became a Jekyll–and–Hyde person. As long as I worked, as long as I got out, I didn't drink. But I had to get back to that first drink somehow. And when I took that first drink, I was off on the usual merry-go-round. And it was my home that suffered. My husband, my children saw the other side of me. So that didn't work.

I figured I'd be all right if I could find something I liked to do. So when the children were in school from nine to three, I started up a nice little business and was fairly successful in it. But not happy. Because I found that everything I turned to became a substitute for drink. And when all of life is a substitute for drink, there's no happiness, no peace. I still had to drink; I still needed that drink. Mere cessation from drinking is not enough for an alcoholic while the need for that drink goes on. I switched to beer. I had always hated beer, but now I grew to love it, bottle after bottle of it, warm or cold. So that wasn't my answer either.

I went to my doctor again. He knew what I was doing, how I was trying. I said, "I can't find my middle road in life. I can't find it. It's either all work, or I drink." He said, "Why don't you try Alcoholics Anonymous?" I was willing to try anything. I was licked. For the second time, I was licked. The first time was when I knew I couldn't live with alcohol. But this second time, I found I couldn't live normally without it, and I was licked worse than ever.

The fellowship I found in A.A. enabled me to face my problem honestly and squarely. I couldn't do it among my relatives; I couldn't do it among my friends. No one likes to admit that they're a drunk, that they can't control this thing. But when we come into A.A., we can face our problem honestly and openly. I went to closed meetings and open meetings. And I took everything that A.A. had to give me. Easy does it, first things first, one day at a time. It was at that point that I reached surrender. I heard one very ill woman say that she didn't believe in the surrender part of the A.A. program. My heavens! Surrender to me has meant the ability to run my home, to face my responsibilities as they should be faced, to take life as it comes to me day by day, and work my problems out. That's what surrender has meant to me. I surrendered once to the bottle, and I couldn't do these things. Since I gave my will over to A.A., whatever A.A. has wanted of me I've tried to do to the best of my ability. When I'm asked to go out on a call, I go. *I'm* not going;

A.A. is leading me there. A.A. gives us alcoholics direction into a way of life without the need for alcohol. That life for me is lived one day at a time, letting the problems of the future rest with the future. When the time comes to solve them, God will give me strength for that day.

I had been brought up to believe in God, but I know that until I found this A.A. program, I had never found or known faith in the reality of God, the reality of His power that is now with me in everything I do.

(8) IT MIGHT HAVE BEEN WORSE

Alcohol was a looming cloud in this banker's bright sky. With rare foresight he realized it could become a tornado.

HOW CAN a person with a fine family, an attractive home, an excellent position, and high standing in an important city become an alcoholic?

As I later found out through Alcoholics Anonymous, alcohol is no respecter of economic status, social and business standing, or intelligence.

I was raised like the majority of American boys, coming from a family of modest circumstances, attending public schools, having the social life of a small midwestern town, with part-time work and some athletics. The ambition to succeed was instilled in me by my Scandinavian parents who came to this country where opportunities were so great. "Keep busy; always have something constructive to do." I did work of all kinds after school and during vacations, trying to find that which would appeal most as a goal for a life work. Then there was wartime service to interrupt my plans, and an education to be picked up after the war. After that came marriage, getting started in business, and a family. The story is not very different from that of thousands of other young men in my generation. It shows nothing or no one to blame for alcoholism.

The drive to get ahead, to succeed, kept me too busy for many years to have any great experience with social life. I would have begrudged the time or money for alcohol. In fact I was afraid to try it for fear that I would wind up like many examples I had seen of excessive drinking in the army. I was intolerant of people who drank, particularly those who drank to an extent that interfered with on-the-job performance.

In time I became an officer and director of one of the largest commercial banks in the country. I achieved recognized and national standing in my profession, as well as becoming a director in many important institutions having to do with the civic life of a large city. I had a family to be proud of, actively sharing in the responsibilities of good citizenship.

My drinking did not start until after I was thirty-five and a fairly successful career had been established. But success brought increased social activities and I realized that many of my friends enjoyed a social drink with no apparent harm to themselves or others. I disliked being different so, ultimately, I began to join them occasionally.

At first it was just that–an occasional drink. Then I looked forward to the weekend of golf and the nineteenth hole. The cocktail hour became a daily routine. Gradually the quantity increased, the occasions for a drink came more frequently: a hard day, worries and pressure, bad news, good news–there were more and more reasons for a drink. Why did I want increasingly greater quantities of alcohol? It was frightening that drink was being substituted for more and more of the things I really enjoyed doing. Golf, hunting, and fishing were now merely excuses to drink excessively.

I made promises to myself, my family, and friends–and broke them. Short dry spells ended in heavy drinking. I tried to hide my drinking by going places where I was unlikely to see anyone I knew. Hangovers and remorse were always with me.

The next steps were bottle hiding, and excuses for trips in order to drink without restraint. Cunning, baffling, powerful–the gradual creeping up of the frequency and quantity of alcohol and what it does to a person is apparent to everyone but the person involved.

When it became noticeable to the point of comment, I devised ways of sneaking drinks on the side. "Rehearsals" then became a part of the pattern, stopping at bars on the way to or from the place where drinks were to be served. Never having enough, always craving more, the obsession for alcohol gradually began to dominate all my activities, particularly while traveling. Drink planning became more important than any other plans.

I tried the wagon on numerous occasions, but I always felt unhappy and abused. I tried psychiatry, but of course I gave the psychiatrist no cooperation.

I was living in constant fear that I would get caught while driving a car, so I used taxis part of the time. Then I began to have blackouts, and that was a constant worry. To wake up at home, not knowing how I got there, and to realize I had driven my car, became torture. Not knowing where I had been or how I got home was making me desperate.

It now became necessary to have noon drinks–at first just two, then gradually more. My hours of work were flexible so that returning to the office was not always important. Then I became careless and returned sometimes when I shouldn't have. This worried me. The last two years of my drinking my entire personality changed to a cynical, intolerant, and arrogant person completely different from my normal self. It was at this stage of my life that resentments came in. Resenting anyone and everyone who might interfere with my personal plans and ways of doing things– especially for any interference with my drinking–I was full of self-pity.

I will never know all the people I hurt, all the friends I abused, the humiliation of my family, the worry of my business associates, or how far reaching it was. I continued to be surprised by the people I meet who say, "You haven't had a drink for a long time, have you?" The surprise to me is the fact that I didn't know that they knew my drinking had gotten out of control. That is where we are really fooled. We think we can drink to excess without anyone knowing it. Everyone knows it. The only one we are fooling is ourselves. We rationalize and excuse our conduct beyond all reason.

My wife and I had always encouraged our children to bring their friends home at any time, but after a few experiences with a drunken father, they eliminated home as a place to entertain friends. At the time this didn't mean much to me. I was too busy devising excuses to be out with drinking pals.

It seemed to me my wife was becoming more intolerant and narrow-minded all the time. Whenever we went out, she appeared to go out of her way to keep me from having more than one drink. What alcoholic can be satisfied with one drink? After every cocktail party or dinner she would say she couldn't understand how I could get in such a drunken stupor on one drink. She of course didn't realize how cunning an alcoholic can be and the lengths to which he will go in finding ways to satisfy the compulsion for more and more drinks after having had the first one. Neither did I.

Finally our invitations became fewer and fewer as friends had more experience with my drinking pattern.

Two years before I joined A.A., my wife took a long trip during which she wrote me she just couldn't return unless I did something about my drinking. It was a shock of course, but I promised to stop and she returned. A year later, while we were on a vacation trip, she packed up to go home because of my excessive drinking, and I talked her out of it with the promise I would go on the wagon for at least a year. I promised, but within two months, I began again.

The following spring she left me one day without giving me any idea of where she had gone, hoping this would bring me to my senses. In a few days an attorney called on me and explained that something would have to be done, as she couldn't face returning to me as I was. Again I promised to do something about it. Broken promises, humiliation, hopelessness, worry, anxiety–but still not enough.

There comes a time when you don't want to live and are afraid to die. Some crisis brings you to a point of deciding to do something about your drinking problem–to try anything. Help you once continually rejected, suggestions once turned aside are finally accepted in desperation.

The final decision came when my daughter, following a drunk of mine that ruined my wife's birthday, said, "It's Alcoholics Anonymous–or else!" Of course, this suggestion had been made before on a number of occasions, but like all alcoholics I wanted to handle my problem my own way, which really meant I didn't want anything to interfere with my drinking. I was trying to find an easier, softer way. By now it had become difficult to visualize a life without alcohol.

However, my low had been reached. I realized I had been going down and down. I was unhappy myself and I had brought unhappiness to all who cared for me. Physically I couldn't take it any more. Cold sweats, jumpy nerves, and lack of sleep were becoming intolerable. Mentally, the fears and tensions, the complete change in attitude and outlook bewildered me. This was no way to live. The time for decision had arrived, and it was a relief to say "Yes" when my family said they would call Alcoholics Anonymous for me–a relief, even though I dreaded it, feeling that this was the end of everything.

Early the next morning a man whose name I knew well, a lawyer, called on me. Within thirty minutes I knew A.A. was the answer for me. We visited most of that day and attended a meeting that night. I don't know what I expected, but I most certainly didn't visualize a group of people talking about their drinking problems, making light of their personal tragedies, and at the same time enjoying themselves.

However, after I heard a few stories of jails, sanitariums, broken homes, and skid row, I wondered if I really was an alcoholic. After all, I hadn't started to drink early in life, so I had some stability and maturity to guide me for a while. My responsibilities had been a restraining influence. I had had no brushes with the law, though I should have had many. I had not yet lost my job or family, even though both were on the verge of going. My financial standing had not been impaired.

Could I be an alcoholic without some of the hair-raising experiences I had heard of in meetings? The answer came to me very simply in the first step of the Twelve Steps of A.A. "We admitted we were powerless over alcohol–that our lives had become unmanageable." This didn't say we had to be in jail, ten, fifty, or one hundred times. It didn't say I had to lose one, five or ten jobs. It didn't say I had to lose my family. It didn't say I had to finally live on skid row and drink bay rum, canned heat, or lemon extract. It did say I admitted I was powerless over alcohol–that my life had become unmanageable.

Most certainly I was powerless over alcohol, and for me, my life had become unmanageable. It wasn't how far I had gone, but where I was headed. It was important to me to see what alcohol had done to me and would continue to do if I didn't have help.

At first it was a shock to realize I was an alcoholic, but the realization that there was hope made it easier. The baffling problem of getting drunk when I had every intention of staying sober was simplified. It was a great relief to know I didn't *have* to drink any more.

I was told that I must want sobriety for my own sake, and I am convinced this is true. There may be many reasons which bring one to A.A. for the first time, but the lasting one must be to want sobriety and the A.A. way of living for oneself.

From the start I liked everything about the A.A. program. I liked the description of the alcoholic as a person who has found that alcohol is interfering with his social or business life. The allergy idea I could understand because I am allergic to certain pollens. Some of my family are allergic to certain foods. What could be more reasonable than that some people, including myself, were allergic to alcohol?

The explanation that alcoholism was a disease of a two-fold nature, an allergy of the body and an obsession of the mind, cleared up a number of puzzling questions for me. The allergy we could do nothing about. Somehow our bodies had reached the point where we could no longer absorb alcohol in our systems. The *why* is not important; the *fact* is that one drink will set up a reaction in our system which requires more, that one drink was too much and one hundred drinks were not enough.

The obsession of the mind was a little harder to understand, and yet everyone has obsessions of various kinds. The alcoholic has them to an exaggerated degree. Over a period of time he has built up self-pity and resentments toward anyone or anything that interferes with his drinking. Dishonest thinking, prejudice, ego, antagonism toward anyone and everyone who dares to cross him, vanity, and a critical attitude are character defects that gradually creep in and become a part of his life. Living with fear and tension inevitably results in wanting to ease that tension, which alcohol seems to do temporarily. It took me some time to realize that the Twelve Steps of A.A. were designed to help correct these defects of character and so help remove the obsession to drink. The Twelve Steps, which to me are a spiritual way of living, soon meant honest thinking, not wishful thinking, open-mindedness, a willingness to try, and a faith to accept. They meant patience, tolerance, and humility, and above all, the belief that a Power greater than myself could help. That Power I chose to call God.

A willingness to do whatever I was told to do simplified the program for me. Study the A.A. book–don't just read it. They told me to go to meetings, and I still do at every available opportunity, whether I am at home or in some other city. Attending meetings has never been a chore to me. Nor have I attended them with a feeling of just doing my duty. Meetings are both relaxing and refreshing to me after a hard day. They said, "Get active," so I helped whenever I could, and I still do.

A spiritual experience to me meant attending meetings and seeing a group of people all there for the purpose of helping each other; hearing the Twelve Steps and the Twelve Traditions read at a meeting; and hearing the Lord's Prayer, which in an A.A. meeting has such great meaning–"Thy will be done, not mine." A spiritual awakening soon came to mean trying each day to be a little more thoughtful, more considerate, a little more courteous to those with whom I came in contact.

To most of us, making amends will take the rest of our lives, but we can start immediately. Just being sober will be making amends to many we have hurt by our drunken actions. Making amends is sometimes doing what we are capable of doing but failed to do because of alcohol–carrying out community responsibilities such as community funds, Red Cross, educational and religious activities in proportion to our abilities and energy.

I was desperately in earnest to follow through and understand what was expected of me as a member of A.A. and to take each step of the twelve as rapidly as possible. To me this meant telling my associates that I had joined Alcoholics Anonymous; that I didn't know what was expected of me by A.A., but that whatever it was, it was the most important thing in life for me; that sobriety meant more to me than anything in this world. It was so important that it must come ahead of anything.

There are many short phrases and expressions in A.A. which make sound sense. "First Things First". Solve our immediate problems before we try to solve all the others and get muddled in our thinking and doing. "Easy Does

It." Relax a little. Try for inner contentment. No one individual can carry all the burdens of the world. Everyone has problems. Getting drunk won't solve them. "Twenty-four hours a day." Today is the day. Doing our best, living each day to the fullest is the art of living. Yesterday is gone, and we don't know whether we will be here tomorrow. If we do a good job of living today, and if tomorrow comes for us, then the chances are we will do a good job when it arrives–so why worry about it?

The A.A. way of life is the way we always should have tried to live. "Grant us the serenity to accept the things we cannot change, courage to change the things we can, and the wisdom to know the difference." These thoughts become part of our daily lives. They are not ideas of resignation but of the recognition of certain basic facts of living.

The fact that A.A. is a spiritual program didn't scare me or raise any prejudice in my mind. I couldn't afford the luxury of prejudice. I had tried my way and had failed.

When I joined A.A., I did so for the sole purpose of getting sober and staying sober. I didn't realize I would find so much more, but a new and different outlook on life started opening up almost immediately. Each day seems to be so much more productive and satisfying. I get so much more enjoyment out of living. I find an inner pleasure in simple things. Living just for today is a pleasant adventure.

Above all, I am grateful to A.A. for my sobriety, which means so much to my family, friends, and business associates, because God and A.A. were able to do for me something I was unable to do for myself.

(9) PHYSICIAN, HEAL THYSELF!

Psychiatrist and surgeon, he had lost his way until he realized that God, not he, was the Great Healer.

I AM A PHYSICIAN, licensed to practice in a western state. I am also an alcoholic. In two ways I may be a little different from other alcoholics. First, we all hear at A.A. meetings about those who have lost everything, those who have been in jail, those who have been in prison, those who have lost their families, those who have lost their income. I never lost any of it. I never was on skid row. I made more money the last year of my drinking than I ever made before in my whole life. My wife never hinted that she would leave me. Everything that I touched from grammar school on was successful. I was president of my grammar school student body. I was president of all my classes in high school, and in my last year I was president of that student body. I was president of each class in the university, and president of that student body. I was voted the man most likely to succeed. The same thing occurred in medical school. I belong to more medical societies and honor societies than men ten to twenty years my senior.

Mine was the skid row of success. The physical skid row in any city is miserable. The skid row of success is just as miserable.

The second way in which, perhaps, I differ from some other alcoholics is this: many alcoholics state that they didn't particularly like the taste of alcohol but that they liked the effect. I loved alcohol! I used to like to get it on my fingers so I could lick them and get another taste. I had a lot of fun drinking. I enjoyed it immensely. And then, one ill-defined day, one day that I can't recall, I stepped across the line that alcoholics know so well, and from that day on, drinking was miserable. When a few drinks made me feel good before I went over that line, those same drinks now made me wretched. In an attempt to get over that feeling, there was a quick onslaught of a greater number of drinks, and then all was lost. Alcohol failed to serve the purpose.

On the last day I was drinking, I went up to see a friend who had had a good deal of trouble with alcohol and whose wife had left him a number of times. He had come back, however, and he was on this program. In my stupid way I went up to see him with the idea in the back of my mind that I would investigate Alcoholics Anonymous from a medical standpoint. Deep in my heart was the feeling that maybe I could get some help here. This friend gave me a pamphlet, and I took it home and had my wife read it to me. There were two sentences in it that struck me. One said, "Don't feel that you are a martyr because you stopped drinking," and this hit me between the eyes. The second one said, "Don't feel that you stop drinking for anyone other than yourself," and this hit me between the eyes. After my wife had read this to me, I said to her, as I had said many times in desperation, "I have got to do something." She's a good-natured soul and said, "I wouldn't worry about it; probably something will happen." And then we went up the side of a hill where we have a little barbecue area to make the fire for the barbecue, and on the way up I thought to myself–I'll go back down to the kitchen and refill this drink. And just then, something did happen.

The thought came to me–This is the last one! I was well into the second fifth by this time. And as that thought came to me, it was as though someone had reached down and taken a heavy overcoat off my shoulders, for that *was* the last one.

About two days later I was called by a friend of mine from Nevada City–he's a brother of my wife's closest friend. He said, "Earle?" and I said, "Yes." He said, "I'm an alcoholic; what do I do?" And I gave him some idea of what you do, and so I made my first Twelfth Step call before I ever came into the program. The satisfaction I got from giving him a little of what I had read in those pamphlets far surpassed any feeling that I had ever had before in helping patients.

So I decided that I would go to my first meeting. I was introduced as a psychiatrist. (I belong to the American Psychiatric Society, but I don't practice psychiatry as such. I am a surgeon.)

As someone in A.A. said to me once upon a time, there is nothing worse than a confused psychiatrist.

I will never forget the first meeting that I attended. There were five people present, including me. At one end of the table sat our community butcher. At the other side of the table sat one of the carpenters in our community, and at the further end of the table sat the man who ran the bakery, while on one side sat my friend who was a mechanic. I recall, as I walked into that meeting, saying to myself, "Here I am, a Fellow of the American College of Surgeons, a Fellow of the International College of Surgeons, a diplomat of one of the great specialty boards in these United States, a member of the American Psychiatric Society, and I have to go to the butcher, the baker, and the carpenter to help make a man out of me!"

Something else happened to me. This was such a new thought that I got all sorts of books on Higher Powers, and I put a Bible by my bedside, and I put a Bible in my car. It is still there. And I put a Bible in my locker at the hospital. And I put a Bible in my desk. And I put a Big Book by my night stand, and I put a *Twelve Steps and Twelve Traditions* in my locker at the hospital, and I got books by Emmet Fox, and I got books by God-knows-who, and I got to reading all these things. And the first thing you know I was lifted right out of the A.A. group, and I floated higher and higher and even higher, until I was way up on a pink cloud, which is known as Pink Seven, and I felt miserable again. So I thought to myself, I might just as well be drunk as feel like this.

I went to Clark, the community butcher, and I said, "Clark, what is the matter with me? I don't feel right. I have been on this program for three months and I feel terrible." And he said, "Earle, why don't you come on over and let me talk to you for a minute." So he got me a cup of coffee and a piece of cake, and sat me down and said, "Why, there's nothing wrong with you. You've been sober for three months, been working hard. You've been doing all right." But then he said, "Let me say something to you. We have here in this community an organization which helps people, and this organization is known as Alcoholics Anonymous. Why don't you join it?" I said, "What do you think I've been doing?" "Well," he said, "you've been sober, but you've been floating way up on a cloud somewhere. Why don't you go home and get the Big Book and open it at page seventy and see what it says?" So I did. I got the Big Book and I read it, and this is what it said: "Rarely have we seen a person fail who has thoroughly followed our path." The word "thoroughly" rang a bell. And then it went on to say: "Half measures availed us nothing. We stood at the turning point." And the last sentence was "We asked His protection and care with complete abandon."

"Complete abandon"; "Half measures availed us nothing"; "Thoroughly follow our path"; "Completely give oneself to this simple program"–rang in my swelled head.

Years earlier, I had gone into psychoanalysis to get relief. I spent five and a half years in psychoanalysis and proceeded to become a drunk. I don't mean that in any sense as a derogatory statement about psychotherapy; it's a very great tool, not too potent, but a great tool. I would do it again.

I tried every gimmick that there was to get some peace of mind, but it was not until I was brought to my alcoholic knees, when I was brought to a group in my own community with the butcher, the baker, the carpenter and the mechanic, who were able to give me the Twelve Steps, that I was finally given some semblance of an answer to the last half of the First Step. So, after taking the first half of the First Step, and very gingerly admitting myself to Alcoholics Anonymous, something happened. And then I thought to myself: "Imagine an alcoholic admitting anything!" But I made my admission just the same.

The Third Step said: "Made a decision to turn our will and our lives over to the care of God as we understood Him." Now they asked us to make a decision! We've got to turn the whole business over to some joker we can't even see! And this chokes the alcoholic. Here he is powerless, unmanageable, in the grip of something bigger than he is, and he's got to turn the whole business over to someone else! It fills the alcoholic with rage. We are great people. We can handle anything. And so one gets to thinking to oneself, "Who is this God? Who is this fellow we are supposed to turn everything over to? What can He do for us that we can't do for ourselves?" Well, I don't know who He is, but I've got my own idea.

For myself, I have an absolute proof of the existence of God. I was sitting in my office one time after I had operated on a woman. It had been a long four- or five-hour operation, a large surgical procedure, and she was on her ninth or tenth post-operative day. She was doing fine, she was up and around, and that day her husband phoned me and said, "Doctor, thanks very much for curing my wife," and I thanked him for his felicitations, and he hung up. And then I scratched my head and said to myself, "What a fantastic thing for a man to say, that I cured his wife. Here I am down at my office behind my desk, and there she is out at the hospital. I am not even there, and if I was there the only thing I could do would be to give her moral support, and yet he thanks me for curing his wife." I thought to myself–What *is* curing that woman? Yes, I put in those stitches. The Great Boss had given me diagnostic and surgical talent, and He has loaned it to me to use for the rest of my life. It doesn't belong to me. He has loaned it to me and I did my job, but that ended nine days ago. What healed those tissues that I closed? I didn't. This to me is the proof of the existence of a Somethingness greater than I am. I couldn't practice medicine without the Great Physician. All I do in a very simple way is to help Him cure my patients.

Shortly after I was starting to work on the program, I realized that I was not a good father, I wasn't a good husband, but, oh, I was a good provider. I never robbed my family of anything. I gave them everything, except the greatest thing in the world, and that is peace of mind. So I went to my wife and asked her if there wasn't something that she and I could do to somehow get together, and she turned on her heel and looked me squarely in the eye, and said, "You don't care anything about my problem," and I could have smacked her, but I said to myself, "Grab on to your serenity!"

She left, and I sat down and crossed my hands and looked up and said, "For God's sake, help me." And then a silly, simple thought came to me. I didn't know anything about being a father; I don't know how to come home and work weekends like other husbands; I don't know how to entertain my family. But I remembered that every night after dinner my wife would get up and do the dishes. Well, I could do the dishes. So I went to her and said, "There's only one thing I want in my whole life, and I don't want any commendation; I don't want any credit; I don't want anything from you or Janey for the rest of your life except one thing, and that is the opportunity to do anything you want always, and I would like to start off by doing the dishes." And now I am doing the darn dishes every night!

Doctors have been notoriously unsuccessful in helping alcoholics. They have contributed fantastic amounts of time and work to our problem, but they aren't able, it seems, to arrest either your alcoholism or mine.

And the clergy have tried hard to help us, but we haven't been helped. And the psychiatrist has had thousands of couches and has put you and me on them many, many times, but he hasn't helped us very much, though he has tried hard; and we owe the clergy and the doctor and the psychiatrist a deep debt of gratitude, but they haven't helped our alcoholism, except in a rare few instances. But–Alcoholics Anonymous has helped.

What is this power that A.A. possesses? This curative power? I don't know what it is. I suppose the doctor might say, "This is psychosomatic medicine." I suppose the psychiatrist might say, "This is benevolent interpersonal relations." I suppose others would say, "This is group psychotherapy."

To me it is God.

(10) STARS DON'T FALL

A titled lady, her chief loss was self-respect. When the overcast lifted, the stars were there as before.

MY ALCOHOLIC PROBLEM began long before I drank. My personality, from the time I can remember anything, was the perfect set-up for an alcoholic career. I was always at odds with the entire world, not to say the universe. I was out of step with life, with my family, with people in general. I tried to compensate with impossible dreams and ambitions, which were simply early forms of escape. Even when I was old enough to know better, I dreamed about being as beautiful as Venus, as pure as the Madonna and as brilliant as the President of the United States is supposed to be. I had writing ambitions, and nothing would do but that I'd write like Shakespeare. I also wanted to be the queen of society, with a glittering salon, the bride of a dream-prince and the mother of a happy brood. Inside, I went right on being a mass of unlovely self-pity, queasy anxiety and sickening self-debasement. Naturally, I succeeded in nothing. Until I reached A.A. my life was a shambles; I was a mess, and I made everybody near and dear to me miserable. I had to go through extreme alcoholism to find my answer.

There was no material or external reason for this. I was born in a castle, in pre-war Austrian territory. My father had a title; there was plenty of means in the family. When I was a baby, my mother brought me to America, and I never again saw my father. But again, the living was easy. My family, on my mother's side, was brilliant, gifted and charming. They were ambitious, successful, strong and famous. They inherited wealth and acquired more.

They did the best they knew how as far as I was concerned. It took me three psychoanalysts and several years in A.A. to really get this through my head.

Up to my early thirties, when my drinking had become a major problem, I lived in large houses, with servants and all the luxuries that I could possibly ask for. But I did not feel a part of my family or a part of the set-up. I got a good non-academic education; my intellectual curiosity was encouraged. I learned how to hold a terrapin fork. Otherwise I got nothing out of it.

Before I started to drink seriously, I tried a couple of other escapes. At eighteen I ran away from home. Showing all the courage and ingenuity that I had not used in a positive way, I covered my tracks and hid from my family so successfully that they did not find me for months. I went out to the West

Coast, waited on table, washed dishes and sold newspaper subscriptions. Like most sick people before me, I was implacably selfish, and chronically self-centered. My mother's heartbreak, or the unpleasant publicity I had caused did not bother my pretty head. After eight months, the family found me. Their telegram was kind and nice. But I was afraid. I was still untrained for any work but washing dishes and waiting on table. So I married a nice, well-meaning young newspaperman, so as not to have to go home. It did not occur to me that marriage might be a job, too. We came back East and met both families. His were good, simple Quaker folk who accepted me with love. But I did not fit into this pattern either. The birth of a daughter filled me with new fears. Responsibility again. Her father became both mother and father to her. At the tender age of twenty-three, I got a divorce. My husband was made miserable by this, but I had already made him and myself miserable. He got half custody of our child, but later kept her during most of the school terms. It was the only real home she knew. I resented this, but I did nothing constructive about it.

Now I had done some living but I hadn't learned a thing. This was where I started my first drinking lessons. Up to this time it just hadn't occurred to me to drink. My Quaker mother-in-law, bless her heart, used to set the Christmas pudding ablaze with lumps of sugar dipped in rubbing alcohol. But now I was a young divorcee, leading a Washington social life. Prohibition meant nothing. My family always bought the best, and the embassies were flowing.

I think I had the physical allergy right away. A drink never gave me a normal, pleasant glow. Instead it was like a tap on the head with a small mallet. I was a little bit knocked out. Just what I wanted. I lost my shyness. Five or six drinks and I was terrific. Men danced with me at parties. I was full of careless chatter. I was so amusing! I had friends.

I got a novel written. It was all about Scott Fitzgerald's little lost debutante, abused, misunderstood and running wild. The book was published, but the reading public said–So what? I did not see that the book dripped with self-pity. I only saw that I had not become Mrs. Shakespeare.

I met a wonderful man. He was the dream prince, the answer. I, who did not know how to give love, was head over heels "in love." I wanted him to love me and make up to me for everything. He was brilliant and ambitious. He was well behaved, and idealistic where women were concerned. But he noticed that I was not a good mother to my child, that I relegated her to nurses when she was with me. He saw that I was unsettled, living away from my family and renting houses here and there. A house in Virginia, during the fox hunting season; a little chalet in Switzerland, during the summer or a place on Long Island–each house complete with cooks, butlers and maids. Above all, he noticed that I drank a good deal, often got tight in his company and told him naughty stories. He did not like naughty stories, so I made them naughtier. He finally decided that he did not love me enough, and soon he told me so and said he was engaged to another girl.

He has since become famous and distinguished, an asset to his country. I saw him recently and he told me that he had always felt guilty, because, after our separation, I had become a serious alcoholic. With ten years of A.A. behind me, I was able to tell him that I'd have been an alcoholic, no matter what; that I had been a sick person, unfit for marriage.

Even then I knew in my heart that I was unfit for the very things I wanted most, a happy marriage, security, a home and love. But when this happened to me, I declared to friends that I would get drunk, dead drunk that very night, and stay drunk for a month. A normal person, hit with adversity, can go on a drinking spree and then snap out of it. But I got drunk that night and stayed drunk, getting increasingly worse until I found A.A. ten years later.

That first night I blacked out at a large dinner party. In the morning, because I was young and healthy, my remorse was worse than my hangover. What had I said? What had I done? I experienced my first real guilt and shame. This was in Virginia, where I had rented a house with stables and a swimming pool, and the fall fox hunting had begun. The people I knew rode hard, and some of them drank hard. Many of them carried a flask and sandwich case, strapped to their saddles so they could stay out all day. But whereas my horse was always equipped with a flask, I merely endured the fox hunting so I could start drinking at lunch time. I would pull out early, and go to the hunt breakfast and the flowing bowl of milk-punch. By two-thirty in the afternoon I was always tight.

During these years, I did acquire some good friends. A few stood by me, at least in their hearts, throughout the whole of my drinking career. Others have come back, others I have lost. But at this time, I began gravitating toward the really hard drinkers, hanging around with them more and more. My old friends showed distress. Couldn't I drink less? Couldn't I stop, after a few? It was nothing to my own inner distress, my self-reproach, and my self-loathing, for was I not bearing out all the horrible things I had always suspected of myself?

I accepted a big tax-free income from the family, but I didn't like it when they told me how to live. I went to Europe to escape them, so I thought. I was really trying, once more, to escape from myself. Imagine my surprise when I came to, in Europe, and discovered I had brought myself along! I rented a beautiful apartment on the banks of the Seine in the winter, and a chalet in Switzerland in the summer. I read sad poetry, cried, drank red wine, wrote sad poetry, and drank some more. I also wrote another novel, all about Scott Fitzgerald's poor, misbegotten, unloved, tipsy little debutante. Even the critics kidded me about this one. I had worked the previous summer on a New York fashion magazine, a job I really enjoyed. I was now with the Paris office. I stayed with them until I got drunk and had a row with the Paris editor.

During this period I married again. This was an Englishman who, at least at this time, drank as much as I did. What we had in common was alcohol. On our honeymoon in Egypt, he cuffed me around quite a bit, and subsequently he hit me some more. I can't blame him. My tongue had become increasingly skilled at venomous home truths. He had not developed this art and had no recourse but his fists.

We went through the two years of deadlock required by the English divorce laws. During this time, you are supposed to behave yourself, but I took a little wine-tasting tour through France, all by myself, with car and chauffeur. Tasting the best of burgundy at a famous restaurant one night landed me passed out on a park bench in the public square. I came to and found a man leaning over me. When he reached for me, I rose and smote him. He, in turn, kicked me so I fell to the ground. Bruised, and deadly ashamed, I told no one. I began, here and now, to fear the answer to the question–what is the matter with me? I had already been to one analyst at home. We had not gotten anywhere. Was my mental state more serious than he said? Was I insane? Was that it? I did not dare to think. I drank and I kept on drinking.

Drunk or sober, I was hectic, unpredictable, irresponsible. At a large party in Geneva, with people from many countries represented, the kind of party that is "protocol" in the extreme, I swayed, laughed hysterically, made naughty remarks in an unhushed voice, and was finally led from the scene. My friends understandably hurt and angry. Why had I done it? Why? I could not tell them. I was afraid to think why. Now I hid when I wanted to drink. I drank alone or with someone, anyone who would stay and drink with me. I passed out frequently in my home, alone.

An American doctor in Paris said I had an enlarged liver. He also said, "You are an alcoholic and there's nothing I can do for you." This went in one ear and out the other. I did not know what he meant. An alcoholic cannot accept the news that he's an alcoholic unless there is a meaningful explanation given, and an offer of help, such as you get in A.A.

I returned from Europe shortly before the war broke out and I never went back. Things were no better with the family, so I moved to New York. Here, also, I had good friends, but I became more and more separated from them. Why did I have to have at least three cocktails to sit through dinner? Other girls whom I had known all my life asked for one weak scotch after dinner. Sometimes they'd put it on the mantel, and forget it. My eye would be glued to that glass. How could anybody *forget* a drink? I would have three quick strong ones in order to endure the evening.

My first analyst said, "You are becoming more and more of an alcoholic," and sent me to another analyst. This good and gentle man, a brilliant research doctor, got nowhere with me fast. I was accepting help with one hand and pushing it away with the other. The liquor counteracted the help I was getting.

Meanwhile I had found another escape. This one was a dandy. It combined running away from my world, and drinking all I wanted to. I had met a bunch of gay young Bohemians who lived in the Village, and were sowing their wild oats. They were all kids, most of them younger than I was. All of them have since settled down to jobs and good marriages. None of them were alcoholics, but at this time they were drinking as much as I was. They introduced me to beer in the morning to kill hangovers. This was the life! I was the center of attention, just what my sick ego craved. They said I was so funny, and told me, with shrieks of laughter, what I'd done the night before. Ribaldry was the substance of the conversation, and I set out to be the funniest and most ribald of them all.

They woke up with hangovers, but with no remorse. I woke up filled with secret guilt and shame. Underneath, I knew this was all wrong. Now it was semi-blackouts every night, outrageous behavior, passing out in some friend's Village studio or not knowing how I got home. The horrors of increasing hangover sickness to occupy the entire day; nausea, dry heaves, the rocking bed, the nightmare-filled mind.

At this stage, I began a daily mental routine. I must drink less, I would tell myself. Or: If I'm really a genius, I must produce a great work, to show why I act like a genius. Or–this is a little too much! I'd better taper off. I must use self-will, self-control. I must go on the wagon for a while. Drink only beer or wine. I used all those well-known phrases. I also thought that I must have *power over myself*. I was an agnostic, so I thought. My new friends made fun of God and all the orthodox beliefs. I thought I was the captain of my soul. I told myself that I had power over this thing. One day soon, the analyses would reveal why I drank and how to stop.

I did not know that I had no power over alcohol, that I, alone and unaided, could not stop; that I was on a downgrade, tearing along at full speed with all my brakes gone, and that the end would be a total smash-up, death or insanity. I had already feared insanity for a long time. Certainly, when I was in my cups, I was not just drunk, I was crazy. Now my whole thinking was crazy. For, after those daily self-punishing sessions with myself, after the vows to stop, I would change entirely as evening came on. I would get wildly excited and look forward to another night of drinking. The remorse would turn inside out, and become anticipatory pleasure. I was going to get drunk again–Drunk!

My child was being exposed to all of this. She was also the victim of my scolding and incessant nagging. I was really scolding my mortal enemy, the inner me. My poor child could not know this. Her father, quite rightly, wanted to put her in a school. When I protested, his lawyer, my lawyer, and my third and last analyst had a conference. She was duly sent to school, away from me.

This new analyst was a woman doctor, one of the best in the country. She did all she could to help this situation and to protect my child. She was endlessly patient as we looked together for an answer. She, more than the others, showed me what ailed me basically, why I was immature and insecure. But I was not able to make use of this knowledge until after I became sober. A.A. had to stop my drinking first. Then I was able to do something about me.

There were a couple of good things. And again these were things that I really profited by after I sobered up. I saw that my Village friends, all of whom had small jobs, were living happily on about a tenth of my sinecure. It had never occurred to me before that I could live simply and be independent of my family. So I did the right thing in the wrong way. I had a drunken quarrel with my family, denounced them, and left them forever. They were awfully good about not cutting me off. It was I who had to tell the bank, after a certain time, to refuse all further deposits. I had saved my allowance. I now had quite a nest egg. I had a tiny trust fund, and I moved into a small apartment where I learned to cook, keep house, and do the things that normal people do. I learned a whole new sense of values. I wrote and sold some short stories. These things were carried out in moments of less severe hangover or short stretches on the wagon. But the money I had saved up went for cases of liquor. I was, when drunk, just as undisciplined and erratic as ever. My new friends had a social conscience. They were bright and well read, they held various political views. In the course of drunken arguments, I found my own views and a sense of responsibility as a citizen. Now it was wartime. But as an air raid warden my attempts to serve my country ended in a drunken and abusive row with a fellow warden.

By this time I had ceased to be the life of the party. I became a menace, the fish-wife, the common scold. I took everybody else's inventory. Finally my new friends told me, one by one, that I could not come around anymore.

Now came the black and endless dismal night. I went to bars alone to drink. There was one Village bar in particular for which I formed an obsession. I had to go there every night. I rarely remembered getting home. The bartenders took care of me, not out of brotherly love, but through enlightened self-interest. An obstreperous woman in a bar is a nuisance, and they wanted no trouble with the police. On the other hand, I was a marvelous customer. For three generations my family had had a charge account in one of the big New York hotels. I stopped at the cashier's any hour of the night on the way to the bar and cashed a check. In the morning I would wake up with a dollar or two. I suspect that those bartenders would wait until I had shot my wad, then call a cab and send me home. This too is how the nest-egg went.

So here, in this dive, this hangout for dead-end alcoholics and neurotics, here was I. In a sick people's place, myself among the sickest. I despised the other barflies and, naturally, they loathed me. In my cups I used to tell them off, giving them lengthy advice on how to lead the right life. They got so they moved their barstools when they saw me coming. The bartenders too, treated me with contempt. Yes I, the queen of them all! The glittering society belle, the modern Shakespeare, the happy wife, the loving and beloved. I, who had dreamed these sick dreams, now reaped the nightmare. What I had secretly believed myself to be all along, this I had become. I was not beautiful or good, as I had yearned to be. I was fat, bloated, dirty and unkempt. Most of the time I was covered with bruises from "running into doors." I wore a man's raincoat, turned inside out, a present from a friend, for now my funds were low. I could not live on that tiny trust fund and still drink all I wanted to. My tweed suit, once a very good one, was shapeless and baggy with bare places worn in the elbows from leaning on the bar.

Once, in a strange gin mill, I stole a bottle from behind the bar. The bartender, a tough Irishman, came around and "gave me the elbow," which means that he raised his elbow and smacked me in the face. I literally hit the sawdust. Luckily a friend was with me, who dragged me out, screaming and cursing, while the bartender threatened to call the police. But I never got into jail. I didn't get into a sanitarium either. I wanted to die and often I would think of ways. I would walk up and down under the 59th Street bridge, trying to get up the nerve to go up there and jump. Once, when I called my analyst, and told her I was contemplating death, she came over and tried to get me into a sanitarium. Frightened and shamed, I refused, and sobered up temporarily. I was not mugged, or manhandled. I did not resort to semi-prostitution for the price of a drink. But all these things *could* have happened. The sanitarium *should* have happened. I was not fit to be on the loose, and there was no one to commit me.

I think now that a God, in whom I did not believe, was looking after me. Perhaps it was He who sent my analyst to a psychiatrist's meeting at which Bill spoke. In those days, psychiatry and A.A. had not gotten together as they have since. My analyst was one of the first to learn of A.A. and to make subsequent use of it in her work. Having heard Bill speak, she was instantly sold. She read this book that you are reading now. She asked me to read it.

"These people all had your problem," she told me.

Anybody who had my problem was beneath contempt!

I read the book and God leapt at me from every page. So this was a group of reformers! What intellectual interests could we have in common? Could they discuss literature or art? I could just hear their sweet, pious talk. Nobody was going to reform me! I was going to reform myself!

I returned the book to my analyst and shook my head. But now a strange thing happened. In my cups I began to say, "I can't stop." I said it over and over, boring my fellow barflies. Something in the book had reached me after all. In a sense, I had taken the first step. My analyst pricked up her ears.

"Why don't you just go down and see Mr. W.?" she asked. "See what you think."

I now said a lucky and wonderful thing. I said, "O.K."

In those days the A.A. Foundation was down in the Wall Street district of New York. As I went in I was dying of mortification. They would all stare at me and whisper! Oh, poor self-centered, sick little me. I did not reflect that half the office was composed of A.A. members, and that I was as unexciting as any client in any office.

Bill was tall, grey haired, with the kind of asymmetrical good looks and pleasant easy manner that inspires confidence in the shaken and afraid. He was well dressed; he was easy going. I could see he wasn't a quack or a fanatic.

He did not take out a folder and say, "What is the nature of your problem?" He said to me, gently and simply, "Do you think that you are one of us?"

Never in my entire life had anyone asked me "Are you one of us?" Never had I felt a sense of belonging. I found myself nodding my head.

He now said that *we* had a physical allergy combined with a mental obsession, and he explained this so that I saw for the first time how this could be. He asked me if I had any spiritual belief, and when I said No, he suggested that I keep an open mind. Then he called Marty and made an appointment for me. I thought, "Aha, he's passing the buck. Now comes the questionnaire." I did not know who this Marty was. I did not want to go and see her, but I went. A friend of Marty's, another A.A. let me in. Marty was late. I felt like a gangster's moll about to be interviewed by the Salvation Army. The strange A.A. put me at ease. The apartment was charming; the shelves were full of books, many of which I owned myself. Marty came in, looking clean, neat, well-dressed and, like Bill, she was neither a bloated wreck nor a reformer. She was attractive; she was like the friends I had once had. Indeed, she had known my cousin in Chicago. Years of drinking and general high jinks had cut her off from old friends. She too had gone to cheap bars to drink. With more physical courage than I had possessed, she had twice tried to take her life. She had been in sanitariums. Her luck had been worse than mine, but not her drinking. I, who had feared questions, now began trying to interrupt and tell *my* story. I couldn't get a word in edgewise! Marty was smart. A load weighing a thousand pounds came off my back. I wasn't insane. Nor was I the "worst woman who ever lived." I was an alcoholic, with a recognizable behavior pattern.

I went to my first meeting with Marty and some other girls. I was sold, intellectually. But my life, even sober, was all askew and so were my emotions. In those days there was only one big meeting a week in New York. On non-meeting nights I was lonesome, or so I told myself. I went to several Village bars, and drank cokes or tea. I had been on the wagon when I came to A.A. and this sobriety-tension eventually popped. Not understanding the twenty-four hour plan, or not wanting to, I began drinking and was off-again on-again, during that first month.

A fellow A.A., called Anne, who had helped me, went on a terrible bender. Priscilla, an A.A. who, like Marty, has become one of my greatest friends, decided that I was a stubborn case. Since they could do nothing with Anne either, Priscilla suggested that I go and look after Anne. Now, I am big and weak, but Anne was bigger than I and strong. Her idea of fun on a bender was to hit sailors and insult cops. We were to go up to our A.A. farm in Kent, and I spent the evening before riding herd on Anne. I was so busy keeping her out of trouble, and so scared she'd swing on me, that I had my last two drinks that night. The farm, in those days, was primitive. There was no central heating, and this was the dead of winter. Anne and I went up in ski clothes and fur coats, and it was so cold we slept in them. I tried to wash a little, but Anne refused to wash at all. She said she felt too horrible inside to be pretty on the outside. This I understood. This was how I had looked and acted a few short weeks ago. I completely forgot about myself in trying vainly to help Anne, whose misery I understood.

On the train going back, Anne's one idea was to get to the nearest bar. I was really scared. I thought it was my duty to keep her from drinking, not knowing that if the other fellow is really determined to drink there is nothing you can do about it. However, I had phoned New York from the farm, appealing for help, and there in the station to meet us were two A.A.'s, John and Bud. They were a couple of normal, sober, attractive men. They took Anne and me to dinner. We, who were dirty, bedraggled and in ski clothes. They did not seem ashamed to be with us, these strangers. They were taking the trouble to try and help. Why? I was astonished and deeply moved.

All these things together brought me into A.A. I got off the so-called wagon, and on the twenty-four hour plan. I had never had the physical courage to shake it out before.

John and Bud became my friends. John said, "Keep going to meetings." And I did. He himself took me to many of them, including the ones out of town.

Except for one short slip, during the first eight months, which was an angry "the world can't do this to me" reaction to a personal tragedy in my life, I have been sober for twelve years. I, who could never stay on the wagon for more than a week. The personality rehabilitation did not come overnight. In the first year there were episodes such as kicking Priscilla in the shins, getting the lock changed on the desk in the A.A. Club, because I, as secretary, didn't want the Intergroup secretary "interfering," and taking an older woman member out to lunch for the express purpose of informing her that she was "a phony." All the people involved in these flare-ups took it with remarkable grace, have teased me about it since, and have become good friends of mine.

A.A. taught me how not to drink. And also, on the twenty-four hour plan, it taught me how to live. I know I do not have to be "queen of them all" to salve a frightened ego. Through going to meetings and listening, and occasionally speaking, through doing Twelve Step work, whereby in helping others you are both the teacher and the student, by making many wonderful A.A. friends, I have been taught all the things in life that are worth having. I am no longer interested in living in a palace, because palace living was not the answer for me. Nor were those impossible dreams I used to have the things I really wanted.

I have my A.A. friends, and I have become reacquainted with my old friends on a new basis. My friendships are meaningful, loving and interesting because I am sober. I have achieved the inner confidence to write quite unlike Shakespeare, and I have sold a good deal of what I have written. I want to write better and sell more. My spiritual awakening in A.A. finally resulted in my joining a church some years ago. This has been a wonderful thing in my life. I consider that I was taking the Eleventh Step when I joined this church. (This was for *me*. Many good A.A.'s never join a church, and do not need to. Some even remain agnostics.)

Every day, I feel a little bit more useful, more happy and more free. Life, including some ups and downs, is a lot of fun. I am a part of A.A. which is a way of life. If I had not become an active alcoholic and joined A.A., I might never have found my own identity or become a part of anything. In ending my story I like to think about this.

(11) ME AN ALCOHOLIC?

Alcohol's wringer squeezed this author–but he escaped quite whole.

WHEN I TRY to reconstruct what my life was like "before," I see a coin with two faces.

One, the side I turned to myself and the world, was respectable–even, in some ways, distinguished. I was father, husband, taxpayer, home owner. I was club-man, athlete, artist, musician, author, editor, aircraft pilot and world traveler. I was listed in *Who's Who in America* as an American who, by distinguished achievement, had arrived.

The other side of the coin was sinister, baffling. I was inwardly unhappy most of the time. There would be times when the life of respectability and achievement seemed insufferably dull–I had to break out. This I would do by going completely "bohemian" for a night, getting drunk and rolling home with the dawn. Next day remorse would be on me like a tiger. I'd claw my way back to respectability and stay there–until the inevitable next time.

The insidiousness of alcoholism is an appalling thing. In all the twenty-five years of my drinking there were only a few occasions when I took a morning drink. My binges were one-night stands only. Once or twice, during my early drinking, I carried it over into the second day, and only once, that I can remember, did it continue into the third. I was never drunk on the job, never missed a day's work, was seldom rendered totally ineffective by a hangover, and kept my liquor expenses well within my adequate budget. I continued to advance in my chosen field. How could such a man possibly be called an alcoholic? Whatever the root of my unhappiness might turn out to be, I thought, it could not possibly be booze.

Of course I drank. Everybody did in the set which I regarded as the apex of civilization. My wife loved to drink, and we tied on many a hooter in the name of marital bliss. My associates, and all the wits and literary lights I so much admired, also drank. Evening cocktails were as standard as morning coffee, and I suppose my average daily consumption ran a little more or less than a pint. Even on my rare (at first) binge nights, it never ran much over a quart.

How easy it was, in the beginning, to forget that those binges ever happened! After a day or two of groveling remorse, I'd come up with an explanation. "The nervous tension had piled up and just had to spill over." Or, "My physical plant had got a little run down and the stuff rushed right to my head." Or, "I got to talking and forgot how many I was taking and it hit me." Always we'd emerge with a new formula for avoiding future trouble. "You've got to space your drinks and take plenty of water in between," or "Coat the stomach with a little olive oil," or "Drink anything *but* those damn martinis." Weeks would go by without further trouble, and I'd be assured I'd at last hit on the right formula. The binge had been just "one of those things." After a month it seemed unlikely that it happened. Intervals between binges were eight months.

My growing inward unhappiness was a very real thing, however, and I knew that something would have to be done about it. A friend had found help in psychoanalysis. After a particularly ugly one-nighter, my wife suggested I try it, and I agreed. Educated child of the scientific age that I was, I had complete faith in the science of the mind. It would be a sure cure and also an adventure. How exciting to learn the inward mysteries that govern the behavior of people, how wonderful to know, at last, all about myself! To cut a long story short, I spent seven years and $10,000 on my psychiatric adventure, and emerged in worse condition than ever.

To be sure, I learned many fascinating things and many things that were to prove helpful later. I learned what a devastating effect it can have on a child to coddle him and build him up, and then turn and beat him savagely, as had happened to me.

Meanwhile I was getting worse, both as regards my inward misery and my drinking. My daily alcoholic consumption remained about the same through all this, with perhaps a slight increase, and my binges remained one-nighters. But they were occurring with alarming frequency. In seven years the intervals between them decreased from eight months to ten days! And they were growing uglier. One night I barely made my downtown club; if I'd had to go another fifty feet, I'd have collapsed in the gutter. On another occasion I arrived home covered with blood. I'd deliberately smashed a window. With all this it was becoming increasingly hard to maintain my front of distinction and respectability to the world. My personality was stretched almost to splitting in the effort; schizophrenia stared me in the face, and one night I was in a suicidal despair.

My professional life looked fine on the surface. I was now head of a publishing venture in which nearly a million dollars had been invested. My opinions were quoted in *Time* and *Newsweek* with pictures, and I addressed the public by radio and television. It was a fantastic structure, built on a crumbling foundation. It was tottering and it had to fall. It did.

After my last binge I came home and smashed my dining room furniture to splinters, kicked out six windows and two balustrades. When I woke up sober, my handiwork confronted me. It is impossible for me to reproduce my despair.

I'd had absolute faith in science, and only in science. "Knowledge is power," I'd always been taught. Now I had to face up to the fact that knowledge of this sort, applied to my individual case, was *not* power. Science could take my mind apart expertly, but it couldn't seem to put it together again. I crawled back to my analyst, not so much because I had faith in him, but because I had nowhere else to turn.

After talking with him for a time, I heard myself saying, "Doc, I think I'm an alcoholic."

"Yes," he said, surprisingly, "you are."

"Then why in God's name haven't you told me so during all these years?"

"Two reasons," he said. "First, I couldn't be sure. The line between a heavy drinker and an alcoholic is not always clear. It wasn't until just lately that, in your case, I could draw it. Second, you wouldn't have believed me even if I had told you."

I had to admit to myself that he was right. Only through being beaten down by my own misery would I ever have accepted the term "alcoholic" as applied to myself. Now, however, I accepted it fully. I knew from my general reading that alcoholism was irreversible and fatal. And I knew that somewhere along the line I'd lost the power to stop drinking. "Well, Doc," I said, "what are we going to do?"

"There's nothing I can do," he said, "and nothing medicine can do. However, I've heard of an organization called Alcoholics Anonymous that has had some success with people like you. They make no guarantees and are not always successful. But if you want to, you're free to try them. It might work."

Many times in the intervening years I have thanked God for that man, a man who had the courage to admit failure, a man who had the humility to confess that all the hard-won learning of his profession could not turn up the answer. I looked up an A.A. meeting and went there–alone.

Here I found an ingredient that had been lacking in any other effort I had made to save myself. Here was–*power*! Here was power to live to the end of any given day, power to have the courage to face the next day, power to have friends, power to help people, power to be sane, power to stay sober. That was seven years ago–and many A.A. meetings ago–and I haven't had a drink during those seven years. Moreover, I am deeply convinced that so long as I continue to strive, in my bumbling way, toward the principles I first encountered in the earlier chapters of this book, this remarkable power will continue to flow through me. What *is* this power? With my A.A. friends, all I can say is that it's a Power greater than myself. If pressed further, all I can do is follow the psalmist who said it long before me: "*Be still*, and know that I am God."

My story has a happy ending but not of the conventional kind. I had a lot more hell to go through. But what a difference there is between going through hell without a Power greater than one's self, and with it! As might have been predicted, my teetering tower of worldly success collapsed. My alcoholic associates fired me, took control, and ran the enterprise into bankruptcy. My alcoholic wife took up with someone else, divorced me, and took with her all my remaining property. The most terrible blow of my life befell me after I'd found sobriety through A.A. Perhaps the single flicker of decency that shone through the fog of my drinking days was a clumsy affection for my two children, a boy and a girl. One night my son, when he was only sixteen, was suddenly and tragically killed. The Higher Power was on deck to see me through, sober. I think He's on hand to see my son through, too.

There have been some wonderful things too. My new wife and I don't own any property to speak of, and the flashy successes of another day are no longer mine. But we have a baby who, if you'll pardon a little post-alcoholic sentimentality, is right out of heaven. My work is on a much deeper and more significant level than it ever was before, and I am today a fairly creative, relatively sane human being. And should I have more bad times, I know that I'll never again have to go through them alone.

(12) NEW VISION FOR A SCULPTOR

His conscience hurt him as much as his drinking. But that was years ago.

I THINK that life, when I was growing up, was the most wonderful life that any kid ever had. My parents were very successful and every new luxury and every new beauty that came into the house was keenly appreciated by all of us. We didn't have things thrown at us. They came little by little.

My parents were both Jews and, in my family life, we were always keenly alive to the beauty of religion, although we were not orthodox. I always saw God as a wonderful force that was a great deal like my father, only magnified to the Nth degree. I once asked my grandfather, when I was a little boy, what God was like. He asked me what my Dad was like. I went into superlatives about Dad because I really loved him so much. He was such a friendly, wonderful father, and so my grandfather said, "Well, your father is the head of your family. God is the head of the entire human family and of the whole universe. But what makes him 'Dear God' is that you can speak to him just as you would talk to your own Dad. He's not only a universal father, but an individual father too." So I'd always had that wonderful comparison of my own father with God.

When they found out that I could create sculpture at a very early age, it made both my parents very happy; my two older brothers were not artists, but they were good students. I was a very bad student and very much an artist. Instead of resenting that, they encouraged my art. So my childhood was really art and music, and I got along at school, usually, by leaving the day before examinations or getting measles or something else like that and being put in the next grade for trial. The teacher of the grade that I left would never take me back under any circumstances.

I was ecstatically happy. My brothers and their friends lived on horses as I did from six years old on. We did everything, all of our playing and wild games on horseback. This was up to World War I. I was about nineteen years old then. I don't think I had any fears at all up to that time.

We were a very close family. Everything was very vital, anything that happened to one happened to another. When war broke out all I could hear in my heart was the echoes of what father and mother had told me so often; how grateful I should be to the United States. Both my grandfathers had come over from the other side, one from Bohemia and one from Prussia, because at that time there was persecution in those countries, and they wanted to live and be a part of the "land of the free." They both had magnificent lives and were able to pull themselves up and live happily and die in luxury. I was very grateful to the United States for that.

I loved my grandparents very dearly and I had watched my father's great financial success. So I felt that I didn't want either of my two brothers to go to war. They were both married, but certainly one of the family should show what we thought and felt about the United States. So I told my folks that I was going to join the army and that scared them to death, but after a while they heard that a nearby hospital was forming a unit and I think my mother had a picture of my going to war with my personal family doctor. Nothing could be more luxurious! So, they gave their consent that I should join the unit, never realizing that you could transfer when you got to the other side.

I was a terrible soldier as far as drilling was concerned, but I had been studying anatomy and dissecting for my art work so a hospital was sort of a second nature to me. I got along very well in that part of the army, very well indeed.

I went through World War I without actually getting drunk. I did learn to drink heavily in France, but it didn't do anything for me or to me. I mean to say I didn't drink for relief or escape, and I was always flattered that I could out-drink almost anybody and take them home. Many of the patients insisted that when they got well they were going to take me down and get me drunk in appreciation. It was usually a hike of two and one-half kilometers to get the patient back to the hospital! These were walking wounded.

I had one bad experience in which a truck that I was in was blown up, and I woke up in Vichy a couple of days later in a bathtub. I thought I was in heaven. The whole room was full of steam. An enormous sergeant came through the steam and said, "Don't move, young fellow." I said, "Where am I?" He told me. I started to upbraid him, "Why shouldn't I move?" He said, "Don't move. That's all." I did, and found it was very painful. I had an injury to my spine. When it was time to get me out of that bathtub that enormous guy just picked me up as though I were a baby and put me on a stretcher. That was about three days before the Armistice.

On Armistice Day everyone pushed all the hospital beds onto the street and had a grand parade of them. Everybody hugged and kissed us and gave us candy and drinks, and the sergeant came along with a glass and said, "The doctor says you're to finish this right away." I turned it upside down and believe me the bed swam from then on. It didn't last very long because as soon as I got something to eat I got over that. But I think that was my very first feeling of being dizzy or drunk.

When I got back from World War I, there didn't seem to be any alcoholic problem at all. I could drink or not drink, but when I did I liked to out-drink other people. This stupid desire to out-drink people, and then drinking more and more myself, was the first sign of my alcoholism.

I married in 1920. In 1928, my wife and I returned to Paris with two children, and I'd get insomnia and get up and go to the dining room and take a glass of brandy and that would put me back to sleep. I thought people took brandy to go to sleep.

Meanwhile, back in this country, I began to notice the family got worried when I was drinking and I didn't like to see them worried. I thought, if it worries them so much, well, I'd drink over at the studio and take my friends over there. Because, by that time, I'd worked up a good, artistic reputation and the critics were particularly kind to me. I had loads and loads of work, all that I could take care of, and I liked work. I always had a long day. To me, sunrise is the most gorgeous time of the day and the most spiritual, and I love to say my prayers and watch the sunrise at the same time. I am grateful for the new day and for the beauty of it.

This drinking over at the studio and then finally at barrooms–anything so as not to drink at the house–became progressively worse. This was when my "guilt complex" started, with this secret drinking. I went to Europe several times and the cycle seemed to be broken each time because I was never drunk over there, except when we lived in Paris after I was actively alcoholic. I was only actually drunk there twice that I know of.

The drinking got heavier and heavier and the compulsion got heavier and heavier. I could still come home without staggering and I was very proud of that. But I was very unhappy too because I was making the folks at home unhappy, and then my legs began to get unsteady and they could see by my bloodshot eyes that I'd been drinking on the sly, and then guilt really started in. And with the guilt there started fears and I was very unhappy, so I decided that I would quit–and then I found that I couldn't quit. This one didn't count. This one was medicine. By that time I was in my thirties. That's just about the time I did such crazy things. I'd sneak away from the house on my motorcycle because I thought I could be wilder and have a grander time on a motorcycle than I could in a car, because a car had four wheels and, incidentally, a motorcycle could go faster. But I found that was very lonely, so I got a sidecar and took a chauffeur. Very often when I'd go out with the chauffeur, he would drive out and I would have to drive him home because he didn't have my capacity.

My wife always had faith that this was only a sickness, but she did worry. She knew nothing about A.A. and I knew nothing of it. But she always realized that this was not her husband, that something had distressed him and that something had to be understood, although I was arrogant and rotten.

After father died in 1934, I drank for oblivion. That was a terrible shock. In my insecurity I thought that all the security in the world had gone with him.

The next few years were really terrible. So many things happened that the net was closing in. One of the most terrible things was that in my guilt I lost God. That was the big thing. I had no right to pray to God. I had no right to go into the temple or church. When we lived in Rome I used to go into one of the cathedrals every night on my way home from work and, to me, a house of God was a house of God and was beautiful and dedicated to His worship. Now I was robbed of God, because I was so ashamed, and so I had no help and I didn't know how to quit. It was very terrible.

We had a dear friend up near us in Westchester by the name of Gabrielle. She had a wash-woman whose son was a cripple. He had created some really beautiful works of art. She asked me if I would go and see his work and help him. I couldn't refuse Gabrielle anything, and I promised her that I would go, and that was really the beginning of the end of my alcoholic experience. I gathered together the most beautiful books of pictures from the Vatican. Like a big shot alcoholic I did everything in style! I got gorgeous new art materials and fine new paper. I couldn't get the train at my own station–that was impossible! I had to go down the line and beat the train by twenty minutes and spend those twenty minutes in a barroom. That held me till I got to 125th Street and the bars were open. So I went to a bar on 7th Avenue and when I got there the welcome was warmer than any welcome I ever received in my life, there were a lot of bar-flies around, and everybody was treating everybody, and I was gulping them down as fast as I could. Finally, when I found myself with sixteen drinks in front of me, still to be taken, and this big package of pictures, I hurried up and finished the sixteen drinks and told the men that I would be back later, that I had to deliver this bundle. Then I began a most peculiar trek down 7th Avenue until I reached where I was going. I stumbled and staggered and fell in area-ways and I became absolutely filthy. I can see to this day the people grabbing their children so that I didn't throw them into the gutter or area-way or knock a baby carriage under a truck. It was almost like a musical comedy when the hero comes downstage and everybody gives way before him.

I finally reached my destination and, to my horror, found that it was on the fifth floor of a walk-up tenement house. How I made the five flights I really don't know. I was just about to put my hand on the doorknob when I realized what a drunken, awful mass of humanity I was. I became thoroughly frightened and instinctively I asked God, "Please help me not to bring further suffering to this family. It's bad enough what they have to go through, but if anything happens to me there, or if I misbehave, think how terrible it would be! Please, please, help me get through these few minutes." Having said that prayer, I straightened myself up and licked my handkerchief and washed my face with it, and slicked back my hair. Then I took off my overcoat and shook it and tried to make myself presentable as best I could, and rang the doorbell. The boy's mother was a sweet, little lady in stiff starched white, absolutely immaculate. The place too was immaculate and the sun was streaming in. I could see the crippled boy in the chair, looking up and watching for me as though I were some great person. I don't know how I did it, but I stayed there two and a half hours. I looked at all of his portfolios and work and showed him how to use the new art material. I told him about the originals of all the pictures in the book and left him, thank God, very happy. When I got out the reaction set in and I took a taxi down to what used to be a speakeasy and was then wide open, and what happened from then on for the next ten days I don't know very much about.

I was in the country and in bed, and the bottle was under the pillow and my hand was firmly around the neck of it. Every time I came to I took another swig and got drunk all over again. During this drunk I had many flashbacks, and I remembered strange things. For instance, I'd seen a play years before called "The Dybbuk," down at the Neighborhood Playhouse. It opened with two rabbis in a sub-sub cellar, talking about another rabbi and they said, "His words have always been so great. From the highest heights to the deepest depths the soul may plunge, but, in itself the plunge contains the resurrection." Those words just came to me. I thought how much further and how much lower can I go? I'm at the bottom; I've taken the plunge. Suddenly I remembered that on the day I had visited my young friend I had prayed before I rang the doorbell, and that God had answered my prayer. I knew that the barrier to prayer was broken, and I turned around in bed and prayed as I had never prayed before. I prayed for instruction and knowledge, not to do something for me because I didn't deserve it, but to do something to me, and to show me the right way so that I could do something for myself. I realized at that moment that alcohol was the basis of all my trouble, that all the rest was fantasy; nothing had happened yet, everything was happening all the time. Nothing was real. I bawled like a baby, as all drunks do, and I cried myself to sleep.

I awakened at dawn, before sunrise even, but it was dawn and very beautiful, and for the first time in years I awakened with a hangover. I didn't have the dry heaves. The bed wasn't full of sweat and all the other horrible things that went with the usual early morning awakening. I had a feeling that I had had a bath in a clean stream, mental, moral, physical, and spiritual. All of a sudden I was clean. And as I lay there in bed trying to understand this feeling, a thought came to me that was foreign to any thoughts I had ever had because of its simplicity, and that thought kept flashing on and off like a neon sign repeating itself, "You're not going to have your last drink. You have had it!" Then, as the sun actually began to rise, the thing dawned on me. The rat race was over and I was ecstatically happy. I went in the next room because I didn't want to disturb my wife. I said so many prayers of thanksgiving that they were all jumbled up. It was the most wonderful feeling because I had read the handwriting on the wall. In my alcoholic fantasy, I had wanted to have a tremendous party, a drunk to end all drunks. I was going to out-Hollywood Hollywood, and I could see myself in the end, up on the model's stand finishing it all up with a Royal Canadian quart and falling back in the arms of some other drunk. That would have been it! But this was simple, beautiful, and real, "I've had my last drink." The release was there.

I was not quite forty at the time, three years after father died. It was in the late spring around Decoration Day, because I had my last drink on Decoration Day.

My doctor put me in the hospital because he wanted me to get over my nervous period. He was very happy that I had stopped drinking, and he put me there in order to help me help myself. He started giving me certain drugs to stop me from shaking, among which was one that was jam full of bromides. I left the hospital very happily after just a couple of days, but about a week later I began staggering and began driving my car so far up on the right hand side that I was practically in the gutter and sometimes on the sidewalk. When I tried walking around the room I'd bump into everything on the right hand side, and then I couldn't walk at all. They finally got a male nurse and put me to bed and a doctor came up from New York, and said, "Oh, yes, I know all about Fred. I've seen them go like that before. There's nothing you can do about it." That didn't satisfy my wife, thank God. That was the doctor that I had recommended, a very nice doctor. Every time I'd tell him about my drinking problem, he helped me drink some cocktails with him and told me to drink as he did. My wife got a really good doctor from New York, just in the nick of time. He suggested my going to a neurological institute that night with him. The minute I got into the hospital the horrors started. They took blood tests at once. By that time I was clear of alcohol, but I was jammed full of bromides. Bromide poisoning had started, and caused a swelling of the brain. I went from bad to worse there, but they started the therapy at once with tons and tons of salt injections, salt water baths and drinking salt. I had to drink seven and a half pitchers of salt water every day. I went into the horrors, which lasted for a whole month. I was in a strait-jacket all the time, in the bathtub and even in the padded cell. I came out of it finally within a month, with the loss of some thirty-five or forty pounds. I was a skeleton when I came out. The horrors were awful, but that never seemed to matter much because I blamed them on the bromides. I felt it was none of my doing. But alcohol was.

I stayed sober for the next ten years. I think I use that word inadvisedly. I should say I stayed dry for the next ten years. I wasn't a nice person. There were certain dividends which were tremendous. My family was very happy believing I was sober. They took almost anything from me, though I was just as emotionally high at times as when I was drinking. But they were so glad I wasn't drinking that they stood for anything. They were terrible years.

It was during World War II, and we had lost two of our nephews. There was death, death in the family, one after the other as the youngsters went. Too, it always seemed to take a toll of two or three of the older members of the family at the same time. They were pretty horrible years, and yet I didn't drink. I didn't drink because I never wanted to break that wonderful covenant that I felt I had made, having gotten a release when I prayed to God for it.

After things were adjusted after World War II, mother died. She died after seeing me sober, or dry, for eight years. She died very happy on account of that. Then old John Barleycorn started to talk to me and say, "Well, you've been dry for ten years now. Isn't that enough?" The severe temptation came when my thinking started telling me that after ten years of not drinking I could certainly drink like a normal human being.

So I planned that on Decoration Day my wife and I would try a bottle of champagne, and that if I stayed sober I could drink with her normally like anybody else, and that would have made her happy too.

A week or ten days before Decoration Day, I was having gasoline put into my car and a very dear friend who had gone to school with me and who had a severe alcoholic problem of his own–he was an A.A., whatever that was–came up to me and instead of just putting the gasoline in and saying, "Good morning, how many gallons of gasoline?", which was his usual daily greeting, he said, "Hello, Fred, how's your alcoholic problem?" I laughed. I said, "I haven't any alcoholic problem. In fact, on Decoration Day my wife and I are going to try a bottle of champagne." He got as white as a sheet, and put his hand on my arm and said, "Look, before you take that first drink will you please come to an A.A. meeting? There's one in town tonight and I'll call for you." I just had to say "Yes." And that was the evening that I was taken into A.A. That man had been wanting to talk to me for ten years about my drinking and never had the courage to mention it. That was about May 20, 1947.

I went to that meeting with my tongue in my cheek. I told my wife I was a joiner again. I said I had to do it, but it was no place for a lady. I'd tell her about it later. I went up there and found so many wonderful people in our little group, so many people who wouldn't normally associate with me and, altogether, such a smiling, happy, delightful group of people that I couldn't believe my eyes and still had to be convinced. The leader was a splendid man, a college man, very quiet, who started the meeting by saying, "Alcoholism is an incurable, progressive disease. Whether you are dry one year, ten years or fifty years, you're still one drink away from a drunk." Then he pulled out his pipe. The floor seemed to give way under me, but immediately it steadied because my reaction was, "Thank God I didn't take that first drink! Thank God I came here!" And I realized at last that, after all these years, before I took that drink, I was going to be told the truth and then make the right choice for myself. The whole experience was so beautiful that I was thrilled by it, and a thing mother had said years before when I had come home drunk and she had seen me, came to my mind. The only time that she ever broke down and wept was that night. She said, "This must be somehow good. This cannot be all negative. Some good must come of it." Mother had been dead two years.

Toward the end of my first A.A. evening, I heard about the Twelfth Step where, as an alcoholic and having gone through the experience, I might be able to reach some other poor alcoholic where doctors, medicine, science and religion by themselves, had failed. Immediately, "That's somehow good," came to my ear. Thank God I have been able to turn it into "Somehow good."

That's my story.

PART III: THEY LOST NEARLY ALL

The twelve stories in this group tell of alcoholics at its miserable worst.

Many tried everything–hospitals, special treatments, sanitariums, asylums, and jails. Nothing worked. Loneliness, great physical and mental agony–these were the common lot. Most had taken shattering losses on nearly every front of life. Some went on trying to live with alcohol. Others wanted to die.

Alcoholism had respected nobody, neither rich nor poor, learned or unlettered. All found themselves headed for the same destruction, and it seemed they could do nothing whatever to stop it.

Now sober for years, they tell us how they got well. They prove to almost anyone's satisfaction that it's never too late to try Alcoholics Anonymous.

(1) JOE'S WOES

These were only beginning when he hit Bellevue for the thirty-fifth time. He still had the state hospital ahead of him; and even after A.A., a heartbreaking test of his new-found faith.

I NEVER DRANK in high school or in college, because I never *went* to high school or college. I've never been to Knickerbocker Hospital, I've never been to Grasslands, I've never been to Town's, that swanky place on Central Park West. But I've been to Bellevue's alcoholic ward thirty-five times. That should qualify me, because they don't take you in the Bellevue alcoholic ward for sinus trouble.

I made a few jails, maybe sixty-five or seventy-five times in my drinking. I made my first trip to Bellevue at the age of seventeen. I was called an alcoholic when I was eighteen or nineteen, but I just couldn't believe it. I didn't know what an alcoholic meant. I had trouble with alcohol, but at that age I wasn't bothering anybody. I was single. I just went on about my business, and made up my mind, "Well, I'll lick this thing my way. Someday I'll be able to stop."

I made up my mind I was going to stop drinking when I got married. In 1926 I met the right girl, and we got married. I thought it would be as easy as the snap of a finger to stop drinking. Well, I didn't stop because I couldn't stop. I couldn't leave it alone. I just went on, but now it went into tragedy drinking, because I had brought three children into the world and it went from bad to worse. It was a matter of hospitals, and jails and that merry-go-round we all go through.

My wife stood for this for about eleven years. Then she got a resentment–she was going to leave me! She had tried to leave me before many times, but it was only to try to get me to sober up. But this time I got home one night in the early evening, and everything was crated ready to go to storage. She was going her way with the three children. I was left to go my way with the bottle.

My sister heard about this, and she came running over to the house and says to my wife, "Now wait a minute, before you do a tragic thing like this and leave my brother! Do you realize he is a sick man?" Boy, I thought that was out of this world–such kind words as "a sick man"! You ought to hear what my family called me before that! My sister says, "Let me stand the expense of taking my brother to the Medical Center to interview one of the best psychiatrists."

I thought I was real ripe for a psychiatrist, because I was beginning to do a lot of things I didn't want to do. I thought I was really going out of my mind. I had gotten to the stage where I'd get up in the morning, and I'd look in the mirror, and then I'd start talking to myself, and I'd say, "For cripe's sake, will you stand still long enough till I shave?"

And then I got to the stage where I'm walking the streets of New York, and my eyes go up to an ad on a great big billboard. The ad read, "Old Dutch Cleanser." Now that's an everyday ad, but on this can of Old Dutch Cleanser there happened to be an old woman with a club. Next thing you know, she got off the sign and chased me into the 51st Street police station. I ran in there for help. She was right behind me. I went up to the lieutenant's desk and said, "Help me, she's out there!" He said, "*Who's* out there?" I start raving "There she is with the club! She's followed me from 54th Street!" He looked me over and says, "Oh, *I* see what you mean, Mac." He hollers for Patrolman Murphy, and Murphy comes out, and this lieutenant says, "Take that bum to Bellevue!" So away I go.

So later on when my sister mentioned the Medical Center and a psychiatrist I thought I had no choice. Next day we walk into the Medical Center and I'm perfectly sober, and we see a certain doctor there. I had made my mind up I would do anything in the world that this man says. So we get appointed to Dr. So-and-so, office so-and-so. We walk in, and there's a little psychiatrist sitting down at his desk. He gets up, and he turns out to be a little squirt about that high. Right away my mind changes! I says to myself, "I'm bigger than this guy." I kept staring at him. I didn't think he knew more than I did. I was bigger than he was. I came to the conclusion in the end, "One good drink would kill that guy!"

He started asking me a lot of questions. He says, "Why do you drink?" My sister is paying fifty dollars for that question! "Why do you drink!" Well, I had interviewed psychiatrists before, and I started asking *him* a lot of questions. He couldn't get to first base with me because I wasn't cooperating. Finally he threw me out of the office and called my wife and sister in and talked to them about an hour. The conclusion was that he suggested that I go to Bellevue! What did Bellevue have for me after being there over twenty-five times?

But I made up my mind to do anything that man suggested. So the next day we walk into Bellevue, and I shocked the doctor that was sitting at the admittance office. He had seen me come in on a stretcher; he had seen me come in on crutches; he had seen me come in with a cop under each arm; and when he saw me walk in with two ladies, he was shocked.

He says, "I don't get this. What is this?" He thought I was really nuts, I guess. "Doctor," I says, "I am having a little trouble with alcohol." I told him about this bird up in the Medical Center that sent me down here to commit myself to a state institution. He says, "You really want to go through with this?" I says, "Yes. I really want to get straight and I think this is going to help me." He says, "Well, all right, I'll draw out a voluntary commitment. You sign it, and you're in!"

He didn't tell me *where* I was in! Ten days later I get on the bus and the first thing I know I'm up in the booby-hatch. Well, I resented that because I thought I was going to one of those drying-out places. I didn't know I was going up there with a lot of nuts.

A few days later another bus came up from Bellevue, and on this bus there happened to be two boys that had made several trips to Bellevue. One of those boys had been in here and knew the ropes. He says, "Don't worry about this place; this ain't the worst place in the world." Well, he was right, because ten days later the three of us were drunk right up there in the booby-hatch!

I left three children and a wife on the outside, absolutely penniless. One of the children, a boy ten years old, wrote me a letter to try to encourage me. He thought I was up there getting shots in the arm and different medicines and that when I came out I would never take another drink. Well, he wrote me a letter, and he says, "Don't worry Dad. Do anything the doctors tell you, no matter how long they keep you there. I hope you come out a dad like my friends have." He could bring boys, his friends, up to the house now, and he couldn't do that while I was drinking because I didn't want anybody around me. I was one of those nasty drunks. He went on in this letter, "Don't worry about the house, because I went into business." His business was that he made himself a shoe-shine box and went out and shined shoes–while I'm up in this hospital drinking!

On one of her visits my wife left me a dollar. I thought it was five dollars. I stuck it in my pocket, and when she left I took it out and saw it was a dollar, and I says, "Why, that cheap so-and-so! What am I going to do here with one dollar for the next two weeks?" Two days later one of the head doctors called me into his office and says, "Do you know your wife had to borrow money to get back to New York, that she left you her last dollar in the world?" He pointed out that my children didn't have the price of a glass of milk the next morning. That made me feel pretty cheap. I says to myself, "*I'm* the cheap so-and-so." I told the doctor, "I'm going to do something about this." He says, "Why don't you sign yourself out–you're able to do that–and go out and get yourself a job, and cut out all this monkey business? Take care of your family. You got a fine little family there. Go out and take care of them." And I swore to God in front of that man that day that I would do that. I swore, "I'll never take another drink as long as I live!"

At the time, I meant it. I did sign myself out, and I did get a job, and for two weeks I did not take a drink. Two weeks is a pretty long period with me. I happened to get paid that first two weeks' pay with a check. I didn't know where to go and cash that check except in a saloon. Nobody knew me, nobody would trust me, only these bartenders. But I knew I couldn't get away with going in there and buying one drink. I says to myself, "So help me God, I won't have any more than three drinks. I'll cash this check and I'll bring this money home." I had my three drinks, cashed the check, picked up the change, and then the bartender says, "Will you have one on the house?" So I did. Well, after that I don't have to tell you what happened. I never got home with a nickel of that money.

I lost my job, but it was easy at the time and I got another one. Then another. And then it was one job after another, until I couldn't beg, borrow or steal any more. Then I think I went as low as a man will ever go. When I couldn't get a job any more, and that kid was still out shining shoes, I used to go around to where he was shining shoes and tell that kid that his mother had sent me over to get the money that he'd made. That kid knew all the time that I wasn't going to bring that money home, but he never refused me. He always gave me all the change he had. And I went out and drank it.

The day came when I finally wound up in Bellevue again. I was in the alcoholic ward and I was pretty sick going in there. One of the doctors ordered a big dose of paraldehyde for me to knock me out. An hour and a half later, three men were trying to wake me up. One of them was the night attendant of the hospital, one was a policeman in uniform, and one was a plain clothes man. The law had been looking for me for four or five days, but they finally caught up with me in Bellevue. It was for something I had done in the blackout that I didn't know anything about. They took me out of the alcoholic ward and took me to the Bellevue prison ward, where I spent quite a few months.

I was up against a very serious charge. I was supposed to go to Sing Sing for between seven and a half to fifteen years for it. But somehow or other, I don't know how it happened–maybe it was through the prayers of my wife, or maybe help by my family, or somehow or other–when I was brought up on trial I was sentenced to the state hospital again instead of Sing Sing. This was in late 1938 when I got back up there. This time I wasn't on my own. I was there with the sentence of three judges.

Early in 1939, when the A.A. book was fresh off the press, I was called into the doctor's office, the chief doctor of the state hospital. One of the founders of A.A. was there with five other men from A.A., trying to get A.A. into the hospital. The way A.A. was put to me, this doctor says to me, "The medical profession has nothing for you. The clergy has nothing for you. There's nobody in God's world can help you. You're a chronic alcoholic, period!" Then he says, "Maybe these men and this book can help you."

I read the book. In the meantime they had meetings in South Orange, New Jersey. There used to be a group from South Orange that would come up to the hospital and take some of the boys down to a meeting and bring them back. I wanted to know what was going on at those meetings. I got one of the boys who was there and I says, "What are these meetings all about?" He says, "It's a bunch of people that get up there and swap stories. They talk to each other and you talk to them. They're all a bunch of ex-drunks. And they're all happy looking. They all have a lot of fun, they're all dressed up, they have a collar and tie. Some are working and some are not, but they're all happy." He says, "Why don't you ask the doctor to let you come down there sometime? You ought to see the spread these people put out after the meeting–chicken sandwiches and..." Oh, he laid out a beautiful picture for me! "Home-made cakes"... something you weren't getting at the hospital! I says, "Gee, that looks pretty good."

I never been to a meeting before in all my life where there was a bunch of alcoholics and nobody didn't have a bottle! So I asked the doctor, and he let me go down to the meeting. I figured, "Well, I'll go down there, I'll get a coupla drinks and I'll beat it, and phooey to A.A. and everything else!" I went down there this first time, and I was introduced to this happy looking bunch of people. They put me in my class with real two-fisted drinkers. They sat me in a corner talking to these guys. I couldn't get away from them. In the meantime, I'm looking for the live wires. Anybody going down towards the water section, I look him over. Well, out of a clear sky there's four rough looking guys over there, and all at once they decide to go down to the water section. Right away I says, "Oops, well, excuse me–I gotta go." And I walked in there figuring as soon as these guys get in there, one of the four is going to pull out a bottle. But I was stunned–I was surprised–no bottle! I says, "What is the matter with these guys?"

I went to A.A. meetings for about seven months and I lost the idea of a drink. I didn't think of it any more. I was amazed when I was called into the doctor's office and told I was going out on parole. I got a year's parole, and on my parole card was "In the custody of your wife and A.A."

My wife used to come to every A.A. meeting with me, but one particular night we got company, and my wife says, "What are we going to do?" I says, "Look, you tend to the company. I wouldn't miss that meeting for the world. It means too much to me."

I went to the meeting that night, and it was a swell meeting until the last speaker got up. This fella says, "As long as you are an alcoholic, you'll never be able to take another drink as long as you live!" Oooh, that was rough! A little later on in the same talk, he says, "And don't forget–not even a glass of beer!" and he pointed his finger right at me sitting in the back. That was it! I says, "Why that bunch of Bible-backed-bums, where do they get that stuff?"

That's one meeting I didn't stay for the Lord's Prayer. The speaker got through and sat down and everybody applauded, and I said, "Phooey!", and went out of the place. I got over to Lexington Avenue and found a saloon. I went in there and I says, "Gimme a glass of beer." I drank it and I walked right out of the place. I stood under a lamp post on the corner there at 59th and Lexington. I stood there maybe fifteen or twenty minutes. I was waiting for something to happen because I had a glass of beer. I thought maybe twenty minutes after you have this beer you get some chemical change in you. Maybe you explode. I didn't know what would happen.

Well, I didn't explode. I didn't do anything. So I jump on the subway up to the Bronx, and when I get off at the subway station instead of going home I automatically walk into a saloon and I have another beer and another beer and another. When the man came up with that seventh beer, I says, "Wait a minute, make that a double whiskey." Well, he did. And to make a long story short, what do you think happened to me? I landed back in the state hospital–that's what!

Don't get me wrong. I didn't wind up in there that night or the next week or the next month. It took me three months, but it was that one glass of beer that started the merry-go-round going.

I asked myself, "Now what am I doing up here again?" In my heart and soul I knew that A.A. had something. I wanted to see where I had made my mistake, and I asked the doctor to please give me that book again to read. My number one mistake was I wasn't honest with myself or with anybody in the world. And I knew A.A. didn't fail me. I failed A.A.

So how do I get honest? I cleaned up. I saw a priest there at the hospital, and I really came clean for the first time in my life. I really worked with A.A. up there in the hospital.

Well, I got out and tried to get a job, but I couldn't. They had opened an A.A. clubhouse on 24th Street, so I used to go out in the morning and look for a job. Then I went down to the Club and helped scrub floors. I helped do everything. I stayed nights for the meeting and I went home when the place closed. That's the way I spent my time.

This went on for about eleven months, and then my wife had got into the family way again for her fourth childbirth. She was told after her third child that she wouldn't be able to have a fourth. But she saw that it meant the world to the children. They were happy, I was happy, she was happy, and I was in A.A. in full swing and getting along fine. So she just ignored the doctor's orders and went through with it. I took my wife to the hospital one night, and the following afternoon I go to visit her. And before I could see her I had to go see the doctor. He says, "Joe, how do you feel?" I says, "I feel pretty good, doctor." He says, "Sit down," and then he says, "How do you feel now?" I says, "I *still* feel pretty good. What are you driving at?" He was trying to tell me my wife was almost ready for delivery, and that they had done everything they could, but that she was in danger. "I'm sure you're doing all you can. What can I do?" I ask the doctor. He says, "Well, your record shows you're a Catholic, so you know how to pray."

I went home, and there was my mother and my mother-in-law, two old ladies waiting for news from the hospital. I never let on what they had told me at the hospital, but my mother-in-law started digging, if you know what I mean. Well I blew my top. I said, "Nuts to it." The next thing I know I'm down in the corner saloon. I got a dollar bill on the bar and I'm ready to order a drink. But A.A. stepped right into this picture, and I says, "Now what am I doing here at a time like this?" I heard in A.A. when you're in trouble, try a little prayer. Well, I was in a lot of trouble and I tried a prayer. When the bartender got tired of waiting for me to order, he hollered at me. "Hey, Mac!" he says, "Didja make up your mind? What're you havin'?" I ordered a ginger-ale and plenty of ice. That's how my prayer was answered.

I went down to the Clubhouse on 24th Street. Some of the boys there talked me out of the idea of a drink. I stayed for the meeting that night and went home and went to sleep.

About one o'clock in the morning I got a telegram from the hospital. I was afraid to open it. I thought it was the last telegram I would ever get about my wife. I paced the living room floor for about half an hour, like a prisoner in his cell, with that telegram in my hand. I was still afraid to open it. I finally got down on my knees and asked God Almighty, I says, "Gimme the courage to open this thing." Then I opened the telegram. My wife had given birth to a girl and everything was all right. Where would I have been, or where would she have been, if I had blown my top and taken a drink at a point like that? I thank God Almighty that I didn't.

It took me seventeen months before I got a job. I kept sober, using what I learned in A.A. Then I got a job that I didn't like very much, and it was keeping me away from A.A. I made up my mind, "If nothing happens within this week, nuts to A.A.!" I planned it out–another drunk for myself. I gave myself a week, see? I just didn't take that drink; I allowed myself a week.

Before that week was up, I go home one night and out of a clear sky there's two old bosses of mine sitting down on the sofa waiting for me. They were two brothers I had worked for a long time before, fellas who swore they'd never have anything to do with me anymore. I'm bringing this out because I want you to know that good news travels in A.A. They heard I was in A.A. and doing all right, back with my family and everything, and they came and asked me to go to work for them. Well, I did go to work for them, and I'm on that job till this very day.

Now then, I'm going back about six years. Something happened again. That boy of mine that was shining shoes at the age of ten, in the meantime he had grown up to be a six-foot-one-inch fella. And almost to the day of his birthday, the sixteenth birthday, I lost that boy in a trolley car accident only two blocks away from my house. I was in Philadelphia when it happened, and they called me up and drove me in from Philadelphia to see my boy. He regained consciousness once in the thirteen hours I was there. He looked up at me and says, "Dad, what happened to me?" I says, "Well, son, you just keep your chin up. You'll be all right." The doctors had told me the boy was going to pull through. He was strong and he was fighting.

Well, the kid didn't make it. He was trying to tell me in that last handshake that he'd lost his battle. He was trying to tell me, "I'm losing this battle, Dad, but don't let this throw you." That's what he was trying to put across to me. I realize it now. But in spite of all of that, when they took that kid away from me, I made up my mind I was going on a suicide drunk. I figured I would go home first and take care of the funeral arrangements. Then I would lock myself in some hotel and drink myself to death. If liquor didn't kill me, I was going to jump out the window.

Before I could do this I get a telephone call. It's an A.A. member in Ohio. How that news travelled to Ohio in thirty-five minutes I don't know till this day. This fella says, "I just heard what happened to you. The reason I'm calling you is I know what's running through your mind. But I hope you don't. I hope you don't take that drink. Nobody in the world or nobody in A.A. can condemn you for it. But don't forget, there's a couple hundred members here, and we all got our fingers crossed; we're all praying for you."

When he got off the wire, somebody else was calling me, somebody from

Connecticut. I was so busy answering calls that I just couldn't get out. While I was still answering calls, one of my A.A. friends walked in. He stayed with me that night, so I didn't have a chance to get out. This fella and I sat in the kitchen all night, smoking cigarettes and drinking coffee.

The next morning the undertaker came up to take me to the hospital morgue to identify my son. This A.A. fella came with me. The undertaker was an A.A. too. Well, when that slab was pulled out for me to identify my son's body, if I didn't have A.A. on my right and A.A. on my left I wouldn't be alive today. I'd be in the same grave with that kid.

So you can see that my length of sobriety wasn't handed to me on a silver platter. If things are going to happen, they're going to happen. But I'm in A.A. and sober for over eleven years now. I had my last drink of alcohol eleven years and seven months ago. Thanks to the good people of A.A., and last but not least by the Grace of God.

And if I can do it, so can you!

(2) OUR SOUTHERN FRIEND

Pioneer A.A., minister's son, and southern farmer, he asked "Who am I to say there is no God?"

FATHER IS an Episcopal minister and his work takes him over long drives on bad roads. His parishioners are limited in number, but his friends are many, for to him race, creed, or social position makes no difference. It is not long before he drives up in the buggy. Both he and old Maud are glad to get home. The drive was long and cold but he was thankful for the hot bricks that some thoughtful person had given him for his feet. Soon supper is on the table. Father says grace, which delays my attack on the buckwheat cakes and sausage.

Bedtime comes. I climb to my room in the attic. It is cold, so there is no delay. I craw under a pile of blankets and blow out the candle. The wind is rising and howls around the house. But I am safe and warm. I fall into a dreamless sleep.

I am in church. Father is delivering his sermon. A wasp is crawling up the back of the lady in front of me. I wonder if it will reach her neck. Shucks! It has flown away. At last! The message has been delivered.

"Let your light so shine before men that they may see your good works–." I hunt for my nickel to drop in the plate so that mine will be seen.

I am in another fellow's room at college. "Freshman," said he to me, "do you ever take a drink?" I hesitated. Father had never directly spoken to me about drinking but he never drank any, so far as I knew. Mother hated liquor and feared a drunken man. Her brother had been a drinker and had died in a state hospital for the insane. But his life was unmentioned, so far as I was concerned. I had never had a drink, but I had seen enough merriment in the boys who were drinking to be interested. I would never be like the village drunkard at home.

"Well," said the older boy, "do you?"

"Once in a while," I lied. I could not let him think I was a sissy.

He poured out two drinks. "Here's looking at you," said he. I gulped it down and choked. I didn't like it, but I would not say so. A mellow glow stole over me. This wasn't so bad after all. Sure, I'd have another. The glow increased. Other boys came in. My tongue loosened. Everyone laughed loudly. I was witty. I had no inferiorities. Why, I wasn't even ashamed of my skinny legs! This was the real thing!

A haze filled the room. The electric light began to move. Then two bulbs appeared. The faces of the other boys grew dim. How sick I felt. I staggered to the bathroom. Shouldn't have drunk so much or so fast. But I knew how to handle it now. I'd drink like a gentleman after this.

And so I met John Barleycorn. The grand fellow who at my call made me a hale-fellow-well-met, who gave me such a fine voice, as we sang, "Hail, hail, the gang's all here," and "Sweet Adeline," who gave me freedom from fear and feelings of inferiority. Good old John! He was my pal, all right.

Final exams of my senior year and I may somehow graduate. I would never have tried, but mother counts on it so. A case of measles saved me from being kicked out during my sophomore year.

But the end is in sight. My last exam and an easy one. I gaze at the board with its questions. Can't remember the answer to the first. I'll try the second. No soap there. I don't seem to remember anything. I concentrate on one of the questions. I don't seem to be able to keep my mind on what I am doing. I get uneasy. If I don't get started soon, I won't have time to finish. No use. I can't think.

I leave the room, which the honor system allows. I go to my room. I pour out half a tumbler of grain alcohol and fill it with ginger ale. Now back to the exam. My pen moves rapidly. I know enough of the answers to get by. Good old John Barleycorn! He can be depended on. What a wonderful power he has over the mind! He has given me my diploma!

Underweight! How I hate that word. Three attempts to enlist in the service, and three failures because of being skinny. True, I have recently recovered from pneumonia and have an alibi, but my friends are in the war or going, and I am not. I visit a friend who is awaiting orders. The atmosphere of "eat, drink, and be merry" prevails and I absorb it. I drink a lot every night. I can hold a lot now, more than the others.

I am examined for the draft and pass the physical test. I am to go to camp on November 13. The Armistice is signed on the eleventh, and the draft is called off. Never in the service! The war leaves me with a pair of blankets, a toilet kit, a sweater knit by my sister, and a still greater inferiority.

It is ten o'clock of a Saturday night. I am working hard on the books of a subsidiary company of a large corporation. I have had experience in selling, in collecting, and in accounting, and I am on my way up the ladder.

Then the crack-up. Cotton struck the skids and collections went cold. A twenty-three million dollar surplus wiped out. Offices closed up and workers discharged. I, and the books of my division, have been transferred to the head office. I have no assistance and am working nights, Saturdays and Sundays. My salary has been cut. My wife and new baby are fortunately staying with relatives. I feel exhausted. The doctor has told me that if I don't give up inside work, I'll have tuberculosis. But what am I to do? I have a family to support and have no time to be looking for another job.

I reach for the bottle which I just got from George, the elevator boy.

I am a traveling salesman. The day is over and business has been not so good. I'll go to bed. I wish I were home with the family and not in this dingy hotel.

Well–well–look who's here! Good old Charlie! It's great to see him. How's the boy? A drink? You bet your life! We buy a gallon of "corn" because it is so cheap. Yet I am fairly steady when I go to bed.

Morning comes. I feel horribly. A little drink will put me on my feet. But it takes others to keep me there.

I become a teacher in a boy's school. I am happy in my work. I like the boys and we have lots of fun, in class and out.

The doctors' bills are heavy and the bank account is low. My wife's parents come to our assistance. I am filled with hurt pride and self-pity. I seem to get no sympathy for my illness and have no appreciation of the love behind the gift.

I call the bootlegger and fill up my charred keg. But I do not wait for the charred keg to work. I get drunk. My wife is extremely unhappy. Her father comes to sit with me. He never says an unkind word. He is a real friend, but I do not appreciate him.

We are staying with my wife's father. Her mother is in critical condition at a hospital. I cannot sleep. I must get myself together. I sneak downstairs and get a bottle of whiskey from the cellaret. I pour drinks down my throat. My father-in-law appears. "Have a drink?" I ask. He makes no reply and hardly seems to see me. His wife dies that night.

Mother has been dying of cancer for a long time. She is near the end now and is in a hospital. I have been drinking a lot but never get drunk. Mother must never know. I see her about to go.

I return to the hotel where I am staying and get gin from the bellboy. I drink and go to bed; I take a few the next morning and go see my mother once more. I cannot stand it. I go back to the hotel and get more gin. I drink steadily. I come to at three in the morning. The indescribable torture has me again. I turn on the light. I must get out of the room or I shall jump out of the window. I walk miles. No use. I go to the hospital, where I have made friends with the night superintendent. She puts me to bed and gives me a hypodermic.

I am at the hospital to see my wife. We have another child. But she is not glad to see me. I have been drinking while the baby was arriving. Her father stays with her.

It is a cold, bleak day in November. I have fought hard to stop drinking. Each battle has ended in defeat. I tell my wife I cannot stop drinking. She begs me to go to a hospital for alcoholics that has been recommended. I say I will go. She makes the arrangements, but I will not go. I'll do it all myself. This time I'm off of it for good. I'll just take a few beers now and then.

It is the last day of the following October, a dark, rainy morning. I come to on a pile of hay in a barn. I look for liquor and can't find any. I wander to a stable and drink five bottles of beer. I must get some liquor. Suddenly I feel hopeless, unable to go on. I go home. My wife is in the living room. She had looked for me last evening after I left the car and wandered off into the night. She had looked for me this morning. She has reached the end of her rope.

There is no use trying any more, for there is nothing to try. "Don't say anything," I say to her. "I am going to do something."

I am in the hospital for alcoholics. I am an alcoholic. The insane asylum lies ahead. Could I have myself locked up at home? One more foolish idea. I might go out West on a ranch where I couldn't get anything to drink. I might do that. Another foolish idea. I wish I were dead, as I have often wished before. I am too yellow to kill myself.

Four alcoholics play bridge in a smoke-filled room. Anything to get my mind from myself. The game is over and the other three leave. I start to clean up the debris. One man comes back, closing the door behind him.

He looks at me. "You think you are hopeless, don't you?" he asks.

"I know it," I reply.

"Well, you're not," says the man. "There are men on the streets of New York today who were worse than you, and they don't drink anymore."

"What are you doing here then?" I ask.

"I went out of here nine days ago saying that I was going to be honest, and I wasn't," he answers.

A fanatic, I thought to myself, but I was polite. "What is it?" I enquire.

Then he asks me if I believe in a power greater than myself, whether I call that power God, Allah, Confucius, Prime Cause, Divine Mind, or any other name. I told him that I believe in electricity and other forces of nature, but as for a God, if there is one, He has never done anything for me. Then he asks me if I am willing to right all the wrongs I have ever done to anyone, no matter how wrong I thought the others were. Am I willing to be honest with myself about myself and tell someone about myself, and am I willing to think of other people, of their needs instead of myself, in order to get rid of the drink problem?

"I'll do anything," I reply.

"Then all of your troubles are over," says the man and leaves the room. The man is in bad mental shape certainly. I pick up a book and try to read, but cannot concentrate. I get in bed and turn out the light. But I cannot sleep. Suddenly a thought comes. Can all the worthwhile people I have known be wrong about God? Then I find myself thinking about myself and a few things that I had wanted to forget. I begin to see I am not the person I had thought myself, that I had judged myself by comparing myself to others and always to my own advantage. It is a shock.

Then comes a thought that is like a voice. "*Who are you to say there is no God?*" It rings in my head; I can't get rid of it.

I get out of bed and go to the man's room. He is reading. "I must ask you a question," I say to the man. "How does prayer fit into this thing?"

"Well," he answers, "you've probably tried praying like I have. When you've been in a jam you've said, 'God, please do this or that,' and if it turned out your way that was the last of it, and, if it didn't, you've said 'There isn't any God' or 'He doesn't do anything for me.' Is that right?"

"Yes," I reply.

"That isn't the way," he continued. "The thing I do is to say 'God, here I am and here are all my troubles. I've made a mess of things and can't do anything about it. You take me, and all my troubles, and do anything you want with me.' Does that answer your question?"

"Yes, it does," I answer. I return to bed. It doesn't make sense. Suddenly I feel a wave of utter hopelessness sweep over me. I am in the bottom of hell. And there, a tremendous hope is born. It might be true.

I tumble out of bed onto my knees. I know not what I say. But slowly a great peace comes to me. I feel lifted up. I believe in God. I crawl back into bed and sleep like a child.

Some men and women come to visit my friend of the night before. He invites me to meet them. They are a joyous crowd. I have never seen people that joyous before. We talk. I tell them of the peace and that I believe in God. I think of my wife. I must write her. One girl suggests that I phone her. What a wonderful idea!

My wife hears my voice and knows I have found the answer to life. She comes to New York. I get out of the hospital and we visit some of these new-found friends.

I am home again. I have lost the fellowship. Those that understand me are far away. The same old problems and worries surround me. Members of my family annoy me. Nothing seems to be working out right. I am blue and unhappy. Maybe a drink–I put on my hat and dash off in the car.

Get into the lives of other people is one thing the fellows in New York had said. I go to see a man I had been asked to visit and tell him my story. I feel much better! I have forgotten about a drink.

I am on a train, headed for a city. I have left my wife at home, sick, and I have been unkind to her in leaving. I am very unhappy. Maybe a few drinks when I get to the city will help. A great fear seizes me. I talk to the stranger in the seat beside me. The fear and the insane idea are taken away.

Things are not going so well at home. I am learning that I cannot have my own way as I used to. I blame my wife and children. Anger possesses me, anger such as I have never felt before. I will not stand for it. I pack my bag and leave. I stay with some understanding friends.

I see where I have been wrong in some respects. I do not feel angry any more. I return home and say I am sorry for my wrong. I am quiet again. But I have not seen yet that I should do some constructive acts of love without expecting any return. I shall learn this after some more explosions.

I am blue again. I want to sell the place and move away. I want to get where I can find some alcoholics to help and where I can have some fellowship. A man calls me on the phone. Will I take a young fellow who has been drinking for two weeks to live with me? Soon I have others who are alcoholics and some who have other problems.

I begin to play God. I feel that I can fix them all. I do not fix anyone, but I am getting part of a tremendous education and I have made some new friends.

Nothing is right. Finances are in bad shape. I must find a way to make some money. The family seems to think of nothing but spending. People annoy me. I try to read. I try to pray. Gloom surrounds me. Why has God left me? I mope around the house. I will not go out and I will not enter into anything. What is the matter? I cannot understand. I will not be that way.

I'll get drunk! It is a cold-blooded idea. It is premeditated. I fix up a little apartment over the garage with books and drinking water. I am going to town to get some liquor and food. I shall not drink until I get back to the apartment. Then I shall lock myself in and read. And as I read, I shall take little drinks at long intervals. I shall get myself "mellow" and stay that way.

I get in the car and drive off. Halfway down the driveway a thought strikes me. I'll be honest anyway. I'll tell my wife what I am going to do. I back up to the door and go into the house. I call my wife into a room where we can talk privately. I tell her quietly what I intend to do. She says nothing. She does not get excited. She maintains a perfect calm.

When I am through speaking, the whole idea has become absurd. Not a trace of fear is in me. I laugh at the insanity of it. We talk of other things. Strength has come from weakness.

I cannot see the cause of this temptation now. But I am to learn later that it began with my desire for material success becoming greater than my interest in the welfare of my fellow man. I learn more of that foundation stone of character, which is honesty. I learn that when we act upon the highest conception of honesty that is given us, our sense of honesty becomes more acute.

I learn that honesty is truth and the truth shall make us free!

(3) JIM'S STORY

This physician, one of the earliest members of A.A.'s first black group, tells of how freedom came as he worked among his own people.

I WAS BORN in a little town in Virginia in an average religious home. My father, a negro, was a country physician. I remember in my early youth my mother dressed me just as she did my two sisters, and I wore curls until I was six years of age. At that time I started school, and that's how I got rid of the curls. I found that even then I had fears and inhibitions. We lived just a few doors from the First Baptist Church, and when they had funerals, I remember very often asking my mother whether the person was good or bad and whether they were going to heaven or hell. I was about six then.

My mother had been recently converted and, actually, had become a religious fanatic. That was her main neurotic manifestation. She was very possessive with us children. Mother drilled into me was a very Puritanical point of view as to sex relations, as well as to motherhood and womanhood. I'm sure my ideas as to what life should be like were quite different from that of the average person with whom I associated. Later on in life that took its toll. I realize that now.

About this time an incident took place in grade school that I have never forgotten because it made me realize that I was actually a physical coward. During recess we were playing basketball, and I had accidentally tripped a fellow just a little larger than I was. He took the basketball and smashed me in the face with it. That was enough provocation to fight but I didn't fight, and I realized after recess why I didn't. It was fear. That hurt and disturbed me a great deal.

Mother was of the old school and figured that anyone I associated with should be of the proper type. Of course, in my day, times had changed; she just hadn't changed with the times. I don't know whether it was right or wrong, but at least I know that people weren't thinking the same. We weren't even permitted to play cards in our home, but father would give us just a little toddy with whiskey and sugar and warm water now and then. We had no whiskey in the house, other than my father's private stock. I never saw him drunk in my life, although he'd take a shot in the morning and usually one in the evening, and so did I; but for the most part he kept his whiskey in his office. The only time that I ever saw my mother take anything alcoholic was around Christmas time, when she would drink some eggnog or light wine.

In my first year in high school, mother suggested that I do not join the cadet unit. She got a medical certificate so that I should not have to join it. I don't know whether she was a pacifist or whether she just thought that in the event of another war it would have some bearing on my joining up.

About then I realized that my point of view on the opposite sex wasn't entirely like that of most of the boys I knew. For that reason, I believe, I married at a much younger age than I would have, had it not been for my home training. My wife and I have been married for some thirty years now. She was the first girl that I ever took out. I had quite a heartache about her then because she wasn't the type of girl that my mother wanted me to marry. In the first place, she had been married before; I was her second husband. My mother resented it so much that the first Christmas after our marriage, she didn't even invite us to dinner. After our first child came, my parents both became allies. Then, in later days, after I became an alcoholic, they both turned against me.

My father had come out of the South and had suffered a great deal down there. He wanted to give me the very best, and he thought that nothing but being a doctor would suffice. On the other hand, I believe that I've always been medically inclined, though I have never been able to see medicine quite as the average person sees it. I do surgery because that's something that you can see; it's more tangible. But I can remember in postgraduate days, and during internship, that very often I'd go to a patient's bed and start a process of elimination and then, very often, I'd wind up guessing. That wasn't the way it was with my father. I think with him it possibly was a gift–intuitive diagnosis. Father, through the years, had built up a very good mail-order business because, at that time, there wasn't too much money in medicine.

I don't think I suffered too much as far as the racial situation was concerned because I was born into it and knew nothing other than that. A man wasn't actually mistreated, though if he was, he could only resent it. He could do nothing about it. On the other hand, I got quite a different picture farther south. Economic conditions had a great deal to do with it, because I've often heard my father say that his mother would take one of the old-time flour sacks and cut a hole through the bottom and two corners of it and there you'd have a gown. Of course, when father finally came to Virginia to work his way through school, he resented the southern "cracker," as he often called them, so much that he didn't even go back to his mother's funeral. He said he never wanted to set foot in the Deep South again, and he didn't.

I went to elementary and high school in Washington, D.C., and then to Howard University. My internship was in Washington. I never had too much trouble in school. I was able to get my work out. All my troubles arose when I was thrown socially among groups of people. As far as school was concerned, I made fair grades throughout.

This was around 1935, and it was about this time that I actually started drinking. During the years 1930 to 1935, due to the Depression and its aftermath, business went from bad to worse. I then had my own medical practice in Washington, but the practice slackened and the mail-order business started to fall off. Dad, due to having spent most of his time in a small Virginia town, didn't have any too much money, and the money he had saved and the property he had acquired were in Washington. He was in his late fifties, and all that he had undertaken fell upon my shoulders at his death in 1928. For the first couple of years it wasn't too bad because the momentum kept things going. But when things became crucial, everything started going haywire and I started going haywire with them. At this point I believe I had only been intoxicated on maybe three or four occasions, and certainly whiskey was no problem to me.

My father had purchased a restaurant, which he felt would take up some of my spare time, and that's how I met Vi. She came in for her dinner. I'd known her five or six months. To get rid of me one evening, she decided to go to the movies, she and another friend. A very good friend of mine who owned a drugstore across the street from us came by only about two hours later and said that he had seen Vi downtown. I said that she told me she was going to the movies, and I became foolishly disturbed about it, and, as things snowballed, I decided to go out and get drunk. That's the first time I was ever really drunk in my life. The fear of the loss of Vi and the feeling that, though she had the right to do as she pleased, she should have told me the truth about it, upset me. That was my trouble. I thought that all women should be perfect.

I don't think I actually started to drink pathologically until approximately 1935. About that time I had lost practically all my property except the place we were living in. Things had just gone from bad to worse. It meant that I had to give up a lot of the things that I had been accustomed to, and that wasn't the easiest thing in the world for me. I think that was basically the thing that started me drinking in 1935. I started drinking alone then. I'd go into my home with a bottle, and I remember clearly how I would look around to see if Vi was watching. Something should have told me then that things were haywire. I can remember her watching. There came a time when she spoke to me about it, and I would say that I had a bad cold or that I wasn't feeling well. That went on for maybe two months, and then she got after me again about drinking. At that time the repeal whiskies were back, and I'd go to the store and buy my whiskey and take it to my office and put it under the desk, first in one place and then in another, and there soon was an accumulation of empty bottles. My brother-in-law was living with us at that time and I said to Vi, "Maybe the bottles are brother's. I don't know. Ask him about it. I don't know anything about the bottles." I actually *wanted* a drink, besides feeling that I had to have a drink. From that point on, it's just the average drinker's story.

I got to the place where I'd look forward to the weekend's drinking and pacify myself by saying that the weekends were mine, that it didn't interfere with my family or with my business if I drank on the weekends. But the weekends stretched on into Mondays, and the time soon came when I drank every day. My practice at that juncture was just barely getting us a living.

A peculiar thing happened in 1940. That year, on a Friday night, a man whom I had known for years came to my office. My father had treated him many years prior to this. This man's wife had been suffering for a couple of months, and when he came in he owed me a little bill. I filled a prescription for him. The following day, Saturday, he came back and said, "Jim, I owe you for that prescription last night. I didn't pay you." I thought, "I know you didn't pay me, because you didn't get a prescription." He said, "Yes. You know the prescription that you gave me for my wife last night." Fear gripped me then, because I could remember nothing about it. It was the first blackout I had to recognize as a blackout. The next morning I carried another prescription to this man's house and exchanged it for the bottle his wife had. Then I said to my wife, "Something has to be done." I took that bottle of medicine and gave it to a very good friend of mine who was a pharmacist and had it analyzed, and the bottle was perfectly all right. But I knew at that point that I couldn't stop, and I knew that I was a danger to myself and to others.

I had a long talk with a psychiatrist, but nothing came of that, and I had also, just about that time, talked with a minister for whom I had a great deal of respect. He went into the religious side and told me that I didn't attend church as regularly as I should and that he felt, more or less, that this was responsible for my trouble. I rebelled against this, because just about the time that I was getting ready to leave high school, a revelation came to me about God, and it made things very complicated for me. The thought came to me that if God, as my mother said, was a vengeful God, he couldn't be a loving God. I wasn't able to comprehend it. I rebelled, and from that time on, I don't think I attended church more than a dozen times.

After this incident in 1940, I sought some other means of livelihood. I had a very good friend who was in the government service, and I went to him about a job. He got me one. I worked for the government about a year and still maintained my evening office practice when the government agencies were decentralized. Then I went south, because they told me that the particular county I was going to in North Carolina was a dry county. I thought that this would be a big help to me. I would meet some new faces and be in a dry county.

But I found that after I got to North Carolina, it wasn't any different. The state was different, but I wasn't. Nevertheless, I stayed sober there about six months, because I knew that Vi was to come later and bring the children. We had two girls and a boy at that time. Something happened. Vi had secured work in Washington. She also was in the government service. I started inquiring where I could get a drink, and, of course, I found that it wasn't hard. I think whiskey was cheaper there than it was in Washington. Matters got worse all the time until finally they got so bad that I was reinvestigated by the government. Being an alcoholic, slick, and having some good sense left, I survived the investigation. Then I had my first bad stomach hemorrhage. I was out of work for about four days. I got into a lot of financial difficulties too. I borrowed five hundred dollars from the bank and three hundred from the loan shop, and I drank that up pretty fast. Then I decided that I'd go back to Washington.

My wife received me graciously, although she was living in a one-room-with-kitchen affair. She'd been reduced to that. I promised that I was going to do the right thing. We were now both working in the same agency. I continued to drink. I got drunk one night in October, went to sleep in the rain, and woke up with pneumonia. We continued to work together, and I continued to drink, but I guess, deep down within our heart, we both knew I couldn't stop drinking. Vi thought I didn't want to stop. We had several fights, and on one or two occasions I struck her with my fist. She decided that she didn't want any more of that. So she went to court and talked it over with the judge. They cooked up a plan whereby she didn't have to be molested by me if she didn't want to be.

I went back to my mother's for a few days until things cooled off, because the district attorney had put out a summons for me to come to see him in his office. A policeman came to the door and asked for James S., but there wasn't any James S. there. He came back several times. Within ten days I got locked up for being drunk, and this same policeman was in the station house as I was being booked. I had to put up a three-hundred-dollar bond because he was carrying the same summons around in his pocket for me. So I went down to talk to the district attorney, and the arrangement was made that I would go home to stay with my mother, and that meant that Vi and I were separated. I continued to work and continued to go to lunch with Vi, and none of our acquaintances on the job knew that we had separated. Very often we rode to and from work together, but being separated really galled me deep down.

The November following, I took a few days off after payday to celebrate my birthday on the twenty-fifth of the month. As usual I got drunk and lost the money. Someone had taken it from me. That was the usual pattern. I sometimes gave it to my mother and then I'd go back and hound her for it. I was just about broke. I guess I had five or ten dollars in my pocket. Anyhow, on the twenty-fourth, after drinking all day on the twenty-third, I must have decided I wanted to see my wife and have some kind of reconciliation or at least talk with her. I don't remember whether I went by streetcar, whether I walked or went in a taxicab. The one thing I can remember now was that Vi was on the corner of 8th and L, and I remember vividly that she had an envelope in her hand. I remember talking to her, but what happened after that I don't know. What actually happened was that I had taken a penknife and stabbed Vi three times with it. Then I left and went home to bed. Around eight or nine o'clock there came two big detectives and a policeman to arrest me for assault; and I was the most amazed person in the world when they said I had assaulted someone, and especially that I had assaulted my wife. I was taken to the station house and locked up.

The next morning I went up for arraignment. Vi was very kind and explained to the jury that I was basically a fine fellow and a good husband but that I drank too much and that she thought I had lost my mind and felt that I should be committed to an asylum. The judge said that if she felt that way, he would confine me for thirty days' examination and observation. There was no observation. There might have been some investigation. The closest I came to a psychiatrist during that time was an intern who came to take blood tests. After the trial, I got big-hearted again and felt that I should do something in payment for Vi's kindness to me; so I left Washington and went to Seattle to work. I was there about three weeks, and then I got restless and started to tramp across the country, here and there, until I finally wound up in Pennsylvania, in a steel mill.

I worked in the steel mill for possibly two months, and then I became disgusted with myself and decided to go back home. I think the thing that galled me was that just after Easter I had drawn my salary for two weeks' work and had decided that I was going to send some money to Vi; and above all else I was going to send my baby daughter an Easter outfit. But there happened to be a liquor store between the post office and the mill, and I stopped to get that one drink. Of course the kid never got the Easter outfit. I got very little out of the two hundred that I drew on that payday.

I knew I wasn't capable of keeping the bulk of the money myself, so I gave it to a white fellow who owned the bar which I frequented. He kept the money for me, but I worried him to death for it. Finally, I broke the last one hundred dollar bill the Saturday before I left. I got out of that bill one pair of shoes, and the rest of that money was blown. I took the last of it to buy my railroad ticket.

I'd been home about a week or ten days when one of my friends asked if I could repair one of his electrical outlets. Thinking only of two or three dollars to buy some whiskey, I did the job and that's how I met Ella G., who was responsible for my coming into A.A. I went to this friend's shop to repair his electrical outlet, and I noticed this lady. She continued to watch me, although she didn't say anything. Finally she said, "Isn't your name Jim S.?" I said, "Yes." Then she told me who she was. She was Ella G. When I had known her years before, she was rather slender, but at this time she weighed as much as she does now, which is up around in the two hundreds or very close to it. I had not recognized her, but as soon as she said who she was, I remembered her right away. She didn't say anything about A.A. at that time, but she did ask about Vi, and I told her Vi was working and how she could locate her. It was around noon, a day or two later, when the telephone rang and it was Ella. She asked me if I would let someone come up and talk to me concerning a business deal. She never mentioned anything about my whiskey drinking because if she had I would have told her, "No" right then. I asked her just what this deal was, but she wouldn't say. She said, "He has something of interest, if you will see him." I told her that I would. She asked me one other thing. She asked me if I would try to be sober if I possibly could. So I put forth some effort that day to try to stay sober if I could, though my sobriety was just a daze.

About seven that evening my sponsor walked in, Charlie G. He didn't seem too much at ease in the beginning. I guess I felt, and he sensed it, that I wanted him to hurry up and say what he had to say and get out. Anyhow, he started talking about himself. He started telling me how much trouble he had, and I said to myself, "I wonder why this guy is telling me all his troubles. I have troubles of my own." He continued to talk and I to listen. After he'd talked half an hour, I still wanted him to hurry up and get out so I could go and get some whiskey before the liquor store closed. But as he continued to talk, I realized that this was the first time I had met a person who had the same problems I did and who, I sincerely believe, understood me as an individual. I knew my wife didn't, because I had been sincere in all my promises to her as well as to my mother and to my close friends, but the urge to take that drink was more powerful than anything else.

After Charlie had talked a while, I knew that this man had something. In that short period he built within me something that I had long since lost, which was hope. When he left, I walked with him to the streetcar line, which was just about a half a block, but there were two liquor stores, one on each corner from my home. I put Charlie on the car, and when I left him, I passed both of those liquor stores without even thinking about them.

The following Sunday we met at Ella G.'s. It was Charlie and three or four others. That was the first meeting of a black group in A.A., so far as I know. We held some two or three meetings at Ella's home, and from there we held some two or three at her mother's home. Then Charlie or someone in the group suggested that we try to get a place in a church or hall to hold meetings. I approached several ministers and all of them thought it was a very good idea, but they never relinquished any space. So, finally, I went to the YMCA, and they graciously permitted us to use a room at two dollars a night. At that time we had our meetings on Friday nights. Of course, it wasn't very much of a meeting in the beginning; most of the time it was just Vi and myself. But, finally, we got one or two to come in and stick, and from there, of course, we started to grow.

I haven't mentioned it, but Charlie, my sponsor, was white, and when we got our group started, we got help from other white groups in Washington. They came, many of them, and stuck by us and told us how to hold meetings. They taught us a great deal about Twelve Steps work too. Indeed, without their aid we couldn't possibly have gone on. They saved us endless time and lost motion. And, not only that, but they gave us financial help. Even when we were paying that two dollars a night, they often paid it for us because our collection was so small.

At this time I wasn't working. Vi was taking care of me and I was devoting all my time to the building of that group. I worked at that alone for six months. I just gathered up this and that alcoholic, because, in the back of my mind, I wanted to save all the world. I had found this new "something," and I wanted to give it to everyone who had a problem. We didn't save the world, but we did manage to help some individuals.

That's my story of what A.A. has done for me.

(4) PROMOTED TO CHRONIC

This career girl preferred solitary drinking, the blackout kind, often hoping she'd stay that way for keeps. But Providence had other ideas.

I WASN'T ALWAYS an alcoholic.

In fact it has been only within the last fifteen years that I changed from a fairly normal, controlled drinker into an alcoholic. I don't mean that I went to bed one night a normal drinker, and awoke the next morning an alcoholic.

It wasn't that simple.

I started drinking socially and at parties and proms when I was about twenty years old. I didn't like it particularly at first, but I did like the effect I got from it. It made me feel quite grown-up and mature, and I think another added attraction was the fact that so far as my family was concerned, it was forbidden, and it had a special attraction for that reason. After a while I really did enjoy drinking and what it did to me, and I became dependent upon it for every occasion. Eventually the day came when I was dependent upon it even when there wasn't any occasion. When I didn't have anything else to do–a dull evening at home–I'd sneak a few drinks upstairs in my room, and that began to be a habit.

In 1939, I went on my first week's bender of solitary drinking, locked up in a hotel room, because my family opposed my coming marriage. I figured that perhaps if I went ahead with that marriage, which I was sure was right for me, that would be the answer to my drinking problem. I thought I would be quite happy and never would I drink too much again. So–I tried that.

(I think my first feeling of fear came with my first week's solitary drinking, locked up in that hotel room. The hotel management, knowing that something was wrong, sent for a doctor. The doctor, apparently realizing that one thing that I certainly needed was sleep, left a bottle of sleeping pills there and in my drunken state I took them all, instead of the one or two he had prescribed. If it hadn't been for an alert hotel maid, I might have died then. From that time on, fear was with me because I realized that not only would I not *remember* what happened to me while I was drinking, but apparently I couldn't *control* what happened. And there didn't seem to be anything to do about it.)

Having passed over the border line, the next five years were filled with fear, failure and frustration. Tragedies during those years that were caused by my drinking, such as the breaking up of my marriage, the death of my child, other things–had little restraining effect. In fact, sometimes they served as good excuses to drink more, to forget. It was in Washington, D.C., that this transition took place, and that the really bad part of alcoholism began happening.

The last Christmas I spent in Washington, fourteen years ago, comes to mind. Only a few days before Christmas I went to the dentist for a periodic check-up. X-rays showed that a couple of teeth had to come out. I hadn't been drinking much about that time, for I had begun to realize that there was something abnormal about my drinking, although as yet, I didn't realize that it was so out of control. On the day set for the extractions, on my way to the dentist's I felt a little nervous, so I had a couple of drinks, and after the teeth were out I was *very* nervous, so I had a few more.

When I got home my mouth was very painful, so I got an ice-bag and went to bed. The next day the ice-bag and I were still in bed–but we had a bottle too! My pattern of drinking at that time had reached the point where once I really started, I would retire to my bed and drink myself into oblivion. The rest of that week is pretty hazy.

And so it went. I remember vaguely violent quarrels with my husband, his finding my liquor supply time and time again and throwing it out. And then my waiting until I was sure he was asleep, and stealing money from him to replenish the supply.

Then I remember him coming into my room one night with a friend, and telling me to get dressed–we were going away.

I fought and struggled, but to no avail. I was taken out of the house and put bodily into a waiting car with nothing on but a robe and gown. We were on our way to New York, where he planned to leave me with my sister. On the way I tried, and I mean really tried, to throw myself out of the car. Finally they stopped and bought me a bottle; they knew so well that would keep me quiet.

We pulled up in front of my sister's house just as dawn broke. There was a long discussion between my husband, my sister, and her husband. It was obvious even to me, in my drunken state, that I wasn't wanted. My parents were due for the holidays that day, and she didn't want them to find their drunken daughter there. So we turned around and started back to Washington. I was too weak and exhausted to even try to throw myself out of the car. The trip back was completed in one of those dead, awful silences.

My husband helped me into the house, packed himself a bag, and gave me some money. He said he didn't care what I did with the money, but there was going to be no more until I was completely sober. He said he was finally and completely through–that he never wanted to see me again.

I was frightened–terribly frightened, and in about three days I was sober. On the day before Christmas I telephoned him and told him I was sober and asked him to come home. He said he'd see. I waited all the rest of that day and paced the floor all that night.

At noon on Christmas Day I called my family in New York, wished them a Merry Christmas, and assured them everything was fine with me. I almost broke down and cried when I talked with them but I didn't. It was the one redeeming act of that Christmas.

Then in a couple of hours, when there was still no word from my husband and no sign of him, I had the feeling we alcoholics all know. "What's the use? What's the sense in trying to do the right thing?" There was that awful alcoholic loneliness.

I went out to a restaurant, found a booth way back in the rear, and started drinking. All afternoon I sat there and drank and played Bing Crosby's recording of "Silent Night" over and over again on the juke box.

To this day I can't hear that song without remembering that awful Christmas.

What happened afterwards I don't know. I completely blacked out. The next recollection I have is of my husband coming into my room (I later found out it was on New Year's Eve) accompanied by two policemen. This time I didn't put up any fight because I knew why they were there and where I was going, the psychopathic ward of the city hospital, where I had been once before.

Did that stop my drinking? Temporarily, but not for long.

Things went from bad to worse, and since I had finally and completely failed at the job of being a wife and a mother, my marriage ended. And then I went back home to live with my parents, and the merry-go-round started again–only this time I didn't have to worry about waking up behind bars in a psychiatric ward.

Instead, I started going to a nice private sanitarium which, after the first visit, turned out to be more like a country club than anything else. After the first two or three days you were allowed the run of the place and it was a lot of fun. Also, after the first visit I learned I could refuse to sign myself in unless they gave me a glass of whiskey in one hand and a glass of paraldehyde in the other. This easy method of sobering up would last at least three days.

There were doctors and psychiatrists there who tried to help me, but at that point I wasn't having help from anyone. I didn't want help. I had decided I was no good–never would be any good, and the sooner I could drink myself out of this life, the better.

My visits to that sanitarium went on for nearly three years, until in March of 1944, my father died and I was too drunk to attend his funeral. At that point everyone decided something drastic had to be done. They held consultations and discussions, and finally decided to give me the "Conditioned Reflex" treatment. I won't go into detail about that, but I can assure you it's no fun.

The idea behind it is that, having taken the treatment, your system is so "conditioned" that the mere sight or smell or taste of alcohol produces a violent reaction, and you become ill. But it didn't condition this girl's thinking.

You may wonder why, since I was having all this trouble, and was having to seek the assistance of others, A.A. hadn't come into the picture. Actually it had, way back in 1940.

The same doctor who had sent me to the psycho had asked my husband, "Why don't you send her to this Alcoholics Anonymous?"

My husband said, "What is A.A.?"

At that time there hadn't been any publicity such as we have now. Even the Jack Alexander *Saturday Evening Post* article hadn't been written, and there was only a tiny group of people in Washington.

So the doctor said, "I really don't know too much about it, but they tell me it is a bunch of drunks who get together..."

My husband interrupted, "She's bad enough now without getting mixed up with a bunch of drunks."

And so, in those following years, whenever A.A. was mentioned I would have no part of it. In my screwed up mind I kept thinking I could have gone to A.A. way back there in 1940, and perhaps saved my marriage and home. I even wanted to–but I wasn't allowed to, so I won't go now.

Finally, however, in November of 1944, at long last I went to A.A.

And A.A. took this wreck of a woman and brought her back to life.

Why did it work for me when all other agencies had failed? Was it because they told me in A.A. that I was an alcoholic?

No, I had known that.

Yes, I even knew I was a "chronic alcoholic."

On one occasion when I was serving time in my favorite drying-out place while I was having a session with the psychiatrist, she left my case history on her desk when she was called away from the room. Sly and crafty, I thought now I'll find out what they think of me here, what they "have on" me, what I've said coming in here drunk. There at the top of the folder was my name, age and address, and underneath were the words, "Periodic Drinker." Only they had been scratched out and over them was written, "Chronic Alcoholic."

As an indication of just how confused and mixed up I was, just as soon as I could I left the office and hurried around to tell other patients that I was getting better. I had been promoted from a periodic drinker to a chronic alcoholic! I honestly didn't know the difference. A.A. didn't teach me I was an alcoholic; rather it taught me that because I was an alcoholic my life had become unmanageable.

It seemed to me that those A.A.'s to whom I talked knew all about me. It is true that the doctors and nurses in the various institutions I attended knew too. But the difference lay in the fact that the A.A.'s knew from their own bitter experience.

In other words, the kindest doctor in the whole world, and I had one such, couldn't help me because I always felt, "You can't know about me–you can't possibly know–you don't even drink!"

But to another woman, the first woman I met in A.A., I could talk. In all the sanitariums and psycho wards I had never met a single woman who said she was an alcoholic. They were always there because of a nervous breakdown, or for a "rest cure"–any reason except because of drinking. (I've met some of these same women since in A.A.) But by listening and talking to these A.A.'s–talking to them as I had never talked to anyone in my whole life,

I saw that it was my *life* that was unmanageable–not just my drinking. With their help I also saw that certainly, because of some of the things I had done during the years, I was bordering on insanity, and so, facing the record, I tried to believe that a Power greater than I could and would restore me to sanity.

The other of the Twelve Steps of Alcoholics Anonymous seemed insurmountable to me at first.

But the older members in A.A. told me, "Easy does it." In the light of subsequent events it became evident that I took their advice far too literally, for, after some months of happy sobriety I drank again. Had I tried honestly and sincerely to practice the Twelve Steps I would have seen from my continuous moral inventory that I was getting off the beam–I would have found that there were some active resentments in my life, a terrific amount of self-pity. But more important, I would have found that once again I was sitting in the driver's seat–I was running the show.

The Higher Power to whom I had turned, and who had sustained me, had once again been thrust into the background, while my emotions were running my life and, as always, my emotions ran me to the bottle.

It came about in this way.

When I first came into A.A., the woman who was my sponsor was the first woman I had ever met who admitted that she was an alcoholic. And she was a charming, delightful, lovely person. She gave me such hope and inspiration that I set her right up on a pedestal. And so for three months this one woman was my A.A. I went to meetings, I spent a lot of time at the clubroom, but it was all centered in this one woman. But she couldn't carry me forever. She realized that, and the way I felt, and so for my own good she gradually began to pull away. Of course, I had the sensitive, hurt feelings of the alcoholic. I thought, "Oh well, these people are just like all the people I've known all my life. They build you up with a lot of false hopes and promises, and rush you around here and there and then, all of a sudden, it's gone." And when she broke a luncheon date with me one Saturday, after I had been in A.A. for about three months, I said, "I'll show *her!* She can't do that to me!" And I got drunk.

Well, you know who I showed. I showed myself. And I landed right smack back in that sanitarium that I had gone to so often. While I was there I realized that I had missed something. I realized that I was trying to pin everything on an individual–not the book or the group or the Higher Power, or anything else. So I concentrated and studied the book during that time, and I liked a lot of the things it said in there. I remember particularly one sentence that seemed to say, "This is for you." It read something like this: "Faith without works is dead. Carry this message to other alcoholics. You can help where no one else can." Here was a book that said I could do something that all these doctors and priests and ministers and psychiatrists that I'd been going to for years couldn't do!

That was over seven years ago, and thank God and A.A., I haven't had a drink since. During these seven years a thing called the Twenty-four Hour Program–a gadget I used to think was only a snare to trap the newcomer–has come to mean much to me, not only as regards my drinking but in the whole pattern of my life.

I realize that all I'm guaranteed in life is today. The poorest person has no less and the wealthiest has no more–each of us has but one day. What we do with it is our own business; how we use it is up to us individually.

I feel that I have been restored to health and sanity these past years not through my own efforts nor as a result of anything I may have done, but because I've come to believe–to really believe–that alone I can do nothing. That my own innate selfishness and stubbornness are the evils which, if left unguarded, can drive me to alcohol.

I have come to believe that my illness is spiritual as well as physical and mental, and I know that for help in the spiritual sphere I have to turn to a Higher Power.

(5) THE PRISONER FREED

After twenty years in prison for murder, he knew A.A. was the spot for him... if he wanted to stay on the outside.

I BEGAN DRINKING as a kid, shortly after I reached my fourteenth birthday. My father was alive, and I had to do as he wanted, so I drank under cover. In 1918, he finally passed away, and the fear of him left me. I didn't have to worry about him any longer. I rolled along with the mob this way, that way and the other way, but in those years nothing really bad happened to me. That was still to come.

On July 23 of 1926 I went on a drunk. When I wended my way home four days later, on the twenty-seventh, there was a detective waiting for me. During the course of that drinking, I had shot and killed one person and almost completed the job on a second one. I was immediately arrested, arraigned in Homicide Court, held without bail, and remanded to the old Tombs Prison to await trial. I was indicted for the crime of murder in the first degree. The trial lasted about a week, and whether or not I was going to the Death House was anybody's guess. However, a verdict was brought in of murder in the second degree. For that crime I received a minimum of twenty years and a maximum of natural life. In the meantime I had been indicted for the second crime, attempted murder. I received an additional fifteen years for that, making a minimum of thirty-five years and a maximum of natural life.

On October 28, I was sent to Sing Sing with a minimum of thirty-three and a half years to serve out of that thirty-five. There was no time off for so-called good behavior, first-timers, or anything else. However, as time went on laws were enacted that reduced the sentence. I spent about six or seven weeks in Sing Sing, and was finally sent off to Dannemora in the Adirondacks. I have spent eighteen years in that institution. An ailment developed in one of my eyes, and I was transferred back to Sing Sing and operated upon. I remained there for about ten months. In September of 1945, I was sent to a place called Wallkill, a so-called rehabilitation center.

I spent my last seventeen months in Wallkill, and it was there that I first got my introduction to A.A. When I had heard about it, it meant nothing but just two letters to me, but some friends of mine in the institution were very active in the program and really believed in it. They kept harping on it, that I go. One evening I decided to go because two of those friends were to speak. I rounded up a few more of my friends and off we went to the meeting, not for anything we would gain from it as much as to make a burlesque out of it. However, before the meeting got started, a group from the outside came in unexpectedly. I had enough decency so that I dismissed the idea of doing any clowning, and I did listen.

After hearing the first speaker I could tell myself that my own lot was rather mild. He had been in and out of Mattewan and many other mental institutions as a result of his drinking. He had gone through the windshields of cars a couple of times and was pretty well banged up. After the meeting was over and we had returned to the cell block again, I was asked how I was impressed. "Oh," I said, "that's not for me! Those poor stiffs probably went to a doctor and were told that if they quit they'd live three weeks and if they didn't they'd die in one." That was my attitude toward A.A. at that time. However, my two friends kept coaxing and cajoling to get me back again. Most of my attendance there was when people would come in from the outside. I clung to the outfit for the balance of my time, and finally I was released on April 5, 1947, after having spent twenty years and nine months behind bars.

I had an advantage in having an idea of what A.A. was about before coming out on the street. It wasn't anything strange to me, and I knew if I wanted to stay on the outside, that would be the spot for me. But after I passed through the gates I took a change of heart and mind. So instead of going near A.A., I just browsed around for that first month. Each time I would make a report to the parole officer he would ask me, "Have you been to an A.A. meeting yet?" I'd say, "No, I don't know where they're at or when they meet. I don't know anyone in the program." After I had made my third report, I stepped downtown, met some of the old crowd, and of course you know the answer.

I staggered home next morning. I couldn't tell you how I got there. When my mother opened the door, I almost fell on my face. She asked me, was I going to do this to her all over again? That really stopped me for a little bit. I said, no I wasn't. She was the one who really helped me to make a go of that twenty years and nine months in prison. She's still alive today at the age of eighty-two.

So I went to an A.A. meeting the first chance I got, and I listened. I started prowling around with a couple of these A.A. boys, which kept me pretty busy and kept my mind off of downtown. I went along pretty well for the next ten months. Then instead of going out with A.A. again I went out with some of the other crowd, and off again I went.

That woke me up. I've stuck pretty close to A.A. ever since then, taken it day by day, not biting off more than I can chew. The days have grown into a little better than four years of sobriety. I don't have any regrets. I don't miss any of the old crowd nor do I miss any of their parties. I have my ups and downs the same as the rest. It's no bed of roses, but somehow or other I've been able to make it, through the kindness of people in A.A. If something does come along that sort of upsets me, instead of walking in and throwing a buck at the barman and asking for a drink, I walk into a telephone booth, drop a dime in the box, and call somebody who was so kind as to give me his name and telephone number to meet such an emergency. I don't have any resentments. I had a rough lot, but I don't worry about that, after hearing the stories of many others. I think I am very lucky that there are people like A.A.'s and an A.A. program to hang on to and carry me through.

(6) THERE'S NOTHING THE MATTER WITH ME!

That's what the man said as he hocked his shoes for the price of two bottles of Sneaky Pete. He drank bayzo, canned heat, and shoe polish. He did a phony routine in A.A. for a while. And then he got hold of the real thing.

I NEVER DRANK because I liked the flavor, but I did like the effect it produced. And one or two little drinks on a Saturday night soon blossomed into three or four. A little bit at a time, I discovered that I enjoyed the stuff. It did things for me that nothing else could do.

I happen to be in the furniture business, and a more miserable business was never invented. In the furniture business you must have a little drink to celebrate an excellent sale. Also you must have a little drink to drown your sorrows when there are not sales. Hah!

First I drank in celebration and in depression, and then I drank all the time. The little three-quarters of an ounce developed into a big fifth. That was during Prohibition, and we had flasks that were about *that* long, and I didn't carry a little bit at a time, I carried it all at once, and it hit me right in the shoulder blades. You could always tell who had the flask by the way he walked around. I liked that! I liked it because they had to come to me to get a drink.

From the little bit of drinking that we'd do on Saturday and on weekends, it went into a long, steady grind of drinking all the time. And little by little I developed a persecution complex. It seemed that everyone was after me. My business associates said I drank too much. I was married to a very charming girl, and she expected me to bring home money on payday. All that silly stuff. I belonged to a golf club over in Jersey in those days, and I didn't play much golf, but I spent a lot of time drinking the liquor. It got so bad that whenever I went into the nineteenth hole for a drink, everybody would move down the other way. Finally they asked me to resign. It seemed I didn't pay my tabs on the first of the month. A miserable bunch of people!

So, a little bit at a time, it began to filter through that I was no longer wanted. I felt very sorry for myself. I knew I was a wonderful fellow. While shaving in the morning, I would look in the mirror and say, "Aaaah, Bill, you're a doll!" Now that's a poor way to go through life, whether you're an alcoholic or not!

So then I decided that I would try will power. All you have to do to stop drinking is precisely that–stop! Well, I didn't drink Tuesday, and I didn't drink Wednesday, and I didn't drink Thursday, and I said to myself, "There's nothing to this!" So I went out Friday and got drunk.

About this time a bartender friend of mine told me about that little drink in the morning. He was a lovely fellow! He gave me this prescription: You take a jigger of gin, the white of an egg, and a dash of orange bitters. Can you picture this trembling drunk pouring out the white of an egg? For a few mornings I would go down to the bar and he'd make this concoction for me and it was wonderful. But pretty soon I dispensed with the egg, I didn't have the bitters handy and there were no small glasses, so I drank the gin right out of the bottle.

My years of flight started from that point. I sold my business, loaded my car with whiskey, and away I went. I didn't stop at five hundred miles. I went out to Seattle. I couldn't go any further because that's the end of the line. I went into business out there, and in twenty months I was bankrupt. I felt awful sorry for myself, because now I'd entered into the "sick" stage. I would get so sick that when I had to get a room in a hotel I'd always get twin beds, one to sleep in and one to be sick in.

It took me nine months to get from Seattle back to New Jersey. I went the long way, by way of San Diego. When I got back I had fifty dollars, a beat-up Oldsmobile, and no whiskey. I felt very sorry for myself. I'd been robbed, lied to and cheated. And, I told myself, it was all their fault!

I wake up one morning and the Oldsmobile is gone and so is the fifty dollars, and I'm standing in the middle of my wardrobe. I have a pair of dungarees with the fanny out of them, a blue shirt, a pair of shoes and no socks. I'm sitting on the end of this bench down in Lincoln Park, and another bum comes along and he says, "Hello, Slim! Hey, that's a fine pair of shoes you have there!" Well, right away I could tell that this fellow knew class when he saw it. I liked this boy. And I started to tell him of my former exploits. Well, he seemed to want to concentrate on the shoes. At that time, shoes were bringing seventy-five cents in pawn. So we went down and pawned the shoes and we got two bottles of Sneaky Pete and a pair of canvas relievers. This was November. There's nothing the matter with me! I'm all right!

I'd gone down to the bottom of the barrel. Not all at once; it took twenty-five years, a lot of money and a lot of heartaches. There we sat on this bench, this bum and I, telling each other of the wondrous things we'd done, and he loved me and I loved him. There's no love like one drunken bum for another. As I looked off into the sky, and the snow started to fall, I said, "You know, it's getting cold on this bench..." and I turned around, and the bum was gone. The dirty dog took the other bottle with him!

Pretty soon another guy comes along, and he says, "If you don't get off that bench you'll freeze to it, and you'll get pneumonia, and you'll die." I always hated to think about dying, because I was such a lovely fellow I knew they'd miss me on earth. He says, "What do you say we go down to Sally?" Well, I didn't know who Sally was, but I knew in my condition she wouldn't care for me. "No," he says, "we'll go down to the Salvation Army." I hope none of you have to resort to the Salvation Army as a means of food and shelter, but they're wonderful people, understanding people. They have a deep love of God that many of us who walk around in our daily business world never will understand. They give just for the glory of giving. They took us in and gave us a bed, and next morning they put us out in the baling room. For that labor we received ninety-five cents a week and our room and board, a magnificent sum for one as dirty as I was. But like all drunks, when they start to sober up for real, I looked around me and I saw all these other bums, and gee! I knew I was head and shoulders over those other guys. I worked hard for two weeks, and finally I got promoted to be the helper on the truck at three dollars a week. A little bit at a time I progressed, until I became a driver. Utopia! I didn't have to sleep in a dormitory where there were two hundred any more. I slept in a room with absolute privacy–there were only six! And now I was getting five dollars a week.

Well, I don't have to tell you what happened. No drunk can stand prosperity. So, I ended up back out in the street, only this time I had a pair of shoes, and a fellow had given me a size forty-six gabardine suit. I have since developed into a forty-long, but a forty-six had always been just a little roomy for me. I wondered what to do then. I didn't believe in God because I knew God was something that had been cooked up for public consumption, mass appeal; you got to have something to keep the dummies in check.

I was going places, and I did. I went from store to store, and from door to door, and I slept under the bridge. I drank bayzo, canned heat, Sneaky Pete, shoe polish, anything that had an alcoholic content. Why I didn't die, God only knows. I didn't wash for weeks on end. I was just a dirty, filthy, slimy thing that came out from under a flat rock. How God in His wisdom let such a thing live only He knows. I don't. No sense of responsibility, no moral code, no sense of ethics–nothing.

One day, on Broad and Market Streets, I ran into my wife. She said, "Well, what happened to you?" I said, "Why–uh–hello, Ma–I–I don't *feel* well. I been a bad boy!"

My wife was raised very tenderly and gently in a parochial school. She never had to work as a young woman. She ended up slinging hash in a dime hash-house to support my daughter and herself.

She took me to a hospital. The doctor said, "Let him try A.A." I stayed in the hospital ten days. I promised her I'd go to an A.A. meeting. She took me home, bought me a fifteen dollar suit, and I went out and got a job working for a guy that used to work for me. And every Wednesday night I'd go down to the A.A. meeting. I'd look in–some guys talking about the grace of God. I'd go home. On the way home I'd stop and have one, two, three, four. When I got home, my wife would ask, "How was the meeting?" and I'd say, "Oh, the meeting's all right; it's just not for women. You know, they have a lot of old bums there. And next to the speakers' table they have another little table, and they got a bowl of cracked ice on the table, and a bottle of rye and a bottle of scotch." She said, "What is all that stuff for?" "Well," I said, "they just put that there to test you." So when I'd come home and she'd smell liquor on my breath, I'd tell her I'd just been testing. And I did test, a little bit at a time, until I came home one night about two o'clock in the morning, drunk as a goat and twice as stinking. I'm pounding on the door, demanding an entrance. My wife opened the door and I fell in. She said, "What happened to you?" And I drew myself up to my full height and I looked down at her–my wife is only about five foot tall–and I said, "Madam, they put me to the test, and I have failed!"

So ends the sordid part of my story. It's not a pretty thing. But I don't want to ever forget, because three quarters of an ounce of whiskey can put me right back there. Now for the story of how I finally got the A.A. program.

It seems that this particular Sunday I'm lying flat on our parlor rung. I know I'm dying. I know this is it. "Oh, God, if I could only try that A.A. again!" So we call up the Alanon Club. A guy answers the phone and says, "Alanon Club, Louie speaking." Right away I knew it was a phony deal. He told me who he was! "Hi!" I said. "This is Mr. G." "Oh, is that so?" "Yes," I said, "This is B.G." "Well," he said, "would you like to come up to the Club?" "Yeh!" "You got a car?" "No." "Well, get on the bus and come on up." And up we go.

The Alanon Club, in 1945, was a big mausoleum with thirteen steps leading up into it and bare as a barn. We walked up, and here was this great big guy about six foot tall, broad as a house, smoking a pipe. "Hiya, boy! My name is Charlie!" This guy I don't want to talk to. I want to see Louie. "Well, that's all right. Meet Joe." Joe's a boy about so broad, bronzed from the sun to the color of a mahogany table. Seems he was a keeper of the greens at a golf club somewhere. "How are you?" he says, "What is your name?" "I'm not gonna tell you!" "Well," he says, "my name's Joe, this is Charlie, and this is Frank." "All right, mine is Bill. But fellows, you don't know how sick I am...." Everybody laughed.

In to see Louie, and then we go into the coffee bar. "Give him some coffee." A meeting upstairs. Joe's on one side, Charlie's on the other. The girls have swept up my wife and taken her off into another room to tell her the facts of life. Their version, not mine. I looked over at my wife and waved, and she looked over at me and waved back. They'd been talking to her, you see. And the meeting started.

The first speaker got up and he started way back at the Boer War and brought us all the way up to the White Cliffs of Dover. Then he took us back into the African campaign, and I said to Charlie, "What does this have to do with being..." and he says, "Shadd-up!" The second speaker told a most poignant story. He had a lovely wife and three beautiful children. It seemed that he just purchased a new electric stove a week before Thanksgiving. She had Thanksgiving dinner cooking on the new electric stove. He had one of his cronies ring the front doorbell, and when she went to answer the bell, he and two other fellows took stove, dinner, and all right out the back door. Oh, did that make me feel good! I looked over at my wife and grinned. I never did *that*!

Finally the meeting is over, and we go home. My wife says, "Sit in the chair and read that A.A. book." "I can't *see*, Ma!" "You sit there and read it!" "What are you gonna do?" "I'm gonna make a nice pot of coffee!" So the night passes. I read a little, drink a little coffee. Very sad.

Somehow ten days pass in rapid succession. I recognize food for what it is. I begin to feel alive again. I was sober for the first time in my life because I had a desire for sobriety greater than any other desire. Meetings and more meetings. Three months went by, and they said, "Bill, get up and say a few words." We had about eight people in the group then, and I looked at these eight people and I stuttered and stammered, and finally I said, "I'm glad to be here!" And I sat down. The applause was tremendous.

At six months I had begun to speak at different meetings. Pretty soon my halo was killing me. My ermine cloak was smothering me. I used to look down and wonder what the other little people did for a living. I didn't walk in, I swept in. All that I'd accomplished in six months was sobriety. I was as dry as dust, and just about as useless. One night we went into the Club and Jack said, "Bill, we're short a speaker, will you say a few words tonight?" "Of course!" The meeting started, and I didn't see Jack any more. They called on the first speaker–and it wasn't me, and they called on the second speaker, and the third speaker–and the meeting was over! I had brought my harp to the party, but I didn't get to play!

That taught me the most important lesson I have ever learned in my entire life. That is that A.A. doesn't need me, but I need A.A. Very desperately, very sincerely, very humbly. Not all at once, because you can't get it all at once, just a little bit at a time. They told me, "You've got to get out and work a little; you've got to give." They told me that giving was living, and that living was loving, and loving was God. And you don't have to worry about God, because He's sitting right in front of your eyes.

You get just a little sobriety, and you get just a little humility. Not much, just a little. Not the humility of sackcloth and ashes, but the humility of a man who's glad he's alive and can serve. You get just a little tolerance, not too much, but just enough to sit and listen to the other guy.

Somewhere along the line, if you've forgotten how to pray, you learn a little about that too. I divorced myself from the Church when I was twenty-two. I got to thinking about that, and I spoke to Father McNulty about it. "Don't worry, Bill," he said, "you'll develop an awareness of God."

We had a basement apartment, and it faced right on the sidewalk, and outside our bedroom window there was a little bush about so high. One morning I awoke, and there was a little city sparrow taking a bath on this little bush. The weight of this tiny creature's body caused the branch to rise and fall. Isn't that a wonderful thing to see? An awareness of God, yes! You're aware of the sunset, you're aware of the blades of grass, you're aware of food cooking on the stove.

You delight in walking down the street, and you see someone you know, and the first thing that enters your mind is, "What is there good about that guy that I know?" You find that big people discuss ideals, average people discuss things, and little people–they just talk about other people. And you realize that if you put this all together, you get a little humility, a little tolerance, a little honesty, a little sincerity, a little prayer–and a lot of A.A.

(7) DESPERATION DRINKING

He was drinking to hold on to his job, to hold on to his wife, to hold on to his sanity. Finally he was drinking to keep away those little men and those strange voices, and the organ music that came out of the walls.

I'M FORTUNATE because I live in an era when A.A. is available, and I'm able to take advantage of it. I'm grateful because that Higher Power led me to A.A. a little over three years ago, when I needed it very badly. My drinking pattern isn't very different from the average you find in A.A. After I came in I found I wasn't an exceptional drunk. I used to think I was. I also thought I was a brilliant drunk. I have my brilliant moments yet, but whenever the boys catch me at it they tell me so very plainly.

When we first come into A.A., many of us are confused because as a general rule we're at the end of our respective ropes, and we don't know what to do. It's like the fellow who came in A.A., and his sponsor said to him, "Listen, buddy, do you believe in a Higher Power?" And the guy said, "Heck, yes, I been married to her for years!" Yes, we find it rather confusing, but as we get around and get to know people in the group, they lead the way and all we have to do is to follow.

I started drinking rather early, at the age of sixteen. I didn't stick at social drinking very long. As I progressed and gained in capacity, I had blackouts. At first they were rather amusing, but a little later on they became serious. And so I got to the swearing off process. That and the morning drink came very early in my drinking career.

A former employer of mine said to me a little over ten years ago, "Pat, you seem to be one of those unfortunate people who at least once every six months must go out and roll in the gutter." That stuck with me for a long time. It was a thorn in my side, because I knew it was the truth, and I hated to hear the truth, especially about myself. So that pattern continued until I went into the army.

The army drinking alone covered a lot of territory. Like many of us who went into the service, I thought it would be a cure-all, a new life. But I came out of the army just as big a drunk as when I went in, if not worse, because now I had a lot more resentments. I remember coming up the Bay in to New York. It was my second arrival in New York. The first had been as a youngster coming out from Ireland. There was a great deal of difference. A lot of the boys had tears in their eyes, they were so happy to be home. For me, it was a little different because I couldn't help thinking about the past, and I saw the future more or less mirrored in the past. It wasn't pretty. Somehow or other I was coming face to face with myself, and I didn't like it. When I landed of course I hit a gin mill, and with three or four good shots under my belt the world began to go into that rosy glow.

I got married to the girl I'd left behind. She certainly wasn't in the dark about my drinking. She had been warned numerous times, not only by her family but by my own mother, that I was a hopeless drunk, that there wasn't anything anybody could do with me, that I'd never stop, and that eventually I'd break her heart. However, she had faith and she had hope, things I didn't have. We were married, and during the first nine months of that marriage I was sober. I was trying for her sake. But at the end of nine months we went to a party one night, and I took the first drink. No one had ever told me it was the first drink that did the damage. And I was off again.

The old pattern reasserted itself, but it was no longer once every six months. The intervals grew shorter. The binges were longer. They were harder to get off. I wasn't the type that could taper off. I had to stop cold. My last binge followed the previous one by two weeks. I had just come off a good one, and I went back on to the next one.

That type of drinking is not pleasant. It is no longer enjoyable. You no longer get the kicks. It is desperation drinking. I was drinking to keep away the shakes, drinking to keep away those little men and those strange voices and the organ music that comes out of the walls. I was drinking to try to hold on to a job, to try and hold on to my home, to try to hold on to my wife, to try to hold on to my sanity.

I had a habit of getting up just prior to the closing time of the saloons, about two or three o'clock in the morning. I'd get downstairs to the gin mill, get enough in to hold me until eight o'clock in the morning, then I'd go out and join that "misery parade" that so many of us know so well. You hit the street about ten minutes to eight, and you walk around the block, God knows how many times, waiting for that joint to open.

One morning I didn't wake up until after four o'clock. I wasn't a happy man that morning, but I'm happy now that it came about. Because as I sat on that bed, I knew that I was in a terrible spot and didn't know how to get out of it. The realization came to me that I *had* to stop drinking, that I *had* to find a way. Either that or end my life. That thought had come to me many, many times. I was afraid that sometime I would get half drunk and go through with it. Of course I really didn't have to worry on that score, because I wasn't the type that got half drunk.

I was at the end of my rope. I knew it, and I turned for help to someone upon whom I had turned my back for many years. I asked God for help. It was the first time that I had asked for help sincerely and honestly. And I got help. I went back to the old family doctor who had helped me the first time I had the D.T.'s back in 1942. At this point, I was no longer the wise boy. I went in there and asked him honestly if he could give me a cure. He just looked at me and said, "Pat, for you there isn't any cure." We talked for a while, and then he sent me down to the Alanon House over on the west side, and there I had my introduction to A.A.

It was a revelation to me to find that there were such people as those I found in Alcoholics Anonymous. It was a revelation when I read that First Step. It was very, very simple. My life had become unmanageable due to the excessive use of alcohol. I had drunk too often and too much. But somehow or other, with my old alcoholic brain, sitting there in that chair, I kept saying to myself, "I wonder if it'll work? I wonder if it'll work for me?"

Then I went to my first meeting. I was a very fortunate drunk. God had been good to me both in my drinking and in my sobriety. Because, thank God, since I came into this program I haven't had any trouble. Oh yes, I get the dry jitters once in a while, but that isn't anything to worry about. It passes away. But I've never come close to that first drink. I took the advice of people I had heard at meetings, the people in the group. And I jumped in with both feet. Someone told me, "When you drank, you didn't get half drunk. You went all the way. In this program there aren't any half way measures. In here you must go all the way too." So I attended as many meetings as possible.

There are steps of recovery, of maintenance. Each one has its own place. We all use them differently. I found a great deal of friendship in this movement. I learned to pray honestly. When you come in here, you find the understanding that you need. A.A.'s Twelve Steps may confuse you when you read them over. But the more meetings you attend, the more people you meet at these meetings, the clearer the Steps become.

We must learn to walk before we can run. That's why we have these slogans. I use that "Easy Does It" every day, to slow me down a little. I have to watch myself all the time. So I don't just take the inventory at night–I take it continually throughout the day. Before I step out and do anything, I stop and check it over first, and then let my conscience be my guide.

For me, A.A. has become a way of life.

(8) ANNIE THE COP FIGHTER

For thirty-five years she fought God, man, and the police force to keep on being what she wanted to be–a drunk. But a telephone call from a gin mill where she was celebrating Mother's Day brought in the nosey A.A.'s to change her life.

I STARTED to drink in 1913, when the women sat in the back rooms. We had a good time in those back rooms. I had two little boys at the time, but my family didn't worry me, because one drunk always led to another. Of course there were days in between when I was sober because I was broke. But mostly I was drunk. So my husband left me and took the two boys; one was six and one was nine. They were going off to school in those days, and it didn't worry me a bit. I loved the liquor and I loved the crowd that I hung out with. As far as my family was concerned, I lost everything of love and respect and everything else.

Believe me, this is no made up story. This is a true story from my own life. When my husband left me, I had to be on my own. I never worked before, but I had to get out and get a job if I wanted to drink. So I got a pretty tough job. I wasn't any chicken, I was a woman of thirty-one when I had my first drink. I got a job as cleaner after mechanics in buildings. I would have done anything to get the money for drink. Any place I threw my hat was home-sweet-home to me. It could be a basement or a cellar or a back yard. I fell plenty low, but if I tell it maybe it will help some gal or some guy so they don't have to get down that low.

Finally one day, as usual, drunk, I was standing on a corner waiting for a streetcar, and a guy comes over to me and he says, "Lady, you're on the wrong side." And I says, "Mind your own business!" And as I looked up, it was a feller in uniform! So we had a few words, and he pushed me, and I wasn't going to let anybody get the best of me, and I shoved him back, and we had a little tussle there, and finally I had two buttons off his overcoat, and he says, "I'm takin' you in!" And I says, "Do as you damn please!" I was a tough piece of furniture in those days; if the Almighty God had come down I'd have done the same thing to Him. So I landed in the 67th Street station house on the east side, and I stayed there all night long. The next day I had to appear, and I was finger printed for molesting a policeman's uniform. So I got five days in the House of Detention. It didn't bother me whatsoever. The only thing I was worrying about was how was the gang making out without me. I thought I was missed all over! But they made out all right.

So I got out, and then I had to grab myself another job again, so what did I get into but hotel work! That was during the Prohibition days, and the bottles were flying all over the place. When I went to work on the floor, my first idea was to look in the guests' closets where the bottles were. I was all right going in, but I was cockeyed drunk coming out. And I'd have the help drunk with me. One time I got so drunk I blacked out and fell asleep in the guest's bed. I had the nerve to go back on the job the next morning–I didn't know what happened the day before–and the housekeeper was right there with her little note and my check. "Your service no longer required." And I had the nerve to ask, "Why?" I was told, all right. Well, in those days you could get jobs any time. It wasn't like today. If they had ever looked for references from me I think I'd never have got a job, because I never stayed in one.

I never hit hospitals, and I don't know why because I was fit for hospitals many a time. All the time I saw queer things crawling up the wall in my bedroom. In 1918, I got pinched again for the same thing. I turned out to be a cop fighter; I thought I could beat the whole force. I landed in the same court, had the same judge, and he asked me was I ever arrested before. I says, "No, your Honor!" Just as brazen as can be. And all he done was give me that sneering look, and he says, "For lying in court," he says, "you're not getting away with five days this trip!" I had gone under an assumed name, and I had forgot that I was finger printed, and I thought, being away for two years, he wouldn't know who I was! Playing so innocent! But I got thirty days then, five days off for good behavior, over on the Island.

Another time I was in court on the same old charge of Drunk and Disorderly. "Thirty days," says the Judge. And I was that mad and disgusting that I reared right up and spit clean in the judge's eye. It was a distance of at least five feet, too! You should have seen him leap. "Another thirty days," he says, "for spittin' in the eye of the Court." "Nuts to you," says I, but I had to serve the whole sixty days just the same.

I was worrying about my liquor and I was worrying about the crowd I hung out with. As far as my family was concerned, they never entered my mind. So I did my twenty-five days on the Island, and all I could do was look through the bars across the East River and see First Avenue and the joints that I hung out in.

When I got out of the workhouse that time I got a domestic job, and it was right up my alley because I got paid every day, and paid by the hour. In my day the women only got twenty-five cents an hour, but the liquor was cheap, and that would be all there was to it–maybe. I had blackouts, and many a night I don't know how I ever got home. I always did say, well, thank God I'm in one piece. But where I had been I would never know.

I had been away from home for fifteen years, and one day I was walking up First Avenue and I met my beloved husband. He called to me and he said, "Where are you going?" I was running like blue blazes to a speakeasy to get a drink, and I didn't know what to say, so I said, "I'm goin' up to the Five and Ten to get hairnets." I wanted to beat it, but he says, "Wait a minute." So I did, and we had a few words, and he looked me over, and he says, "You smoke, too, don't you?" He didn't know what all I was into; he should have known the rest! I said, "Listen here, you! This is my body and soul, and I can do as I please about it! I have been on my own for all these years, and I can still do as I please!" He didn't get angry over it, and then finally he popped the question to me: "Would you like a drink?" Whooh! There's what I was running for! And I says, "Sure, I would." So we went into a speakeasy up along the line and we had quite a few drinks, and we talked things over and I went back home with him.

But believe me, when I went back home it was too much of a decent life for me to lead. I didn't want the decent, clean life. I wanted to be what I was, a drunk. So I spent more time over on First Avenue than I did at home. Of course when I went back home, my two boys were raised, which I will give my husband the credit for. He raised them as gentlemen. The oldest boy was married, and the youngest boy was going to Delehanty's–to become a policeman! Brother! Well, it was all right. I had to take it and accept it. But every time I thought of that uniform, it killed me! After he had been in the force one year he got married. I was invited to that wedding with his father. But I invited myself to the old gin mill over on First Avenue again, and celebrated his wedding with my crowd that I hung out with. That's the kind of mother I was.

I went back home again anyway. I was always forgiven, somehow or other. But I wasn't back home very long before it was the same old round-about–back again to the friends and the blazes with the family. When the doors opened up for the women to sit at the bars, I thought that was the terriblest thing–for a woman to sit at the bar! Well, it didn't take me a long while until I got myself initiated to the bar. I was thrown off those stools so often that, believe me, it wasn't funny.

I had everybody's answers. I butted in to everybody's conversation. If a guy would fall asleep and leave his change on the bar, I was handy to help myself. He couldn't sleep and spend his money, so what was I waiting for? And I'd hang around like an old jackass until I got loaded. Brother, was I black and blue! I was kicked and I was banged and pulled by the hair. I'm surprised today that I'm not lame or something like that, the way I was knocked and kicked.

Then I got so low that I hung out with the guys and gals that were on the Bowery. I was loused up too. My whole clothes on my body were full of lice. How low can a woman get!

I got in tow with a gal named Irene, and we used to drink. When we had good money, we'd drink the best, but when we had only a little bit, beer was good enough. So one day in 1946, I happened to go into our hangout again as usual, and I asked Irene what she was drinking. She says, "Anna, to tell you the truth, I can't take the first drink. I'm havin' coke." (She nearly knocked me dead!) I says, "Saints above! What happened to you?" She says, "I can't take the first drink." "Well," I says, "nuts to you. I'm havin' mine!" "But," she says, "I'm gonna get you yet!" I says, "Over me dead body!"

She got into A.A. in March of 1946, and in May of that year, Mother's Day was on the 12th. The day before that I was having a good time in a gin mill again, and I don't know whatever come over me, but I asked some of the younger folks that could dial the phone to call Irene. I don't remember doing it. This was all told to me after. The next day was Mother's Day, and like everyone else I wanted to be such a wonderful mother that I had to buy a gardenia for my coat. I went up to this same gin mill to celebrate Mother's Day. I sat on the stool drinking and pretty soon in comes my friend.

"Oh!" I says, "Hello, Irene!" She says, "Hello my eye! You got me lookin' all over the town for you! You made a date with me yesterday!" I says, "*I?*" She says, "Not you, but the crowd in here had the ears rung off me with the telephone. They said that you wanted to meet me tonight and you wanted me to take you where I go on Sunday nights." "Hmmmm," I says, "That's news to me. Have a drink?" "No," she says, "I can't take the first drink. There's a cab there waitin' for me to take you down to A.A."

So down to the old 41st Street Club House I landed. In those days they used to have three meetings a week–Sunday, Tuesday, and Thursday. So I went down to that A.A. meeting that night. They took me to the beginners' meeting. I don't know what was said, but I do remember that when the meeting was over, when the door of the 41st Street Club House opened, I sobered up that very night after thirty-two years of knocking liquor around. I drank coke there that night, and I went back and forth to the meetings for eight months.

I was sober for eight months, physically, but not mentally. I never mingled with a soul in the meetings. I never shook hands or said hello to my neighbor sitting alongside of me. I never stopped for coffee. I just ran in and ran out. In the meanwhile I got married the second time. I picked a swell partner, another drunk like myself. I would come home from the meetings and tell him all about these stories, about these women hitting all the jails so often and all the hospitals so often, and he says, "You old so-and-so, you should've been there yourself!" That's what I got for an answer. But it didn't bother me.

Then one night a little argument started. I think I was waiting to start something. It was a foolish thing, over pig's knuckles, believe it or not. I was waiting for that pig's knuckles argument. He told me he was gonna have the gang up to eat up my sauerkraut and pig's knuckles for Saturday night, and I said, "You will in a pig's eye!" And I went out and got a fine load on. I only drank for two days, but I carried enough for a year in those two days.

I got off that two-day drunk through the A.A.'s. The nosey A.A.'s caught up with me somehow or other. They went to the place where I worked. The woman there was very interested in alcoholics. She said to me, "You're drinking." I says, "How do you know?" She said, "Come on in–sit down a while and rest yourself." She says, "Charlie called up." I says, "That son-of-a-gun! He's got me so advertised that this damn organization knows my whole business! Nobody stepped over my territory before in my life! Now I gotta get into a thing like this and they know it all!" "Don't get excited," she says.

"They're comin' up to see you tonight." I nearly dropped dead.

They came up all right. And I humbled myself. I felt so guilty. I don't know what A.A. does to you, but you never can drink the same again. So they suggested to me to go up to a farm in Connecticut, nothing but wide open spaces in the Berkshire Hills. It was a beautiful place. I stayed up there two days, and I came back a new woman.

Today I have a lot to be thankful for. A.A. has taught me the way of life. It has given me back my respect. It has given me back the love of everybody I know. It has taught me to show gratitude, which I never did before. It has taught me to be humble when I have to be humble.

I am what you call a lucky woman. I live alone now. I have a television which my boys have treated me to, and now I have a telephone too! I do love to go to A.A. meetings, and I meet with everybody, the old and the new. I'm a twenty-four hour person. I live on that twenty-four hour plan. I am five years and seven months without a drink, but I could go out tonight, but for the grace of God, and get drunk. There's another thing I must remember, that once an alcoholic always an alcoholic. I don't mind the name of alcoholic, because I was called a son-of-a-this and a son-of-a-that, and alcoholic is a good enough name for me. So I'm very, very happy. To newcomers I say, go to meetings, and God take care of each and every one of you!

(9) THE CAREER OFFICER

A British officer, this Irishman–that is, until brandy "retired" him. But this proved only a temporary setback. He survived to become a mainstay of A.A. in Eire.

I AM AN Irishman and I was forty-nine when I joined A.A. I belonged to one of the Irish families who, more or less traditionally, sent their boys to the British armies.

I had a very happy upbringing at home. When I look back, I can't see anything that would have predisposed me towards being either a neurotic or a drunk. I went to a very good public school run by Jesuits. I got along well there. I was going to be sent to the Indian Civil Service, which, in those days, meant that people thought you had a certain amount of brains. I was very fond of music. I was one of the star singers in the choir and one of the leading violins in the orchestra. I liked games. There was nothing in my school life that I can look back on which was responsible for anything that happened afterwards.

Then I had a year in Germany at school–that was, incidentally, when I got drunk for the first time. But that was just a mistake. I went out and drank some German wine and it went to my head. When I came back, I told the priest, the Chaplain of the place, exactly what I thought of him and he didn't like it. He reported to the Headmaster and the Headmaster was going to expel me. But I pointed out to him that as I was the first British boy who had been to the school, it wouldn't be a very good advertisement for him, so I got over that all right. The term was nearly over and we parted on fairly friendly terms.

I had two years at Dublin University, and then in 1916, I got a nomination for Sandhurst, the British Military College. The war was on and it was a fairly short course, about eight months. Up to that time, drinking didn't really mean anything to me at all. In fact, I couldn't have told you the difference between sherry and brandy. But as soon as I got out on my own in France, I started drinking. At first, like everybody else, I could keep control when I drank, but if I did start to drink, even in those days, I was always one of the last to leave the party.

When the war was over, we had about a year in Germany, occupying the place. When I came home to ordinary garrison life in England, I found that I was drinking rather more than most people of my age. It didn't worry me very much, because at that time I could shut off for a couple of months without taking a drink or even wanting one, and without feeling that I was giving anything up. I should say there was less drinking in the army than I thought at that time. Lots of the older people had taken to drinking quite a good deal more during the war, but the younger generation was, I think, about the same. In my own generation I stuck out, I can see that now, as being a very much heavier drinker than the average man. But as long as you did your work and didn't disgrace yourself, you were socially acceptable and nobody really intruded on your private life very much.

I was still very fit and good at games.

Then I went over again to Germany for four years on an occupation job. I got a job by myself which suited me down to the ground, because there was nobody really to interfere with what I did, one way or the other, and I usually had my nerves in good trim when anybody was coming around to inspect. The gradual result was that I was drifting into making drinking one of the more important parts of my life. I was alone by myself in that job and for a long time.

Then I was sent out to India and from then on drinking just increased and increased, and I started having two or three day spells instead of just the ordinary concentrated one day.

India lent itself to drinking then, if you were disposed to drink, because you lived in bungalows; you didn't live all together as you do at home in an Officer's Mess. We had a minor campaign or two and that helped distract attention from my drinking. By and large, I got through. I was still very good at games. I was up to international standards in one particular game, and that again covered quite a lot of my sins. Then a change in management took place in the regiment and the new O.C. didn't like me very much and I didn't like him, and he started to lie in wait for me. He didn't have to lie in wait very long, but fortunately by that time, I had acquired friends upstairs and they covered me for quite a time.

The Abyssinian war broke out just as things were going very badly for me, and I went off to Egypt on a job there. Strangely enough, right through to the end of my twenty-six years in the army, I was still being offered very good and important jobs in spite of the fact that my superiors must have known that I wasn't thoroughly reliable. However, I kept that job in Egypt and Palestine for about two years, and then I changed over to the other battalion in my regiment. They weren't quite so up-to-date on my history and I got away with about four years with them. Then I had about six months on a small island in command of the troops there. I left because I had a contretemps with the Governor. I went to a dinner he gave one night, rather drunk. I buttonholed him after dinner and gave him a few tips on how to run his colony better and the result of that was about a fortnight or so later I was shipped back to my regiment. But on the other hand, I was terribly fortunate because that should have been a court martial offense and I should have been out on my ear. I was lucky again. I had three or four very uncomfortable months with my regiment then on the Suez Canal. The Commanding Officer only spoke to me when he wanted to tell me exactly who I was and what I was and how little I counted in the scheme of things and how glad he would be if I went away. Even at that, he spoke quite often.

Then Hitler's war broke out, and again, I was given a really important job on the Suez Canal, dealing with military shipping. I lasted at that for four months, chiefly on alcohol, because I never seemed to find any time to eat. At the end of that time, they shipped me back to my regiment again. I think the Commanding Officer was rather tired of this particular chicken coming back to roost so often because he very soon wrote in to the medical authorities to tell them that they had to get me into hospital, to be thoroughly examined for drinking. They brought me in and of course, they hadn't very much trouble in finding that I was an alcoholic. But that didn't mean anything to me. I didn't know what an alcoholic was. I was down in the Sudan by this time. They kept me in hospital for two months, and then they sent me up to Egypt, a three days journey. They sent me up with an attendant, and the attendant and I both arrived at the Egyptian Hospital rather the worse for wear. I was there for another couple of months and then, after a few more adventures in the East, I was shipped home.

About three months after that, my record reached home and I got a letter telling me I was retired from the army, they put it very kindly, on medical grounds. But I knew that they knew what the medical grounds were, and that they had put a big black mark against my name. I was never to be allowed back. I had two or three feelings about that. In part, it was a feeling of intense shame at having to leave the army during the war, but mostly it was resentment that this kind of thing should happen to me for, strange as it may seem, up to then I still thought I could control drinking. I thought, well, now that I've been put out for drinking, I'll just show them that they were completely wrong, so I went off on the biggest bout I had been on up to then, involving about a fortnight's blackout.

I was a civilian now. I was in a world that I knew nothing at all about, and I felt intensely afraid. I put myself into a home. I stayed there just long enough to work up a real good resentment against the doctor in charge, who I didn't think was doing anything at all except collecting fees, and I left there fully determined that I'd never put myself in the power of medical people again.

I stopped off just to have one drink to see if it tasted the same on the way back to London, and that night I was carried back to bed again. So I decided I'd go back and live in Ireland to try the geography cure.

When I arrived back in Dublin, I had no friends left. Everybody I had known in the old days had gone. I had no work to do and I was at an age where it seemed too late to start anything new. In any case, I made myself believe that, so I just drifted about, existing on my retired pay, drinking, and living at home.

That went on for about six years. Things were getting worse and worse. I went to hospitals, I went to retreats and doctors, and finally my mother asked me to go and see a specialist of her own choosing. I talked to him for quite a long time and at the end, he said, "Well, you're not quite mad enough to be shut up for good yet, but you soon will be if you live long enough." That put a scare in me for about a fortnight. I was terribly afraid that I was actually going mad, if I hadn't gone mad already.

I couldn't understand myself. I was intensely unhappy the whole time, but I didn't seem to be able to do anything about it, and the worst part to me was the realization that all this was going to happen again and again until I died. I couldn't see that there was any way out of it, and I got absolutely despairing. My only hope was to try and get through what was left of life as best I could, but I could never visualize doing that without drinking. The thought of stopping drinking just never occurred to me.

As I say, this specialist put a scare in me for about a fortnight or three weeks, then I started my last bout, which went on and off for about three months. Finally, my mother came and said she had kept me at home for six years because she thought she could help me, but that now she had come to the conclusion that I wasn't even worth trying to help. I was to pack and go and get out of their lives for good. That morning was the first time I really realized where I'd got to in my life. I couldn't think of anything at all to do. It was no use talking of putting myself into a home, a hospital, or of going to see a doctor again, or of going to see a priest or anyone else. I had played all that out long ago. She really meant business this time. This was the only time in my life that I'd ever known my mother to be almost pitiless, but she couldn't be blamed for that.

Just as I was wondering what on earth I could do–I was too drunk even to pack a handkerchief–the memory of an A.A. write-up that I had seen in the Evening Mail flashed across my mind–and I thought to myself, this is something I haven't tried yet. So I did manage to get myself down to an A.A. meeting that night. Providentially, this was a Monday night when the Dublin Group met in those days, and my family agreed that if A.A. could do anything for me at all, that I'd be allowed to stay on at home on probation. But if I came back in the usual state, then I'd have to go off for good the next day.

Having made that bargain, I immediately began to feel I'd been trapped into it and I went out and had some drinks–four glasses of gin, I remember. I was taking benzedrine and paraldehyde quite impartially during the day then, and by the time I arrived at my first A.A. meeting, I was pretty drunk and certainly doped up to the eyes and completely jittery. I had been using paraldehyde more or less like ordinary drink for the last six years though, occasionally, I'd bounce back to phenobarbital and things like that.

When I arrived at The Country Shop, which was a restaurant where they met in Dublin, I found about thirty-five or forty people in the room. It was their open night meeting, but of course I thought they were all alcoholics; I couldn't imagine why anybody else would want to go there, and my first reaction was, well, I've come to something that's not for me. People seemed to be carefully dressed, too happy, too normal. My mind was too screwy to be able to understand much of what was being said. But I did understand this eventually, that these people had been through a lot of drinking experiences just as I had, and had managed to make a job of it. What struck me most was that they all seemed to be quite pleased with having made a job of it and having stopped drinking. That gave me my first bit of hope. I thought that if these kind of ordinary people can do it, a man of my brains ought to find it much more easy, and I joined. I suppose I had reached my spiritual gutter that night, but I have never had what you could call a real urge to drink again.

Since I joined on that April night, A.A. has done more for me than just stop me from drinking; it has brought me back to life again. It has made me understand that I must be one of my world, that I cannot exist in any happiness as a rebel by myself. It has taught me that I can best keep my sobriety by sharing it out with others; that I must *bring* that sobriety to others who need it, in my own interest. It continues to try to teach me the real charity, the charity that gives time and good will and service, and not just money. It has shown me, through the tragic stories of so many other alcoholics, the utter futility of self-pity. It has taught me that success and failure are never final, and that neither count for very much in the final assessment of any man who has done his best. It has brought me back to a realization of my Maker and my duties to Him. It has made me very happy.

My mother lived on for five years after I joined A.A., the last two in complete blindness. Not least of my debts to A.A. is the knowledge that in that time when she wanted me most, I was there–and that I wasn't drunk.

(10) THE INDEPENDENT BLONDE

The lady was blonde, self-supporting, and self-sufficient. Then she began slamming doors, kicking shins, and waking up in psychopathic wards. At last the day came when all this changed.

I HAVE TO TELL you a little of the way I lived before I got into A.A. so you can see why I made the choice that I did. I started drinking at the age of seventeen, but I was in trouble with myself long before that. I never got along at home, and at the age of thirteen I stepped off and decided I'd go out for myself. I decided that no one loved me and I didn't love them, and I was going off and make myself independent.

My father brought us up to give no quarter and seek no quarter, and that was just the way I lived. I gave nothing, and I took nothing. I suppose I lived mostly for pleasure, or what I knew of pleasure, which to me was just going out at night. I worked all day, and went out and stayed out at night. That was about as much as I knew about life. I rebelled against everything I'd ever heard as a child, and I lived to suit myself.

I never thought much about settling down. I thought anyone who got under the dominance of another human being was pretty foolish, but when I was twenty-nine I did get married. I was never trained to live with anyone else, and I took on a pretty big job I wasn't capable of handling. After I was married I was in much more trouble with myself and I drank a great deal more, but now I had someone to blame it on. All my life I had blamed everything that ever happened to me on someone else, and I usually could find someone. Now I have a husband. If I was drinking worse now, it must be his fault.

One night I was out drinking by myself, which I didn't do as a rule. I sat in a bar drinking martinis for a long time, and somewhere on the way home I fell down in the street, and a cop came along and picked me up and took me to St. Vincent's Hospital. They pronounced me Drunk and Disorderly and took me over to Bellevue.

When I came to the next morning, I was in the psychopathic ward. The doctor who tested me and asked me a few personal questions was a psychiatrist. I asked him to call up where I worked and tell them I wouldn't be in. I thought they'd just give me my clothes and let me leave quietly. They told me that I was not able to go out on the street alone, that I was not a responsible citizen. They said someone would have to call for me. To someone is arrogant as I was, who is taking care of herself, that was kind of rough.

I thought I would never get in such a situation again, and I thought the way to get over it would be not to drink. I was so naive that I thought that would be possible–by just wishing not to drink! I didn't take a drink for three months, but on New Year's Eve everybody was drinking, and about two-thirty in the morning I started. In about one hour I was drunker than anyone there. I kicked someone in the shins and slammed the door on his fingers. I knew I shouldn't be drinking, and I was scared to death. I was in real trouble. I didn't know why I was drinking, and I didn't know why my behavior had changed so. I thought if I left my husband things would be different. I thought I would be different if I could live by myself again. Which I did–and proceeded to drink worse than ever before.

Then I decided that I was in trouble because I was living in New York and everyone knew me, and I used to drink too much with people, and maybe I didn't know the *right* people. So I moved away. I never thought about changing myself, I always thought about changing people, or changing places.

I went down to Virginia, of all places, to stop drinking. I was down there one month when I bumped into a fellow I knew from Greenwich Village who was on the same army post. We were glad to see each other, and he invited me out, and I said "Oh, I can't go out. I don't drink anymore." I really thought if you didn't drink, you couldn't go out! And he said, "Oh, that's all right. Come on over to the Club and have a few beers." And I said, "Well, that I can do." About midnight that night, when they wanted to close up the Club, they announced that if anybody was missing his companion, she was in the ladies' room, passed out. That was me, in my brand new environment, with the right people!

So I left there and went to another army post, where some Red Cross workers took me out on a date with some British officers. I got drunk with the British officers, and I don't need to tell you what I told the British officers, I being Irish. I left the next day, telling my boss that I needed a very serious operation, and he agreed with me. I never had the courage to wait to be fired. I left every place I'd ever been. I ran away from life. I never knew myself until I got into A.A.

I had heard about A.A. about a year before I came in, but I thought it was some organization that helped you out financially, and I was always too independent for that. But at that time I had lost all of that kind of independence. I had been drunk for nine days, sick and alone and desperate. They didn't have to tell me that alcoholism was a sickness. When you take a bottle and lock that door and go in by yourself, that is death.

This day I decided to give up. I don't know why you give up one day and not another–I have never been able to understand that. I had suffered on drunks before, but as they explained it to me in A.A., that particular day I hit bottom. I decided to call up A.A., but I didn't know that the Clubhouse didn't open until noon. So I kept drinking and calling up, and drinking and calling up. Finally, I got someone on the telephone, and I told her I was in trouble and asked what I should do. The girl asked me if I could walk. And I said to myself, "My God, how understanding! Somebody who knows that you couldn't walk and why you couldn't walk!" I said to her, "I don't know, I haven't tried." She said, "Well, the only reason I ask is, if you can't we'll come over to you." And I reared up in all my arrogance and I said, "You'll never come to me, but I'll go to you!" It took me until four o'clock that day to get there.

I never shall forget how comforted I fell that there was a building, there was a place, there were people who were interested in what was wrong with me. I walked in that door and the girl asked me my name, and I said, "I'd rather not give you my name." She said, "We don't care if you haven't got a name, just so you have an alcoholic problem!" Well, I was put to shame, and I told her my name. She assigned me to another girl who took me upstairs. I looked into this girl's eyes, and I thought, "If only my eyes would ever be that clear again, then I'd be grateful for that alone." Little did I ever think that many more things would happen to me than clear eyes.

The first thing I learned that day was that if I never took another drink I would never have another problem with alcohol. That went over in my mind like a Victrola record. I had never thought about that first drink. I had schemed and stolen drinks, but it was never the first one. And here I had a very simple problem–one drink, and that's all I was able to understand.

About seven o'clock someone came over to this girl and asked her to speak at a meeting in Brooklyn. I was scared this girl would leave me. It was the first time in my life I ever had *needed* someone, and I knew it. I looked at her to see what she would say. She looked at me and said, "Would you like to go to Brooklyn?" I don't like to go the Brooklyn when I'm cold sober! But I wanted to stay sober, and I went to Brooklyn. I don't know who spoke first, last, or what, but someone got up and said he had been in Bellevue thirty-five times. I thought, "Oh, my God! I'll look like St. Cecilia here!" I was so glad to be able to tell this dark secret that I had had for eight years that I nudged a man alongside of me and said, "Mister, do you know I was in Bellevue once?" He said, "Okay, girlie, you'll get the program." I guess he figured I was just another psycho!

The next day I started back for the Clubhouse. On my way over, that thick head of mine started saying to me, "I don't know that you're such a drunk. I think you're far too dramatic about this whole thing. Why do you have to go over there with that bunch of people?" I was walking along a Bowery sort of street, with music playing and those awful neon lights all around, and suddenly a little man started to follow me. Not the kind of man that follows nice girls. And suddenly I said to myself, "Listen, Toots, there's something the matter with you when a guy like that follows you, and you better get over to the Clubhouse and find out what it is!" I always like to say that on my second day I was "wolfed" into A.A.

I heard that I had to make amends, and do something good for someone–that I was too self-centered. I thought of a girl friend who had a brand new baby, and she used to like to get drunk on Saturday night. And I thought, "That'll be it. That'll be good." I called her up and told her I'd mind the baby while she went out and got drunk. That's how much I knew about doing good! The next day I called my boss and told her what had happened to me and asked her if she would take me back to work. It was the first time in my life that I ever showed any sort of humility, that I ever asked anybody for anything. And I went back there to work. I learned that going back and facing something unpleasant, regardless of how tough it is at the time, is a lot easier than running away.

I went to meetings every night in the week, because I'm that kind of person. I either do a thing or I don't do it. I didn't have to give up very much, because my life before A.A. was very empty, very lonely, and very superficial. Then I was always afraid of being a sucker, for some unknown reason–I always thought people were taking advantage of me.

One day a call came in to the clubhouse for someone to go out and do a Twelve Step job. And they looked at me and said, "How long are you in?" and I said, "A week or so." And they said, "Oh, you can't go. You have to be sober three months." And then I realized that here I had spent all of my life afraid that people were trying to get something out of me, and I had nothing to give! Now I was in an organization where they needed someone that had something I didn't have; someone who was sober three months, who had some sort of stability; someone that had kindness in their hearts for other human beings, and compassion for their suffering. I had to wait until these people gave it to me so that I could go out and give it away.

Then I began to have trouble with myself, and I went to see Dr. Silkworth and he explained to me what honesty was. I always thought honesty had something to do with telling other people the truth. He explained that it had to do first with telling *myself* the truth. I spent most of my life worrying about myself, thinking that I was unwanted, that I was unloved. I've learned since being in A.A. that the more I worry about me loving you, and the less I worry about you loving me, the happier I'll be.

I discovered a fellowship of human beings that I'd never seen before. I learned how to have self-respect through work that A.A. gave me to do. I learned how to be a friend. I learned how to go out and help other people–there was nowhere else I could have done that. I have learned that the more I give, the more I will have; the more I learn to give, the more I learn to live.

(11) HE WHO LOSES HIS LIFE

An ambitious playwright, his brains got so far ahead of his emotions that he collapsed into suicidal drinking. To learn to live, he nearly died.

I REMEMBER the day when I decided to drink myself to death quietly, without bothering anyone, because I was tired of having been a dependable, trustworthy person for about thirty-nine years without having received what I thought was a proper reward for my virtue. That was the day, that was the decision, I know now, when I crossed over the line and became an active alcoholic. Perhaps a better way of saying it is that, on that day, with that decision, I no longer fought drinking as an escape. Rather, I embraced it–I must in honesty admit it–with a great sense of relief. I no longer had to pretend. I was giving up the struggle. Things weren't going as I thought they should, for my greater enjoyment, comfort and fame; therefore, if the universe wouldn't play my way, I wouldn't play at all. I, a man of steel, with very high ideals, well brought up, an honor student and the recipient of scholarships and prizes, a boy wonder in business–I, Bob, the author of this essay, looked and saw that the universe was beneath my contempt, and that to remove myself from it was the only thing of dignity a man could do. Since, perhaps, suicide was a bit too drastic (actually, I was afraid), dry martinis were chosen as the slow, pleasant, private, gradual instrument of self-destruction. And it was nobody's business, nobody's but mine. So I thought.

Within a month, the police, the hospital authorities, several kind strangers, most of my friends, all of my close relatives, and a few adepts at rolling a drunk and removing his wrist watch and wallet had been involved. (There was a time, for about three months, when I bought a ten-dollar wrist watch every payday–that is, every two weeks. Since it was wartime, I explained to the somewhat startled shopkeeper that I had many friends in the service whom I was remembering with a watch. Perhaps, without realizing it, I was.)

On that day of decision, I didn't acknowledge that I was an *alcoholic.* My proud southern blood would have boiled if anyone had named me such a despicable thing. No, it can best be explained in a little phrase I coined and sang to myself: "What happened to Bob? Bob found alcohol!" And having sung that phrase, I'd chuckle with amusement, turning into irony turning into self-contempt turning into self-pity, at the sad fate of Bob, that wonderful, poor little motherless boy who was so smart in school and who grew up to accept responsibility so early and so fast and who staggered under his burdens without a whimper until the time came when he thought he was too good for this world and so he ought to be out of it. *Poor Bob!*

That was one aspect of it, and a true one. There were several others. There was loneliness. There was the necessity for sticking to a job I hated, a dull, repetitive job performed in association with other men I had nothing in common with... performed for years on end, because the money was needed at home. There was the physical aspect; to be the youngest and the runt of the brood of children, to have to wear glasses very early and so to be teased, to be bookish and bored in school because the captain of the football team *could not* translate Virgil and yet was the school god while you, *you*, you little shrimp, were the school egghead, junior size and an early model.

There was the father one lost respect for at the age of eleven, because the father broke his solemn word in a circumstance where you, eleven years old, had assumed guilt when you were innocent but the father would not believe you, no matter what; and to ease his suffering you "confessed" and were "forgiven," only–months later–to have your "guilt" brought up–only he and you knew what he was talking about–brought up in front of the stern grandmother. The sacred word was broken and you never trusted your father again, and avoided him. And when he died, you were unmoved. You were thirty-five before you understood your father's horrible anguish, and forgave him, and loved him again. For you learned that he had been guilty of the thing he had accused you of, and his guilt had brought suffering to his entire family; and he thought he saw his young son beginning his own tragic pattern.

These things were all pressures. For by thirty-five I had been drinking for a few years. The pressures had started long ago. Sometimes we are told in AA. not to try and learn the reasons for our drinking. But such is my nature that I must know the reason for things, and I didn't stop until I had satisfied myself about the reasons for my drinking. Only, having found them, I threw them away, and ordered another extra dry martini. For to have accepted the reasons and to have acted on them would have been too great a blow to my ego, which was as great, in reverse, as my body was small.

In my twenties, I found Edna St. Vincent Millay's verse:

"Pity me the heart that is slow to learn
What the quick mind sees at every turn."

That couplet contains most of my reasons for drinking. There was the love affair which was ridiculous–"imagine that midget being able to fall in love!"–and my head knew it while my heart pumped real, genuine anguish, for it hurt like hell, and since it was first love, things have never been quite the same. There was the overweening ambition to be the world's greatest author, when–at thirty-nine–I had nothing of importance to say to the world. There was the economic fear which made me too timid to take any action which might improve my circumstances. There was the sense of being "misunderstood," when as a matter of fact by my middle twenties I was quite popular, although I hadn't grown much bigger physically. But the feeling was a crutch, an excuse. It was my "secret garden"–bluntly, it was my retreat from life, and I didn't want to give it up.

For a while, for a long time, we can endure the intellect's being ahead of the emotions, which is the import of Millay's couplet. But as the years go by, the stretch becomes unbearable; and the man with the grown-up brain and the childish emotions–vanity, self-interest, false pride, jealousy, longing for social approval, to name a few–becomes a prime candidate for alcohol. To my way of thinking, that is a definition of alcoholism; a state of being in which the emotions have failed to grow to the stature of the intellect. I know there are some alcoholics who seem terribly, terribly grown-up, but I think that they are trying to make themselves *think* they are grown-up, and the strain of their effort is what is causing them to drink–a sense of inadequacy, a childish vanity to be the most popular, the most sought after, the mostest of the most. And all this, of course, is, in the popular modern jargon, "compensation" for immaturity.

I wish I knew a short cut to maturity. But I wanted a cosmos, a universe all my own which I had created and where I reigned as chief top reigner and ruler over everyone else. Which is only another way of saying, I had to be *right all the time*, and only God can be that. Okay, I wanted to be God.

I still do. I want to be one of His children, a member of the human race. And, as a child is a part of his father, so do I now want to be a part of God. For always, over and above everything else, was the awfulness of the lack of meaning in life. Now, for me, and to my satisfaction, I know the purpose of life: The purpose of life is to create and the by-product is happiness. *To create:* Everyone does it, some at the instinct level, others in the arts. My personal definition, which I submit as applying only to myself (although everyone is welcome to it who wants it), includes every waking activity of the human being; to have a creative attitude towards things is a more exact meaning, to live and to deal with other human beings creatively, which to me means seeing the God in them, and respecting and worshipping this God. If I write with the air of one who has discovered the obvious, which is to say, the eternal truths which have been offered to us since the beginning, forgive my callowness; I had to find these things out for myself. Alas for us men toward whom Shaw hurled his cry, "Must a Christ be crucified in every generation for the benefit of those who have no imagination?"

My serious drinking covered about seven years. In those years I was in jail nine times, in an alcoholic ward, overnight, twice; and I was fired from three jobs, two of them very good ones. As I write these words, it seems incredible that these things should have happened to me, for they are, truly, against all my instincts and training. (Well! I started to cross out that last sentence, but decided to let it stand. What a revelation of ego and arrogance still remaining in me–as if *anyone*, instinct and training apart, *likes* to be in jail or in an alcoholic ward or fired from his job. After nearly eight years of sobriety in A.A., I still can set down such thoughts, "against my instinct and training," showing that I still consider myself a "special" person, entitled to special privileges. I ask the forgiveness of the reader; and from now on I shall try to write with the humility I honestly pray for.)

A pattern established itself. I never was a "secret" drinker, and I never kept a bottle at home. I'd visit one bar after another, having one martini in each, and in each hoping to find some one interesting to talk to. Actually, of course, I wanted someone to *listen* to me, because when I had a few martinis inside, I became the great author I longed to be; and the right listener was in for some pretty highflown theories of literature and of genius. If the listener were drunk enough, the lecture might go on through several martinis, which I was glad to pay for. If he were still sober, chances are that very quickly I put him down as a Philistine with no appreciation of literary genius; and then I went on to another bar to find a new victim.

So it was that in alcohol I found fulfillment. For a little while, I was the great man I wanted to be, and thought myself entitled to be just by reason of being me. I wonder if ever there has been a sillier reason for getting drunk all the time. Sobering up, the mind that was ahead of the emotions would impel the question: What have you written or done to be the great man? This question so insulted the emotions that clearly there was only one thing to do, go and get drunk again, and put that enquiring mind in its proper place, which was oblivion.

Depending on the stage of drunkenness, eventually I either fought or went to sleep. Brandishing my "motto," which was "A little man with a stick is equal to a big man," sometimes I varied the literary lecture by a fight with a big man, selected solely because he was big and I was little. I bear a few scars on my face from these fights, which I always lost, because the "stick" existed only in my mind. So did the waterboy on the high school football team attempt to revenge himself on the big brother who was the star quarterback; for I was the waterboy and my brother was the star quarterback, innocent of everything except the fact that he was a star quarterback.

When sleep overtook me, my practice was to undress and go to bed, wherever. Once this was in front of the Paramount Theatre in Times Square. I was down to my shorts, unaware of wrong-doing, before the ambulance got there and hauled me off to a hospital from which anxious friends rescued me, later that night.

Still another friend and temporary host received me at four in the morning from the charge of a policeman who had found me "going to bed" in a garage far from the last place I could remember having been, a fashionable bar and restaurant in the theatrical district of New York, to which I had repaired after my date for that evening, a charming lady of the theatre who had refused my company for obvious reasons. This time, whoever had rolled me had taken my glasses as well (they were gold). When the policeman released me to my stupefied and exasperated friend at four in the morning, I went to my traveling bag and groped until I found–well, let the officer speak: "Ah," said the policeman, "he's got anuder pair, t'ank God!" Thank *you*, Mr. Policeman, wherever you are now.

I mentioned that this friend was my temporary host. Need I add that such was the case because I had no money to provide a roof over my head? Still, I had had funds sufficient to get plastered because that, of course, was more important than paying my own way.

Once, or even twice, such incidents might be amusing. Repeated year on end, they are horrible–frightening and degrading, a chronicle of tragedy which may be greater because the individual undergoing the tragedy, myself, knew what was happening, and yet refused to do anything to stop it. One by one, the understanding friends dropped away. The helpful family finally said, over long distance, that there would be no more money and that I could not come home.

I say, "refused to do anything to stop it." The truth is, I did not know how to stop it, nor did I want to, really. I had nothing to put in the place of alcohol, of the forgetfulness, of the oblivion, which alcohol provides. Without alcohol, I would be *really* alone. Was I the disloyal sort who would turn his back on this, my last and truest friend?

I fled, finally, after having been fired from my war job by a boss who wept a little (for I had worked hard) as he gave notice for me to clear out. I went back home, to a job of manual labor where for a little while I was able to keep away from alcohol. But not for long; now, for five Friday nights in a row, I went to jail, picked up sodden with beer (which I always disliked, but which was the only drink available); in jail five consecutive Friday nights in the town where I had grown up, where I had been an honor student in high school, where a kindly uncle, bailing me out, said, "Bob, our family just doesn't do this sort of thing." I had replied, "Uncle, give the judge ten dollars, or I'll have to work it out on the county road." I was in hell. I wandered, craving peace, from one spot to another of youthful happy memory, and loathed the man I had become. I promised on the grave of a beloved sister that I would stop drinking. I meant it. I wanted to stop. I did not know how. For by now I had been exposed once to A.A., but I had treated it as a vaudeville and had taken friends to meetings so that they too could enjoy the fascination of the naked revelation of suffering and recovery. I thought I had recovered. Instead, I had gotten sicker. I was fatally ill. A.A. had not worked for me. The reason, as I learned later, was that I had not worked for A.A. I left this home town, then, after I had made a public spectacle of myself in the presence of a revered teacher whose favorite pupil I had been. I could not face the boy and youth I was in the reality of the contemptible man I had become.

Back to the big city, for another year of precarious living, paid for largely by one or two friends I still had not milked dry or worn to exhaustion with demands on their bounty. I worked when I could–piddling jobs I thought them. I was not capable of anything better. I stumbled agonizedly past the theatre where in years gone by a great star had played my play. I had even borrowed money from her, over her protest: "Bob, please don't ask me to lend you money–you're the only one who hasn't." I took her money, though; I had to have it. It paid for a ten-day binge which was the end of my drinking days. Thank God that those days are gone.

On another small borrowed sum, I went up into the country to the home of a doctor I had known since boyhood. We worked in five below zero weather, fixing on an elm tree a wrought iron device which modestly proclaimed that he was indeed a country doctor. I had no money–well, maybe a dime–and only the clothes I stood in. "Bob," he asked quietly, "do you want to live or die?"

He meant it. I knew he did. I did not remember much of the ten-day binge. But I remembered the years of agony preceding the binge, I remembered the years I had thrown away. I had just turned forty-six. Maybe it was time to die. Hope had died, or so I thought.

But I said humbly, "I suppose I want to live." I meant it. From that instant to this, nearly eight years later, I have not had the slightest urge to drink. I choose to believe that the Power greater than ourselves we ask for help, wrapped my shivering body in loving warmth and strength which has never left me. The doc and I went back into the house. He had a shot of brandy against the cold and passed me the bottle. I set it down and made myself a cup of coffee. I have not had a drink of anything alcoholic since.

Please do not think it ended so simply and so easily. Simply, yes, it did end; for I had changed my mind about alcohol, and it stayed changed. But for the next years, I worked hard and exultantly in A.A. In the nearby little town there was a plumber who once had tried to get an A.A. group going. I went over and met him, and we two started the group up again. It is going strong still, these eight years later, and some of its members have been of great influence for good in state-wide A.A. work. I myself have been lucky enough to help out. I have had the joy of seeing many a human being, down and out, learn to stand straight again, and to proceed under his own power to happiness in life. I learned the true meaning of bread cast upon the waters.

There were debts totaling nearly ten thousand dollars to be paid off. They are almost paid; the end is in sight. I have been allowed to build an entirely new career in a field I had never worked in. I have published a book covering certain aspects of this field which has been well-reviewed and which is helping other people. I have been appointed to the faculty of my old school, to teach in my new field. All of my family and loved ones, all of my friends, are nearer and dearer to me than ever before; and I have literally dozens of new friends who say they cannot believe that a short eight years ago I was ready for the scrap heap. When I remark that I have been in jail nine times, and in an alcoholic ward twice, they think I'm kidding, or possibly dramatizing for the sake of a good yarn. But I know I'm not. I remember how horrible jails are, how dreadful a thing it is to be behind steel bars. I wish we did not have to have jails; I wish everyone could be in A.A. and if everyone were there would be no need for jails, in my opinion.

For I am happy. I thought I could never be happy. A happy man is not likely to do harm to another human being. Harm is done by sick people, as I was sick, and doing dreadful harm to myself and to my loved ones.

For me, A.A. is a synthesis of all the philosophy I've ever read, all of the positive, good philosophy, all of it based on love. I have seen that there is only one law, the law of love, and there are only two sins; the first is to interfere with the growth of another human being, and the second is to interfere with one's own growth.

I still want to write a fine play and to get it on. I'd gladly do it anonymously, as I have done this brief account of my struggle with alcohol– merely to present certain ideas for the consideration of the reader. I don't care too much about personal fame or glory, and I want only enough money to enable me to do the work I feel I can perhaps do best. I stood off and took a long look at life and the values I found in it: I saw a paradox, that he who loses his life does indeed find it. The more you give, the more you get. The less you think of yourself the more of a person you become.

In A.A. we can begin again no matter how late it may be. I have begun again. At fifty-four, I have had come true for me the old wish, "If only I could live my life over, knowing what I know." That's what I am doing, living again, knowing what I know. I hope I have been able to impart to you, the reader, at least a bit of what I know; the joy of living, the irresistible power of divine love and its healing strength, and the fact that we, as sentient beings, have the knowledge to choose between good and evil, and, choosing good, are made happy.

(12) FREEDOM FROM BONDAGE

Young when she joined, this A.A. believes her serious drinking was the result of even deeper defects. She here tells how she was set free.

THE MENTAL TWISTS that led up to my drinking began many years before I ever took a drink, for I am one of those whose history proves conclusively that my drinking was "a symptom of a deeper trouble."

Through me efforts to get down to "causes and conditions," I stand convinced that my emotional illness has been present from my earliest recollection. I never did react normally to any emotional situation.

The medical profession would probably tell me I was conditioned for alcoholism by the things that happened to me in my childhood. And I am sure they would be right as far as they go, but A.A. has taught me I am the result of the *way I reacted* to what happened to me as a child. What is much more important to me, A.A. has taught me that through this simple program I may experience a change in this reaction pattern that will indeed allow me to "match calamity with serenity."

I am an only child, and when I was seven years old my parents separated very abruptly. With no explanation at all, I was taken from my home in Florida to my grandparents' home in the Midwest. My mother went to a nearby city to go to work, and my father, being an alcoholic, simply went. My grandparents were strangers to me, and I remember being lonely, terrified, and hurt.

In time I concluded that the reason I was hurt was because I loved my parents, and I concluded too that if I never allowed myself to love anybody or anything, I could never be hurt again. It became second nature for me to remove myself from anything or anybody I found myself growing fond of.

I grew up believing that one had to be totally self-sufficient, for one never dared to depend on another human being. I thought that life was a pretty simple thing; you simply made a plan for your life, based upon what you wanted, and then you needed only the courage to go after it.

In my late teens I became aware of emotions I'd not counted on: restlessness, anxiety, fear, and insecurity. The only kind of security I knew anything about at that time was material security, and I decided that all these intruders would vanish immediately if I only had a lot of money. The solution seemed very simple. With cold calculation I set about to marry a fortune, and I did. The only thing this changed, however, was my surroundings, and it was soon apparent that I could have the same uncomfortable emotions with an unlimited checking account that I could on a working girl's salary. It was impossible for me to say at this point, "Maybe there is something wrong with my philosophy," and I certainly couldn't say, "Maybe there is something wrong with *me*." It was not difficult to convince myself that my unhappiness was the fault of the man I had married, and I divorced him at the end of a year.

I was married and divorced again before I was twenty-three years old, this time to a prominent band leader–a man that many women wanted. I thought this would give me ego-strength, make me feel wanted and secure, and alleviate my fears, but again nothing changed inside me.

The only importance in all of this lies in the fact that at twenty-three I was just as sick as I was at thirty-three, when I came into A.A. But at that time I apparently had no place to go because I had no drinking problem. Had I been able to explain to a psychiatrist the feelings of futility, loneliness, and lack of purpose that had come with my deep sense of personal failure at this second divorce, I seriously doubt that the good doctor could have convinced me that my basic problem was a spiritual hunger. But A.A. has shown me this was the truth. And if I had been able to turn to the church at that time, I'm sure they could not have convinced me my sickness was within myself, nor could they have shown me the need for self-analysis that A.A. has shown me is vital if I am to survive. So I had no place to go. Or so it seemed to me.

I looked around me at people who seemed happy and tried to analyze their happiness, and it seemed to me that without exception these people had something or somebody they loved very much. I didn't have the courage to love; I was not even sure I had the capacity. Fear of rejection and its ensuing pain were not to be risked, and I turned away from myself once more for the answer, this time to the drinks I had always refused before, and in alcohol I found a false courage.

I wasn't afraid of anything or anybody after I learned about drinking. It seemed right from the beginning that with liquor I could always retire to my little private world where nobody could get at me to hurt me. It seems only fitting that when I did finally fall in love, it was with an alcoholic, and for the next ten years I progressed as rapidly as is humanly possible into what I believed to be hopeless alcoholism.

During this time, our country was at war. My husband was soon in uniform and among the first to go overseas. My reaction to this was identical in many respects to my reaction to my parents leaving me when I was seven. Apparently I'd grown physically at the customary rate of speed, and I had acquired an average amount of intellectual training in the intervening years, but there had been no emotional maturity at all. I realize now that this phase of my development had been arrested by my obsession with self, and my egocentricity had reached such proportions that adjustment to anything outside my personal control was impossible for me. I was immersed in self-pity and resentment, and the only people who would support this attitude or who I felt understood me at all were the people I met in bars and the ones who drank as I did. It became more and more necessary to escape from myself, for my remorse and shame and humiliation when I was sober were almost unbearable. The only way existence was possible was through rationalizing every sober moment and drinking myself into complete oblivion as often as I could.

My husband eventually returned, but it was not long until we realized we could not continue our marriage. By this time I was such a past master at kidding myself that I had convinced myself I had sat out a war and waited for this man to come home, and as my resentment and self-pity grew, so did my alcoholic problem.

The last three years of my drinking, I drank on my job. The amount of will power exercised to control my drinking during working hours, diverted into a constructive channel, would have made me president, and the thing that made the will power possible was the knowledge that as soon as my day was finished, I could drink myself into oblivion. Inside, though, I was scared to death, for I knew that the time was coming (and it couldn't be too remote) when I would be unable to hold that job. Maybe I wouldn't be able to hold any job, or maybe (and this was my greatest fear) I wouldn't care whether I had a job or not. I knew it didn't make any difference where I started, the inevitable end would be skid row. The only reality I was able to face had been forced upon me by its very repetition–*I had to drink*; and I didn't know there was anything in the world that could be done about it.

About this time I met a man who had three motherless children, and it seemed that might be a solution to my problem. I had never had a child, and this had been a satisfactory excuse many times for my drinking. It seemed logical to me that if I married this man and took the responsibility for these children that they would keep me sober. So I married again. This caused the comment from one of my A.A. friends, when I told my story after coming into the program, that I had always been a cinch for the program, for I had always been interested in mankind–I was just taking them one man at a time.

The children kept me sober for darn near three weeks, and then I went on (please God) my last drunk. I've heard it said many times in A.A., "There is just one good drunk in every alcoholic's life, and that's the one that brings us into A.A.," and I believe it. I was drunk for sixty days around the clock, and it was my intention, literally, to drink myself to death. I went to jail for the second time during this period for being drunk in an automobile. I was the only person I'd ever known personally who had ever been in jail, and I guess it is most significant that the second time was less humiliating than the first had been.

Finally, in desperation, my family appealed to a doctor for advice, and he suggested A.A. The people who came knew immediately I was in no condition to absorb anything of the program. I was put in a sanitarium to be defogged so that I could make a sober decision about this for myself. It was here that I realized for the first time that as a practicing alcoholic, I had no rights. Society can do anything it chooses to do with me when I am drunk, and I can't lift a finger to stop it, for I forfeit my rights through the simple expedient of becoming a menace to myself and to the people around me. With deep shame came the knowledge too that I had lived with no sense of social obligation nor had I known the meaning of moral responsibility to my fellow man.

I attended my first A.A. meeting eight years ago, and it is with deep gratitude that I'm able to say I've not had a drink since that time and that I take no sedation or narcotics, for this program is to me one of complete sobriety. I no longer need to escape reality. One of the truly great things A.A. has taught me is that reality too has two sides; I had only known the grim side before the program, but now I had a chance to learn about the pleasant side as well.

The A.A. members who sponsored me told me in the beginning that I would not only find a way to live without having a drink, but that I would find a way to live without *wanting* to drink, if I would do these simple things. They said if you want to know *how* this program works, take the first word of your question–the "H" is for honesty, the "O" is for open-mindedness, and the "W" is for willingness; these our *Big Book* calls the essentials of recovery. They suggested that I study the A.A. book and try to take the Twelve Steps according to the explanation in the book, for it was their opinion that the application of these principles in our daily lives will get us sober and keep us sober. I believe this, and I believe too that it is equally impossible to practice these principles to the best of our ability, a day at a time, and still drink, for I don't think the two things are compatible.

I had no problem admitting I was powerless over alcohol, and I certainly agreed that my life had become unmanageable. I had only to reflect on the contrast between the plans I made so many years ago for my life with what really happened to know I couldn't manage my life drunk or sober. A.A. taught me that *willingness to believe* was enough for a beginning. It's been true in my case, nor could I quarrel with "restore us to sanity," for my actions drunk or sober, before A.A., were not those of a sane person. My desire to be honest with myself made it necessary for me to realize that my thinking was irrational. It had to be, or I could not have justified my erratic behavior as I did. I've been benefited from a dictionary definition I found that reads: "Rationalization is giving a socially acceptable reason for socially unacceptable behavior, and socially unacceptable behavior is a form of insanity."

A.A. has given me serenity of purpose and the opportunity to be of service to God and to the people about me, and I am serene in the infallibility of these principles that provide the fulfillment of my purpose.

A.A. has taught me that I will have peace of mind in exact proportion to the peace of mind I bring into the lives of the other people, and it has taught me the true meaning of the admonition "happy are ye who know these things *and do them*." For the only problems I have now are those I create when I break out in a rash of self-will.

I've had many spiritual experiences since I've been in the program, many that I didn't recognize right away, for I'm slow to learn and they take many guises. But one was so outstanding that I like to pass it on whenever I can in the hope that it will help someone else as it has me. As I said earlier, self-pity and resentment were my constant companions, and my inventory began to look like a thirty-three-year diary, for I seemed to have a resentment against everybody I had ever known. All but one "responded to the treatment" suggested in the steps immediately, but this one posed a problem.

This resentment was against my mother, and it was twenty-five years old. I had fed it, fanned it, and nurtured it as one might a delicate child, and it had become as much a part of me as my breathing. It had provided me with excuses for my lack of education, my marital failures, personal failures, inadequacy, and of course, my alcoholism. And though I really thought I had been willing to part with it, now I knew I was reluctant to let it go.

One morning, however, I realized I had to get rid of it, for my reprieve was running out, and if I didn't get rid of it I was going to get drunk–and I didn't want to get drunk anymore. In my prayers that morning I asked God to point out to me some way to be free of this resentment. During the day, a friend of mine brought me some magazines to take to a hospital group I was interested in. I looked through them, and I saw a banner across one featured article by a prominent clergyman in which I caught the word *resentment.*

He said, in effect: "If you have a resentment you want to be free of, if you will pray for the person or the thing that you resent, you will be free. If you will ask in prayer for everything you want for yourself to be given to them, you will be free. Ask for their health, their prosperity, their happiness, and you will be free. Even when you don't really want it for them and your prayers are only words and you don't mean it, go ahead and do it anyway. Do it every day for two weeks, and you will find you have come to mean it and to want it for them, and you will realize that where you used to feel bitterness and resentment and hatred, you now feel compassionate understanding and love."

It worked for me then, and it has worked for me many times since, and it will work for me every time I am willing to work it. Sometimes I have to ask first for the willingness, but it too always comes. And because it works for me, it will work for all of us. As another great man says, "The only real freedom a human being can ever know is doing what you ought to do because you want to do it."

This great experience that released me from the bondage of hatred and replaced it with love is really just another affirmation of the truth I know: I get everything I need in Alcoholics Anonymous–and everything I need I get. And when I get what I need, I invariably find that it was just *what I wanted all the time.*

APPENDICES

THE A.A. TRADITION

To those now in its fold, Alcoholics Anonymous has made the difference between misery and sobriety, and often the difference between life and death. A.A. can, of course, mean just as much to uncounted alcoholics not yet reached.

Therefore, no society of men and women ever had a more urgent *need* for continuous effectiveness and permanent unity. We alcoholics see that we must work together and hang together, else most of us will finally die alone.

The "12 Traditions" of Alcoholics Anonymous are, we A.A.'s believe, the best answers that our experience has yet given to those ever-urgent questions, "How can A.A. best function?" and, "How can A.A. best stay whole and so survive?"

On the next page, A.A.'s "12 Traditions" are seen in their so-called "short form," the form in general use today. This is a condensed version of the original "long form" A.A. Traditions as first printed in 1946. Because the "long form" is more explicit and of possible historic value, it is also reproduced.

THE TWELVE TRADITIONS

One—Our common welfare should come first; personal recovery depends upon A.A. unity.

Two—For our group purpose there is but one ultimate authority—a loving God as He may express Himself in our group conscience. Our leaders are but trusted servants; they do not govern.

Three—The only requirement for A.A. membership is a desire to stop drinking.

Four—Each group should be autonomous except in matters affecting other groups or A.A. as a whole.

Five—Each group has but one primary purpose—to carry its message to the alcoholic who still suffers.

Six—An A.A. group ought never endorse, finance or lend the A.A. name to any related facility or outside enterprise, lest problems of money, property and prestige divert us from our primary purpose.

Seven—Every A.A. group ought to be fully self-supporting, declining outside contributions.

Eight—Alcoholics Anonymous should remain forever nonprofessional, but our service centers may employ special workers.

Nine—A.A., as such, ought never be organized; but we may create service boards or committees directly responsible to those they serve.

Ten—Alcoholics Anonymous has no opinion on outside issues; hence the A.A. name ought never be drawn into public controversy.

Eleven—Our public relations policy is based on attraction rather than promotion; we need always maintain personal anonymity at the level of press, radio and films.

Twelve—Anonymity is the spiritual foundation of all our traditions, ever reminding us to place principles before personalities.

THE TWELVE TRADITIONS

(The Long Form)

Our A.A. experience has taught us that:

1.–Each member of Alcoholics Anonymous is but a small part of a great whole. A.A. must continue to live or most of us will surely die. Hence our common welfare comes first. But individual welfare follows close afterward.

2.–For our group purpose there is but one ultimate authority–a loving God as He may express Himself in our group conscience.

3.–Our membership ought to include all who suffer from alcoholism. Hence we may refuse none who wish to recover. Nor ought A.A. membership ever depend on money or conformity. Any two or three alcoholics gathered together for sobriety may call themselves an A.A. group, provided that, as a group, they have no other affiliation.

4.–With respect to its own affairs, each A.A. group should be responsible to no other authority than its own conscience. But when its plans concern the welfare of neighboring groups also, those groups ought to be consulted. And no group, regional committee, or individual should ever take any action that might greatly affect A.A. as a whole without conferring with the trustees of the General Service Board. On such issues our common welfare is paramount.

5.–Each Alcoholics Anonymous group ought to be a spiritual entity *having but one primary purpose*–that of carrying its message to the alcoholic who still suffers.

6.–Problems of money, property, and authority may easily divert us from our primary spiritual aim. We think, therefore, that any considerable property of genuine use to A.A. should be separately incorporated and managed, thus dividing the material from the spiritual. An A.A. group, as such, should never go into business. Secondary aids to A.A., such as clubs or hospitals which require much property or administration, ought to be incorporated and so set apart that, if necessary, they can be freely discarded by the groups. Hence such facilities ought not to use the A.A. name. Their management should be the sole responsibility of those people who financially support them. For clubs, A.A. managers are usually preferred. But hospitals, as well as other places of recuperation, ought to be well outside A.A.–and medically supervised. While an A.A. group may cooperate with anyone, such cooperation ought never to go so far as affiliation or endorsement, actual or implied. An A.A. group can bind itself to no one.

7.–The A.A. groups themselves ought to be fully supported by the voluntary contributions of their own members. We think that each group should soon achieve this ideal; that any public solicitation of funds using the name of Alcoholics Anonymous is highly dangerous, whether by groups, clubs, hospitals, or other outside agencies; that acceptance of large gifts from any source, or of contributions carrying any obligation whatever, is unwise. Then too, we view with much concern those A.A. treasuries which continue, beyond prudent reserves, to accumulate funds for no stated A.A. purpose. Experience has often warned us that nothing can so surely destroy our spiritual heritage as futile disputes over property, money, and authority.

8.–Alcoholics Anonymous should remain forever nonprofessional. We define professionalism as the occupation of counseling alcoholics for fees or hire. But we may employ alcoholics where they are going to perform those services for which we might otherwise have to engage nonalcoholics. Such special services may be well recompensed. But our usual A.A. "12 Step" work is never to be paid for.

9.–Each A.A. group needs the least possible organization. Rotating leadership is the best. The small group may elect its secretary, the large group its rotating committee, and the groups of a large metropolitan area their central or intergroup committee, which often employs a full-time secretary. The trustees of the General Service Board are, in effect, our A.A. General Service Committee. They are the custodians of our A.A. Tradition and the receivers of voluntary A.A. contributions by which we maintain our A.A. General Service Office in New York. They are authorized by the groups to handle our overall public relations and they guarantee the integrity of our principal newspaper, the A.A. Grapevine. All such representatives are to be guided in the spirit of service, for true leaders in A.A. are but trusted and experienced servants of the whole. They derive no real authority from their titles; they do not govern. Universal respect is the key to their usefulness.

10.–No A.A. group or member should ever, in such a way as to implicate A.A., express any opinion on outside controversial issues–particularly those of politics, alcohol reform, or sectarian religion. The Alcoholics Anonymous groups oppose no one. Concerning such matters they can express no views whatever.

11.–Our relations with the general public should be characterized by personal anonymity. We think A.A. should avoid sensational advertising. Our names and pictures as A.A. members ought not be broadcast, filmed, or publicly printed. Our public relations should be guided by the principle of attraction rather than promotion. There is never need to praise ourselves. We feel it better that our friends recommend us.

12.–And finally, we of Alcoholics Anonymous believe that the principle of anonymity has an immense spiritual significance. It reminds us that we are to place principles before personalities; that we are to practice a genuine humility. This to the end that our great blessings may never spoil us; that we shall forever live in thankful contemplation of Him who presides over us all.

SPIRITUAL EXPERIENCE

The terms "spiritual experience" and "spiritual awakening" are used many times in this book which, upon careful reading, shows that the personality change sufficient to bring about recovery from alcoholism has manifested itself among us in many different forms.

Yet it is true that our first printing gave many readers the impression that these personality changes, or religious experiences, must be in the nature of sudden and spectacular upheavals. Happily for everyone, this conclusion is erroneous.

In the first few chapters a number of sudden revolutionary changes are described. Though it was not our intention to create such an impression, many alcoholics have nevertheless concluded that in order to recover they must acquire an immediate and overwhelming "God-consciousness" followed at once by a vast change in feeling and outlook.

Among our rapidly growing membership of thousands of alcoholics such transformations, though frequent, are by no means the rule. Most of our experiences are what psychologist William James calls the "educational variety" because they develop slowly over a period of time. Quite often friends of the newcomer are aware of the difference long before he is himself. He finally realizes that he has undergone a profound alteration in his reaction to life; that such a change could hardly have been brought about by himself alone. What often takes place in a few months could seldom have been accomplished by years of self-discipline. With few exceptions our members find they have tapped an unsuspected inner resource which they presently identify with their own conception of a Power greater than themselves.

Most of us think this awareness of a Power greater than ourselves is the essence of spiritual experience. Our more religious members call it "God-consciousness."

Most emphatically we wish to say that any alcoholic capable of honestly facing his problems in the light of our experience can recover, provided he does not close his mind to all spiritual concepts. He can only be defeated by an attitude of intolerance or belligerent denial.

We find that no one need have difficulty with the spirituality of the program. *Willingness, honesty and open mindedness are the essentials of recovery. But these are indispensable.*

"There is a principle which is a bar against all information, which is proof against all arguments and which cannot fail to keep a man in everlasting ignorance–that principle is contempt prior to investigation."

–Herbert Spencer

THE MEDICAL VIEW ON A.A.

Since Dr. Silkworth's first endorsement of Alcoholics Anonymous, medical societies and physicians throughout the world have set their approval upon us. Following are excerpts from the comments of doctors present at the annual meeting [*1944*] of the Medical Society of the State of New York where a paper on A.A. was read:

Dr. Foster Kennedy, neurologist: "This organization of Alcoholics Anonymous calls on two of the greatest reservoirs of power known to man, religion and that instinct for association with one's fellows... the "herd instinct." I think our profession must take appreciative cognizance of this great therapeutic weapon. If we do not do so, we shall stand convicted of emotional sterility and of having lost the faith that moves mountains, without which medicine can do little."

Dr. G. Kirby Collier, psychiatrist: "I have felt that A.A. is a group unto themselves and their best results can be had under their own guidance, as a result of their philosophy. Any therapeutic or philosophic procedure which can prove a recovery rate of 50% to 60% must merit our consideration."

Dr. Harry M. Tiebout, psychiatrist: "As a psychiatrist, I have thought a great deal about the relationship of my specialty to A.A. and I have come to the conclusion that our particular function can very often lie in preparing the way for the patient to accept any sort of treatment or outside help. I now conceive the psychiatrist's job to be the task of breaking down the patient's inner resistance so that which is inside him will flower, as under the activity of the A.A. program."

Dr. W.W. Bauer, broadcasting under the auspices of The American Medical Association in 1949, over the NBC network, said, in part: "Alcoholics Anonymous are no crusaders; not a temperance society. They know that they must never drink. They help others with similar problems... In this atmosphere the alcoholic often overcomes his excessive concentration on himself. Learning to depend upon a higher power and absorb himself in his work with other alcoholics, he remains sober day by day. The days add up into weeks, the weeks into months and years."

Dr. John F. Stouffer, Chief Psychiatrist, Philadelphia General Hospital, citing his experience with A.A., said: "The alcoholics we get here at Philadelphia General are mostly those who cannot afford private treatment, and A.A. is by far the greatest thing we have been able to offer them. Even among those who occasionally land back in here again, we observe a profound change in personality. You would hardly recognize them."

The American Psychiatric Association requested, in 1949, that a paper be prepared by one of the older members of Alcoholics Anonymous to be read to the Association's annual meeting of that year. This was done and the paper was printed in the *American Journal of Psychiatry* for November 1949.

(This address is now available in pamphlet form at nominal cost through most A.A. groups or from Box 459, Grand Central Station, New York, NY 10163, under the title "Alcoholism the Illness.")

THE LASKER AWARD

In 1951 the Lasker Award was given Alcoholics Anonymous. The citation reads in part as follows:

"The American Public Health Association presents a Lasker Group Award for 1951 to Alcoholics Anonymous in recognition of its unique and highly successful approach to that age-old public health and social problem, alcoholism... In emphasizing alcoholism as an illness, the social stigma associated with this condition is being blotted out... Historians may one day recognize Alcoholics Anonymous to have been a great venture in social action; a new therapy based on the kinship of common suffering; one having a vast potential for the myriad other ills of mankind."

THE RELIGIOUS VIEW ON A.A.

Clergymen of practically every denomination have given A.A. their blessing.

Edward Dowling, S.J., [*Father Ed, an early and wonderful friend of A.A., died in the spring of 1960.*] of the Queen's Work staff, says, "Alcoholics Anonymous is natural; it is natural at the point where nature comes closest to the supernatural, namely in humiliations and in consequent humility. There is something spiritual about an art museum or a symphony, and the Catholic Church approves of our use of them. There is something spiritual about A.A. too, and Catholic participation in it almost invariably results in poor Catholics becoming better Catholics."

The Episcopal magazine, *The Living Church*, observes editorially: "The basis of the technique of Alcoholics Anonymous is the truly Christian principle that a man cannot help himself except by helping others. The A.A. plan is described by members themselves as 'self-insurance.' This self-insurance has resulted in the restoration of physical, mental and spiritual health and self-respect to hundreds of men and women who would be hopelessly down and out without its unique but effective therapy."

Speaking at a dinner given by John D. Rockefeller Jr. to introduce Alcoholics Anonymous to some of his friends, Dr. Harry Emerson Fosdick remarked: "I think that psychologically speaking there is a point of advantage in the approach that is being made in this movement that cannot be duplicated. I suspect that if it is wisely handled–and it seems to be in wise and prudent hands–there are doors of opportunity ahead of this project that may surpass our capacities to imagine."

HOW TO GET IN TOUCH WITH A.A.

In the United States and Canada, most towns and cities have A.A. groups. In such places, A.A. can be located through the local telephone directory, newspaper office, or police station, or by contacting local priests or ministers. In large cities, groups often maintain local offices where alcoholics or their families may arrange for interviews or hospitalization. These so-called intergroup associations are found under the listing "A.A." or "Alcoholics Anonymous" in telephone directories.

At New York, USA, Alcoholics Anonymous maintains its international service center. The General Service Board of A.A. (the trustees) administers A.A.'s General Service Office, A.A. World Services, Inc., and our monthly magazine, "The A.A. Grapevine."

If you cannot find A.A. in your locality, a letter addressed to Alcoholics Anonymous, Box 459, Grand Central Station, New York, NY 10163, USA, will receive a prompt reply from this world center, referring you to the nearest A.A. group. If there is none nearby, you will be invited to carry on a correspondence which will do much to insure your sobriety no matter how isolated you are.

Should you be the relative or friend of an alcoholic who shows no immediate interest in A.A., it is suggested that you write the Al-Anon Family Groups, Inc., 1600 Corporate Landing Parkway, Virginia Beach, VA 23456, USA.

This is a world clearing house for the Al-Anon Family Groups, composed largely of the wives, husbands and friends of A.A. members. This headquarters will give the location of the nearest family group and will, if you wish, correspond with you about your special problems.

Made in the USA
Monee, IL
18 September 2023

42923462R00184